# THE MATRIFOCAL FAMILY
## *Power, Pluralism, and Politics*

# THE MATRIFOCAL FAMILY

## *Power, Pluralism, and Politics*

**RAYMOND T. SMITH**

Routledge
New York   London

Published in 1996 by

Routledge
29 West 35th Street
New York, NY 10001

Published in Great Britain by

Routledge
11 New Fetter Lane
London EC4P 4EE

Library of Congress Cataloging-in-Publication Data

Smith, Raymond Thomas,
    The matrifocal family: power, pluralism, and politics/Raymond T. Smith.
      p.  cm.
    Essays originally published 1956–1987 plus two conference papers presented in Dec. 1992 and Aug. 1993.
    Includes bibliographical references and index.
    ISBN 0-415-91214-8 (hard). — ISBN 0-415-91215-6 (pbk.)
    1. Matriarchy—Caribbean Area. 2. Matrilineal kinship—Caribbean Area. 3. Family—Caribbean Area—Social conditions. 4. Caribbean Area—Ethnic relations. 5. Caribbean Area—Social policy.
    I. Title.
GN564.C37S65  1995
306—dc20                                     95-13171
                                                    CIP

# CONTENTS

*Cover:* This late eighteenth century engraving, entitled "The voyage of the Sable Venus from Angola to the West Indies," was made to accompany a poem of thirty verses written in 1765 and entitled *The Sable Venus; an Ode.* The poem makes indirect reference to Botticelli's Venus, and dwells upon the beauty of the archetypical African woman with verses such as:

> Her skin excell'd the raven plume,
> Her breath the fragrant orange bloom,
> Her eye the tropic beam:
> Soft was her lip as silken down,
> And mild her look as ev'ning sun
> That gilds the COBRE stream.

It appears in Volume 2 of Bryan Edwards' *The History Civil and Commercial, of the British Colonies in the West Indies,* at the end of the chapter on "Present Inhabitants" and immediately before the chapter dealing with slavery, a chapter that begins by condemning slavery, pointing out that most slaves have been "torn from their native country and dearest connections, by means which no good mind can reflect upon but with sentiments of disgust, commiseration, and sorrow" [Edwards 1793, Vol. 2, p. 34]. The contrast of the images of cruelty and degradation on the one hand and idealized womanhood on the other, in the form of the "Sable Venus," is cynically cruel in its own right, but it encapsulates in a striking manner the convoluted meanings surrounding the whole concept of the "matrifocal family" with its qualities of sexual exploitation, female oppression and racist embodiment.

# ACKNOWLEDGMENTS

Chapter Two is excerpted from Raymond T. Smith, *The Negro Family in British Guiana: Family Structure and Social Status in the Villages,* published in 1956 by Routledge and Kegan Paul Limited, London, and reproduced here by permission of Routledge.

Chapter Three was originally published as "Culture and Social Structure in the Caribbean: Some Recent Work on Family and Kinship Studies," in *Comparative Studies in Society and History,* Vol. VI., No. 1, (October 1963), Copyright 1963 by the Society for the Comparative Study of Society and History. It is reprinted here with the permission of Cambridge University Press.

Chapter Four was originally published as "The Matrifocal Family" in *The Character of Kinship* (pp. 121-44), edited by Jack Goody (1973), copyright Cambridge University Press. It is reprinted here with the permission of Cambridge University Press.

Chapter Five was originally published as "Hierarchy and the Dual Marriage System in West Indian Society" in *Gender and Kinship: Essays Toward a Unified Analysis,* (pp. 163-96) edited by Jane Fishburne Collier and Sylvia Junko Yanagisako, copyright 1987 by the Board of Trustees of the Leland Stanford Junior University. It is reprinted here with the permission of Stanford University Press.

Chapter Six was originally published as "Family, Social Change, and Social Policy in the West Indies" in *Nieuwe West-Indische Gids: New West Indian Guide,* Vol. 56, Nos. 3 & 4, 1982, (pp. 111-42). It is reprinted here with the permission of KITLV Press, Leiden, The Netherlands.

Chapter Seven was originally published in *New World: Guyana Independence Issue 1966,* edited by George Lamming and Martin Carter and published by New World Group Associates, Georgetown, Guyana.

Chapter Eight was originally published as "Caste and Social Status among the Indians of Guyana" in *Caste in Overseas Indian Communities* (pp. 43-92), edited by Barton M. Schwartz and copyright 1967 by Chandler Publishing Company, San Francisco.

Chapter Nine was originally published as "Race and Class in the Post-Emancipation Caribbean" in *Racism and Colonialism: Essays on Ideology and Social Structure* (pp. 94-119), edited by Robert Ross and copyright 1982 by Martinus Nijhoff Publishers, The Hague. It is reprinted here by permission of Kluwer Academic Publishers.

Chapter Ten was originally presented at a conference on "Ethnicity, Ideology, and Colonial Legacy in the Caribbean" held at Brigham Young University on December 7 and 8, 1992. It is also published in *New West Indian Guide,* Vol. 69, Nos. 3 & 4, 1995, by arrangement with KITLV Press, Leiden, The Netherlands.

Chapter Eleven was originally presented at the University of Guadalajara Conference on "La Lucha por el Status: La Formacion de Groupos de Status y la Produccion de la Cultura" held in Ajijic, Jalisco on August 7, 1993.

# PREFACE

The essays reprinted in this volume were written over a period of more than forty years and published in a wide variety of books, journals, and collections. Over that considerable time span my indebtedness for help, guidance, criticism, and cooperation has grown beyond my capacity to acknowledge it, but certain elements of that debt demand recognition.

Among academics it is conventional to refer to colleagues as "the student of" a particular individual, and while I do not resist having the late Professor Meyer Fortes referred to as my "mentor," he was only one—albeit an important one—among many individuals who influenced my early work. In Cambridge, John Peristiany, Reo Fortune, Talcott Parsons, and Edmund Leach were—along with Meyer Fortes—salient faculty members in the late 1940s and early 1950s, while fellow students Jack Goody, Colin Rosser, Derrick Stenning, Kathleen Gough, and Al and Grace Harris were stimulating companions at one time or another. However, I consider that the education most relevant to the problems discussed in these essays began soon after I disembarked from a banana boat in Kingston harbor, Jamaica, in the spring of 1951. I was met at the ship by Lloyd Braithwaite and Leslie Robinson of the then University College of the West Indies (both eventually became Pro-Vice-Chancellors of the independent University of the West Indies), and taken to a small residence for unmarried members of the university staff. I stayed there for the next three weeks during which I obtained an intensive course in the history, economics, politics, and social problems of the West Indies from a remarkable group of young, and predominantly West Indian, scholars. Lloyd Braithwaite and Elsa Goveia (later to be appointed the first Professor of West Indian History at the University of the West Indies), were major influences. I maintained a voluminous correspondence with Elsa Goveia throughout the subsequent year of field research in British Guiana, a correspondence that was invaluable in refining my understanding of colonialism in general and British Guiana in particular. Subsequent residence in Jamaica as a member of the faculty of the University of the West Indies was crucial in deepening and broadening that understanding by working with people such as Lloyd Best, Roy Augier, William Demas, Gladstone Mills, George Roberts, David Edwards, M.G. Smith, George Beckford, Herman and Hermione McKenzie, Alister MacIntyre, Archie Singham, and more recently Donald Robotham, Patricia Anderson, Norman Girvan, Elsie LeFranc, Barry Chevannes, and Derek Gordon—whose tragic premature death cut short what would have been a brilliant career and further research collaboration.

I first met Chandra Jayawardena in early 1956 when he arrived in the then British Guiana to work with me on a study of the East Indian population. Chandra studied two sugar estates while I spent one year in the rice-growing community of Windsor Forest. During that year we met frequently to discuss our respective field studies, and subsequently collaborated in the writing of a number of articles dealing with that research (Smith & Jayawardena 1958, 1959, 1967). One of those articles, "Caste and Social Status Among the Indians of Guyana" is reprinted here as Chapter Eight. After completing his doctorate at the London School of Economics, Chandra took up a post in Australia and subsequently worked in Fiji and Indonesia. In 1975 we planned to carry out a restudy of our respective field sites in Guyana, and met in Trinidad before going on to Guyana. Unfortunately he had to return to Australia with only a quick visit to his plantations, though I was fortunate enough to be able to spend over six months on the restudy. I never saw Chandra again since he died in Australia in 1981 at a distressingly early age. Chapter Five was originally delivered as the Chandra Jayawardena Memorial Lecture at the University of the

West Indies in March 1982, a small and inadequate tribute to a scholar from whom I learned an enormous amount, and whose dedication to the cause of equality suffused all his writings to the very end.

In Guyana I have accumulated a mountain of indebtedness, not only to the people of the communities in which I have worked over the years, but also to many individuals and organizations in Georgetown, the capital, and elsewhere. During my first weeks in British Guiana in 1951 I met both Dr. Cheddi Jagan and Mr. Forbes Burnham, each of them to become leading figures in the formation of the new nation of Guyana, and each of whom were both friends and facilitators of my research. Dr. Frank Williams was friend, physician, and perceptive instructor about the complexities of Guyana and the Caribbean generally. My wife Flora has, over the years, contributed an enormous amount as field collaborator and critic, and continues to be deeply enmeshed in a worldwide network of Guyanese and West Indian interchanges.

I moved to the University of Chicago in 1966 partly at the urging of David M. Schneider, but also because its Department of Anthropology was then the most intellectually stimulating place to be, with a collection of anthropologists working on precisely the kind of problems raised by these essays. Although I have disagreed with him in several major ways, David Schneider has always been a valued friend, a constructive critic, and a generous collaborator who has been a major influence on my thinking about the problems of kinship in particular. Clifford Geertz, Lloyd Fallers, Bernard Cohn, Manning Nash, Stanley Tambiah, Terence Turner, and later John and Jean Comaroff, along with an exceedingly talented body of graduate students, worked on similar problems in widely disparate areas of the world, creating a continuing tradition of research and writing on "new nations" that has almost imperceptibly developed into work on post-colonialism, late capitalism, globalization, and transnationalism.

The several years I spent collaborating on a study of the effects of poverty on family life in Chicago were more difficult. As the only anthropologist among a group of coinvestigators and research assistants (who were mainly trained in a particular kind of quantitative sociology, and committed to the study of problems defined by William J. Wilson, the principal investigator on the project, and laid out in his book *The Truly Disadvantaged*), I much-too-frequently found myself in opposition to major aspects of the study. Professor Wilson was always open to suggestions, or to the use of project resources for ethnographic-type field research, but the problem of communication across a deep theoretical divide was impossible to solve. However, a major collection of case studies was accumulated under my direction and I expect that they will form a part of various studies resulting from the project, including my own; I have used some of those data here in Chapter Eleven. That chapter is also influenced by the earlier studies of kinship in Chicago that I carried out in collaboration with David Schneider.

Finally, I must thank Marlie Wasserman, Executive Editor for Social Sciences at Routledge, who suggested this collection and has patiently seen it through publication, and to the various publishers who have given permission for the reprinting of these essays. I have not changed any of them significantly, beyond correcting obvious errors and making the style and spelling uniform throughout the book.

# CHAPTER ONE

## *Introduction*

The publication of this collection of essays provides an opportunity to suggest the relevance of Caribbean ethnography to recent discussions of social theory, and to forge a link between that ethnography and the study of urban problems in the United States. For many anthropologists the Caribbean has been an area of fragmented cultures, odd survivals, juxtaposed social segments, explicable only by reference to some authentic point, or points, of origin outside the region, or in terms of the chaotic conflict of plural entities. Some of the island societies, like Cuba and Puerto Rico, were populated as extensions of the Spanish reoccupation of Spain itself following the expulsion of the Moors, but most were created in the ferment of early capitalist adventurism and driven by the technical rationality of plantation agriculture, a development that eventually overwhelmed all the territories of the region. Modernity, one might say, was built into their foundations and they were incorporated into a global, or transnational, order from their inception. On that account alone the experience of these Caribbean societies is an instructive case study in colonialism and its late-twentieth-century sequels—post-colonialism and postmodernism.

As in many of the North American colonies, egalitarian ideologies struggled against the hierarchical imperatives of plantation structures and technical rationality was profoundly modified by ideologies of race. Across the Caribbean there were many differences in the patterns of settlement and in population composition, but everywhere concepts of race and birth status emerged as dominant considerations in the structuring of social status.

My own field experience has been mainly in Guyana and Jamaica, so that these essays, although they were selected for their relevance to the central themes of the collection, draw heavily on material pertaining to those societies. Jamaica, with a current population of over two and a half million, is the largest of the British ex-colonies in the Caribbean, with a rich history that was, prior to 1776, closely intertwined with that of the North American colonies. Its sugar plantation economy was based firmly on African slavery and although some immigration from India, China, and the Middle East has complicated the picture, the fundamental categories of race on which the social divisions of the population were originally based, were black, white, and mixed, or colored. While the correspondence of social status and presumed race has been gradually eroded, the majority of the population is descended from Africans imported against their will to work on the sugar plantations and there are very powerful Afrocentric movements both at the level of what is usually styled "popular culture" and among academics. The population is estimated to be 76 percent of African descent, 15 percent of mixed African and European descent, 3 percent European, about 3 percent descended from immigrants from India, and even smaller proportions descended from immigrants from China and the Middle East. A British colony until 1962, Jamaica is now an independent member of the British Commonwealth.

Guyana is one of the three "Guyanas"—British, Dutch, and French—lying on the northeast shoulder of South America between Venezuela and Brazil. The country is mainly forest and savannah, but a low-lying fertile coastal strip was reclaimed from the sea by the Dutch in the mid-eighteenth-century and quickly became a major sugar plantation area worked by African slaves.

Acquired by the British in the early nineteenth-century, the colony's sugar industry survived the abolition of slavery by instituting schemes of importation of indentured labor from Portuguese Madeira and China, but most notably from India. Portuguese and Chinese immigration was limited, but large numbers of Indians were introduced between 1848 and 1917 so that their descendants are now the largest single racial group. In 1946 East Indians (as they are termed to distinguish them from Amerindians) constituted 43.5 percent of a total population of just 375,701 individuals. Persons of African descent constituted 38.2 percent, while Mixed, Amerindians, Portuguese, Chinese and European made up the rest.

Over the next twenty years the population increased rapidly and the East Indian population increased faster than any other. By 1964 the Guyana Year Book estimated a total population of 638,480 made up of 50.1 percent East Indians, 31.3 percent African, 11.9 percent Mixed, 4.6 percent Amerindian, 1.1 percent Portuguese, .6 percent Chinese, and .4 percent European. These racial classifications are an expression of social divisions remaining from the colonial regime, and are closely linked to political conflict, as discussed in Chapters 10 and 11 particularly. The colony of British Guiana became the independent state of Guyana in 1966, and was declared the Co-operative Republic of Guyana in 1970. No census figures have been published recently and racial classifications are no longer given in official statistics. However, massive migrations during the 1970s and 1980s—to Canada, Britain, and the USA mainly but also to neighbouring countries in the West Indies and Suriname—have probably offset any natural increase. The Central Intelligence Agency on-line Fact Book estimates the 1994 population to be 729,425 made up of East Indians 51 percent, Black and Mixed 43 percent, Amerindians 4 percent, and Europeans and Chinese 2 percent.

Running throughout the essays several themes are insistent. One, deriving from my earliest work in British Guiana (referred to as Guyana when discussing the period since 1966) and continuing through the most recent research in the United States, questions the common view of African-American family life as being "disorganized" and pathological. Without minimizing the severe problems that beset the poor and oppressed, or the undoubted social pathologies of modern urban life, it is abundantly clear that the remarkable strength, resilience, and diversity of African-American kinship has been almost willfully ignored, simply because it does not conform to the cramped ideals of the so-called middle class.

It has been convenient to create statistical models that establish causal links between the supposed breakdown of the African-American family and the conditions of poverty and deprivation in which large numbers of people are obliged to live, without ever considering the constitutive relations between affluence and deprivation—between the extravagance of the rich and the desperation of the poor. That desperation is no longer as deeply rooted in starvation, disease, and physical deprivation as it was (though there is still a scandalously generous amount of those things), but it is no less deeply felt because it is produced by scorn, humiliation, and the lack of what Adam Smith referred to as "not only the commodities which are indispensably necessary for the support of life, but whatever the *custom of the country* renders it indecent for creditable people, even of the lowest order, to be without" (Smith 1976, Vol. 2, p. 399, my emphasis). He cited linen shirts and leather shoes as necessary commodities for the maintenance of self-respect in the late eighteenth century, and we can easily compile an updated list for our own time. However, there are few late-twentieth-century voices raised in support of according respect to the poor.

Fortunately, and not a little ironically, "mainstream" family practice is beginning to approximate, in some respects at least, the previously despised patterns of poor African Americans, so that pejorative expressions such as "born out of wedlock" are losing their capacity to injure. However, the stereotyped denigration of African-American kinship continues to be an integral part of discourse on social policy, especially in the United States, and the by-now extensive body of ethnographic material establishing a more positive view continues to be ignored. Also ignored, or accorded a less than positive appreciation, is the revolutionary change in the relations between men and women, with its far-reaching consequences for marriage, familial relations, and the care of children. The easiest, and most common, reaction is to assert the value— or the absolute necessity—of "traditional" family values, which means a traditional nuclear family with a male breadwinner and a female "homemaker."

The anthropological study of kinship has always been a direct path to the understanding of political issues, though in modern state systems that path is not always obvious. Kinship is the anchor of racial and class differentiation. While macro-sociological analysis may yield complex models illuminating processes of class formation and social mobility, it is the fine-grained study of family connections that yields the data on which an understanding of status dynamics depends.

Over the past ten or fifteen years the debate over welfare policy in the United States has taken a dangerous turn, greatly stimulated by the revival of eighteenth-century ideas embedded in Charles Murray's reasonable-sounding (but largely incorrect) assumption that public assistance for the poor encourages dependence and immoral behavior (Murray 1984), and his less reasonable-sounding, but equally seductive, writing on race and genetic differences (Murray and Herrenstein 1994). In spite of the barrage of statistical evidence marshalled to refute these claims, the idea of cutting public assistance is as attractive now as it was when Jeremy Bentham produced his plan for reforming the Poor Laws of England almost two centuries ago (see Bahmueller 1981). The difference now is that the discussion is inflected with a deep racism that no amount of statistical evidence, or arguments about genes versus environment, can hide. I have not discussed these recent debates in this volume, but the research carried out in Chicago (discussed in Chapter Ten) was formulated with them in mind and many of the essays in this volume speak directly to the issues they raise.

A second theme running through this work is the assertion that race is neither the natural basis of social differentiation nor the inevitable starting point for cultural distinctions. This is a position widely (but not universally) acceded to in theory but generally denied in social practice. As the process of globalization has accelerated there has been, throughout the world, a counter process of ethnic assertion and what is now generally called "identity politics." It is not an exaggeration to say that analysis of this process—social integration accompanied by the assertion of cultural exclusiveness—has been the major focus of academic controversy in Caribbean studies for almost half a century. Rancorous, and often *ad hominem,* debate has swirled around the question of whether Caribbean societies are "plural" or "unitary" societies; that is, whether they are made up of sections that are culturally and institutionally distinct, or whether their very marked internal differentiation is itself the result of a particular mode of societal integration that actually creates, or perpetuates and exaggerates, conceptions of cultural difference. These are not merely academic questions; recent events in Bosnia, Sri Lanka, most of Africa, and many other places are eloquent testimony to the deadly potential of the ideological projection of "ethnicity" into the political domain. The Caribbean is a particularly interesting area because its societies are almost wholly made up of immigrants, and formally dedicated to the creation of unitary national states.

In this they have been inspired by, and have emulated, the founders of the United States, but have been forced to confront the corrosive ideology of race in different ways, while undertaking the task of nation building within the claimed sphere of influence of an expansionist and dominating superstate. Working in Guyana during the 1950s, 60s, and 70s provided me with an illuminating view of the effect of United States and British policy during the period of the Cold War, and the way in which that policy interacted with local power struggles to produce tragic and lasting exacerbation of racial and "ethnic" conflict. Perhaps even more fascinating was the way in which academic theorizing became involved in the power struggles, stripping away any pretension of value neutrality in the research process. This is discussed further below, but it is worth noting here that the United States government has refused, after the normal forty years, to open the archives relating to United States activities in British Guiana during this period. If, eventually, it is established that policy was directed deliberately toward inciting racial conflict as a means of combatting communism, there will be little satisfaction in having suspicions confirmed.

The essays collected here are not presented in the chronological order of their publication, nor has it been possible to separate them strictly in terms of the matters they deal with since the same themes of kinship, class, and race generally appear in all. Therefore the division into two parts labelled "kinship and family structure," "conflict and difference," is conveniently approximate.

## Part One: Kinship and Family Structure

Part One begins with an excerpt from my first major publication on African-American kinship in Guyana (then British Guiana). Published in 1956, it took a firm stand against interpreting family forms either in terms of pathology or in terms of an assumed cultural continuity from Africa. Instead it proposed to view domestic life in the context of the color/class system of a racist and exploitative colonial social order, and through analysis of the developmental cycle of domestic groups that had been refined by Meyer Fortes in his studies of the Tallensi and Ashanti. That first book of mine, *The Negro Family in British Guiana,* has long been out of print, and this section begins with an abbreviated version of chapter nine, "Hypotheses and the Problem of 'Explanation'." The chapter was intended to summarize the main argument of the book by setting the main features of the family system against the relevant aspects of the overall status system of colonial society to support the conclusion that the characteristic focus of domestic and familial relations upon the mother is produced by the marginalization of husband-fathers, whose status and functions as household heads is depressed because of their lowly status in the society as a whole.

The final manuscript of that book was prepared at the University of the West Indies, where I had accepted an appointment at the Institute of Social and Economic Research with the express intention of returning to British Guiana in order to broaden my work to include the large population descended from indentured immigrants from India. In January of 1956 I began a twelve month period of field research in a large rice-growing community while my colleague, Chandra Jayawardena, studied two sugar estate communities over a period of eighteen months. We devoted a great deal of time to the study of kinship and family life in those various East Indian communities and published a number of papers on kinship and marriage (Smith & Jayawardena 1958, 1959; Jayawardena 1960, 1962, 1963). Those papers are quite long and contain the kind of ethnographic detail more appropriate to a specialized work, so they have not been included in this collection, though some material on marriage and the family will be found in Chapter Eight,

"Caste and Social Status Among the Indians of Guyana." The relevant point here is that the research on East Indian communities demanded a major reconsideration of the hypotheses developed in *The Negro Family in British Guiana.*

To put the matter as simply as possible, both Afro- and Indo-Guyanese had entered colonial society in the same lowly status as plantation labor. Although East Indian workers were indentured servants rather than chattel slaves, the difference was hardly palpable; indeed, Indian laborers commonly referred to themselves and their brethren as "slaves." Over the years since the ending of indentures in 1917 they had faced enormous hurdles in the attempt to raise their status in colonial British Guianese society; even in 1956 they could not be regarded as anything but a low-status group. However, their family system, while showing some of the apparent "instability" common to low-income groups in other places, was fundamentally different from that of Afro-Guyanese. In 1957 I presented a paper at a seminar on plantation systems showing that the model that I had developed for the explanation of Afro-Guyanese kinship just does not work when applied to other groups (Smith 1959b). That paper, "Family Structure and Plantation Systems in the New World," is not reprinted here, but it reviewed material from Jamaica, Puerto Rico, and British Guiana to show that plantation labor is compatible with markedly different patterns of domestic and familial organization. Therefore the earlier conclusion that matrifocal kinship and male domestic marginality are produced by low economic status had to be reconsidered. The problem now was to find an alternative explanation without resorting to the theoretically unacceptable assumption that each "ethnic group" in Guyana is the bearer of a traditional culture that determines the structure of the institutions it practices.

It seemed clear to me that Africans and East Indians in Guyana (or Trinidad, Suriname, Guadeloupe, etc.), are part of a complex creole system in which their existence is defined in contrastive relation to each other, not in terms of primordial identity. The solution to the problem of why they responded differently to similar economic conditions had to lie in a closer examination of the structure of the society in which these groups are contained, of the relations between the groups, and the political, economic, and cultural practices that constituted them and their supposed differences.

Some readers of my early work found it convenient to characterize it as "integrationist"—as opposed to the "pluralist" approach of M.G. Smith (see Part Two)—but these simplifying labels hardly do justice to either position. To speak of "the structure of the society in which these groups are contained" does not necessarily mean that we are looking for "norms," in the sense of rules for behavior, nor "common values" in the sense that all members of a society must think and act alike. A structure can embrace dialectical opposition or contradiction and common values can certainly be the source of conflict in the process of social action. The fact of conflict does not make a structure "plural" either. Structures may be built on the very premise of conflict; relations of the parts of a structure may be relations of opposition. The logic of the emerging system of family and kinship relations was created at a very early point in the development of the Caribbean colonies, and it bound together the whole population, black and white, slave and free. It was that system, that structure that had to be elucidated, and I increasingly employed two means of doing so. The first was the study of the present-day ideology of kinship and its relation to social action; the second was the study of the historical development of that system. But first I undertook a review of the state of Caribbean kinship studies. That paper, "Culture and Social Structure in the Caribbean," is reproduced here as Chapter Three. It provides an overview of what I was thinking about kinship and the family after spending three years teaching at the University of Ghana, and just a few years before a major reorientation of my research agenda.

In 1966 I left the University of the West Indies to join the Department of Anthropology at the University of Chicago and immediately began to plan for a quite different kind of kinship research in Jamaica, Guyana, and Chicago. David Schneider and Raymond Firth had been working for some time on a comparative study of kinship in London and Chicago, a study that was premised on the observation that virtually no attention had been paid to genealogy and extended kinship networks in European and American studies of the middle-class family. Firth and his students had actually undertaken some work on genealogy in London in the 1950s (see Firth 1956), but the comparative project was more carefully planned and it eventually resulted in two studies that were only nominally comparable because of the very different theoretical assumptions that informed them (Schneider 1968; Firth, Hubert & Forge 1969). To put the matter simply (and therefore not very accurately), Schneider was more interested in his informants' kinship *concepts*, while Firth and his associates concentrated on the actual *social relations* among the relatives recognized by their informants. In principle both studies collected material on concepts *and* relations but the different emphases resulted in very different analyses.

In 1967 I began a series of field investigations in Jamaica and Guyana that were, informally at least, conceived as an extension, to a very different part of the world, of the Firth-Schneider project. Although I adopted the method of intensive case studies and the construction of detailed genealogies in a manner that permitted comparison with the English and American data, the project was quite self-contained as a study of West Indian kinship, and was eventually presented as such in a book entitled *Kinship and Class in the West Indies: a Genealogical Study of Jamaica and Guyana* (Smith 1988).

The field research in Guyana and Jamaica was already in progress when I was asked to contribute to a festschrift being prepared by Jack Goody to honor Meyer Fortes on his retirement from the William Wyse Chair in Social Anthropology at the University of Cambridge. This became an excellent opportunity to review the changes in my approach to the study of West Indian kinship and to offer some comments on Fortes's work in the light of my own studies. That paper, "The Matrifocal Family," was published in 1973 and is presented here as chapter four. It makes a number of important points that still need to be emphasized since some recent students of Caribbean kinship appear to be unaware of them. Easily the most important is the unequivocal break with the idea that the "nuclear" or "elementary" family of a man, his legal wife, and their legitimate children is both a universal and necessary human social institution. This idea, so deeply embedded in the commonsense assumptions of European and North American societies, had been central to Meyer Fortes's theoretical work, as it had been in the work of Malinowski, George Peter Murdock, Talcott Parsons, and many others. "The Matrifocal Family" makes a clear break with these assumptions and seeks to demonstrate that the complex patterns of West Indian kinship, domestic organization, and mating are not distorted forms of a basic nuclear family system, but a rich and viable system in its own right. The paper also clarifies the meaning of "matrifocal," sharply separating it from any confusion with "female-headed households."

Of course, it is one thing to show that a particular kinship system can accord relatively low priority to conjugal relations within the whole complex of kinship and domestic relations, and another to situate such a system in its full social and historical context. It had always been recognized that there is some connection between the observed peculiarities of African-American family life and the calamitous history of slavery and exploitation. Even Herskovits recognized that if African custom had "survived" in the New World it must have been profoundly altered by the traumatic experience of slavery and oppression. However, the general assumption was that one could understand "African-Americans" as a bounded group, rather like an organism adapting to its environment, a metaphor frequently used in the discussion of "racial" or "ethnic" groups.

From the time of my very earliest work in the Caribbean I had insisted that each such group must be understood in the context of the society of which it is a part, but from the beginning of this new phase of analysis based on the field research of the late 1960s and 1970s, I began to explore those interdependencies more thoroughly. The chapter on "Hierarchy and the Dual Marriage System" presented here was written for a conference on gender and kinship that provided an opportunity to present some of the research into the historical development of kinship in the Caribbean, and to show the complex interrelations among individuals of different class and racial categorization in the development of these societies. That work has been carried much further by younger scholars with whom I have been privileged to work (Douglass 1992; Lazarus-Black 1994), so that we are now in a position to reject categorically any suggestion that we are dealing with discrete kinship systems in a plural society.

The final chapter in Part One, "Family, Social Change, and Social Policy in the West Indies," addresses explicitly the way in which policy pronouncements have consistently misconstrued the matrifocal family as a *cause* of poverty, rather than seeing it as an integral part of a complex system of class and status relations. Although the discussion in this chapter is focused mainly on the West Indies, many of the arguments are relevant to contemporary discussions of African-American kinship and "family breakdown" in the United States. The paper provides a detailed examination of the way in which family and kinship norms become institutionalized and, whatever their strengths or weaknesses, resist attempts to change them that are based on a simple-minded "rational choice" theory of human behavior.

## Part Two: Conflict and Difference: Race, Culture, and Politics

The studies of kinship and the family presented in Part One raised all the issues of class, race, and "pluralism" at the level of the most intimate social relations. However, the conflicts that followed the ending of colonial rule in the British Caribbean were pitched in a much higher register, transforming intimacy into strident denunciation or—sometimes—into physical violence. As explained above, the theory of "plural society" quickly became a convenient explanation for struggles over power and prestige, and a pretext for intervention by Britain and the United States. In the late 1950s I was invited by the Royal Institute of International Affairs to write a book on British Guiana that would place contemporary social and political conflict in a general framework of historical and economic forces. That book, *British Guiana,* was published in 1962 by Oxford University Press and was subsequently reissued by Greenwood Press in 1980. Its contents are not reproduced here, but its central theme was that British Guiana, like other British West Indian societies, had developed a creole society and culture in which all the constituent groups were integrated into a coercive and hegemonic social order ranked by race and purported approximation to the "civilized" customs of the dominant—British—group. With the ending of British rule several developments were possible. One was that the groups created by the colonial social order, variously termed races or ethnic groups, could mobilize to assume the position of dominance being vacated by the British. And those tendencies were quite clearly evident. A more

hopeful, and constructive, possibility was that the ending of colonialism would provide an opportunity for a complete transformation of the colonial order and the establishment of a society
based on some form of egalitarian individualism and on democratic principles in which race and
other forms of particularistic status would be of minor significance.

This was not a new choice for Caribbean societies; political reformers had oscillated between
a vision of "back to Africa," as in the case of the Garvey movement, and of building a truly egalitarian society on the ruins of colonialism (see Post 1978: 2–5 for an account of the "class versus
race" debate in the Jamaica of the early 1930s). British Guiana was fortunate in developing a
sophisticated leadership for an inclusive political party dedicated to building a socialist state that
would encompass racial and sectional differences. It is easy to look back from the mid-1990s and
assume that any such socialist state was doomed to failure, another fiasco to set beside the long
list of failed experiments in colonial transitional regimes. But of course none of those regimes
existed in isolation; they were, inevitably, casualities of the Cold War, victims of superpower politics. Guyana was no exception.

Among the more durable Caribbean visionaries, Lloyd Best is one of the most intelligent and
most optimistic. While living in British Guiana as economic advisor in 1963, he founded the
New World Group, dedicated to finding rational solutions for the development of British
Guiana, and for the Caribbean generally. Upon his return to the University of the West Indies in
Jamaica in 1964, Best established an offshoot New World Group that became a major influence
among West Indian academics, especially through the publication of *New World Quarterly*. When
Guyana became formally independent in 1966 the New World Group commissioned the
Barbadian novelist George Lamming and the Guyanese poet Martin Carter to edit a special *New
World* Guyana Independence Issue, to which I was invited to contribute an article. This was a sig-
nal honor since the volume included essays by a distinguished body of West Indian intellectuals,
writers, poets, politicians, and even the odd historical figure such as Sir Walter Raleigh. I chose
to examine the original formulation of the theory of the plural society by J.S. Furnivall and the
very different use to which it had been put by M.G. Smith in his studies of the Caribbean and
other parts of the world such as South Africa. When I submitted the essay with a long and typically academic title, George Lamming wrote back that the title did not convey anything about
the contents of the essay and therefore he was changing it to "People and Change." It appears
here, under the more informative title "Plural Society Theory," as Chapter Seven and I continue
to think that it shows J.S. Furnivall to be a much more farsighted and realistic analyst than the
vast majority of those who have misused his ideas.

Furnivall had written, as long ago as 1910, that the free play of economic forces in European
colonies creates multiracial societies based solely on economic competition and lacking in any
overall moral cohesion, or culture. M.G. Smith had taken this idea and developed it into a full-
fledged theory that argued for the existence of a special class of societies in which culturally distinct groups, each with its own institutions, are aggregated by politically dominant powers into
hierarchically ordered "plural societies" held together only by the force of political coercion. Any
change in such a society results merely in a reordering of the hierarchy. Through a more careful
examination of Furnivall's later work I was able to show that he had a much more optimistic view
of the future possibilities of colonial societies than that embedded in M.G. Smith's vision. While
questioning the efficacy of welfare programs grounded in economic development, he urged the
necessity of inventing new modes of integration appropriate to these multiracial societies created

through colonial domination. Those new modes of integration would, he thought, require the fostering of new forms of nationalism through which new moral orders could be built and new forms of social cohesion forged. Thus, far from arguing for the permanence of pluralism he envisioned processes of cultural creation and convergence. These abstract-appearing discussions were highly relevant to the then-current situation in the Caribbean generally, and Guyana in particular.

The emergent conflict in Guyana focused on the supposed cultural differences between Guyanese of African descent and those whose ancestors were imported from India to work as indentured labor on the sugar plantations. A series of works by United States scholars had begun to argue that the East Indian populations of Guyana and Trinidad were, as the bearers of "Indian culture," so profoundly different from the African-descended population (sometimes referred to as Creoles) that they must be thought of as Indian rather than West Indian (Despres 1967; Singer 1967; Klass 1988 [1961]). The conclusions reached by Chandra Jayawardena and myself, based upon our extensive field research in Guyana, were totally different. In 1967 we contributed an article to a volume on Caste among Overseas Indians, a collection in which these controversies over pluralism were played out in many of the articles. Our article, "Caste and social status among the Indians of Guyana," is reproduced here as Chapter Eight. In it we argue forcefully that in spite of the segregation and low status of the immigrant Indian population in the colonial society of British Guiana, profound cultural changes had taken place—including a loss of effective caste distinctions—as the Indian population had been brought within the legal, educational, and political framework of British Guianese society. At the same time the very structure of colonial society created "racial" groups as the constituent units of the state, so that it was hardly surprising that each such group should begin to emphasize the worth of its particular historic "culture," rediscovering and, if necessary, inventing traditions. That process has continued, and even accelerated, in the years since we wrote that essay. Brackette Williams has documented with great skill and insight the way in which "race" and "culture" are deployed in the quotidian processes of social life in modern Guyana (Williams 1991).

The paper reproduced here as Chapter Nine, "Race and Class in the Post-Emancipation Caribbean" was prepared originally for a conference on racism and colonialism held in the Netherlands at the Leiden Centre for the History of European Expansion. It pursues the general themes of this collection in its examination of the cultural meaning of race as this developed and changed with the ending of slavery, focusing primarily upon Jamaica, but drawing upon comparative data when necessary. Although it may appear, at first glance, to veer off into historical discourse, it deals with theoretical issues that are crucial for the understanding of present-day social relations in the Americas. Most importantly it explores the independent significance of ideology in structuring social relations. It refutes the idea that racism emerges directly out of economic structures as a rationalization of economic exploitation, nor does it countenance the idea that racial categories are rooted in essential biological differences or even in the perception of "somatic norm images" (see Hoetink 1967). Instead, I explore the historical process through which the British government attempted to create a new basis for social relations after it forced the ending of slavery in 1838. Slaves were transformed into subjects equal before the law and a system of apparently liberal egalitarianism was created, concurrent with a determined effort to convert the ex-slaves into Christians. However, there was embodied within the very structure of the ideology of liberal egalitarianism a continuing system of racial concepts that ranked persons according to their color, and also according to their perceived ways of thinking, behaving, and speaking in terms of their approximation to the dominant English patterns. A subtle transformation made it impossible for a person of color ever to be considered authentically English in culture, so that the apparently universalist political order set strict boundaries that served to maintain the hierarchical structure of colonial society (see Holt 1992 for a recent argument along the same lines).

The final two essays in this section have been written in the more recent past. The first, "Living in the Gun-Mouth," is a reconsideration of the "racial" conflict that has marked Guyanese history since the country became independent, and it places in more specific political context some of the theoretical issues raised in the other chapters in this section. Its appearance is particularly timely, since the ending of the Cold War and the return to office of Dr. Jagan as President of Guyana have stimulated a reexamination of the events of the 1950s and 1960s, when intervention by Britain and the United States destroyed an incipient democracy and resulted in a long period of repressive government. However, the most important issues examined in this essay have to do with the way in which *a priori* categories influence the selection of material for anthropological analysis. The decision to study "African" or "Indian" communities is shown to deflect attention from the complex interrelations between people living in such communities. One has to be aware of the extent to which political struggle can mobilize the myths of primordial identity, but people living in societies like Guyana—which is in all major respects like other societies in this hemisphere—are well aware of the ties that bind them together as well as of the potential for conflict. Responsible social science cannot adopt the very language of political conflict that it purports to analyze, and I have suggested that a revisionist reading of Max Weber's analytical categories of class and status group provide a more adequate framework for understanding status and power struggles in the modern world than the increasingly meaningless term "ethnicity."

This argument is pursued further in the last essay of the collection, "On the Disutility of the Notion of 'Ethnic Group' for Understanding Status Struggles in the Modern World," but this time focussing on the modern urban United States, and the perennial discussion of supposed cultural differences among "ethnic groups." Drawing upon material collected as part of the University of Chicago Urban Family Life and Poverty Project, the paper explores the complexity of the intersection of class and status among the poor of Chicago, and in the process demonstrates the way in which use of the blanket term "ethnic group" conceals that complexity. That concealment is particularly important in the United States where class differences are so frequently obscured beneath a tissue of assumptions about the special characteristics of "racial" or "ethnic" groups. The problem is not to relegate group cultural differences to a position of insignificance, but to understand how they are deployed, created, or perpetuated in contexts of class oppression or political struggle.

Unlike sociologists, anthropologists rarely become involved in advocating domestic social policy, confining their lobbying activities mainly to drawing attention to the plight of small minority populations that are the victims of "development" policies or genocide. The case of the African-American family in the western hemisphere is an exception, although the writings of anthropologists are little heeded by politicians and other formulators of social policy. This final essay can hardly be construed as a vigorous advocacy of one or another social policy, but it does speak to the issues of "family disorganization" and "ethnicity," and the way in which they are constructed as objects of policy formulation.

# PART ONE

## *Kinship and Family Structure*

# CHAPTER TWO

# Hypotheses and the Problem of Explanation (1956)

In the preceding chapters we have examined most of the features of Guianese society that are necessary to the type of correlation we wish to make, and this chapter outlines our main hypothesis.* We also deal briefly with the problem of "explanation" as it has been conceived in relation to West Indian family life.

## STATUS DIFFERENTIATION IN THE TOTAL SOCIAL SYSTEM AND THE INTERNAL STRUCTURE OF THE HOUSEHOLD GROUP

The crux of our argument lies in this:

We maintain that the matrifocal system of domestic relations and household groupings in the villages we have studied can be regarded as the obverse of the marginal nature of the husband-father role. We further argue that there is a correlation between the nature of the husband-father role and the role of men in the economic system and in the system of social stratification in the total Guianese society. Men, in their role of husband-father, are placed in a position where neither their social status nor their access to, and command of, economic resources are of major importance in the functioning of the household group at certain stages of its development.

Such an argument requires a good deal of elaboration and we shall begin by attempting to summarize the main features of the status system and the family system as follows:

### Features of the Status System

A. There is a scale of color values at the extremes of which the "white" or European complex is given positive value, and the "black" or Negro complex is given negative value, and this serves as a basis for the hierarchical ranking of persons, and groups of persons, according to the "color" characteristics ascribed to them.

B. The other main basis of evaluation of a person's status is in terms of his performance in economic or occupational roles, thereby making it possible for a limited number of persons to achieve higher status than that which is initially ascribed to them on the basis of their "color," though the ethnic component of a person's social character is never completely effaced as a factor in status placement. Achieved status is secondary to ascribed status, especially at the extreme ends of the color scale, but the evaluation of performance in jobs, educational attainment, etc., can serve as a basis for upward mobility especially in the middle zone of the color scale.

C. We may speak of a color/class system in-so-far as the internal differentiation of the social system allocates differential facilities and rewards largely on the basis of position on the scale

---

* This essay is an abbreviated version of chapter nine of my book *The Negro Family in British Guiana,* a chapter that sets out the major theoretical framework of the book as a whole. It introduced the term "the matrifocal family," a term that has been widely used (and misused) since. The book has long been out of print.

of socially evaluated color differences, but the fact that performance criteria are taken into account keeps the system "open" to a degree where we can speak of "classes" which do not have an absolute one-to-one relation to ethnic factors.

D. Ethnic groups such as the Portuguese, Chinese, and East Indians, that do not fit readily into the color/class hierarchy, are able to infiltrate at all levels and to take over special functions where a relative lack of status-consciousness is an advantage, particularly in the retail and distributive trades. The development of a separate collectivity, primarily oriented towards a function implying the predominance of economic achievement, such as business enterprise, competition, and efficiency, really conflicts with ascribed membership of groups, and it would seem to have been fortuitous that these ethnic groups came from societies where there was already a tradition of trading, shopkeeping, moneylending, and so on. The market nexus of petty trading in British Guiana is interstitial to the ascriptively based social groupings, but it has not developed very far towards becoming organized, or forming a primary focus of attention for the ordering of social relations, and in any case the larger scale marketing operations have been controlled by the higher status ethnic groups. The very multiplicity of operators in the lowest level of the marketing system (especially vendors of garden produce, fruits, etc.), is an indication of the tendency to spread the functions and prevent specialization from developing to a point where it would conflict with the ascribed low status of the operators. One special feature of a differentiated group in market operations is the necessity for "affective neutrality," and this could most readily be found in the Chinese and Portuguese groups, where all other sections of the population did in fact regard them as being neutral in terms of the scale of color values, and the symbolism connected with it (see Parsons 1952: 59–61).

E. In the villages studied, the model of the total social system tends to repeat itself, but since the village is only a section of the total society, it does not have the same degree of internal differentiation. The village "upper class" is either occupationally or ethnically differentiated in the sense that its members are either non-Negroes, or in high-status white-collar (usually government) jobs, and it shows its difference by means of "diacritical" signs such as dress, speech pattern, marriage pattern, etc.[1]

F. The main village group tends to be solidary *vis-à-vis* the rest of the society, and status differentiation within it is discouraged since this would conflict with the main status differentiations within the total social system. However, there are both non-hierarchical differentiations (segmentations), and minor differential prestige positions within it, as well as the inevitable age and sex differentiations which are not directly relevant to the present discussion.

G. There is a variation in the degree of internal differentiation as between the three villages.

## Main Aspects of Family Structure

A. The household group tends to be matrifocal in the sense that a woman in the status of "mother" is usually the *de facto* leader of the group, and conversely the husband-father, although *de jure* head of the household group (if present), is usually marginal to the complex of internal relationships of the group. By "marginal" we mean that he associates relatively infrequently with the other members of the group, and is on the fringe of the effective ties that bind the group together.

B. Household groups normally come into being when a man and a woman enter a conjugal union (legal or common-law marriage), and set up house together in a separate dwelling. Either or both partners may have children who were born prior to the establishment of an effective conjugal union.

C. During the period when the woman is bearing children she will be most dependent on her spouse for economic support and most subject to his authority and control, but as her children grow older she becomes much more independent and acquires much greater security in her status as "mother."

D. Common-law marriage is a cultural characteristic of the lower class, and can be regarded as a permissive deviation from the norms of the total social system. The non-legal nature of the tie reflects the reluctance to establish a conclusive bond and is in accordance with the primary emphasis upon the mother-child relationship rather than the conjugal relationship.

E. There is a variation in the incidence of different types of conjugal union as between the three villages.

These two paradigms have been constructed in an attempt to compress into a more manageable form the relevant features of the two complexes we wish to correlate, and they are only intended as a brief summary of our previous descriptions.

It would seem that whilst biological relatedness is taken as a major focus of status ascription in the total social system, the unit of kinship which is emphasized in this respect is not the nuclear or extended family as such, but rather the widest possible kinship unit which is the ethnic group itself. Within this group two other points of reference become foci of differentiation in descending order of importance (from this point of view). They are territorial affiliation (membership of the local community), and matrifiliation. Matrifiliation as a basis of status ascription has a long history in the West Indies, and under the slave regime it was taken as defining legal status. The child of a slave woman and a free man always took its mother's legal status and became a slave (see Cousins 1935). In the contemporary situation the relation to the mother almost invariably determines the place of residence of the child, for it is the services rendered to the child by the mother, such as "care" in its broadest sense, which are amongst the main functions of the household group. In this respect it is significant that any woman will give any child a little food, and children quite often eat at their playmates' homes or at the houses of kinsfolk if they happen to be there at meal times.

There is a sense in which we can take for granted the fact that the mother-child relationship will be a close one in any society, and the real problem then begins to center on the way in which masculine roles are integrated into the family system, and the way in which the mother-child relationship is structured to fit in with the general structure including the masculine role pattern (see Radcliffe-Brown 1950: 77).

In societies where kinship provides the basis for practically all the differentiation within the social system, the positions of prestige and control are almost invariably and totally vested in adult males and no matter whether the system is patrilineal, matrilineal, or based on double unilineal descent, it is males in whom the principal rights over property and services are vested. The varying patterns of domestic organization may place these rights in different contexts, and even where the rights themselves are formally vested in women, as amongst the Hopi, it is still the males who control the exercise of these rights, and who hold positions of primary managerial authority (see Eggan 1959).

It is clear from our discussions in previous chapters that the role of husband-father is by no means absent in lower-class Negro society in British Guiana, nor is it reduced to such insignificant proportions as we find in certain extreme matrilineal societies such as the traditional Nayar (Gough 1952) or Menangkabau (Josselin de Jong 1951).

Amongst the Nayar a woman resides in the joint household *(taravad)* of her matrilineage, and is visited by a series of lovers with whom she has sexual relations. Her children remain with her in the taravad where they come under the authority of the eldest male member of the group, who may be the woman's brother, mother's brother, or even mother's mother's brother. The child's father, who is an outsider to the group (he may even belong to a different caste), has no economic, political, or ritual functions in relation to the taravad of his children. His relationship to his child is confined to presenting certain customary gifts at the time of the birth. The role of husband-father is not completely absent from the Nayar system, but it is reduced to extremely limited proportions.

However, men do have vital economic, political, status, and ritual functions in relation to their own taravad, and it is the existence of a tightly organized unilineal descent group—having strongly corporate functions and laying stress upon the close interdependence of a set of brothers and sisters—that makes the Nayar system completely different from that with which we are dealing in British Guiana. The Nayar are able to reduce the husband-father role to minimal proportions precisely because male roles in relation to the taravad are so highly developed and the supportive activities of males in relation to women and children are embodied in the structure of the taravad. Virtually the only activities of men in relation to women which are left outside the sphere of the matrilineage are those concerned with sexual activity and procreation.

In the bilaterally organized kinship system of the villages with which we are dealing in British Guiana, men are essential providers of economic support for women and children. Women can, and do, engage in money-making activities, but they cannot be economically self-sufficient. The question then arises as to how men's supportive functions shall be tied in to the family system. There are thus two distinct problems to be considered. The first concerns the male role in society, and here we have indicated that men are expected to earn money to contribute to the support of women and children. We have described in some detail the difficulties which men face in a society where there is little prospect of steady employment, and we have also stressed the fact that there is little occupational differentiation and correspondingly little hierarchical status differentiation amongst the village men. The second problem concerns the direction in which men are to offer their economic support, and this is the main problem we are to consider here. Economic support for women and children is located in a series of statuses, the principal ones being those of son, husband, and lover. It is not located in a group, for in a bilaterally organized kinship system there is no enduring kinship-group structure available. For any particular woman with children the problem is to find a male in one of the above statuses to provide the necessary support. Chance factors inherent in the birth and death incidence render the likelihood of there being an individual *always* available to fill a given status somewhat uncertain, and therefore a situation such as the one in British Guiana has to be sufficiently fluid to permit of a choice of alternative persons. This is particularly the case in bilateral systems of narrow range.

One way of resolving this difficulty is to vest the functions of economic support in a husband-father who is selected from a wide range of possible individuals, and this is precisely what happens in our case. However, the importance of the economic function of the husband-father becomes diminished as the woman passes her period of maximum dependence and becomes freed for economic activities of her own and as her sons begin to take over supportive functions. The reasons for this must be sought in the economic and stratification systems of the total social system.

In a society where the range of effective kinship ties is narrowed to a point where the nuclear family becomes a highly significant and relatively isolated unit, as in urban middle-class groups in the United States, then the position of the husband-father in the primary status-determining occupational system—rather than in an extended kinship system—is a crucial one. In such a situation, hierarchical mobility is normal and the husband-father determines the social status of the whole unit by virtue of his position in the occupational system. He becomes the peg on which the whole unit hangs.

In British Guiana the male member of the village groups neither has exclusive control over property and services, including the means of production for the livelihood of the household group, nor does he determine its status in the social system by virtue of his position in a graded occupational hierarchy, since this is already determined to a large extent by "race" or "color," plus membership of the territorial unit which is the village. The important fact is that occupations are not hierarchically graded to any significant extent within the main Negro village groups, though the occupations of the Negro men are ranked low in the total occupational system in the same way that Negro men are ranked low in the color scale. The male's participation in the occupational system does not affect the status of the other members of the household group, which is already defined by their racial characteristics and territorial affiliation. This is a very broad statement and only holds good for the relatively undifferentiated lowest status group. As soon as one approaches the upper fringe of this group, where prestige factors begin to operate, or get into the higher-status village group, then the occupation of the husband-father becomes significant, and there is a quite definite tendency for his position in the household group to be established, and for him to become a reference point for the other members of the group. In the urban middle class, certain other factors may intervene to tend to bring the focus of solidarity of the group back to the mother, particularly where the man marries a lighter-colored woman who then becomes a focus of attention for status placement on the color scale (see Braithwaite 1953). In the middle class there is always this interplay between occupational factors, and "color" and/or "cultural" factors. In the lowest status group the only basis for male authority in the household unit is the husband-father's contribution to the economic foundation of the group, and where there is both insecurity in jobs where males are concerned, and opportunities for women to engage in money-making activities, including farming, then there is likely to develop a situation where men's roles are structurally marginal in the complex of domestic relations. Concomitantly, the status of women as mothers is enhanced and the natural importance of the mother role is left unimpeded.

Although we have had to present our argument rather forcefully in order to make it clear, there are certain reservations which must be entered. The analysis of family structure has shown quite clearly that the elementary family, consisting of a conjugal pair and their offspring, is not atypical in the groups we have been considering, but is in fact the *normal* unit of co-residence, particularly at the stage when a father-figure is important in the socialization of the children. It is not within our competence to discuss the psychological implications of this fact but in any discussion of socialization it should be borne in mind that we are dealing with a social system wherein the normal unit of child-rearing is an elementary family unit. In particular cases of mental development, it would be important to look for the deviations from this norm and, in discussing the psychological component of values, it may be necessary to bear in mind the nature of the father-child and mother-child relationships. In the three villages we have been discussing it would not be justifiable to treat these questions as if the normal pattern were for children to grow up without any kind of relationship to a father or father-surrogate, and high illegitimacy rates are not an indication of these relationships.

## THE CULTURE-HISTORICAL APPROACH TO NEW WORLD NEGRO FAMILY ORGANIZATION

Writings on New World Negro family organization have tended to concentrate to some extent on the controversy as to whether the form of the New World Negro family is the result of the peculiar conditions obtaining on the plantations during the period of slavery or whether it can be seen as a modified survival of an "African" family pattern. Equally plausible theories supported by historical evidence have been advanced on either side, and the polemical discussions have brought to light a considerable body of information and have been productive of many profound insights. It would seem, though, that there is a need for synchronic analysis, which attempts to understand the working of the system without any preconceptions as to its previous states. There is always a danger that the prior task of sociological analysis may be side-stepped when historical factors are prematurely introduced as "explanatory" devices.

Professor and Mrs. Herskovits were, in a very real sense, the pioneers of anthropological study in the Caribbean area, and their work has had a profound influence on subsequent investigators, so that it is impossible to discuss the problems of the area without considering their work. It is beyond the scope of this book to offer a critical examination of the highly developed theoretical approach they brought to their studies, and we shall confine our discussion to the interpretations they present of some of the institutions of West Indian society. More particularly we shall consider those interpretations concerning the village of Toco in Trinidad which most nearly resembles August Town, Perseverance, and Better Hope [the British Guiana villages in which this study was carried out] (M.J. and S.F. Herskovits 1947).

The Herskovitses are primarily concerned with the problem of law in history, or the processes of social change, and they suggest that two different drives work together to fashion civilization.

> There are first of all the forces that, without reference to cultural form as such, are constantly at work to maintain the balance between stability and change in every culture or, where different cultures are in close and continuous contact, to accelerate change. Then there are the unique historical sequences of events which, in any given instance, determine particular reactions in specific situations, and through this the particular forms that the institutions, beliefs, and values in a given culture will take at a given moment in its history (M.J. & S.F. Herskovits 1947: 5–6).

In discussing Toco, they state explicitly that it will be necessary to comprehend both the general laws of cultural dynamics, and the particular historical forces bringing about change in Toco. These "general laws of social dynamics" are relatively simple and are set out at length by Professor Herskovits in other publications. Principally they concern the idea of "cultural focus," "cultural retention," and "reinterpretation" of "borrowed" items of culture (M.J. Herskovits 1945). Fundamental to the whole theory is the assertion that culture is learned, and culture is an all-embracing concept of which social organization is one "aspect" (M.J. Herskovits 1952). They demonstrate quite convincingly in the opening section of *Trinidad Village* that one way of explaining the importance of women in the family structure of Toco is to see this structure as a persistence of a part of the form of African family organization. In Africa each wife has her own hut which she inhabits with her children, and whilst those aspects of African social organization which were the field of male activity (the clan, and the extended family) were impossible to maintain under slavery conditions, this basic structure of a woman and her children persisted through all the vissicitudes of slavery. The role of the father continued to be remote from the children and the wife as it was in Africa. Unfortunately there is an equally convincing "explanation" of how this situation involving the importance of women in the family system might have arisen. Franklin Frazier has carefully documented the disruption in family life brought about by slavery and demonstrated how the natural unit of a woman and her children was the one most likely to survive, no matter what the antecedent form of family life might have been (Frazier 1939).[2]

## CONCLUSION

Without extending the range of our discussion any further it is evident that we have raised many fundamental problems merely by juxtaposing the material from several different "culture areas" as we have done. What we have done, essentially, is to take two main features of the social systems we have dealt with—social stratification and family structure—and describe some aspects of their interrelations in the different societies. We started out by trying to understand the structure of the family in three village communities in British Guiana, and an attempt was made to analyze this structure as fully as possible in the main section of this work. Inevitably we came up against the old problem of whether the nature of family relations in New World Negro society is to be explained in terms of historical factors such as the survival of African patterns of behavior, the peculiar conditions existing on the slave plantations, or whether we could advance more plausible hypotheses in terms of the functional requirements of an ongoing social system. It has been remarked that there is a fundamental similarity between the types of family structure found in Negro communities all over the New World, and of course if one regards this unit as a clearly defined "culture area" there is a tendency to try to explain its unity and peculiar characteristics in terms of a set of factors peculiar to it alone. The very concept of culture held by the majority of scholars who have worked in the area has tended towards this type of analysis, for culture in this sense is essentially an historical concept, and culture contact becomes a process of exchange of culture traits over a period of time. The same type of analysis has been employed by scholars working in the Latin-American field, and it seems truly remarkable that the two areas–Latin American and New World Negro—should have been treated in such a completely separatist manner. If the same kind of approach had been adopted towards the problems of African anthropology it is difficult to see how the advances in comparative social structure in Africa could have developed. Had societies been classified according to their complexes of culture traits alone, without reference to their structure, then presumably a book such as *African Political Systems* or *African Systems of Kinship and Marriage* could never have been written (Fortes and Evans-Pritchard 1940; Radcliffe-Brown and Daryll Forde 1950).

Throughout Latin America and the Caribbean area we are dealing with societies that all exhibit similar structural features, and this gives the whole region a unity which is not to be found in a comparison of the particular cultural symbols through which that structure is given meaning. Admittedly, both areas have been subject to not-dissimilar sequences of historical events, since both have been areas of colonization of European powers. But since quite different "cultures" have been involved, Amerindian and African, we should expect the resulting situation to be quite different in the two areas. In terms of our definition of culture, we do in fact find that the contemporary "cultures" in the two areas are very different indeed. Radcliffe-Brown speaks of a "cultural tradition" as the process of handing down knowledge, skills, ideas, belief, tastes, and sentiments, which are thus acquired by other persons through the learning process (Radcliffe-Brown 1952: 4). A more precise and systematic statement, and one with which we would substantially agree, is made by Talcott Parsons, when he says, "It is [such] a shared symbolic system which functions in interaction which will here be called a *cultural tradition*" (Parsons 1952: 11). If culture is a system of shared symbolic meanings which make communication possible in an ordered social life, then it is *the way* in which actions are carried out that interests us when discussing "culture." Thus, in the Peruvian village of Moche studied by John Gillin in 1944, when a Mochero dies the church bells are rung in almost the same way that they are in August Town in British Guiana, but when the *velorio* is held on the night following the death, although it seems to have exactly the same functions as a Guianese "wake" in expressing a sense of communal loss, etc., the details of the way in which the body is laid out, the women weep, and so on are quite different.

If we look at all the societies we have mentioned in this section [in the original book they include Trinidad, Haiti, the United States, Jamaica, Peru, Mexico, Guatemala, and Scotland] we find a correlation between low social status in a stratified society, and a type of family system in which men seem to lack importance as authoritarian figures in domestic relations. These are facts of social structure, and the arrangement of these structural elements is basically similar despite marked variations in their corresponding cultural complexes in different societies. We are really dealing with subsystems of the several societies, although certain aspects of the total societies are basically comparable. In all cases the subgroups with which we are most immediately concerned constitute relatively solidary groups, differentiated with respect to other groups in the society, but internally relatively undifferentiated so far as status is concerned.

If our analysis is correct then it raises certain issues of general importance. It would suggest that there is a rewarding field for comparative study between Latin American and West Indian societies using a structural frame of reference. The relations of racial or ethnic groups become special cases of a general theory of social stratification, and "acculturation" has to be seen in the light of continuing social differentiations of a certain kind.

Cultural traditions of certain ethnic subgroups may be found to persist as indices of status differentiation rather than as a result of geographical isolation. Leach has graphically shown how even linguistic differences can persist between households in one local community provided there is a structural base for such cultural differentiation, and his conclusion that culture and structure appear to vary independently is borne out by our researches, though there is always the possibility that the independent variability is merely apparent at the particular level of abstraction at which we are working (Leach 1954: 288–90).

# CHAPTER THREE

# Culture and Social Structure in the Caribbean (1963)

The territories of the circum-Caribbean region contain some of the most complex societies in the world. Their complexity lies not in their size, degree of internal differentiation, or technological development, but in the dependent and fragmented nature of their cultures, the ethnic diversity of their populations, the special nature of their dependent economies, the peculiarities of their political development, and the apparent incoherence of their social institutions. It has been suggested that many Caribbean societies have no history of their own but should be viewed as an extension of Europe. Dr. Eric Williams, Prime Minister of Trinidad and Tobago, has recently written in reference to his country:

> On August 31, 1962, a country will be free, a miniature state will be established, but a society and a nation will not have been formed (Williams 1962: 284).

His words are an almost exact echo of those of a former Governor of Trinidad, Lord Harris, who wrote in 1848:

> [A]s the question now stands a race has been freed but a society has not been formed (Burn 1937: 370).

When Lord Harris wrote, he was particularly concerned with the problem of creating a society out of a population consisting of recently freed Negro slaves, their white masters, and an intermediate group of colored persons created out of the irregular unions between white men and Negro women. By the time Dr. Williams came to face the same problem, Trinidad had acquired a large population of East Indians and sizable minorities of Chinese and Portuguese. Each Caribbean territory faces something of the same problem that faces Trinidad, but national unity is further compromised by sharp differences in standard of living between rich and poor—standards that often coincide with ethnic divisions. This incoherence of the national and societal image within each unit is to some extent a reflection of the recent growth of the very idea of national independence, and of an attempt to establish an image different from that of the metropolitan countries; but Haiti and some of the Latin American countries show that the condition is not cured by simple political autonomy.

The study of kinship and family structure reflects these difficulties and uncertainties; throughout the region we find ambiguity in normative prescriptions and variability in behavior patterns even within ethnic and class units. Most of the work on kinship and family structure has been concentrated upon lower-class Negro groups and a number of recent publications continue this bias (see Mintz & Davenport 1961; M.G. Smith 1962). Some general descriptions of non-Negro groups in Puerto Rico have been published but as Mintz says,

> In Puerto Rico, in spite of the large number of papers and books dealing directly or tangentially with rural family life, there is nothing permitting rigorous comparison with the excellent studies of domestic social structure carried out in Jamaica, Trinidad, British Guiana and elsewhere (Mintz 1961: 528).

Studies of East Indian family structure in Trinidad and British Guiana have not really been brought into the same comparative framework as yet, though they are crucial cases for assessing the relative effect of cultural tradition and structural constraint, and for the testing of other hypotheses.[1] Even if analysis is confined to Negro groups, the number of variables that have to be taken into account is considerable. A brief discussion of the development of family studies in the region will show that some unsolved problems and unresolved conflicts still dominate present-day discussions.

The first real family studies to be made in the Caribbean were an offshoot of studies of the American Negro, and they were carried out as a result of Professor Herskovits's scheme for plotting the persistence of Africanisms in the New World (see Herskovits 1937, 1945; Herskovits and Herskovits 1934, 1947). They were not studies of Caribbean family structure, nor even of Haitian or Trinidadian family structure, but of family forms among the descendants of Africans, and of the relation of those forms to the general structural features of African societies. Professor Franklin Frazier had formulated some significant generalizations about the effects of slavery upon the family life of American Negroes (Frazier 1939). Unlike Professor Herskovits, he did not regard New World Negroes as being primarily displaced Africans, but rather as Americans trying to build a stable life after the almost total social disorganization of slavery and in a society which continues to be hostile and discriminatory. He argued that deviations from normal American patterns of behavior (including normal family patterns) can best be seen as a failure to achieve proper adjustment because of continuing obstruction. Gunnar Myrdal put it even more strongly when be said,

> In practically all its divergencies, American Negro culture is not something independent of general American culture. It is a distorted development, or a pathological condition, of the general American culture (Myrdal 1944: 928).

Myrdal is making a deliberate statement of value which he proposes as a basis for practical action but the general point is similar to that made by Franklin Frazier.

This controversy between Herskovits and Frazier was introduced into the earliest studies in the British West Indies and fitted itself into the emerging preoccupation with welfare problems that came with the post-war movement towards greater political autonomy. It was very noticeable, for example, that Jamaica had an illegitimacy rate of over seventy per cent of all live births and this caused considerable concern as soon as a more active interest began to be taken in the well-being of the lower classes. Was this evidence of massive social disorganization or was there something wrong with a view that measured "legitimacy" according to "English" or "upper class" standards? It had long been known that women exhibited a high degree of independence both in the West Indies and among Negroes in the United States, and Frazier had referred to the "matri-centric" family based on a mother and her children, and to a "type of matriarchate" based upon a group consisting of an old woman, her daughters, and their children. The primacy of the relationships between mother and children was remarked upon by both Frazier and Herskovits. Frazier saw this unit of mother and children as the one primary group which had persisted throughout the slavery period, while Herskovits derived its structural importance from the domestic organization of African societies, where the mother-children group forms a separate cell within the framework of the polygynous family. Both spoke of the destruction of male roles in relation to the domestic group during the slavery period and Frazier tried to show with a wealth of historical material that American Negroes had rebuilt a stable family life with strong paternal authority whenever they had been able to do so. That is, whenever they could get decent jobs that enabled them to provide the economic foundations for a reasonable family life in the American fashion. In looking at West Indian societies it was natural to adopt the points of view developed in these studies since the family arrangements seemed to be quite similar to those described by Frazier, and there was ample evidence of African cultural survivals. But there were other factors involved in the West Indies. The atmosphere of these developing societies was such that it predisposed students to examine the contemporary situation rather than its historical derivation. Professor Simey did as much as anyone to set the pattern for future studies by his use of simple distribution figures for various family "types," taking his data from a survey conducted by Lewis Davidson in Jamaica. Both Simey (Simey 1946) and Henriques (1953) directed attention to the color-class system and to the fact that there seemed to be a close relation among color, occupational or economic level, and family type. By the time Henriques's book was published in 1953, the idea was firmly established that there are a number of different family types, each of which is "normal" within the stratum in which it occurs. A slight variant of this idea was put forward by Dom Basil Matthews on the basis of a number of years work in Trinidad (Matthews 1953). Focussing attention upon what he called "the non-legal union," he tried to show that the persistence of this form of mating in the New World is related to the continued importance of plantation agriculture, which dominates the economies and the social life of so many territories. He wrote:

> The persistence of the non-legal union has to do essentially with the persistence in the social system of those elements which produced it in the first instance. On the impersonal or material side, the effective agents or factors comprise the geographic, economic, moral and social conditions built into the free plantation economy, heir to the physical and social traditions of the plantation in slavery. On the personal and formal side, the deciding factor was, and is, the free choice of the people. It must, however, be conceded that in their choice the people were confronted with an overmastering set of social and economic conditions which it was morally impossible, that is to say, extremely difficult, for them to overcome.

> The social and economic setting and background of the non-legal union everywhere suffice to explain its social origins and its social structure. And this setting and historical background are the same for all peoples in the New World, even for those who did not themselves undergo the ordeals of slavery (Matthews 1953: 104).

This was an important variant upon the themes of color and poverty because it introduced the idea that high illegitimacy rates and unstable family forms are not peculiar to the Negro lower classes but are related to the existence of a form of social organization found in the non-Negro areas of Latin America as well. There is also the suggestion here that the plantation economy produced a peculiar type of social system wherever it occurred, a type of social system with a distinct value configuration which would affect all those who became involved in it irrespective of their contact with plantation life itself.

Here then by the early 1950s the main shape of future studies had been blocked out. This is by no means a complete survey of the work that had been published up to that time. A fuller bibliography can be assembled from the summaries by Mintz and Davenport contained in *Working*

*Papers in Caribbean Social Organization.*[2] No attempt has been made here to examine the often penetrating commentaries by contemporary writers for the slavery and post-slavery periods. Extracts such as the following show that many of the ideas we work with today are really quite old:

> I have known them [the slaves] point to things of this description, for the purpose of shewing that it is impossible for them to marry. Over their children it is obvious that they could have no authority resembling that which parents in a free country possess: they could only leave them the same wretched inheritance which they received from their ancestors. Hence those who have children are careless in respect to the habits they form, and the lives they lead. They know they can never sink lower in the scale of society than they already find themselves placed, and they have no hope of rising. A regular line of orderly conduct may save them from the lash but it can effect no radical change in their conditions (*Negro Slavery* 1823: 57–58).

By the early 1950s a clear distinction had been made between cultural persistence as an explanatory device and the study of contemporary structural arrangements and interconnections. Some writers like Simey, Henriques, and Matthews adopted a two-dimensional approach but without pushing very far in either direction. The obvious need was for more detailed studies, both historical and of contemporary structure; the main emphasis in recent work has been on the latter for the simple reason that material is more easily available. Mr. George Robert's work in demographic problems is perhaps an exception in that he has done considerable research on archival and census material, but he too has been concentrating upon surveys to provide supplementary data in recent years (Roberts 1957; Roberts & Braithwaite 1959, 1960, 1961a, 1961b, 1962). Almost all recent discussions have been based upon the analysis of quantitative data of the kind presented in my own work on British Guiana and in Miss Clarke's study of Jamaica (Smith 1956; Clarke 1957). In the Mintz-Davenport volume, *Working Papers in Caribbean Social Organization,* four out of the five papers concentrate upon analysis of quantitative material on household composition while M.G. Smith's book *West Indian Family Structure* is an extended comparison of statistical data on household composition and mating from five samples—two in Jamaica, two in Grenada, and one in Carriacou. One of the reasons for the concentration upon domestic organization was that since it had been usual to speak of lower-class family life as being "disorganized" it was important to establish whether any patterning existed at all, and whether the "disorganization" was not primarily a matter of definition. From our general knowledge of other societies we know that unstable marriage, separate residence of spouses, or even the complete whittling away of the marriage relationship, as among the Nayar, is not necessarily a sign of social instability or of pathological development. In an important paper published in 1949, Fortes had shown that a wide range of variability in household composition among the Ashanti could be understood as the result of the varying strength of two major forces: the pull of matrilineal kinship ties on the one hand, and the tendency for the nuclear family to establish itself as a separate unit on the other (Fortes 1949b). It was pointed out that while economic factors and missionary teaching tended to reinforce the claims of nuclear family relationships at the expense of the matrilineal tie, the conflict was not new, but must be rooted in the very nature of matrilineal systems. Audrey Richards made much the same point in an essay on Central African matrilineal societies published in 1950 (Richards 1950). Fortes also demonstrated that the shape of households is bound to change over time since households are constituted around the process of physical and social reproduction and are therefore tied to biological birth, maturation, and death—a point which he has made even more elegantly in a recent publication (Fortes 1958). Much the same techniques of analysis have been used in recent studies in the Caribbean but the problem has been to determine the forces which are at work giving shape to domestic group structure. Another way to put it is to ask how social reproduction is accomplished and how it fits with other activities which in many societies are embedded in domestic organization—activities such as mating, domestic services such as cooking, washing, the provision of economic support, and so on. In my studies of three Negro villages in British Guiana, *The Negro Family in British Guiana*, I paid particular attention to the developmental cycle of household groups and tried to see the extent to which the ideal form of nuclear family domestic group is realized in practice and what patterning there is in the deviations from this form. Nancie L. Solien drew attention to the fact that in view of the many relationships which seem to exist in some Caribbean societies between individuals who reside in *different* households, including nuclear family relationships, more attention should be given to investigating these relationships and a clear distinction should be made between domestic organization and family structure (Solien 1960). M.G. Smith takes this point and makes it the basis of his analysis, though the nature of much of his survey data, which was collected during brief interviews, makes it impossible for him to deal in depth with extra-residential relationships. As more field studies are made available it is becoming clear that we need to reconsider the whole question of the relation between nuclear family relationships, socialization, and domestic structure; new questions have arisen and new investigations will have to be carried out, but unless we are to revise the whole of current family theory it will not be possible to ignore nuclear family relationships as one important constellation of roles which has functional as well as formal implications.

Another major variable, or set of variables, that has been investigated for its effect upon family and domestic organization is "the economy" or economic factors. Earlier writers such as Frazier, Simey, and Henriques had discussed the effect of "poverty" in producing or perpetuating unstable family forms. One of Miss Clarke's main objectives in conducting the West Indian Social Survey (which was actually a study of family life and child rearing in Jamaica) had been to measure the effect of varying economic background upon family structure. In order to do this she chose communities in a) a sugar plantation area, b) a poverty-stricken peasant farming area and c) a relatively prosperous community of citrus farmers (Clarke 1957). Miss Clarke's collaborator in this study, Dr. Madeleine Kerr, transformed the idea of "poverty" into that of "social deprivation" by adding other dimensions to it and has since carried out comparative work in a Liverpool slum area which yields surprisingly similar conclusions about the effect of such deprivation upon personality (Kerr 1952). Most of the conclusions of these studies are incorporated in Davenport's excellent discussion of the Jamaican family system (Davenport 1961). Cumper's paper on Barbados and Wilson's on Providencia Island both treat of economic and status factors as the prime variable affecting domestic and family relations but none of the papers in *Working Papers in Caribbean Social Organization,* nor in M.G. Smith's book, deal adequately with the whole question of status and societal and subcultural norms, mainly because all the studies limit themselves to Negro subsectors of these societies.

The other major variable to receive considerable attention recently is the organization of mating relations. From one point of view this is an integral part of the discussion of nuclear family relationships. In the Caribbean it must receive special attention because of the prevalence of unstable mating, of a widespread distinction between legal and non-legal unions, and the existence of mating unions which do not involve common residence. Studies by Roberts and Braithwaite (1961a, 1961b, 1962), Judith Blake (1961), and M.G. Smith (1962), focus upon the variability in mating relations and its effect upon family structure, and M.G. Smith's book raises anew the whole question of African heritage versus slavery by his derivation of present mating forms from slavery. In the following discussion these varying aspects of Caribbean family structure and its social milieu are dealt with one by one in an attempt to take stock of recent contributions.

## THE NUCLEAR FAMILY AND KINSHIP STRUCTURES

Since Murdock published his *Social Structure* in 1949 there has been considerable controversy over the question of the universality of the nuclear family and over Murdock's statement:

> The family is a social group characterized by common residence, economic cooperation, and reproduction. It includes adults of both sexes, at least two of whom maintain a socially approved sexual relationship, and one or more children, own or adopted, of the sexually cohabiting adults (Murdock 1949: 1).

It has been pointed out that in many cases husbands and wives habitually live in separate households, or that in some societies nuclear families are so absorbed in wider units that they can hardly be said to exist as separate organizational complexes at all. Despite these objections there has been a convergence upon the view that the basic functions of the family are those of socialization and the regulation of personality, whatever other activities the family may engage in, and for these functions the role structure of nuclear family relationships seems to be both required and universally present in all societies.[3] According to some variants of this view it is not necessary that every "family" should be a concretely coresidential nuclear family group, but the role system of nuclear family relationships should be institutionalized and in the normal cases enough interaction should exist to carry out the functions and to maintain the system. In particular cases nuclear family relationships exist across the boundaries of household groups, household groups take on a great many other activities than those of child-care and sexual interaction, and nuclear family roles may be performed by individuals other than "real" family members, but empirically there seems to be a close correspondence between "family" activities and domestic group organization. As Fortes says, "In all human societies, the workshop, so to speak, of social reproduction, is the domestic group" (Fortes 1958: 2). These views would seem to mean that the nuclear family is more than a fortuitous by-product of sexual mating and physical birth; that it has positive functions and is in a sense "required" if societies of human beings are to continue. Even Leach in his discussion of the variability of ideologies of reproduction and genetic transmission seems to assume that underneath the differing types of relationship of incorporation and alliance actual nuclear family relationships exist (Leach 1961: 17–26). Even if the theory exists that mothers and sons are like affines, they do not engage in sexual intercourse and there would appear to be more to it than the simple fear of committing adultery, even though this might fit very nicely at the formal structural level. There is something more than psychological dogma or the slavish copying of Freud to the idea that the relationship between a mother and her children is of a particularly close kind, even if at other levels of behavior the relationship is played down. With the father-child relationship the position is rather different and even those theorists who base their arguments for the universality of the nuclear family upon personality theory admit a great deal of variability in this relationship. Apart from their domestic and familial roles, men in most societies have important statuses in wider social systems and therefore the husband-father role is particularly responsive to variations in the external situation.

Analysis of the Caribbean material is affected by these changing views of nuclear family functions and it provides evidence bearing upon those views. Solien's insistence upon the distinction between household and family arose out of her experience of family arrangements among the Black Carib of Guatemala. She says:

> The nuclear family unit among the Carib may be scattered in several different households. For example, the husband-father may be living with his own mother, one or more children may be with their maternal relatives or with non-Caribs, while the mother may be working and "living in" as a maid in one of the port towns (Solien 1960: 104).

Her observations could be duplicated from every report that has ever been written on lower-class Negro family life, and it is quite true that the concentration of attention upon the household as a functioning unit of child care and economic organization has tended to divert attention from the networks of relationship linking households to each other. It is important that these relationships be studied with as much exactitude as possible but it would be ridiculous to regard the household in a purely negative way, or to forget that "family" functions require frequent social interaction and not merely a token recognition of consanguineal or deactivated conjugal relationships. It is also important to know the frequency with which the patterns of divided residence occur and the intensity of the relationships maintained across household boundaries. This problem is discussed again below in relation to mating.

The study of household composition has shown that a variety of kinship ties may be activated to bring people together into the same dwelling unit, and considerable attention has been given to charting the shape of kinship systems and the strength of the various relationships within them. Both Davenport and Solien have analyzed "non-unilineal descent groups" as a structural type and Solien has identified such formations among the Black Carib as well as suggesting that they probably exist elsewhere in the Caribbean. M.G. Smith speaks of patrilineages in Carriacou (though his use of the term "lineage" is somewhat idiosyncratic) and Bastien stresses the importance of patrilineal joint families in Haiti. Davenport's discussion of the lower-class Jamaican Negro kinship system is couched in general terms but provides an excellent overview which is applicable to most British West Indian territories. He characterizes it as being based upon "kindred organization." By this he means that there are no corporate kin groups, as such; that kinship is reckoned bilaterally; and that kinship rights and obligations are relative to individuals. What is equally clear is that "Parents, parent's siblings, first cousins, children, sibling's children (both sexes referred to as 'niece') and grandchildren form a hard core of close kin that is sometimes described as 'near family', in order to distinguish it from more distant relatives, called 'far family.' A person's kindred then will be defined as his near family, plus any other kin with whom he may have special relationships" (Davenport 1961: 422). It is clear from this that kindred ties arise out of domestic relations, mating, and local community ties. Within the kindred, relationships are further modified by emphasis upon siblingship and mother-child relations in much the same way as previously described for British Guiana (Smith 1956: 151–59).

So far as Carriacou and its "patrilineage" organization is concerned we are dealing with a miniature society with a whole series of special features. Carriacou is an island dependency of Grenada, which is itself dependent upon the British Government's grants even to balance its budget. Carriacou has a population of about 6,800 and an area of thirteen square miles. A large proportion of its male inhabitants are off the island working at any one time. As M.G. Smith describes it there is no significant class differentiation within this small population, and the island is so small that most people must know each other personally. The majority of households are headed by women but since there are two-and-one-half times as many adult women as men resident on the island this is perhaps not surprising. The "bloods" or "patrilineages" appear to be name groups consisting of those agnatic kin between whom extended family relations exist. The development of these groups seems to be related to the stability of local relations, the regulation of mating in a very small community, and the performance of family rituals—the family being not only ideally but actually paternalistic. Not dissimilar name lines of even greater depth can be found in isolated and economically stagnant Guianese Negro villages, but the units carrying out ritual activities are the close kindred on the one hand and the whole village community on the other. It is clear from M.G. Smith's descriptions that it is not merely the existence of "bloods" which makes paternity important within the family system, but also the strong emphasis upon legal marriage and the status conferring functions of paternity plus the channeling of male economic support through the husband-father role. In other words, it is not the "lineage" that determines male domestic roles, but other variables.

More extensive groups of kin, settled on "family land" as in Jamaica or constituting extended family clusters as in Haiti, arise out of common interests in land, and Davenport offers an excellent summary of the situation in Jamaica. He stresses the fact that "family land" represents a focus of interest for absent kindred and, while rights in family land are vested in all the members of the kindred, there is, inevitably, a number of mechanisms for limiting the actual exercise of claims.

To sum up: The kinship system is bilateral and not very extensive. The most important relationships within it arise out of coresidence, cosiblingship, and the coincidence of neighborhood and kinship ties. The special strength of the mother-child relationship compared to the easy diminution of father-child ties has been noted by all writers but the reasons for this cannot be located merely in the definition of kinship relations. Similarly the emergence of short matri-lines consisting of mother, daughters, and daughter's children is an important feature of the system though M.G. Smith asserts that this has been greatly exaggerated in the literature (M.G. Smith 1962: 243). Elizabeth Bott's comments on the conditions necessary for the emergence of these female solidarities are interesting especially since they are based upon work in Britain rather than in the Caribbean. She says that

> the psychological consequences of being brought up in a family having marked segregation of parental roles does not of itself produce groups of women within a kinship network. All it produces is a close emotional tie between mother and children, particularly between mother and daughter. Before there can be a group there must also be several related women in the same place at the same time. If groups of grandmother, mothers, and daughters are to be formed, women should get married young, they should have plenty of children, preferably girls, they should live for a long time, and all the women concerned should continue to live in the same local area. The formation of such groups also depends on certain negative factors—on the absence of rights to land or other economic advantages through the father and his relatives....

To phrase the discussion in general terms: whenever there are no particular economic advantages to be gained by affiliation with paternal relatives, and whenever two or preferably three generations of mothers and daughters are living in the same place at the same time, a bilateral kinship system is likely to develop a matrilateral stress, and groups composed of sets of mothers and daughters may form within networks of kin (Bott 1957: 137–38).

The special relationship between "two sisters' children" which was reported for British Guiana (Smith 1956) and which M.G. Smith has included under the more general term "materterine" kinship (a term first suggested in Schapera 1957: 154) is, in the societies we are dealing with, clearly derivative from the kind of female grouping within bilateral networks that Bott has described. The placement of children with their mother's sister or mother's sister's daughter is a logical procedure once such female groups have existed.

## MARRIAGE AND MATING

What is the nature of the mating system and what is the significance of high illegitimacy rates? This is the most vexed question in the whole literature on Caribbean family systems. It would be impossible to discuss it fully here but certain broad features are clear. Legal, Christian, monogamous marriage is everywhere accepted as the correct and respectable form of mating relationship by all sections of the population of Caribbean societies, with the exception of the East Indian groups in Trinidad and British Guiana. In practice the majority of children are conceived and born *outside* such marital relationships. Some of these children are born to couples who live together in non-legal unions, and some are born to women who are not in coresidential unions and who enjoy varying degrees of stability in their relations with the father of their children. M.G. Smith refers to all these latter as "extra-residential unions," ignoring the differences between them except when they become so unstable as to constitute promiscuity, and he further maintains that a specific type of parental role is associated with such a form of mating though he does not tell us what it is. A more sophisticated treatment in quantitative terms has been carried out by Roberts and Braithwaite, who use the term "visiting union" and try to distinguish degrees of stability within this broad category (Roberts & Braithwaite 1961). A recent book by Judith Blake dealing with Jamaica discusses the whole question of extra-residential mating in a clear and lively way (Blake 1961). It is obvious that the existence of visiting unions and the birth of children to women in such unions must affect household composition and—despite Dr. M.G. Smith's assumptions to the contrary—this has been recognized by all previous writers on the subject. The problem is—why do extra-residential mating and coresidential, non-legal unions occur and how stable are such forms of mating? Among the Ashanti, extra-residential mating is a recognized form clearly associated with the strength of matrilineal ties, and it is based upon clearly recognized marital relationships which include properly defined mutual rights, duties and obligations. Among the Nayar it is again related to matrilineal ties and the need for their protection. In the Caribbean, extra-residential mating is clearly associated with the *avoidance* of responsibilities and rights and obligations. Full acceptance of responsibility involves coresidence, but even here there is a variation in the degree of assumption of responsibility from the minimum amount involved in short-term, unstable unions up to that of stable marital unions. M.G. Smith joins a long, and respectable, line of writers who attribute the non-legal mating patterns of West Indians to customs laid down during slavery, plus (in order to account for the absence of common-law marriage in Carriacou) the varying success of the churches in enforcing lawful marriage in different areas (M.G. Smith 1962: 255–65). He is doubtless correct and there is no reason for not recognizing also that there is an equal likelihood that West African patterns of extra-residential mating have persisted into the present. Mintz states very clearly the case for further historical research which will have as its object the elucidation of structural relations at various stages of Caribbean history; the progressive development of different types of structural arrangements has been worked out for Puerto Rico, but very little along these lines has been done for the British Caribbean as yet. But even if more attention is devoted to historical research (as opposed to speculation) Schapera's point will remain valid—"I do not imagine that we shall ever abandon completely the study of the social present, and in a study of that kind history is at best an aid to understanding and not the only means of understanding" (Schapera 1962: 154). If we recognize the existence of a direct connection between slave society and the present and between the present lower-class Negro family system and that of the slave plantation, what accounts for the persistence of those patterns? Is it cultural inertia or the existence of a separate folk-culture in a plural society, or is something else involved? Numerous answers have been given to this question and their consideration brings us to the next stage of the discussion.

## ECONOMIC AND STATUS FACTORS

It has been a matter of common knowledge for a very long time that there is some sort of association between mating patterns and family structure and the level of income and status. Frazier made this association the basis of his analysis and both Simey and Henriques laid primary emphasis upon poverty and low status as causal factors in producing mating and family patterns which deviate from the societal ideals. It has always been assumed that in the "middle" and "upper" classes (however they may be defined) legal Christian marriage is the rule, that it is an essential prelude to child-bearing, and that the typical domestic unit consists of a nuclear family group. As Davenport says, "…it will be assumed [for lack of data to the contrary] that the middle- and upper-class family systems are homogeneous and indistinguishable from those of comparable class strata in England and the United States" (Davenport 1961: 420). There is good reason to believe that this is not wholly true. In the first place we know that kinship ties are recognized to a much wider degree in the Caribbean than in the U.S. or Britain, partly because of the immobility of the higher status groups and their concentration in a few urban centers. There is also a well-marked pattern of extramarital mating on the part of higher status males. Along with the middle class emphasis upon respectable patterns of behavior that differentiate them from the lower classes, there is an old and pervasive pattern of sexual license for men. The idea of the Caribbean as a place of hot passions, sensuous music, and provocative calypso is not something dreamed up by the tourist agencies. The Europeans set the pattern of mating outside marriage by their willingness to take black or colored mistresses, and the existence of a large population of mixed-bloods testifies to the importance of the pattern set by the upper classes. The ambivalence about stable marriage, for men at least, is probably found at all levels of the society. Certainly more research needs to be done on attitudes toward marriage among the higher status groups in Caribbean societies, and its possible contribution to attitudes of permissiveness at all levels of the society. Judith Blake, in her recent book on Jamaica, argues that her interview data show that the vast majority of Jamaican women wish to marry, that everyone in the society regardless of class level or culture regards marriage as the right framework for mating, but that men are able to exploit the ignorance and the economic insecurity of women to enjoy regular sexual associations without the responsibility of marriage. She considers that the family structure is weak and that the present conditions reinforce this weakness, that there is no sub-norm of preference for non-legal unions, and that if "economic development and adequate opportunities within the system of social stratification" develop then it is possible that the family system will develop enough control to propel people into marriage at the proper time (Blake 1961: 147). Before examining this idea further, what sort of variation do we actually find according to economic and status differences?

Edith Clarke's work in Jamaica as presented in *My Mother Who Fathered Me,* showed that the variation in mating and household types between her three field centers was quite complex and depended upon more than simple differences in income level. The nature of the community structure and the type of economic base on which the family is erected also affect the picture. For example, the high incidence of both concubinage and one-person households in Sugartown is not associated simply with low incomes, but with a whole pattern of mobility, casual labor, individualism, absence of wide kinship networks, and a particular kind of community authority structure. In both Mocca (the peasant hill community) and Orange Grove (the prosperous farming area) the household group is a unit of agricultural production in addition to any other functions it may have. The extent of cooperation between families was small in Mocca and extensive in Orange Grove, according to Miss Clarke, and it is interesting that the type of community activity found in Orange Grove is that associated with "development" and is therefore in conformity with wider societal values. The building of a Community Hall, organizing a Savings Union, Agricultural Society Branch, Egg Cooperative, Cricket Club, and the like were obviously related to the level of agricultural prosperity and the striving after a greater sense of social worth. Marriage rates were higher in Orange Grove than in the other two centers, but there was also a higher proportion of extended families of all types, including those with a female head. This is related to the fact that in this community there is an adequate economic base for the growth of more extensive kinship units, so that older women as well as men are able to build up sizeable household groups. Without such a base, including a house, it is difficult for households to grow beyond a certain size, and once a family passes a certain socioeconomic level there is presumably an incentive to reduce the size of the household in order to alter the style of life and to facilitate upward mobility.

The most detailed treatment of the relation between "economic" data and household composition is provided by Cumper both in his earlier work on Jamaica and in his "Household and Occupation in Barbados" which is one of the essays in the Davenport-Mintz volume (Cumper 1958, 1961). Although he works with a relatively simple model which relates the household to the occupational system through the boundary role of the household head, he is not simply dealing with "economic" factors as Davenport suggests (Davenport 1961: 381). His sample of 1,296 Barbadian households (a random sample of one in forty-two of the island's population) is divided into eight groups based upon the occupation of the household head. While not attempting to measure "status" apart from income it is clear that in Barbados occupation is a good index to status. For example, the difference in income between skilled workers and non-farm laborers is very small, but skilled workers are probably a higher status group and this is reflected in the higher incidence of common-law marriages among laborers.

It would be impossible to summarize Cumper's very detailed data on Barbados here but certain key points are worth noting. The group of households in which the head is a white-collar worker conform reasonably closely to the societal ideal of a nuclear family group based upon stable legal marriage. Barbados has a large white population, and it is possible that the picture for the white-collar group is affected by the fact that there is a large racially white element included in it. However, Dr. Cumper is of the opinion that the majority of families in this group are non-white, though he has no statistical data on this point (personal communication). At the other end of the comparative scale Cumper places a group of "peasant proprietors" whose households appear to be typically stable units, a high proportion of them based on legal marriage but containing a relatively high proportion of the children of unmarried daughters. (Peasant proprietors in Barbados, like those in British Guiana, generally live in close proximity to sugar plantations and depend upon them for part-time work.) In all peasant households, both male and female headed, male earnings constitute the bulk of household resources, and female heads of households are usually widows or women whose spouses are away or have deserted them. Peasant proprietors are a stable population living in their own houses and able on this account, and because of the relative security of their economic base, to sustain three-generation domestic groups. Cumper shows very ingeniously that the intermediate occupational categories and their households can be dynamically related to each other and to the peasant types through a consideration of the life chances and experiences of their members. It is the same method of analysis which Cumper used so successfully in his study of the symbiotic relationship between sugar plantations, hill peasant communities, and urban migration in Jamaica, and it demands a consideration of development over time including occupational mobility.

The intermediate categories with which he deals consist of:

1. "Renters" — a group of agricultural laborers who erect their own moveable houses upon rented land.

2. Landless laborers (agricultural).

3. Domestic servants.

4. Own-account workers.

5. Non-farm laborers.

6. Skilled workers.

What Cumper suggests is that the "renters" and landless laborer categories are being constantly augmented by young men with their way to make in the world—young men who are incapable of meeting the prescriptions of the role of married household head. Their compromise solution is to enter into non-legal unions of varying degrees of stability; the acquisition of a house without land is, for example, considered to be a sufficient basis for establishing a common-law marriage, or a young man may join the household of a woman and her mother, where he can receive various kinds of domestic services as well as enjoy sexual relations in exchange for his contribution to the household economy. The instability of these unions produces female-headed households of either the two- or three-generation type and of the same general nature as those termed "denuded" by Miss Clarke. Some young men move from the agricultural laborer or peasant groups into skilled labor but in these cases the men concerned are likely to acquire new mobility aspirations and to adopt new cultural norms in relation to marriage and family formation. Or to put it another way, they may feel, because of their higher-status occupation, that they are better able to live up to the role prescriptions of the family norms accepted by the whole society as being correct. On the other hand many men and women remain in the renter and landless laborer groups for life, and as they grow older they too may try to meet the cultural prescriptions of the total society by getting married. The possession of even a moveable house on rented land seems to increase the potentiality of the household developing into a three-generation group, but among the landless laborers households are held together mainly by women. These women, living in rented or free quarters, manage by their own, their children's, or their daughters' lovers' labor to provide an economic base for the continued existence of domestic units.

In the non-agricultural sector, the categories of "own-account worker" and "domestic" are in some senses the counterpart of "renter" and "landless laborer" occupations. The households with domestics as heads are naturally female headed, since domestic service is a female occupation in the West Indies, but many of these women have been, or are, in unions of some kind. About ten per cent of the households contain a common-law husband of the head and "a third or more...receive some support from a man who is, or has been, the husband or lover of the head" (Cumper 1961: 397). Other important contributions flow in from remittances and pensions. The own-account worker group contains a varied collection of people from small jobbing contractors to seamstresses, petty shopkeepers, and female traders. This group is generally economically less secure than any other non-agricultural group despite its economic independence, and it contains a high proportion of older men living alone, and women from broken unions.

Cumper recognizes that his material is limited in many respects, but he shows very clearly the sort of control that is necessary before one can generalize about "urban" and "rural" groups in the West Indies. If one compares Cumper's work with that of Dr. M. G. Smith, as set out in his *West Indian Family Structure,* one is immediately conscious of the shortcomings of Smith's generalizations about urban and rural patterns in Jamaica. By lumping together the sample populations on a geographical basis and speaking of status only in terms of a "folk" typology, Smith, if Cumper's arguments are correct, confuses important differences within these groups. Davenport too recognizes the importance of economic and occupational differences in Jamaica when he says:

> Land and wealth are almost synonymous to the lower class countryman. When he is landless he is poor, with nothing to fall back on in time of need, and no place to go to when wage work is done. Under these dire circumstances, households, as we have seen, tend to be small or incomplete, with their members dispersed throughout related households which are better able to support them" (Davenport 1961: 450).

## SOCIAL CLASS AND THE PLURAL SOCIETY

So far we have dealt mainly with studies of family structure among lower status Negro groups for the simple reason that this is where most work has been done. In most societies in the Caribbean, Negroes constitute the lowest status groups for historical reasons and it is therefore very difficult to determine whether the pattern of family and mating relations found among them is due to economic and status factors alone or whether residues of African and slave plantation culture constitute the determining factors. What complicates the matter further is that dark skin color is itself a status factor in all Caribbean societies. This is a contemporary fact and not simply a "survival." Theoretically the study of family structure among East Indians should provide us with a crucial test since in Trinidad, British Guiana, and Jamaica, East Indians constitute (or did until recently) a special low-status group. A number of studies have been carried out in recent years which show conclusively that the East Indian family pattern is quite distinct from that of the lower-class Negro groups (see note 1). Morton Klass in his book *East Indians in Trinidad: A Study of Cultural Persistence* chooses a deliberately cultural bias in his analysis and sees the East Indians of Trinidad as people who have, in the face of considerable difficulty, re-established an Indian village way of life. Studies by Roberts and Braithwaite in Trinidad, and by Smith and Jayawardena in British Guiana (see note 1), show that there are considerable differences between the kinship structure of Indians in these territories and a pure Indian system (if there is such a thing). What is distinctive about East Indian family and kinship structure is the early age at which marriage takes place, the absence of extra-residential mating and the position of the husband-father in the domestic organization. All these factors are certainly associated with a continuing Indian subculture, though all of them are also consonant with the ideal pattern of the total society. In practice they are considerably modified by circumstances. Early marriage takes place, but it is usually customary religious marriage and not legal marriage, and the incidence of breakup of first unions is high both in British Guiana and in Trinidad.[4] Even if these first unions are regarded as proper marriages and not equivalent to common-law marriages among Negroes, subsequent unions are apt to be simple common-law unions. There is also considerable variation in the internal relations of domestic units. Jayawardena shows that in the sugar estate communities paternal authority is considerably modified in situations where sons, wives, and daughters contribute substantially to household income (Jayawardena 1962). But the crucial point is that the role of husband-father among Indians is defined in a quite different way than it is in the rest of the society. A household which does not have a man to represent it in community affairs, in religious organizations and at *rites-de-passage* is socially deficient. The authority and status of the husband-father within the family does not depend solely upon his ability to provide for his family and to achieve a certain standard of consumption, nor does it depend upon his ability to participate in activities characteristic of higher-class groups; it depends upon his ability to represent his family within the Indian community, and that community's specialized associations, though the man's earning capacity and his occupational status are becoming more important as Indians become more closely integrated into the societies of which they are now a part.

Various attempts have been made to place the discussion of Caribbean family systems in a wider comparative framework; a framework not of historical comparisons designed to trace cultural derivations, but a structural framework in which crosscultural comparisons could be made. Such a comparative framework was suggested in *The Negro Family in British Guiana* and a more elaborate comparative scheme was suggested some years ago by William J. Goode in his paper on "Illegitimacy, Anomie and Cultural Penetration" (Goode 1961). Goode treats illegitimacy as an index to familial disorganization under certain circumstances. In European countries where illegitimacy rates are high, this is usually associated with freedom in courtship and delays in getting married rather than with casual or unsanctioned mating. In Africa the high illegitimacy rates are found mainly in urban areas and are to be seen as a result of the effects of migration and the subsequent weakening of tribal community sanctions. In the New World communities of Latin America, the Caribbean, and the southern United States, special conditions have been created by massive cultural penetration and the destruction of traditional social systems. Goode suggests that a four-phase development is likely under such circumstances:

1. Pre-contact situation with low illegitimacy rates.

2. Intense contact in cities with high urban illegitimacy rates.

3. Beginnings of assimilation in the urban areas and spread of contact to rural areas results in a drop in urban illegitimacy rates below those of the rural areas.

4. The development of a unitary social system and uniformly low illegitimacy rates.

In the Americas south of the Rio Grande the destruction of traditional cultures was accompanied by a period of economic stagnation in which there was little opportunity for the development of upward mobility. A relatively integrated Western group dominated many anomic communities in which the peasants had a low commitment to Western values, while their old values had been undermined. Goode also adopts Merton's idea that anomie can result from the failure to master instrumental norms which are necessary for adherence to cultural norms, so that low educational levels, absence of skills, and so forth impede social integration around new norms. This paper is a reasonable attempt to generalize over a wide range of data, but it necessarily by-passes many difficulties. The problem of measuring national integration is much *more* difficult than is suggested and continuing sharp status differentiations are often related to the maintenance of given economic and political systems rather than to some disembodied process of cultural contact and assimilation.

Goode's analysis raises the crucial question of what constitutes "anomie." Are we dealing with a state of normlessness in badly integrated societies; are these "plural societies" in which the population segments "mix but do not mingle," as Furnivall said; or are they societies of a peculiar type in which a special mode of integration of a differentiated population obtains? This is a fundamental problem for upon its solution depends the kind of analytical framework one adopts for the examination of family structure and mating. Dr. M.G. Smith takes a "plural society" view so that for him extra-residential mating and common-law marriage are patterns of "folk culture"— at least so long as they appear to have statistical stability. Miss Blake takes the opposite view and, as a result of attitude measurement, concludes that all Jamaicans hold the same values but many are prevented from realizing those values in action owing to a breakdown in social control and to the unfavorable position in which women find themselves. The fact is of course that lower class West Indian Negroes hold contradictory views about what is desirable or possible for them; otherwise one can hardly explain the fact that although couples live together without benefit of clergy they usually do marry eventually or in times of stress.[5] The problem is to uncover the source of this patterned deviance from societal values.

There is a fundamental dissonance between the accepted ideals of these societies and the objective possibility of their realization by the majority of people. This is not due simply to a failure to master instrumental norms; it has to do with the mode of integration of colonial or ex-colonial societies around the acceptance of white superiority, while at the same time political power was deployed for the maintenance of a relatively fixed pattern of social and economic relations. It was, and in many cases still is, a far more rigid stratification than that of nineteenth-century England, and it produced a family system much closer to Engel's picture of proletarian family life than Europe ever did. Even the special position of East Indians is due to their relative isolation on plantations and to a deliberately pursued policy of encouraging them to retain Indian customs instead of becoming Christianized, educated, and assimilated to creole society; a policy that was only partially successful.

## CONCLUSION

The work reviewed here shows that the study of Caribbean kinship and family structure raises a host of general theoretical problems. Most obviously there is the problem of determining just what is the structure of family relations, how it fits into the domestic organization, and how it is related to generalizations about the family as universal social institution. The adoption of statistical measures of frequency in types of domestic, kinship, and mating relations and the use of developmental cycle models have revealed some very complex patterns. It is to be expected that controversy will continue over the question of whether a number of discrete "types" of family structure or of household composition are involved or whether actual variations can be seen as the resultant of the interaction of a limited number of organizational principles. There is room for considerable refinement in the application of statistical techniques. Most early studies were case studies of particular communities employing 100-percent surveys or using very large samples. Now that investigators are beginning to work with national samples or at least with samples covering very large populations, it is imperative that proper tests of significance be applied. While the tendency to apply statistical measures over a larger area of the social map is a very welcome trend, it is also necessary to extend the study of family and kinship relations in depth by doing more case studies. Although the records of social agencies, mental hospitals, and clinics may contain some interesting case material, no systematic work has been done on such records. One suspects that the records are really inadequate. Because of the inarticulateness of the lower classes, the relative dearth of literary work dealing with lower class life, and the limited number of people who receive any kind of psychotherapy, we know little of a really intimate nature respecting the personal and family life of Caribbean peoples. Field anthropologists have so far been trying to understand a wide range of behavior and have not had the time for a close study of a limited number of cases. The biographical studies by Mintz (1960), M.G. Smith (1957), and Oscar Lewis (1959) are valuable, but we need studies comparable to those carried out in England by Elizabeth Bott. This would deepen our understanding of lower class motives, feelings, frustrations, and values. Judith Blake is right in her contention that we do not understand people's values well enough, but more is needed than simple, short, attitude surveys, especially since there is so much conflicting evidence.

The major problem is what it has always been: to relate patterns of familial, domestic, and mating behavior to other factors in the contemporary social systems and to the cultural traditions of the people concerned. Here progress has been less impressive because we are still unclear about the nature of these societies. William J. Goode speaks about degrees of political integration, Dr. Eric Williams voices his doubts about whether Trinidad is a society at all, and Dr. M.G. Smith asserts that we are dealing with "plural societies." These are not mere idle speculations; they determine what factors we shall consider important for their effect upon family relations. It is possible to start with a close look at families and to move outwards, exploring the systems of action in which family members are enmeshed, and we can construct theories of the middle range—or models of limited mechanisms. But eventually we shall have to make decisions about such questions as these: What is the meaning of blackness in societies integrated around the dominance of whiteness? What is the meaning of being Indian in societies where prestige is defined in terms of Spanish culture? What does it mean to be an East Indian in Trinidad? To answer these questions calls for models of total social systems no matter what kind of models they may be. It is an urgent task to find out more about the mode of integration of these societies, both for its intrinsic interest and as the proper framework for family and kinship studies.

In the meantime it is a pleasure to record the considerable progress that has been made in recent years and the growing interest in the Caribbean to which the studies reviewed here testify. A special debt of gratitude is due to the Research Institute for the Study of Man and to its director Dr. Vera Rubin, for the assistance they have given to most of the recent studies discussed here.

# CHAPTER FOUR

# THE MATRIFOCAL FAMILY (1973)

I regard it as now established that the elementary components of patrifiliation and matrifiliation, and hence of agnatic, enatic, and cognatic modes of reckoning kinship are, like genes in the individual organism, invariably present in all familial systems. ...I regard the succession of generations in the process of physical and social reproduction focused in the relationships of filiation and descent as the keystone of kinship structure. For this process to go on, institutionalized forms of alliance are not essential. What is indispensable is parenthood, and for this any form of permitted procreative cohabitation is sufficient. —Meyer Fortes, *Kinship and the Social Order: The Legacy of Lewis Henry Morgan.*

Throughout his writings on kinship Meyer Fortes has been concerned to isolate the "elementary components" of kinship and family structure. Despite careful qualification and meticulous attention to ethnographic exceptions, consistently he has found those components within the elementary family of parents and children, which more often than not constitute a domestic group, which is in "all human societies the workshop, so to speak, of social reproduction..." (Fortes 1958: 2). While he recognizes evidence which shows that social placement does not always depend upon legitimate paternity, he continues to believe that patrifiliation is a universally required social attribute.

This brings us back to the proposition that no one can become a complete social person if he is not presentable as legitimately fathered as well as mothered. He must have a demonstrable *pater*, ideally one who is individually specified as his responsible upbringer, for he must be equipped to relate himself to other persons and to society at large bilaterally, by both matri-kinship and patri-kinship. Lacking either side, he will be handicapped, either in respect of the ritual statuses and moral capacities that every complete person must have (as in Australia) or in the politico-jural and economic capacities and attributes that are indispensable for conducting himself as a normal right-and-duty bearing person (Fortes 1969: 261–62).

This insistence upon the importance of bilateral affiliation as a moral principle of universal significance serves to reestablish the nuclear family (or something very like it) as the universally necessary matrix for the reproduction of social beings. It also forges a strong link in the theoretical chain between domesticity and kinship, and comes dangerously close to reintroducing the confusion between biology and kinship.

These ideas seem to run counter to the understanding of kinship which Fortes has been developing over the past decade. For example he identifies the "axiom of amity" as the irreducible principle of morality on which kinship rests, and he rejects the "genealogical fallacy" that kinship derives from some actual network of biological ties. But he then qualifies these conclusions by saying "It is conceivable—and I for one would accept—that the axiom of amity reflects biological and psychological parameters of human social existence" (1969: 251). It is difficult to see why biological and psychological parameters should be introduced into what is presented as a purely analytical distinction unless there is a lingering feeling that the kinship domain grows out of the domestic domain, which is *par excellence* the domain of child-rearing and social reproduction.

In this chapter I wish to explore the implications of Fortes's argument through a reconsideration of the concept of "matrifocality," a concept I first used in the early 1950s as a means of characterizing certain features of the domestic organization of Guyanese coastal villagers (Smith 1956). Meyer Fortes has drawn on some aspects of that work to support his view of the importance of patrifiliation (Fortes 1969: 259–69, fn. 17), and so the reexamination of these data and their analysis may feed directly into his ongoing theoretical concerns.

## II. DERIVATION OF THE TERM "MATRIFOCAL"

During the summer of 1952, I made a preliminary analysis of material collected in the course of a field study of the social structure of a community of Guyanese descendants of African immigrants whose ancestors had established a free village in the early 1840s, soon after the abolition of slavery. I decided to concentrate upon the analysis of household composition, marriage, and child rearing, because of the increasing theoretical interest in West Indian family structure and also because of the supposed practical problems of illegitimacy and family stability. The subject was hardly new, since it had been treated extensively by North American sociologists (Frazier 1939; Herskovits 1941; Drake and Cayton 1945), and Professor and Mrs. Herskovits had devoted attention to it in their work on Suriname, Haiti, and Trinidad (1934; 1937; 1947).

The model for my own analysis was Fortes's pioneering use of quantitative data in "Time and Social Structure: An Ashanti Case Study" (1949b). My data showed that these Guyanese villagers lived in households with a high proportion of female heads, a situation curiously similar to that in the two villages studied by Fortes in the Ashanti area of Ghana.[1] In both areas the ideal form of household appeared to be that established by a man upon marriage, consisting of himself, his wife, and their children. Another striking similarity was in the strength of the mother-child relationship, and in the tendency for the unit of a woman, her children, and her daughter's children to emerge as a particularly solidary unit, often constituting the core of a domestic group. Fortes reports that an Ashanti man of means would always be expected to set up a house of his own, but interestingly enough this could be done not to provide shelter for himself, his wife, and their children but because "[o]ne of the strongest motives is the desire, among both men and women, for domestic independence of the effective minimal lineage consisting of the children and daughters' children of one woman" (Fortes 1949b: 68).

With all these similarities there were notable differences, the major one being the absence in Guyana of unilineal descent groups. Fortes's analysis stressed the complex consequences for domestic group composition of the contrary pulls of marriage and lineage ties and he suggests "that the type of domestic unit found in any particular case is a result of the balance struck between the obligations of marriage and parenthood on the one hand and those due to matrilineal kin on the other" (1949b: 70). The situation in Guyana was quite different because race and social class, not lineage ties, were of major importance in defining social position in systems "external" to the domestic domain.

The key to understanding the Guyanese system seemed to lie in the recognition that male occupational and class roles constitute the point of intersection of domestic and politico-jural domains, while female roles are primarily confined within the domestic domain. Those male occupational and class roles are relatively independent of familial or kinship roles, so that the two domains do not articulate in the same way as they would in the Ashanti case.

The aspect of Fortes's work which proved most relevant was his emphasis upon family structure and domestic organization as a process in time with a cyclical development through the genesis, maturation, and decay of domestic groups parallel to the physiological processes of the individual's life cycle. My problem was to determine the "normal" developmental cycle for the groups with which I was concerned. In retrospect it is easy to see that much room for error lay in the choice of procedures for establishing this normal pattern. Even though Fortes's essay had been written as a solution to the problem of establishing "norms," it left a number of issues unresolved.

The central question is whether one can derive the "norms" which govern behavior and give "structural form" to a particular aspect of social life from the examination of tables showing the frequency of particular items of behavior. Fortes leaves unclear the nature of the relationship between cultural principles, which were to be grasped "qualitatively," and structure, which is "meaningful in terms of magnitude" (1949b: 57). One possible interpretation of his argument is that in stable and homogeneous societies there is no difference between culture and structure: principles are expressed directly in action so that one may "arrive at the 'norms' by comparison of and induction from repeated instances" (1949b: 58). In more complex societies norms have to be established by the application of statistics because the comparison of, and induction from, repeated instances is too difficult to achieve directly. Here again "structure" and "culture" become different ways of arriving at the same thing, and therefore "norms" and "behavior" are ultimately the same thing. However, Fortes is not consistent for he contrasts a "'paradigm' or cultural 'norm' sanctioned by law, religion, and moral values" (60) with structure "governed by internal changes as well as by changing relations, from year to year, with society at large" (1949b: 60). Then to make everything more complex he states that because modern Ashanti is neither stable nor homogeneous "there *appears* to be no fixed norm of domestic grouping" but it can be discovered by "rigorous methods of a statistical kind" (1949b: 61).

Fortes has raised a crucial theoretical problem, but he has not resolved the question of the relationship between the normative elements and the frequency of actual behavior; certainly he has not derived or discovered normative principles by rigorously statistical methods. At best he has demonstrated the effects of certain moral norms, such as matrilineal loyalty or conjugal attachment, upon the patterns of household composition.[2]

A similar problem surrounds the analysis of the Guyanese materials. In order to construct a model of the developmental cycle, one must first settle upon the generative principles which are assumed to produce the variations seen in the frequency tables. The dominating assumption in my original discussion of Guyanese lower-class household composition was that child-rearing is the central function of domestic organization and that the "nuclear family" is both an ideal form and one which is approached as a part of the "normal" developmental cycle. Variations from the normal pattern are produced by the failure of male domestic roles to be supported by male performance in the occupational and status systems (Smith 1956: 112).

The developmental sequence was presented as follows (1956: Chaps. V & VI). Households come into being when a man and a woman set up house together, and this is the normal starting point of the developmental cycle. Either or both partners may have had children already and some of them may be brought into the new household. During the period of early cohabitation (which may or may not be based on legal marriage), the woman is fully occupied with child-rearing and maximally dependent upon her spouse, but while men contribute to the support of the household they do not participate very much in childcare or spend much time at home. As the children grow older, they gradually begin to drop out of school to help with household tasks or with jobs on the farm and running errands. The woman is gradually freed from the constant work of childcare and when the children begin to earn, they contribute to the daily expenses of the household. It is at this stage that one begins to see more clearly the underlying pattern of relationships within the domestic group; whereas the woman had previously been the focus of affective ties she now becomes the center of an economic and decision-making coalition with her children. This increasing "matrifocal" quality is seen whether the husband-father is present or not, and although the proportion of women who are household heads increases with age—principally because of widowhood—matrifocality is a property of the internal relations of male- as well as female-headed households.

In choosing the term "matrifocal" in preference to such descriptive terms as "matri-central," "matriarchal," "female-dominated," "grandmother family," and so on, I specifically intended to convey that it is women *in their role as mothers* who come to be the *focus* of relationships, rather than head of the household as such. In fact it was central to my argument that the nuclear family is both ideally normal, *and* a real stage in the development of practically all domestic groups.

The "normal" developmental sequence of household groups is rounded out by noting that young men and women begin to engage in love affairs while they are still in their parents' homes. If children result they may be assimilated to a filial relationship to the maternal grandmother, and in this way household groups are often extended to three generations. Upon the death or desertion of the male household head, his spouse simply assumes headship, and the cycle comes to an end with her death. Sometimes a widower will manage to keep a household together with the aid of a mature daughter, or a group of siblings may hold together for a year or two, but household groups normally dissolve upon the death of the focal female.

The argument which I then developed to account for the configuration of this developmental cycle was that both late entry to coresidential unions and early decline in effective male domestic authority are due to the discrepancy between ideal and possible performance of male domestic roles. Men's low status and power in the economic and class systems reacts back upon their roles in the domestic system, making it impossible for them to live up to the norms. The obvious next step was to see whether similar cases existed in other societies. Although the material I examined in *The Negro Family in British Guiana*—on Latin America and Scotland—was very sketchy, the fact that I chose cases where there were neither high illegitimacy rates, female-headed households, nor marital instability shows clearly that my definition of matrifocality included none of these things (Smith 1956: 240–54) .

## III. DEVELOPMENT OF THE CONCEPT OF MATRIFOCALITY

It would be neither easy nor profitable to review every version of the concept of matrifocality. I have already reviewed some of the developments in the study of Caribbean kinship (Chapter Three), and will confine myself here to some of the theoretically more important issues.

Among the earliest comments on *The Negro Family in British Guiana* was the criticism that it had confused household composition with family structure and, through lack of rigorous definition, had obscured the importance of familial relations between those who lived in separate households.[3] There is some merit to this criticism; unfortunately Solien and M.G. Smith, whose comments were the most carefully considered, each introduced other problems instead of clarifying the issues. Solien's arguments are particularly diffuse and although she raised an important issue, she rushed into a collection of errors from which she did not manage to extricate herself through a series of articles and the belated publication of her Ph.D. thesis (Solien 1959a; 1959b; 1959c; 1960: Solien de González 1961; 1965; González 1969). In discussing her own fieldwork she argues that Black Carib society exhibits a "type" of household organization which includes a series of "forms," the most important of which are (1) consanguineal (the members related by consanguineal ties and "no two members bound together in an affinal relationship") and (2) affinal (where there is an affinal tie between any two members) (1969: 4). Solien de González jumps to the mistaken conclusion that I had used the term "matrifocal" to identify her "consanguineal" family form, and that matrifocal families in Guyana are always female-headed.[4] I cite this only because it represents a more general tendency in the literature to use the term "matrifocal" to refer to either female-headed households or households composed exclusively of blood-kin. All such usages can be summarily dismissed as being pointless since there is nothing to be gained by coining a new term for these easily designated types. The classic statement of this misguided point of view is a paper by Kunstadter (1963). Although the shortcomings of the paper were pointed out by Randolph (1964), this has not prevented it from being the most cited source on the matrifocal family, and therefore a constant source of confusion.[5]

González, in the rest of her analysis, sets up the consanguineal household as a special type and then tries to relate its frequency of occurrence to migrant wage labor and demographic factors in what she calls "neoteric" societies (1969: 10). This seems to be merely a lower level and more rigid specification of the general principles set out in my original association of matrifocal family structure with color/class factors in Guyana.[6]

M.G. Smith also draws attention to the relationships existing across household boundaries, and particularly those which have come to be designated Visiting Unions (M.G. Smith 1962). He argues that it is variations in mating relations which produce different types of parental roles and give rise to variations in the composition of domestic groups. Despite the complexity of his presentation the argument is quite simple; it is predicated on the assumption that the nuclear family based on legal marriage is a normal form providing adequate "parenthood." In the West Indies, "The persistence of high illegitimacy rates, unstable unions, and anomalous forms of domestic groups...are all due to the same conditions" (1962: 260). The conditions are the past existence of slavery and the failure of the church to do anything more than introduce legal marriage as an *alternative* form of mating. M.G. Smith does not depart very far from the ideas and the methods set out in *The Negro Family in British Guiana;* he distinguishes between family relations and domestic structure and argues that family relations are prior to and determinate of, domestic organization, but the principles of family structure are derived from "the analysis of domestic groups [and] we can use the data on household composition to verify or illustrate them" (M.G. Smith 1962: 9). Furthermore, he sees the different configurations of family and domestic relations which are revealed by his analysis as being substitute forms of parental care. The focus is thus shifted from a developmental model of a normal type of household composition, to an array of alternative forms which emerge to supplement, or substitute for, "marginal parenthood" (1962: 219). And where "marginal parenthood" exists, it is as a result of the persistence into the present of forms of mating which originated in slave society. Matrifocality is not an issue for Professor M.G. Smith; he is concerned only with household headship and where a situation exists of male headship coexisting with the complex of authority and organizational elements I called matrifocal, he assumes that a condition of instability has arisen which will soon lead to disintegration. The appearance of complexity in M.G. Smith's work is produced by an empty formalism which insists upon multiplying categories, a procedure well expressed in this statement:

> Given a mating system which contains three equally valid alternative forms, there will be six divergent forms of parenthood, one for each sex in each type of union (1962: 219).

Elizabeth Bott's well-known study of urban family structure in England (Bott 1968 [1957]) is more relevant to the issues being considered here than is most of the work on the Caribbean. The question with which she was concerned is the effect upon domestic family relations of role performance in external systems; in order to determine this she chose to make a detailed examination of the family life of twenty couples. Her book *Family and Social Network* has been widely discussed and I shall deal with only a small part of it.

She points out that the literature on American *and* English working-class family life often characterises the husband-father as "authoritarian" while at the same time the family structure is "mother-centred." These apparently contradictory statements can be reconciled if it is recognized that such couples generally exhibit "segregated conjugal roles"—a concept which she develops at some length. In short it means that they have separate spheres of activity within the family and interact separately with friends and kin outside the family. Discussing one of her case families she shows that while her husband has a network of friends with whom he spends time at the pub, in cycle racing, or playing cricket, the wife's close contact is with neighbors and above all with her mother, her mother's sisters, and her maternal grandmother.

> These women and their children formed an important group, helping one another in household tasks and child care, and providing aid in crises....Within the network of relatives, there was thus a nucleus composed of the grandmother, her daughters, and her daughters' daughters; the relationships of these women were sufficiently intense and distinctive to warrant the term "organized group" (Bott 1968 [1957]: 69).

The emergence of these groups of female kin depends most immediately upon the pattern of segregation of conjugal roles, which is a special case of marked sex-role differentiation. Despite their greater prevalence in the working class, they may appear anywhere in the status scale. Close emotional ties between mothers and children are to be expected but are not sufficient to account for the emergence of these clusters of female relatives.

> To phrase the discussion in general terms: whenever there are no particular economic advantages to be gained by affiliation with paternal relatives, and whenever two or preferably three generations of mothers and daughters are living in the same place at the same time, a bilateral kinship system is likely to develop a matrilateral stress, and groups composed of sets of mothers and daughters may form within networks of kin....[T]hese groups of mothers and daughters have no structural continuity. They do not last for several generations; they are not named; they tend to break up when the grandmother dies, and they are readily dissolved if their members are separated from one another (Bott 1968 [1957]: 137–38).

If Bott's analysis is correct then we should expect to find this matrilateral stress in kinship ties occurring in many different societies. The reason for the lack of "structural continuity" is that the ties originate and have meaning within the domestic domain; they are rooted in the identity of interests and activities of women whose principle role is that of mothers. This is very close to the assumption that underlies my own analysis of the Guyana materials; the difference there is that the surrounding complex of male roles produced significant differences in domestic group structure.

The real question then, is whether the emergence of this "matrilateral stress" is in itself sufficient to warrant the application of the special term matrifocal, and whether that term should be applied to the system of familial relations or to domestic organization.

A number of other studies have identified matrifocal family structure in societies as widely separated as Java, Mescalero Apache, and the poorer sections of the population of Naples (Geertz 1961; Boyer 1964; Parsons 1969). In all these cases we find the same combination of an expectation of strong male dominance in the marital relationship and as head of the household, coupled with a reality in which mother-child relations are strongly solidary and groups of women, daughters, and daughters' children emerge to provide a basis for continuity and security. The writers offer various explanations and hypotheses to account for this state of affairs, but essentially the issues raised are as I have set them out above.

## IV. CULTURAL PRINCIPLES, NORMS, AND SOCIAL BEHAVIOR

In all the reports of matrifocal family structure that I have cited there is the suggestion that this structure is somehow anomalous. It is rarely made clear whether the anomaly exists for the people being studied or for the investigator, and while all the investigators tend to stress the positive or adaptive value of matrifocal tendencies, only Bott treats them as being "normal." In this section I shall reconsider some of my earlier conclusions about Caribbean kinship in the light of further work carried out in Guyana and Jamaica between 1967 and 1969.[7]

This more recent study was designed to explore in greater depth, and more directly, cultural values and norms in their relation to behavior. The method used involved repeated interviews with a small number of informants rather than wide-ranging surveys using predetermined questions. This method is statistically limited but it elicits material from which one may better arrive at those basic axioms, cultural paradigms, and accepted principles which are fundamental to an understanding of "norms." The first task I set myself was the accurate determination of informants' cultural conceptions in the domain we refer to as "kinship."[8]

I have already touched upon some of the difficulties of Fortes's discussion of norms, and before going further I should make clear some of the analytical distinctions made in this study.[9] Schneider, following Talcott Parsons, has argued that it is important to analyze cultural systems in their own right as systems of symbols and meanings, distinct from, but empirically related to social systems. The cultural system is "abstracted" from norms which are the rules and regulations for proper behavior. The cultural system:

> ...consists in the system of symbols and meanings embedded in the normative system but which is a quite distinct aspect of it and can easily be abstracted from it. By symbols and meanings I mean the basic premises which a culture posits for life: what its units consist in; how those units are defined and differentiated; how they form an integrated order or classification; how the world is structured; in what parts it consists and on what premises it is conceived to exist, the categories and classifications

of the various domains of the world of man and how they relate one with another, and the world that man sees himself living in (Schneider 1972: 38).

But the cultural system is held to be separable into two parts—a "pure" level and a "conglomerate" level. The conglomerate level brings together elements from different "pure" domains into models for the action of "persons"; thus the person "father" will be a conglomerate of elements from the kinship domain, the sex-role domain, the status and age role domains, etc.

> The conglomerate system is oriented toward action, toward telling people how to behave, toward telling people how-to-do-it under ideal circumstances. It is thus much closer to the normative system. The pure system, however, is oriented toward the state-of-being, toward How Things Are. It is in the transition from How Things Are and How Things Ought To Be to the domain of If That Is So, How Then Should One Act that the pure systems come together to form the conglomerate systems for action (Schneider 1972: 42).

I have quoted Schneider at some length since I have employed his distinction between analytically separable cultural and social system levels. However, Schneider nowhere explains the difference between the conglomerate and the normative system except to say that the former elements are found in a normative matrix which also contains social system elements (Schneider 1972: 44). While it is analytically convenient to separate "basic assumptions" from "normative rules," and to recognize a measure of continuity in the array of symbols which are transmitted from one generation to the next, one must recognize that those symbols acquire their meaning from the experience of social life and not from some inherent property of the timeless principles and axioms. It is precisely the device of separating the "is" from the "ought"—as in the quotation from Schneider above—that lies at the root of the sterile philosophical dispute between idealism and positivism. The issue was dealt with by Marx in his extensive notes on Hegel's *Philosophy of Right*, and by Feuerbach who summed up the issue in his contention that "space and time are modes of existence... Timeless feeling, timeless volition, timeless thought are no-thing, monsters" (Feuerbach 1843: quoted in Avineri 1970: 11).

I shall assume that norms, by their very nature, are subject to variation; they are developed in the process of understanding particular situations in terms of cultural assumptions and prescriptions, knowledge of system requirements, and calculation of individual and group interests. They are ideas-in-action and have to be treated as such. Useful though it may be for us as anthropologists to construct an intermediate "conglomerate" level which indicates to us the manner in which social actors combine cultural elements from different domains in the processes of social interaction, we should not assume that they constitute unvarying "models for action."

Let us now examine our data and the concept of matrifocality in the light of these considerations.

## Cultural Principles

There are persistent reports in the literature on Caribbean kinship of a belief that "blood" is transmitted exclusively through one or the other parent. Writing of land tenure in Jamaica, Edith Clarke states that rights to family land may be inherited "through the blood" or "by the name," which suggests a conceptual distinction between inheritance of "blood" through females and "name" through males (Clarke 1957: 44, 48). In fact Miss Clarke footnotes an extensive quote from Rattray on the Ashanti distinction between blood inherited matrilineally, and spirit or semen inherited patrilineally (1957: 71). Although she does not say so directly, the point of the quote would seem to be to suggest that there is some continuity of African concepts. African concepts do survive in the New World, of course, but the question is; how widespread are they and to what extent do they constitute a set of beliefs which dominate thinking about kinship at the present time?[10] The evidence from our studies shows unequivocally that all our informants, irrespective of class or race, and whether Guyanese or Jamaicans, share the assumption that "blood" is transmitted to the child from both parents and that conception follows a single act of sexual intercourse during which the male seed is implanted in the female womb there to fertilize an egg which grows into a baby. There is considerable variation and confusion about the precise anatomical and physiological details of this process, but the general idea is clear.[11] It is believed that both father and mother contribute physical material to the formation of the child and transmit to it such intangible features as gestures, manner of walking, speech patterns and temperament. This is amply confirmed by informants' discussions of the transmission of racial characteristics, a topic of central interest in the Caribbean.

Within this general framework one may find differential stress upon the matrifilial and patrifilial ties, as when Jamaicans assert that "mother-blood is stronger than father-blood." But all these distinctions are made within the framework of a general ideology of bilateral affiliation. It is interesting that when Miss Clarke reports the distinction between inheritance through the blood and by the name, she does so in the context of a discussion of the *equivalence* of these two methods of inheritance. Blood relationship is believed to flow from the natural act of conception and each individual has one "real" father and one "real" mother. Many children grow up apart from one, or even both, "real" parents, but the believed-in *physical* bond cannot be destroyed entirely

Relatives "by law" constitute the second important component of the culturally defined kin-universe of West Indians, but the meaning of "law" is extremely complex. Although legal marriage creates the model "in-law" relationship, in fact relatives by law are simply those who have "come into the family" through the establishment of any kind of conjugal union. The term "bye-family" is used (though rarely by members of the middle class) as a general category for all those who have "come into the family" either through the establishment of conjugal unions or through the adoption of behavior appropriate to kinsmen.[12]

It is well-known that in the Caribbean non-legal unions are common, though it is often suggested that these unions are quite different from legal marriage in terms of the relationships they generate (as we saw M.G. Smith suggesting in the quotation on page 44 above), and that they are institutionalized only among "the folk" or the lower class. Neither contention is correct; one finds unions of all types among all classes and racial groups (though the incidence of occurrence certainly varies) and our data show that legal marriages do not generate proportionately more kinship links than other forms of union. This can be illustrated by reference to Table 1, which compares the proportions of affines of consanguineals, and their kin, generated by various kinds of union.

The "kin-type chain" is arrived at by tracing the links on the genealogy from Ego to each person on the genealogy, and noting each time a change is made from a consanguineal to an affinal tie. For example, if one is tracing the relationship from Ego to his mother's brother's wife's sister's daughter's husband's brother's child, then the first consanguineal chain (C) runs from Ego to

**TABLE 1** *Affinal composition of kin-type chain by union type*

| Kin-type chain | Kingston Jamaica middle-class | | Kingston Jamaica lower-class | | Jamaica rural areas | | Guyana East Indians | | Guyana all others | | All cases | |
|---|---|---|---|---|---|---|---|---|---|---|---|---|
| | No. | % | No. | % | No. | % | No. | % | No. | % | No. | % |
| CA (Legal) | 400 | 90.0 | 308 | 57.7 | 305 | 60.1 | 99 | 88.4 | 411 | 67.5 | 1523 | 69.0 |
| CA (Common-law) | 14 | 3.1 | 108 | 20.2 | 105 | 20.7 | 10 | 8.9 | 115 | 18.8 | 352 | 15.9 |
| CA (Visiting) | 24 | 5.4 | 110 | 20.6 | 88 | 17.4 | 3 | 2.7 | 76 | 12.5 | 301 | 13.6 |
| CA (Unspecified) | 6 | 1.4 | 8 | 1.5 | 9 | 1.8 | 0 | 0 | 7 | 1.2 | 30 | 1.3 |
| Total CA | 444 | 100.0 | 534 | 100.0 | 507 | 100.0 | 112 | 100.0 | 609 | 100.0 | 2206 | 100.0 |
| CA (Legal) C | 699 | 96.5 | 239 | 44.7 | 388 | 56.7 | 35 | 100.0 | 226 | 87.5 | 1587 | 71.0 |
| CA (Common-law) C | 2 | 0.3 | 142 | 26.5 | 193 | 28.2 | 0 | 0 | 123 | 5.0 | 350 | 15.6 |
| CA (Visiting) C | 22 | 3.0 | 153 | 28.6 | 103 | 15.0 | 0 | 0 | 19 | 7.4 | 297 | 13.2 |
| CA (Unspecified) C | 1 | 0.2 | 0 | 0 | 0 | 0 | 0 | 0 | 0 | 0 | 1 | 0.2 |
| Total CAC | 724 | 100.0 | 534 | 100.0 | 684 | 100.0 | 35 | 100.0 | 258 | 100.0 | 2235 | 100.0 |
| CA (Legal) CA+ | 512 | 99.4 | 73 | 51.7 | 136 | 44.6 | 9 | 100.0 | 88 | 83.8 | 818 | 76.0 |
| CA (Common-law) CA+ | 0 | 0 | 33 | 23.4 | 133 | 43.6 | 0 | 0 | 10 | 9.5 | 176 | 16.3 |
| CA (Visiting) CA+ | 2 | 0.4 | 35 | 24.8 | 36 | 11.8 | 0 | 0 | 7 | 6.7 | 80 | 7.4 |
| CA (Unspecified) CA+ | 1 | 0.2 | 0 | 0 | 0 | 0 | 0 | 0 | 0 | 0 | 1 | 0.2 |
| Total CACA+ | 151 | 100.0 | 141 | 100.0 | 305 | 100.0 | 9 | 100.0 | 105 | 100.0 | 1075 | 100.0 |

Note: The analytical technique of tracing kin-type chains is adapted from the unpublished manuscript by Schneider and Cottrell, *American Genealogies.*

**TABLE 2** *Union types*

| Union type | Kingston Jamaica middle-class | | Kingston Jamaica lower-class | | Jamaica rural areas | | Guyana East Indians | | Guyana all others | | All cases | |
|---|---|---|---|---|---|---|---|---|---|---|---|---|
| | No. | % | No. | % | No. | % | No. | % | No. | % | No. | % |
| **1. Extant Unions** | | | | | | | | | | | | |
| Legal | 1701 | 98.3 | 923 | 73.7 | 1133 | 83.6 | 269 | 93.0 | 1110 | 84.9 | 5136 | 86.6 |
| Common-law | 17 | 1.0 | 241 | 19.2 | 196 | 14.4 | 18 | 6.2 | 144 | 11.0 | 616 | 10.4 |
| Visiting | 11 | 0.7 | 88 | 7.0 | 26 | 2.0 | 2 | 0.8 | 53 | 4.0 | 180 | 3.0 |
| Total | 1729 | 100.0 | 1252 | 100.0 | 1355 | 100.0 | 289 | 100.0 | 1307 | 100.0 | 5932 | 100.0 |
| **2. Extant and Terminated** | | | | | | | | | | | | |
| Legal | 2005 | 97.5 | 1062 | 71.4 | 1284 | 78.4 | 306 | 93.1 | 1261 | 81.7 | 5918 | 83.9 |
| Common-law and Visiting | 50 | 2.5 | 425 | 28.5 | 353 | 21.6 | 23 | 6.9 | 283 | 18.3 | 1134 | 16.1 |
| Total | 2055 | 100.0 | 1487 | 100.0 | 1637 | 100.0 | 329 | 100.0 | 1544 | 100.0 | 7052 | 100.0 |

**TABLE 3** *Kin living and dead by sex*

| Vital status | Kingston Jamaica middle-class | | Kingston Jamaica lower-class | | Jamaica rural areas | | Guyana East Indians | | Guyana all others | | All cases | |
|---|---|---|---|---|---|---|---|---|---|---|---|---|
| | No. | % | No. | % | No. | % | No. | % | No. | % | No. | % |
| Living | | | | | | | | | | | | |
| Male | 1171 | 46.4 | 1336 | 45.3 | 1171 | 43.4 | 259 | 42.9 | 1172 | 41.5 | 5109 | 44.1 |
| Female | 1201 | 48.0 | 1256 | 43.6 | 1176 | 43.5 | 234 | 38.8 | 1202 | 42.6 | 5078 | 43.8 |
| Unknown | 138 | 5.4 | 354 | 12.0 | 352 | 13.0 | 110 | 18.2 | 444 | 14.7 | 1398 | 12.1 |
| Total | 2519 | 100.0 | 2946 | 100.0 | 2699 | 100.0 | 603 | 100.0 | 2818 | 100.0 | 11585 | 100.0 |
| Dead | | | | | | | | | | | | |
| Male | 469 | 46.2 | 285 | 50.6 | 406 | 50.3 | 41 | 60.2 | 236 | 55.6 | 1437 | 50.0 |
| Female | 368 | 36.2 | 208 | 36.9 | 324 | 40.1 | 21 | 30.8 | 175 | 41.2 | 1096 | 38.2 |
| Unknown | 177 | 17.4 | 70 | 12.4 | 76 | 9.4 | 6 | 8.8 | 13 | 3.0 | 342 | 11.8 |
| Total | 1014 | 100.0 | 563 | 100.0 | 806 | 100.0 | 68 | 100.0 | 424 | 100.0 | 2875 | 100.0 |
| Total Living | 2519 | 71.2 | 2946 | 83.9 | 2699 | 77.0 | 603 | 89.8 | 2818 | 86.9 | 11585 | 80.1 |
| Total dead | 1014 | 28.6 | 563 | 16.0 | 806 | 22.9 | 68 | 10.1 | 424 | 13.0 | 2875 | 19.9 |
| Grand total | 3536 | 100.0 | 3510 | 100.0 | 3506 | 100.0 | 671 | 100.0 | 3242 | 100.0 | 14460 | 100.0 |
| Number of cases | 12 | | 14 | | 11 | | 1 | | 12 | | 51 | |
| Mean Size | 295 | | 251 | | 319 | | 335 | | 270 | | 284 | |
| Largest case | 733 | | 606 | | 661 | | 265 | | 1106 | | 1106 | |
| Smallest case | 41 | | 52 | | 121 | | 206 | | 80 | | 41 | |

**TABLE 4** *Composition of consanguineal kin*

| Kin type | Kingston Jamaica middle-class | | Kingston Jamaica lower-class | | Jamaica rural areas | | Guyana East Indians | | Guyana all others | | All cases | |
|---|---|---|---|---|---|---|---|---|---|---|---|---|
| | No. | % | No. | % | No. | % | No. | % | No. | % | No. | % |
| Blood Kin—Father's side | 569 | 48.3 | 639 | 47.4 | 522 | 38.8 | 143 | 42.8 | 886 | 57.3 | 2759 | 48.0 |
| Blood Kin—Mother's side | 445 | 37.7 | 439 | 32.5 | 487 | 36.2 | 92 | 27.5 | 402 | 26.0 | 1865 | 32.4 |
| Siblings and direct descendants of self and siblings | 164 | 13.9 | 269 | 19.9 | 334 | 24.8 | 99 | 29.6 | 257 | 16.6 | 1123 | 19.5 |
| Total consanguines | 1178 | 100.0 | 1347 | 100.0 | 1343 | 100.0 | 334 | 100.0 | 1545 | 100.0 | 5747 | 100.0 |

mother's brother where an affinal tie intervenes, (A) and then another consanguineal chain runs from the wife to her sister's daughter (CAC), another affinal link and a final consanguineal chain from the husband's brother's child. Thus the total kin-type chain in this case is CACAC. By noting the type of union involved in these chains we can compare the propensity to recognize consanguineal relatives of spouses of different types—legal, common-law, or visiting. In order to make the comparison meaningful we must know the proportions of each union type occurring in the sample as a whole, and this information is provided in Table 2.

Taking all cases it would appear that relatives by common-law and visiting unions are somewhat *more* likely to be recognized than relatives through legal marriages, but this varies by class and race, as a close examination of the tables will show. The general point to be made is that non-legal unions certainly do generate recognized kinship ties, especially among lower-class informants.

Both legal and non-legal unions create blood ties through the birth of children, but there is also another principle at work. Despite the primary distinction between blood kin and relatives "by law," informants consistently tend to reduce the distinction between consanguines and affines by stressing the assimilation of affines to "the family." This seems to be part of a more general cultural process among the lower class in which there is an emphasis upon creating and keeping open as many relationships of diffuse enduring solidarity as possible (see Schneider and Smith 1978).

One crude measure of the shape and extent of the area of social relationships embraced by "kinship" is a simple count of the persons recognized by informants as being in some way connected to them by ties of consanguinity and affinity. Table 3 presents the gross figures for those cases which were considered to be complete enough for this kind of analysis.

The very method of collecting genealogies tends to filter out relationships which, while lacking a basis either in consanguinity or in a sexual union, nonetheless share the general code for conduct of diffuse, enduring solidarity, and are regarded by informants as being "like family." In some cases such relationships were included on the genealogies because the informant asserted that a kinship tie existed even though they could not say just how, but we must assume that many "kin-like" relationships are in fact excluded.

The range of variation in the size of kin universe between informants raises some interesting questions. For example, the largest case in the Guyana group, containing 1,106 individuals, was collected from a forty-one-year-old woman from a large, predominantly black coastal village in which intravillage conjugal unions have been common for over a century. Therefore many of the people she knows *as fellow villagers* she also knows to be connected to her by some kinship tie. For the inhabitants of this village it is axiomatic that village territorial ties are kinship ties at a certain level—an axiom summarized in such statements as "All August Town is one family" (see R.T. Smith, 1956: 203–20). Whether one regards village ties as kinship ties, or genealogical ties as being recognized because of territorial ties, is of little significance at this level. Both are characterized by ideal relations of diffuse, enduring solidarity. One of the reasons, then, for the variation in genealogy size is the differential experience of individuals in growing up in local communities of varying size and kinship composition.

Another interesting aspect of Table 3 is that while the ratio of males to females among recognized living relatives is close to normal for this population, informants consistently recognize slightly more dead males than females. This might partially be accounted for by an actual preponderance of dead males available to be recognized within the shallow generation depth of these genealogies, but the fact is significant as a counter to the idea that females are somehow more important across the total social field.

Table 4 reinforces some of the impressions gained from Table 3. The proportion of blood kin on the father's side is consistently higher than on the mother's side. Again it is possible that there were more patrilateral than matrilateral consanguines actually available to be recognized, but the finding is suggestive in dispelling the notion that West Indians do not recognize patrilateral kin ties as much as those through the mother.

## Norms and behavior

So far it would appear that these Caribbean data support Fortes's contention that bilateral filiation is a universal aspect of kinship; at least they do not contradict it. However, it is vital to distinguish between the conceptual dogma of bilateral filiation, which is a cultural assumption of a particular kind, and the structure of the norms which mediate behavior in the process of social interaction; it is here that the distinction between cultural conceptions and norms comes into play. These norms do not require bilateral filiation in the sense implied by Fortes's assertion that a person "lacking either side...will be handicapped, either in respect of the ritual statuses and moral capacities that every complete person must have...or in the politico-jural and economic capacities and attributes that are indispensable for conducting himself as a normal right-and-duty bearing person" (Fortes 1969: 262). Fortes's own presentation of material on Ashanti kinship and marriage leads me to doubt the generality of this statement. He has stated unequivocally that "an Ashanti woman need not be married in order to have legitimate children. Once sexually liberated [by performance of the nubility ceremony], she is free, as we have already seen, to produce offspring for her lineage, provided she does not violate the incest prohibitions, which is one reason why she must be able to cite a licit genitor" (Fortes 1969: 209). We are somewhat handicapped by the absence of detailed case material, but it would appear that the important consideration is not the establishment of a pater for the child, but rather the avoidance of the suspicion that the woman has engaged in an incestuous relationship.

Even if we take Ashanti as exemplifying the generalization that both patrifiliation and matrifiliation are invariably present in all kinship systems, Fortes's work makes it clear that it is quite unjustifiable to move from the cultural dogma that every child must have two parents (which, incidentally, I do not believe to be universal), to the assumption that it is normatively prescribed that children should be brought up in two-parent households, or that the nuclear family is a normal configuration based upon the functional requirements of child-rearing. The early studies of household composition and the developmental cycle in household groups in Ashanti made it clear that the contrary pulls of marriage and lineage attachment could result in a wide range of outcomes, a fact which renders the idea of the empirical universality of nuclear families as coresidential child-rearing units quite erroneous.

Here our data from the Caribbean are clear: they show that there is nothing anomalous in the apparent complexity of household composition, the shifting of children between households, or the changing patterns of mating relations. The lower-class West Indian family is not based on marriage or on the nuclear family, and our informants show no concern about implementing some abstract norm, or value, of nuclear family solidarity. This is true even though marriage is a statistically "normal" pattern of mating, and the nuclear family is the most frequently occurring form of domestic group. The documentation of this by means of extensive case material will have to be left for future publication, but once we abandon the *a priori* assumption that the complex household and mating patterns are distorted forms of a basic nuclear family system, then many of the supposed problems of interpretation disappear. Child-rearing is doubtless an important task, as is the provision of support for women and children. but these things do not require a nuclear family unit for their accomplishment. The evidence for this is super-abundant, and one need only examine the average lower-class genealogy to appreciate the impossibility of arranging the individuals on it into coresidential nuclear families.

In view of the foregoing discussion is there any point in retaining the designation "matrifocal" for this family system, and if so, what should we mean by it?

In 1956 I stated that the mother-child relationship is the basic unit of all kinship systems, and that we should examine the way in which males' roles are structured in relation to it. This Radcliffe-Brownian view of kinship now seems less useful, since I believe that the question of what constitutes the elementary units of all kinship systems should be left open for further investigation. The elements which have been included in the matrifocal complex can be more adequately understood as follows.

*(a) Domestic relations:* in any system of marked sex-role differentiation where men are excluded from participation in child-rearing, cooking, washing, and other domestic activities, women will be "dominant" within this sphere. Such a statement does not presuppose any particular kin ties between the women, or between the women and the children; it merely asserts the segregation of adult males from the major activities of the domestic domain. Adult males are likely to relate to female-focussed domestic groups as consumers of services, providers of support, and as linking elements between the domestic group, and the "external" systems of social, economic, political, and ritual activity.

These are all functional, or social system, considerations which arise in a situation of marked sex-role differentiation where men are marginal to domestic activities. Such marginality may be expressed in the physical absence of men from the physical environs of the house for most of the time, or it may be expressed in the form of spatial segregation within the house or compound. To the extent that sex-role differentiation excludes women from participation in "external" systems they will be correspondingly dependent upon males to relate them to such systems. It will be clear that I am using the concept of domestic domain here in a way similar to Fortes, who sees it as the setting for the performance of familial roles as opposed to the jural roles of the external kinship system.

Thus we can find "matrifocality" in domestic relations in a wide range of situations, from those where males virtually monopolize political, economic, and ritual life—as in China and India—to those where women are active in all or some of those spheres—as in the Caribbean, Java, or West Africa—and there will be a range of variation within this continuum. The reason that the domestic relations are mother-focussed rather than simply female-focussed is that "mothering," or child-rearing, is the central activity of the domestic domain and is productive of the intense affective relations which pervade it.

There can be considerable variation in the manner in which particular women relate to particular men within the system of reciprocal dependencies of the division of labor by sex. Women may be under the authority and protection of the men of a group defined as being a consanguineal entity, as in the case of the Ashanti *abusua,* while having sexual relations with "lovers" or husbands from other groups; they may develop exclusive attachment to a husband; or they may be related to a number of men, simultaneously or serially, in a number of different ways. There is no inherent or systematic limitation on this.

The "Bott effect"—the development of solidary but non-permanent groups of mothers and daughters—is a subsidiary effect of the system of sex-role differentiation when it is combined with geographical propinquity and the absence of countervailing pressures such as status or property considerations. It does not appear in India for example, because the ideal there is to make a sharp break between a woman and her kin at marriage.

(b) *Familial relations:* by far the most important element producing a matrifocal quality in lower-class West Indian kinship is the low priority of solidary emphasis placed upon the conjugal relationship within the area of "close family" ties.[13] There has been a tendency in the literature on the Afro-American family to attribute this to the residual effects of slavery, or to the effects of "poverty" in rendering males ineffective as the sole support of wife and children. As a kind of functional compensation, it is suggested, women are inclined to spread the risk of failure among a number of different men. This is not a particularly convincing explanation, even though it is certainly true that in the practice of social life under conditions of economic deprivation and insecurity, the failure of men to meet the responsibility of supporting their wives and children could lead to marital conflict, or breakup. But quite apart from this functional consideration, what we find is priority of emphasis placed upon the mother-child and sibling relationship, while the conjugal relationship is expected to be less solidary, and less affectively intense. It is this aspect of familial relations which is crucial in producing matrifocal family structure.

In this paper I have paid relatively little attention to the controversial topic of marriage which has so dominated the discussion of Caribbean kinship, so it may be well to conclude with some observations on it.

Most writers on Caribbean kinship make a sharp distinction between legal, religiously-sanctioned marriage and non-legal unions. I have already referred to M.G. Smith's elaborate typology distinguishing various types of parenthood according to the sex of the parent and the status of the union. Few writers adopt such formalistic rigidity, but many share the same basic idea which misrepresents the situation in important ways. There is no essential difference in the nature and quality of the relationship between those in various types of union where both partners are lower-class. The distinction between legal and non-legal unions is entirely in terms of their status and legal significance, and this latter may be of minor importance to the majority of lower-class people. Marriage is an act in the status system and not in the kinship system.[14]

It is frequently assumed that visiting unions and common-law unions are distinctively "lower class" or "folk" institutions, and that insofar as lower-class people marry, this is an indication of their internalization of middle-class values and culture. Again this is untrue. Marriage, common-law unions, and visiting unions form a coherent series in which each one is defined by contrasting it with the others. All forms of mating are practiced at all class levels (though with different frequencies), but higher status males marry status equals, or superiors, and mate extra-legally with status inferiors. Among the lower class where status differences are constricted, this rule becomes transformed into the idea that marriage is an act conferring prestige, to be entered into when the partners can afford it. Marriage as a public act of status affirmation is quite distinct from the process of contracting and entering conjugal unions, which is almost casual. The situation is in some ways reminiscent of that reported by Yalman for the poorer inhabitants of Terutenne in

Ceylon, who often dispense with marriage altogether (Yalman 1967: 133–34; 150–88). Such informality in the making and breaking of unions is associated with status group endogamy, absolute bilaterality in inheritance, and a marked segregation of conjugal roles with relatively little concern over sexual fidelity.

All these conditions hold for the West Indian lower class; the conjugal relationship, ideally, is one of mutual respect and consideration rather than intense affect, but the most important fact is that conjugal ties rank below other primary kinship ties in the hierarchy of solidarity. If we consider this fact in conjunction with the segregation of males from the activities of the domestic domain, it is easy to see why conjugal unions can be unstable without markedly affecting family structure, and why visiting unions are a perfectly viable form. Visiting unions embody the same core relationship as that in marriage or common-law unions, but here the union is separated from the domestic domain. The relationship which remains strong throughout life is that between mother and child, or between the child and the woman who "mothered" or "grew" him.

*(c) Stratification* and economic factors: poverty, racism, and marked status distinctions are a palpable fact of life in the West Indies, as in many other parts of the world, and all these factors affect the day-to-day relationships in which people are involved. However, I do not think that they are the sole reason for the development of matrifocal family relations. Theoretically, such a system should be capable of maintenance in a variety of economic settings. The absence of property and status considerations is particularly conducive to the development of a matrifocal system, but this need not imply poverty. It is possible that groups of unequivocally high status and ample property are so secure and so tolerant of unstable marriage that they develop a system very similar to that described for the West Indian lower class. In such groups women may hold and manage property equally with men, and be quite capable of holding together a diverse household group, or providing the focus for a complex familial network.

Traditional Ashanti, with a very different economic system, came very close to having a matrifocal family system. However, despite the frequency of occurrence of female-headed household groups, the close linkage between the familial system and the wider politico-jural system—a linkage effected solely by men in the status of brother, or mother's brother, to the women of the household—shifts the focus of the kinship system away from mothers, to mothers' brothers, despite the structural prominence of the mother role. Similarly, once the maintenance or demonstration of status, or the transmission of crucial property, is effected through marriage, then the focus of the familial systems tends to swing back onto the marital tie and paternal authority, despite the intensity of affectual relations between mother and children.

## V. CONCLUSION

The coining of terms does not solve problems, and may in fact obscure more than clarify. The concept of matrifocal family and domestic relation is a difficult one because of the complexity of the factors involved. In this paper I have tried to set out the major dimensions of the problem as I see them, rather than attempting a "definition" of matrifocality. A subsidiary purpose was to demonstrate the existence of a family system in which legitimate paternity is not a pre-requisite for the development of full social personality (or psychological health), and in which the central relationships can tolerate an attenuation or elimination of the conjugal bond without becoming pathological. In doing so I was led to question some of Meyer Fortes's generalizations about the elementary structures of kinship, and particularly his idea that the bilaterality of kinship systems universally arises out of the experience of parenthood and procreative cohabitation.

The West Indian kinship system is clearly bilateral: children are believed to share common substance, "blood," with both parents and their respective consanguineal kin, and all kinship relations are believed to be properly imbued with prescriptive amity. These beliefs, assumptions, general concepts, or cultural principles, remain the same no matter what the particular circumstances of individuals' particular lives may be. They are not a projection of domestic experience on to other levels. Furthermore they do not transform simply and directly into "norms" which then "govern" behavior, any more than behavioral regularities are crystallized into norms, which are then rationalized into concepts or mythical charters. The process is much more complex and can only be understood by focusing attention upon that point at which cultural assumptions and moral axioms are brought into conjunction with other aspects of reality in the process of social life. This above all is the lesson one learns from the richness of Fortes's field material, and from his example in pursuing the analysis of data even into their inconsistencies.

# CHAPTER FIVE

# Hierarchy and the Dual Marriage System in West Indian Society (1987)

## THE PROBLEM AND THEORETICAL CONSIDERATIONS

The Caribbean has always been a test case for theories of the family and of woman's role in society. High illegitimacy rates, unstable conjugal unions, and a high proportion of female-headed households pose a problem for theories which assume that nuclear families are necessary in all societies and that men are the natural heads of families. Those theories generally adopt the distinction between "domestic" and "politico-jural" domains, assigning women to the one and men to the other. Because of its deep roots in European culture, that distinction continues to be a preoccupation of modern feminist writing, but the Caribbean case shows that it obscures more than it illuminates.

In the period after 1945—the period of postwar nationalist sentiment, the phenomenal expansion of social science research, and a general yearning for change—broad agreement was reached on "the facts." Negro, black, Afro-American, or lower-class (the terms were often used interchangeably or linked together, as in "Negro lower-class") family relations were said to be characterized by unstable conjugal unions, a high incidence of illegitimate births, and a high proportion of female-headed households. Sharp differences in the explanations of why this should be so, coupled with the acrimonious nature of the debate, concealed a surprising level of agreement on unstated assumptions.

Virtually all investigators treated the "Negro lower class" as an entity that could be defined (if somewhat imprecisely) and bounded for purposes of discussion. Apart from Melville J. Herskovits, who saw contemporary family forms as reinterpretations of surviving African forms, social scientists assumed that deviations from a normal family pattern were the product of class position or poverty. It was agreed that even lower-class West Indians value a Christian, monogamous family life, and that they would like to live as the middle class was believed to live. The conclusion was inescapable: circumstances prevent them from establishing stable families. They are forced to "stretch their values," as one writer put it (Rodman 1963). The middle class was believed to be quite different—to be the cultural heirs of the British colonial upper class—although little or no attempt was made to understand the actual social practices of the class to which the eighteenth- and nineteenth-century whites belonged or to examine the exact genealogy of the modern middle class.

It has always been assumed that upper-class West Indians had a family life that was essentially "English" and that it was very different from the disorganized conjugal and family patterns of the black and colored population. This chapter will show that the apparently "English" upper class was intimately involved in the creation and maintenance of a system of marriage and domestic relations that embraced all sections of the population. It has been customary to think of a "normal" system of legal, Christian marriage from which certain sections of the population deviated for one reason or another: because slaves were forbidden to marry legally; because of poverty; or because of the persistence of other cultural forms. I argue that these supposed "deviations" are an integral part of one marriage system that included alternate forms appropriate to different class and racial groups, or to certain inter-class and inter-racial relations. I refer to this as the "dual marriage system."

### Structure and Function

The idea that the lower class is deviant (both historically and in the present) was reinforced by another set of shared assumptions, theoretical this time, concerning the functional necessity of a "nuclear family relationship complex" in all human societies. Talcott Parsons (1955) gave a plausible account of why this should be so, George Peter Murdock (1949) declared that the nuclear family is found in all human societies, and Meyer Fortes (1949a, 1949b, 1958, 1969, 1978) refined Bronislaw Malinowski's view of family dynamics, integrating it with new ideas about the "kinship polity," or external politico-jural domain. The analysis of West Indian family structure in the period after the Second World War was informed by this developing structural-functional theory, and the results were used, in turn, to validate and support that theory (see Fortes 1953: 3–8; Fortes 1956: xiii; Fortes 1969: 255, 259; Parsons 1955: 13 n.11).

Structural-functional theories of the family and kinship now face mounting criticism. Attempts to save and even improve them either refine definitions to accommodate marginal cases—such as the Nayar and the Ashanti—that threaten the idea of a universal nuclear family, or they seek to break apart clusters of variables tied together by previous theorists. The most notable attempts are those of Jack Goody and Terence Turner. Goody has redirected attention from the "necessary functions" of nuclear family relations to what are supposed to be the actual "similarities in the way that domestic groups are organized throughout the whole range of human societies" (Goody 1972: 124). Taking note of some empirical complications, he has left intact the essential features of the functional model proposed by Fortes and Parsons (see R.T. Smith 1978a: 338–39). Turner's reformulation is more theoretically ambitious, attempting to synthesize the work of Meyer Fortes, Claude Lévi-Strauss, Talcott Parsons, and Jean Piaget by making their several "contributions" part of a more abstract model, which he hopes will rise above the low-level confusion of family and domestic group and embrace a wide range of empirical variation by redefining it as "surface structure" produced by "generative mechanisms" (Turner 1976). It is impossible to do justice to Turner's complex text here, but he too ends up arguing for certain substantive "reference points"—sexuality, the life cycle, the mother-child dyad—that are always culturally "appropriated and transformed." The analysis remains faithful to Parsons's view that family and domestic groups perform essential functions, "the replacement and integration of individuals into the society as socially and psychologically mature adults, and, at the level of social organization, the regeneration of the social groupings within which these functions are accomplished" (Turner 1976: 440). Revisionist structural-functional theories such as these carry forward the idea of domains, the primacy of the mother-child relationship, and, ultimately, the linking of sex role distinctions to domain distinctions.

Feminists analyzing West Indian family life tend to adopt this paradigm, and many writers are preoccupied with the idea of a "value stretch." Most feminists try to correct male bias by focussing on women and their problems. Since lower-class women bear the brunt of economic deprivation and the responsibility for child care, they remain the center of attention. Although it is agreed that "family life and the domestic domain [are] spheres of particular importance and relevance to female status" (McKenzie 1982: vii), increased attention is being paid to the resources women are able to—or are forced to—mobilize from wage labor, from productive economic activity such as farming, or from "external networks."

Some feminist criticisms of domain distinctions have been simplistic to a fault, suggesting that the whole idea of domains is invalid just because men have roles in the domestic sphere and women engage in market activities (see, for example, Bourguignon 1980: 338). A major exception is Verena Martinez-Alier's 1974 analysis of marriage patterns in nineteenth-century Cuba, which argues that the hierarchical relation among races, and not poverty or males' inability to provide for their families, produces the "sexual marginalization" of women (see R.T. Smith 1978a: 349–50 for further discussion). It also reinforces a concern with class relations that was evident in some earlier studies.

## Cultural Analysis and History

The racial hierarchy has not disappeared, and it continues to affect marriage and the family, as can be shown from studies carried out under my direction in Jamaica, Guyana, and Trinidad over the past fifteen years or so. These studies collected extensive genealogies, detailed family histories, and material on occupation, education, race, and social status.[1] Other case materials, collected to supplement wide-ranging survey data (Roberts and Sinclair 1978), or to stress subjective factors in understanding familial behavior (Brodber 1982; Gonzalez 1982), also throw new light on interclass linkages and the dual marriage system. My view of Caribbean kinship assumes that ideology, or culture, is an important part of the system of social relations and not a mere rationalization of them. I argue that a creole kinship structure was established in the formative stage of West Indian society, and that women occupied a peculiar position in it. Although they were jural minors and linked ideologically to "domestic" activities, they played crucial economic, political, and status roles; these social roles and the meaning of "domesticity" itself are part of a unique social formation that was, and is, West Indian creole society.

## Marriage and Concubinage

From the beginning of the development of the slave regime, a marriage system was in place that included both legal marriage and concubinage, a system in which the elements were mutually and reciprocally defining and which articulated with the racial hierarchy. White men married white women but entered into non-legal unions with women who were black or "colored," that is, of mixed race. The laws governing marriage, legitimacy, and inheritance were, in all the English colonies, based upon English common law, but each colony introduced significant modifications to deal with the particular circumstances of a slave regime.[2] The term "concubinage" is a general one, contrasting with "marriage" in terms of legality, but it includes practices ranging from short-term sexual relationships that did not involve coresidence to permanent unions that differed from marriage only in terms of the legal status of the spouses and children. While a few lower-class white women migrated to the colonies—usually as indentured servants—and some of them bore out-of-wedlock children resulting from casual unions, the overwhelming majority of non-legal unions were between white men and black or colored women, and between those women and black or colored men. Slaves were almost always forbidden to marry or to become

Christianized. The incorporation of free blacks and colored people into the churches was extremely uneven prior to the beginning of the nineteenth century, depending a great deal upon local circumstances and the waxing and waning of missionary efforts. It is difficult to generalize because of the many exceptions that were made. For example, in Jamaica during the eighteenth century it was possible for the illegitimate children of wealthy planters to be declared legally white by an act of the Assembly, thus entitling them to inherit property and to enjoy all the social status of free whites. When the number of such special acts became excessive, and appeared to be a threat to the slave regime itself, a law was passed limiting such possibilities. Throughout all the variation however, the central opposition between legal marriage and concubinage, and its association with the racial hierarchy, remained the same. Indeed an act of the Assembly declaring a person of color to be "white" merely reflected the existence and strength of the system itself.

This system did not arise and continue just because it was useful or practically necessary. It is often supposed that a shortage of white women forced white men to take concubines for "natural" reasons, a supposition that does not survive close examination. The cultural system did indeed invest concubinage with a degree of "naturalness" in contrast to the "civilized" institution of marriage, but that is part of the data, not of the analysis. Marriage to a white woman did not preclude non-legal unions with black or colored women, nor was it permissible for a white woman, even if single or widowed, to indulge in "natural" sexual relations with a black or colored man.[3] The limits of possible action were contained within the structure of the meaning of the system, and at its core was the set of contrasted meanings attaching to marriage and concubinage. Far from being anarchic, this was a finely regulated system in which the meaning of different types of union was, and is, widely recognized.

Because the dual marriage system permitted white men to have "outside" unions with black and colored women, while being married to white women, it wove a complex tapestry of genetic and social relations among the various segments of creole society. Once established (in the earliest period of settlement of the New World), it was capable of ordering conjugal relations outside the simple black-white conjunction; it could generate the forms of sexual and conjugal behavior appropriate to equals and unequals of all kinds. In its most general form it embodied the rule that men marry status equals and have non-legal unions with status inferiors; since slaves were property, slave men and women could only engage in non-legal relations. The legal and overt bases of status differentiation are vastly different today, but the general structural principles of the marriage system are not.

I have not attempted to establish structural continuities in detail, but my analysis recognizes the pivotal role played by women, and their status concerns, in maintaining the dual marriage system in both historic and modern periods. Just as the slave or Free Coloured woman accepted concubinage for the benefits it might confer upon her and her children, so today lower- and working-class women accept non-legal conjugal relationships in place of the idealized norms of legal marriage because they believe that they "cannot do better," a belief that derives from their self-conception as "poor sufferers" in a social system that continues to be hierarchical in its most basic structure. Middle-class West Indian women of all races have, since the latter part of the nineteenth century, been the most vocal opponents of "outside" unions, but they implicitly accept the supposed inevitability of male extramarital affairs. However, it is wrong to explain a structured system of social practices in terms of the motives of the individuals who act within it; the motives themselves are partially derived from the structure that sustains and reproduces them.

In this case the dual marriage system is an integral part of a structure that has been, in its most general form, persistent over a long period of time. In order to understand its nature I will now look more closely at the range of practices found during the crucial period of the formation and development of the system. That is, during the period of slavery. The exposition moves between data from archival research and modern field study.

## THE GENESIS AND NATURE OF THE DUAL MARRIAGE SYSTEM

### Racial and Class Hierarchies in the Slave Regime

*Upper Class Whites:* The tentative nature of domestic life among the earliest West Indian settlers may be gauged from the following inventories of two Barbados estates in 1635: "A Captain Ketteridge had five white servants, a Negro slave, and six hundred acres, yet his total household furnishings consisted of an old chest, six hammocks (the Negro slept on the ground), some empty barrels, a broken kettle, an old sieve, some battered pewter dishes, three napkins and three books. Matthew Gibson, with four servants, possessed even less: a chest, a cracked kettle, two pots, several barrels, a sieve, a glass bottle and a pamphlet without covers" (Dunn 1972: 54). By 1680, sugar cultivation using slave instead of indentured labor had already supplanted the incipient tradition of European small farmer agriculture. The population of Barbados, and of the other British colonies such as Antigua, St. Kitts, Nevis, and Montserrat, grew rapidly, as did that of Jamaica, acquired from Spain in 1655. Although these were not true settler colonies, the increased immigration of upper-class white women meant that family life was possible, and by the early eighteenth century there was already a creole white population. White women of lower social status who came to the colonies as domestic or indentured servants sometimes married the owners of small plantations, thus moving up in the social scale.

Wills and parish registers in Jamaica show that, contrary to much speculation in the literature, there was an orderly social life among white settlers, with proper Christian celebration of births, marriages, and deaths. Because the creole white population was small, cousin marriage seems to have been common—as it was in other New World colonies (Farber 1972; Lewin 1981)—and the high mortality rate resulted in multiple marriages and complex families with half siblings. In an interesting discussion of the descendants of Dr. Robert Dallas—a prominent eighteenth-century landowner, physician, and member of the Jamaican Assembly, Michael Ashcroft (n.d.) mentions cousin marriage, arranged marriages, and elopement as well as the existence of extra-marital unions and "outside" children among whites themselves.

What kind of people were these West Indians? Janet Schaw, visiting Antigua in 1774, reported on the character of the white inhabitants, declaring the creole women to be

> the most amiable creatures in the world...amazingly intelligent and able to converse with you on any subject. They make excellent wives, fond attentive mothers and the best housewives I have ever met with. Those of the first fortune and fashion keep their own keys and look after everything within doors; the domestick Economy is entirely left to them.... A fine house, an elegant table, handsome carriage, and a croud of mullatoe servants are what they all seem very fond of.... While the men are gay, luxurious, and amorous, the women are modest, genteel, reserved, and temperate (Andrews and Andrews 1923: 113).

By the second half of the eighteenth-century, the "great houses" of wealthy West Indians had come to constitute important statements about the wealth, power, and prestige of their owners, who devoted much time to entertaining. The "domestic life" of the West Indian upper-class cannot be equated with anything so mundane as cooking or child-rearing. These activities were delegated to the large numbers of servants, almost all black or colored slaves or freedmen, who lived in or near the main house, constantly at the beck and call of the whites for all kinds of purposes (see Buisseret 1980 on "great houses").

On small plantations with few slaves, the owners' wives generally took an active part in running the property. A widow might be left in a position that forced her to take over management or to remarry quickly—not so easy when properties were entailed. For example, when Robert Elbridge died around 1727, he left his share of the Spring Plantation in Liguanea, Jamaica, to his wife Mary for her life. Upon her death it was to revert to his lawful heir, who happened to be his elder brother's daughter's husband. Other persons having shares in the plantation agreed to Mary's managing it for the rest of her life, which she did with considerable skill. As she wrote rather angrily to the legal heir, Henry Woolnough, on June 20, 1739, in response to his veiled hint that she was not playing straight with the plantation accounts, "I have laboured on this plantation for 12½ years and Can prove by the Accounts that I have made more money of it and Saved more than ever was under any person Management" (BRO: AC/WO 16[17]e). Mary Elbridge was not unusual; many of the 4,000 white settlers on small Jamaican farms in 1792 (mostly cattle, ginger, pimento, coconut, and coffee properties) were women (Brathwaite 1971: 146).

Dunn has noted that English colonists in Barbados were "not transferring to the tropics the strong family structure they established in...mainland America" (Dunn 1972: 109–10). By "strong family structure," he means households established through stable, legal marriages that comprised parents, large numbers of legitimate children, and few servants. The West Indian pattern is different because of slavery and the existence of concubinage alongside marriage. Concubinage was found in Britain, of course; it was common enough for members of the upper class, not excluding royalty, to have large numbers of bastard children. In the West Indies, the practice was much more widespread and inextricably intertwined with the special nature of the social hierarchy.

When Janet Schaw referred to the creole men as "amorous," she was noting the most important feature of the kinship system. These men

> have their share of failings, the most conspicuous of which is, the indulgence they give themselves in their licentious and even unnatural amours, which appears too plainly from the crouds of Mullatoes, which you meet in the streets, houses and indeed every where; a crime that seems to have gained sanction from custom.... The young black wenches lay themselves out for white lovers, in which they are but too successful. This prevents their marrying with their natural mates, and hence a spurious and degenerate breed, neither so fit for the field, nor indeed any work, as the true bred Negro. Besides these wenches become licentious and insolent past all bearing. (Andrews and Andrews 1923: 112)

Janet Schaw's indignation is directed more to the black "wenches" than to the white men and contrasts sharply with the view that their irregular unions were the result of coercion, or even rape. Some recent literature on slavery and the origin of the modern black family has revived the image of white slave owners or overseers raping slave women, forcing them against their will to submit to brutal sexual advances and perhaps tearing them away from slave lovers or husbands. Yet this image, which gained currency in the antislavery literature of the eighteenth and nineteenth centuries, does not accord with most contemporary accounts or with the picture Barry Higman painstakingly put together from Jamaican plantation records. His study shows that black women who bore children for white men rarely had black children prior to the birth of their first child of mixed race and were likely to continue bearing colored children. His conclusion is that there is little evidence of women being torn away from slave husbands: "It was very rare for a slave woman to bear children darker than herself.... Mulatto, sambo, and black women...sometimes had children of different colours at different stages of their lives. For all these women the movement was from white towards black fathers.... [I]t would appear that the process of miscegenation followed rules known and obeyed by the whites as well as the slaves and that direct physical compulsion was perhaps unimportant relative to the psychosocial imperatives" (Higman 1976: 152–53).

By contrast, there is much evidence that the "laying out" that Janet Schaw observed became institutionalized. For example, in the 1820s, a man who presented himself as a "Slave Driver" who had put aside the whip to take up the pen described the following scene in a work of fiction: "[The young plantation employee, Marly,] was interrupted by a rather strange form of application, from an elderly negro woman, accompanied by a young negro girl about sixteen or seventeen years of age, who she said was her daughter, requesting Marly to take this young girl for his wife,—the girls who live with the white people being so called" (Anonymous 1828: 80). Twenty years earlier Henry Bolingbroke had observed in Demerara that every European male in the West Indies finds it necessary to provide himself with a "housekeeper, or mistress": "The choice he has an opportunity of making is various, a black, a tawney, a mulatto, or a mestee; one of which can be purchased for 100£ or 150£ sterling, fully competent to fulfil all the duties of her station.... They embrace all the duties of a wife, except presiding at table; so far decorum is maintained and a distinction made" (Bolingbroke 1809: 26–27). Bolingbroke was not the only writer to mention that "housekeepers" did not preside at table, so we may infer that this symbolic activity was reserved for the wives alone. However, it was not essential for a man to have a wife in order to establish himself as a man of substance and a lavish host; his housekeeper was not to preside at table (we do not know how rigorously this rule was observed), but she was responsible for the household and its hospitality.

William Codrington, later to become the first baronet of the Codrington line, was grandson of the first of the West Indian Codringtons. Until about 1715, William was resident at Betty's Hope, his plantation in Antigua that had a complement of 322 slaves (125 men, 126 women, forty-one boys, and thirty girls). Just before he left Antigua in 1715 to return to England and the life of an absentee, William Codrington wrote a long and detailed letter of attorney to The Hono. Wm. Byam, Esq., Mr. Jos. Jones, and Capt. John Lightfoot, who were to be entrusted with the care of his properties. The four pages of closely written instructions, preserved in Sir William's letter book, state his wishes regarding the running of his estates and the treatment of his house servants who are, presumably, slaves.

> I earnestly desire that Babe, Judy, Beck, and Florah be not molested or troubled in their Grounds or provisions by anybody much more my own people, and that they live alltogether there and that Beck and Florah they have each one barrel of beef and 200 lbs of good salted cod fish.... That they have

always the Negroes they have now. That the above wenches have particular care taken of them when sick and to have anything they want from my Plantation Doctor.... That Sackey's Sary be kept in the house at Betty's Hope and that her child might be cloathed as may be proper.... That Unoe the wench who lived with my Couz Bates be always kept in the great house which is what Mr. Bates desired of me about 2 hours before he dyed. That Moll and Unoe be allways kept at the great house at [my adjacent plantation] The Cottin and no others. That my two boys Quashie and Johnoe Ham be put to the Carpenter's trade.

The instructions go on and on, and Codrington keeps reverting to Babe, Judy, Beck, Florah, and to his boys Quashie and Johnoe Ham: specifying the horses they shall be allowed to use, providing for their passage to England should they wish to "come home," and repeatedly reminding his attorneys that "the wenches are not to be ill-used by anybody and you have nothing to do with the house Negroes" (GRO 347: C2).

Once back in England, William married Elizabeth, daughter of William Bethell, owner of considerable estates in Swindon, Yorkshire. She brought to the marriage not only her own "fortune" or dowry but also an alliance between Sir William and her brother Slingsby Bethell, a powerful London merchant, member of Parliament, alderman, and lord mayor of London. The four sons and three daughters she bore him inherited their father's property and status. He did not forget his Antigua connections, for we find him writing again in 1717, complaining that his instructions have not been followed properly and repeating that only Babe, Judy, and Florah are to live in the great house and to have all its keys. It is possible that he visited Antigua again sometime between 1722 and his death in 1738, but nothing is yet known of the fate of those he mentioned in his 1715 instructions.

For a man as wealthy as William Codrington, the possibility of settling down permanently with a slave or free colored woman was quite remote. However, he left behind an elaborate establishment at Betty's Hope and The Cottin. The days of Captain Ketteridge and Matthew Gibson were long past. The 1715 inventories show the houses to be well furnished and equipped; the lists of items shipped from Bristol to Betty's Hope include one hundred Delft plates, thirty jelly glasses, sweetmeat plates, sconces, and large numbers of prints, looking glasses, damask curtains, tablecloths, and napkins. Assuming that the "wenches" referred to by name were either house slaves or free colored servants (Moll and Unoe are listed elsewhere as "House Negroes," but Babe, Beck, Judy, and Florah cannot be identified as such), they obviously enjoyed positions of trust and must have been skilled in the management of a large household. At least one of them had children by William Codrington, and it is not unlikely that other children by other white men, perhaps attorneys or managers with their own creole wives, formed part of this large ménage.

As this example clearly shows, the West Indian marriage system included alternative forms of union that mutually defined each other and related directly to the color/class hierarchy. This does not mean that class differences in marriage were unimportant. For the upper class, marriage meant alliance between status equals, and its specific values included permanence, religious sanction, and the maintenance and reproduction of status; concubinage was defined in terms of "service" and patronage.

The question is whether this structure dominated the whole of West Indian society and whether those lower in the social scale attached different values to that structure. To answer that, and the larger question of how we can understand the relation between structure and process, we must look first at the other social elements in slave society and then consider the change in the relationships among classes effected by the abolition of slavery.

*Slaves:* Female members of the slave field gangs differed most from upper-class white women. On a large West Indian plantation, sex was not a primary factor in deciding how labor was to be divided. The "great gang," engaged in the hardest labor, was made up of the healthiest men and women working side-by-side in the fields. Many aspects of "domesticity" were communal. The main meal of the day was prepared by cooks and served to the field gangs; small children were taken care of by old women while their mothers worked (breaks being given for breastfeeding); medical care was provided by the plantation physician and his slave assistants in the hospital; rewards and punishments were dispensed by the overseer.

This invites reconsideration of the supposed universal necessity of domestic groups and nuclear families, but it does not mean that slaves had no domestic life, no independent fields of action, nor any norms in their kinship relations. The cultivation of provision grounds and the marketing of vegetables and small stock were important slave activities even in the seventeenth-century. Slaves would not allow their owners to arrange the details of their sexual lives and would not be bound to lifelong unions arbitrarily arranged by the master. Conversion to Christianity and Christian marriage practices made little headway until the first decades of the nineteenth-century, but slaves had their own customs.

In 1776, Adam Smith recorded that Greek and Roman as well as West Indian slaves "were hindered from marriage. They may cohabit with a woman but not marry, because the union between two slaves subsists no longer than the master pleases. If the female slave does not breed he may give her to another or sell her. Among our slaves in the West Indies there is no such thing as a lasting union. The female slaves are all prostitutes, and suffer no degradation by it" (A. Smith 1978: 451). Adam Smith's view from the top of the system is echoed in recent work by Orlando Patterson (1969: 159–74; 1982: 139–43), although there is no evidence that slaves regarded their own familial relations in these terms.

In his detailed discussion of the Montpelier and Shettlewood estates in early-nineteenth-century Jamaica, Higman identifies three major categories of family and household organization among slaves, categories which he believes have wide validity. In the first type of household, formed largely by old people and Africans without kin, slaves lived alone or with friends. In the second, the "great majority of the seventy percent of slaves who did possess family links lived in simple family households, most of them nuclear units" (Higman 1976: 168). In the third type, favored mostly by creoles, slaves lived in extended family households. Although believing this third category to be "relatively unimportant" (a conclusion based solely upon its infrequent occurrence in the house lists), Higman provides information based on more than simple counts of who lived in which house. At Montpelier and Shettlewood, "ten of the groups of 'families and dependents' [were] occupying two or three houses. Most of the latter were type 2 housefuls, containing coloured and skilled slaves; they generally had the use of relatively large areas of provision grounds and possessed considerable numbers of livestock. It is evident that these slaves had more than one house not because of their numbers but because of their privileged occupations and relative prosperity" (Higman 1976: 168–69). This fascinating information pertains to the elite of the slave population. Some of these families could have been based on the privileged position of men who had polygynous extended family households, although it seems that actual polygynous compounds were rare. It is more likely that drivers, skilled tradesmen, and the like were able to build up extended family units in which both men and women played important roles as the nucleus of household groups. At the same time, the dominant males established unions with women in other places, thus creating households that appeared to be both female-headed and matrifocal. Women played a crucial part in creating and maintaining this structure because they too were selectively entering unions with men resident in other households—some of them white men.

*Lower-Class Whites and Free People of Mixed Race:* The number of unions between white men and black or colored women may have been small, as was the number of households resulting from these unions, but their importance is much greater than their frequency of occurrence would suggest. They embodied the structural contrast between legal and non-legal unions, and the households were archetypically matrifocal. Contemporary observers said frequently that the colored women's preference for unions with white men made it impossible for colored men to marry. This is an exaggeration; both marriage and Christianization gained among free colored people during the nineteenth century as civil rights were gradually extended under pressure from Britain. What is important is that black and colored men in positions of prestige, either members of the slave elite or freedmen, reproduced the whites' pattern of marital behavior. That is, they might marry—either legally or according to some customary form (Smith 1956: 171–72)—but they would also have "outside" unions, and those usually with women of lower status in the racial hierarchy (see Higman 1976: 146–47).

We now have a great deal of information about social and plantation hierarchies, the role played in their creation by the sexual unions of white men with black and colored women, and the emergence of the population of mixed racial origin as an important element in those hierarchies. But an analysis of modern West Indian kinship is incomplete without an account of the history of the "colored middle class" and of the ideologies created in the course of its emergence as the politically dominant element in West Indian life.

"Lesser whites" such as overseers, bookkeepers (a local term used for field supervisors), and skilled tradesmen on large plantations were usually recruited as single men and forbidden to marry so long as they were employed, presumably on the assumption that marriage would distract them from their duties and require a larger outlay for housing. Almost all soon acquired a mistress (not least to nurse them back to health when they succumbed to tropical disease). Most often the woman was a slave, also forbidden to marry because of her status as property, and any children that resulted from their union shared the mother's slave status. Although slaves, these "Persons of Colour" were set apart, believed to be unsuitable for field labor. The men were usually apprenticed to skilled tradesmen and the women employed as domestic servants, washerwomen, or seamstresses. Fathers often tried to improve the status and life chances of their bastard children; how much of that effort was prompted by the mothers we shall never know.

For example, John Hugh Smyth of Bristol gave permission on a number of occasions between 1765 and 1797 for slaves to be manumitted on his Jamaica plantation, The Spring, by having them replaced with new slaves. On September 3, 1765, he wrote to his attorneys, "As you think letting Mr. SEWARD put an able Negro on the estate in place of the Mulatto girl will be an advantage, I readily acquiess in granting her freedom." Again on May 1, 1797, he wrote to Hibbert and Taylor, his attorneys, "As you recommended and Messrs Rothley and Stratton have consented I can have no objection to authorize you to join in manumissing [sic] the Negro

Woman Slave named Margaret and her Mulatto Son named Peter on condition the proposal made by the Executor of the late Mr. Stewart's will be complied with in placing in their room two prime new Negroes" (BRO: AC/WO 16[37]).

Not well-endowed with property (by definition), white men with low status were oriented toward material and social improvement, observing the hierarchical distinctions of race and servitude with scrupulous care. They attached the same value to marriage as did the upper class; when plantation employees formed long-lasting liaisons with colored women, marriage was rare even if the man managed to leave plantation employment and acquire a small property of his own. Although such unions and attempts at manumission were common and continued through the slavery period, it is not clear that the unions created a "family," and it is certain that "domestic groups" were not always constituted thereby.

The free colored population comprised slaves who had been manumitted because they had performed faithful service (usually as house slaves) or because they were the offspring of non-legal unions, plus those born to free colored parents. Free status was a prized and jealously guarded possession, not easy to maintain if one was black in a slave society that equated blackness with servitude. If legal status distinguished the free colored from the slave, "complexion" separated the colored from the whites and imposed other civil disabilities. Those disabilities did not bar the free colored from legal and Christian marriage, but their position in the status hierarchy caused them to experience the marriage system in a different way.

Women of mixed race, slave or free, were preferred as concubines by white men, and so long as the slave regime persisted these women were disposed to prefer a non-legal union with a white man to marriage to a colored man. In 1794 Bryan Edwards discussed the situation of the Jamaican free colored population at some length, remarking that the women are often accused of incontinency for accepting the position of kept women without entertaining the hope of marriage. But "in their dress and carriage they are modest, in conversation reserved; and they frequently manifest a fidelity and attachment towards their keepers, which, if it be not virtue, is something very like it. The terms and manner of their compliance…are commonly as decent, though perhaps not as solemn, as those of marriage;…giving themselves up to the husband (for so he is called) with faith plighted, with sentiment, and with affection" (Edwards 1794, II: 23). His explanation for their behavior was complex but as interesting as most of those we find today: "Excluded as they are from all hope of ever arriving to the honour and happiness of wedlock, insensible of its beauty and sanctity; ignorant of all christian and moral obligations; threatened by poverty, urged by their passions, and encouraged by example, upon what principle can we expect these ill fated women to act otherwise than they do?" (Edwards 1794, II: 22).

Other observers noted that colored women, exploited though they might have been, seemed to enjoy considerable freedom: "Though the daughters of rich men, and though possessed of slaves and estates, they never think of marriage; their delicacy is such, for they are extremely proud, vain and ignorant, that they despise men of their own colour; and though they have their amorous desires abundantly gratified by them and black men secretly, they will not avow these connections" (Moreton 1790: 124–25, quoted in Brathwaite 1971: 177). This passage draws attention to the important and neglected fact that colored women often had white fathers who were powerful, rich, and sufficiently interested in the welfare of their children to leave them substantial property. To what extent these men concerned themselves with their daughters' unions— or left this matter to the mothers—we do not know. Mavis Campbell reports that a white man entering into a union with a free woman of color often signed a bond, similar to a marriage settlement, providing for her maintenance in case of death or separation (Campbell 1976: 53ff). A colored woman who was mistress of a white man probably had her own household and more freedom to come and go than if she were married. Colored women also seemed to have dominated huckstering, small shopkeeping, and the management of hotels and inns.

Although social convention depicted the slave, colored, and white groups as discrete social entities, in fact "segments" were defined, differentiated, transformed, and dynamically interrelated through a series of exchanges and interactions. One can never find the "essence" of each group. An African became a Negro only in the context of the slave regime, just as a creole or a mulatto acquired his or her social being only in this particular social formation. Field slaves learned to speak creole English quickly; the customs and manners of the upper classes were not unknown to them, just as the creole whites were well versed in the speech patterns, "superstitions," music, and folklore of the slaves. These were small societies, but all groups did not converge upon a uniform culture; new modes of conflict and distance developed out of the cleavages and contradictions of creole society, and the constant influx of new immigrants was absorbed with difficulty. But a distinct society was created, and upon its basis, modern social forms were built.

## STRUCTURAL REPRODUCTION AND TRANSFORMATION IN THE NINETEENTH CENTURY

We have seen that the West Indian system of kinship and marriage was an extension in cultural logic and social action of the dominant structural element in creole society, the racial hierarchy—an element that pervaded every aspect of social life: economic, political, religious, and domestic. In the late eighteenth and early nineteenth centuries, that society began to feel the impact of profound changes taking place in Europe: the rapid growth of industrial production, the increasing power of the bourgeoisie, the expansion of overseas enterprise into new areas of the world, and the triumph of new political ideologies espoused in the American and French Revolutions. When, in 1791, a West Indian visitor wrote a letter from New York where she, her mother, and husband had recently arrived as "Travellers of Observation in this Land of Equality and Independence," she was being ironic but also communicating the complex sentiments of the West Indian planter class; admiration for colonists willing to stand up to Britain over unjust taxation, and fear of the consequences of espousing doctrines of freedom and equality in a society based on slavery (GRO 351: D1610, C22).

The gradual decline of the mercantile system, the emergence of powerful interests dedicated to the destruction of the slave regime, and the changing patterns of world trade and world markets eventually were to transform many aspects of the internal economy of West Indian colonies. Those movements cannot be discussed here, nor is there space to detail the ways in which the planter class managed to maintain its domination and ensure that structural change in the racial hierarchy and in the economic system were more apparent than real (see Hall 1959; Brathwaite 1971; R.T. Smith 1982b; Campbell 1976; Heuman 1981). Instead, we may take the most dramatic of the apparent changes and examine their implications for kinship.

### The Ending of Slavery

The abolition of the slave trade in 1807 set in train a series of demographic changes, the most important of which was the rapid increase in the proportion of people of mixed race in large colonies such as Jamaica (Higman 1976: 153). As the economics of tropical agriculture shifted, and as opportunities increased in the expanding economies of Europe and in new areas of enterprise such as Australia, New Zealand, southern Africa, and North America, the proportion of whites in the West Indian population began to fall. The cessation of African immigration ensured that the black population was predominantly creole by the 1830s, except in areas of new settlement such as Demerara, Essequibo, Berbice, and Trinidad.

Missionary activity, gathering momentum from about 1820, hastened the creolization of the slave population. Slavery was abolished throughout British possessions in 1838, following a few years' transition to wage labor. The event was experienced as a great transformation, ideologically at least, even though social relations changed at a very slow pace indeed. Two aspects of this change are particularly relevant to our discussion of kinship.

Suddenly there ceased to be any distinction in law based upon race, color, or servile status. On September 21, 1834, the secretary to the lord bishop of Jamaica issued an order instructing all parishes to use the same registers of births, marriages, and deaths for the whole population since all were now free. An order-in-council announced in the *London Gazette* of September 8, 1838, set out procedures for marriage in the colonies and confirmed the validity of the marriages of slaves, or even of free colored people, solemnized prior to emancipation. If people had married *de facto,* provision was now made for them to solemnize the union simply by signing a declaration (*London Gazette,* No. 19656: 2004–2005). There was no rush to legalize unions. But over the next forty years or so, there was an important shift in the position of the various groups in the class system, and nothing is more interesting than the changing position of the colored woman.

The free colored population had attained a prominence and new political significance in many colonies long before the abolition of slavery. As early as the latter part of the eighteenth century there had been advocates of the automatic manumission of colored slaves and the extension of more civil rights to qualified people of color. Many free colored people were themselves owners of slaves, since the bequest of a few slaves was a favorite means of granting a continuing (and perhaps increasing) source of support. But despite their privileged position and economic importance, this group did not become a significant and active political force mediating between white and black until the 1830s (see Campbell 1976; Handler 1974; Heuman 1981).[4] By 1850 a proportion of the colored population was firmly established as a new elite, the vanguard of the so-called "coloured middle class." Prominent members of this group were active in politics, in journalism, and in such professions as law, but not all colored people were suddenly elevated into an economically based middle class. The reality is different and has a great deal to do with the complexity of today's relation between race and class.

Free colored and free black people who owned small numbers of slaves or small plantations faced the same economic problems that white planters faced once slavery had been abolished and as the markets for tropical produce became constricted. As the upper levels of the society came to be filled with expatriate officials, managers, and professionals, the class status of the creole white and colored population began to converge. This took time, and the process intertwined class and kinship factors in a complex way.

The changes of the mid-nineteenth-century also began to produce a literate, devout core of churchgoers from the ex-slave population, the "peasantry" often referred to at the time as the stable foundation of the new order. They were generally small farmers growing minor crops such as coffee, ginger, arrowroot, plantains, pimento—crops traded through middlemen who became prosperous produce dealers. In Jamaica, banana was to become the favored crop after the North American market opened in the 1870s.

Most of the ex-slaves constituted an impoverished rural proletariat, and even those who managed to acquire some marginal cultivable land found it little different from the "provision grounds" to which they had had access as slaves. They still had to work for wages on the surviving plantations and engaged in an increasingly bitter struggle over the conditions and rewards of their labor. Those with land suitable for semisubsistence farming appeared to be cushioned from the full force of industrial discipline, but it is a mistake to think of them as peasants working only occasionally for wages. Their lives were shaped by the plantation system, and the legacy of resentment created by the whites' refusal to permit a radical transformation of the society and its economy is embedded in much of present-day West Indian life.

### Changes in the Dual Marriage System and Class Structure

Was the marriage system transformed during this period, and if so, in what ways? The rich planters of the eighteenth century were mostly gone by about 1850, soon to be replaced by corporate capital, operating larger, consolidated plantations staffed by "expatriates." Many European and creole whites continued to operate small plantations, especially in Jamaica and Barbados. Preliminary historical research strengthens the impression, derived from genealogical study, that an upwardly mobile colored population and the downwardly mobile remains of the white planter class converged in the formation of the modern West Indian "middle class." In Jamaica, at least, both groups became increasingly urban from the mid-nineteenth-century onward, leaving the less successful family members in the rural areas. The continuing vitality of the dual marriage system, linked in complex ways to the changing definitions of status and class, resulted in a new concern among the upwardly mobile with lower-class "illegitimacy," a concern that has lasted into the present. That concern was a displacement onto the lower class of issues that were central in the life of the middle class. In order to understand it one must follow the changing structure of class itself, which will also throw light on the question of whether the marriage system was transformed or not.

Wills filed in the Jamaica Island Record Office show that the custom of open concubinage of white men and colored women did not end with the abolition of slavery. The will of "John Smith, a native of Scotland now residing at Cape Clear Pen in the Parish of Metcalfe" (formerly and subsequently St. Mary) and styling himself "Planter" was entered at the Island Record Office on January 22, 1870 (JIRO: Wills, Lib. 131, f. 88). In it he leaves to Bridget French Kilkelly, now residing at Cape Clear, "one hundred pounds sterling and one moiety or half share of my table knives, silver forks, silver spoons, furniture," and other goods. However, it is his "natural daughter, Janet East, daughter of the said Bridget French Kilkelly," who is to be his residual legatee after various monetary bequests are made to nephews and nieces in Scotland and in Canada. This natural daughter is married to one Patrick East and the mother of John Smith's grandchildren, John Slater East and Isabella East. Although it is possible that Bridget French Kilkelly is white, the chances are very much against it. No attempt has been made to follow the subsequent career of John Smith's grandchildren, but it is reasonable to infer that they moved into the emergent middle class, a class increasingly preoccupied with respectability and increasingly based in urban bureaucracy.

More characteristic, perhaps, is the fate of the O'Sullivan family of Clarendon, Jamaica, as revealed in Albinia O'Sullivan's diary covering the years 1872 and 1873 (IJMC: MS 1604). This small leather-bound book contains little in the way of diary entries but quite detailed copies of letters sent and received by the daughter of John Augustus O'Sullivan of Highgate Park, Jamaica, and formerly of Richins Park, Buckinghamshire, England. At one time provost marshall of Jamaica and owner of considerable acreage and two houses in St. Catherine, O'Sullivan died in June 1871, leaving three daughters and five sons by his late wife Jane, daughter of Sir Charles Taylor of Cothrell in County Glamorgan, Wales. Albinia's diary begins with an accurate and complete transcription of her father's will (entered JIRO: Wills, Lib. 131, f. 202, Nov. 7, 1871), which leaves one hundred acres to each of the four younger sons and a grandson; a house and the income from a £5,000 life insurance policy to the daughters; and the residue of the estate—including pictures, books, family heirlooms, and the family great house at Highgate Park—to his eldest son and heir, Augustus.

The letters that follow reveal the family's plight. Augustus, who has taken holy orders, emigrates to Nova Scotia with his wife and children. In a letter dated May 17, 1872, he urges his brothers and sisters to join him, rent a farm, and make a new start: "Tell [the boys] to come to Canada. Put Pride in their pockets or leave it in a yam hill and go to work like 1000ds of others are daily doing in a few years they may be sure of having a thriving farm each of their own and a jolly wife apiece to churn butter make cheese too. I implore them not to waste their lives in Jamaica." They declined this invitation, and indeed it is not long before Augustus brings his family back to Jamaica with plans for revitalizing the old Highgate Park property—with the capital of his brothers and sisters. The problem is that they do not have enough capital; indeed, Albinia and her sisters have been obliged to sell the piano and sundry other possessions just to keep going. Brother Edward, who lives in Four Paths, is so hard up that he has to walk four miles to his office each day; brother George is trying to make a go of cattle farming; the most successful brother is living in Richmond Park and has a steady job in business, but he cannot afford the £40 to £50 per annum that it would cost to send his son Benji to be educated by a private tutor in Kingston.

Again, although I have not followed the O'Sullivans' fortunes further, interviews with the living descendants of similar families suggest that in many cases the more energetic and successful family members moved to the urban areas or even migrated to North America, leaving behind a deteriorating property on which the others struggled along, having "outside" children, and sometimes even marrying darker-skinned partners (see Craton 1978 for an excellent discussion of cases of this kind). Such marriages were contrary to the structural principles of the system, yet they certainly occurred, particularly in the rural areas where decreasing numbers of whites, downwardly mobile in economic terms, were absorbed into the colored population.

## Illegitimacy Redefined as a Class Problem

Because very few slaves married before about 1830 (relaxation of the laws barring slave marriages was uneven until the institution of apprenticeship in 1834), "illegitimacy" was a meaningful concept only among the rich. Certainly it was not defined as a social problem, since it was an integral part of the whole slave system. In the approximately 150 years since the ending of slavery, illegitimacy rates have remained high and remarkably stable. In Jamaica, for example, the rate has varied between sixty and seventy percent of live births ever since reliable records were first kept in the 1870s. As George Roberts points out, these rates have been tied to the marriage rate, which is quite low (1957: 288). Many lower-class West Indians defer marriage until they have several children, but this is not just a system of deferred marriage pending the accumulation of resources for a proper ceremony. Simple "economic" theories have been employed to explain West Indian patterns of kinship and marriage, converting the "problem" of illegitimacy into an exclusively lower-class matter, but many errors could have been avoided had Bishop Nuttall's statement of 1886 been noted.

In the mid-1880s there was an upsurge of sentiment in Jamaica favoring legislation to mitigate the evil of illegitimacy and check immorality. Led by clergymen, it is fair to assume that its most active supporters were the influential members of their congregations, among whom women of the new middle classes were prominent. Partly a colonial reflection of the social purity and antiprostitution movement in Britain (see Walkowitz 1980), it nonetheless addressed what was coming to be seen as a local problem. During 1885, the governor of Jamaica received a number of petitions expressing concern over illegitimacy. One, from a conference led by Bishop Nuttall, suggested the enactment of a law containing the following provisions:

- That, so far as possible and practicable, registration be made of the father of every illegitimate child.
- That some Public Officer in each district (to be defined) be charged with the duty of securing such registration, and be held responsible for the taking, or causing to be taken, the necessary steps preliminary to registration.
- That among such preliminary steps should be the proving of such paternity before competent authority in all cases where such paternity is not acknowledged by the father.
- That every mother of an illegitimate child be required, under penalty, to give information to such Officer with a view to the ultimate registration of the father of such child.
- That it also be made the duty of such Officer to see to the strict carrying out of the Law for the maintenance of illegitimate children in every case where there is an attempt to evade the obligations imposed by that Law (IJMC: MST 209, No. 13, p. 2, minute signed by H. W. Norman, Governor).

The governor declined to take action on these proposals, saying that they would be impossible to carry out in practice. The bishop was provoked into writing a pamphlet entitled "Public Morality: An Appeal, by the Bishop of Jamaica" (IJMC: MST 209, No. 13). In the course of a lengthy reply to the governor, Bishop Nuttall declared, "Let no man drag into this debate questions of class and colour, or suspect this agitation of any class sympathies or antagonisms. It is a question of the social life of a whole people. It has nothing to do with class. The immoral lives of numerous Englishmen, Scotchmen, and Irishmen in Jamaica, for generations past, are quite sufficient to silence those who want to get rid of this subject by the convenient insinuation that the blame for our present condition of things rests exclusively upon them [the lower class]" (p. 4).

His warning was quite forgotten, and over the ensuing years marriage came to be the mark of "middle-class" status, whereas the lower classes were considered to have "disorganized" family relations marked by unstable marriages and high illegitimacy rates. It was precisely the colored women with middle class status who now became the most vocal critics of vice and immorality and the most staunch defenders of the sanctity of marriage. However, their indignation was largely directed against the immorality of the lower classes and they accepted with relative passivity the continuing "outside" unions of their own menfolk.

Despite this newfound concern in the West Indies for respectability, the dual marriage system itself did not change; there was just a reallocation of positions within it. The pattern of men forming "outside" unions with women of lower status did not disappear; indeed it is an intrinsic part of present-day life. The dual marriage system is not a faint memory from the past but a living reality (R.T. Smith 1978a; R.T. Smith 1978b; R.T. Smith 1982a). It continues to disturb, but not destroy, relations within middle-class families. The woman who feels its full impact is the lower-class woman of limited means attempting to raise several children, forced to work if and when she can, and often passing through a series of unions with men who appear to be as transitory as the white bookkeepers of slavery days.

It is remarkable that social scientists should have adopted the class view of this system, attributing its major characteristics to poverty, adaptation, even African culture—anything, in fact, but its obvious relation to the overall structure of class society itself. Several aspects of the contemporary system make it difficult to understand the way in which the dual marriage system operates. Because it had its genesis in the relations between high-status men and lower-status women there is a tendency to suppose that such interclass relations would be necessary for it to continue, and that it is the non-legal unions of such men and women that constitute the system. This is not so. Although cross-class non-legal unions continue to be common, the phenomenon of primary interest to sociologists and social planners alike is the coexistence in the lower class of legal and non-legal unions, and the high proportion of illegitimate children born to lower-class women. Only a small proportion of these children are fathered by middle- or upper-class men.

Once the system was in place the structure became more general than the specific practices that gave rise to it. If one considers the situation within the free colored population during slavery, it is evident that the rule enjoining marriage to a status equal and non-legal union with an inferior had to be implemented in a way different from that found within the white group. Whereas white women did not (with few exceptions) enter non-legal unions, colored women were reputed to prefer concubinage with a white man over marriage to a colored man. Within the colored group, the principles embodied in the dual marriage system were transformed into the rule that legal marriage and concubinage were *alternative forms* even between status equals. For black slaves, legal marriage was forbidden and by virtue of that fact was institutionalized *for them* as a superior form. After emancipation some white men continued to have colored mistresses, but the white population declined rapidly in most colonies while the class position of the colored group was greatly improved through the growth in professional and bureaucratic employment. The whole system was shifted down one register, so to speak, without any basic alteration. For blacks, who were now enjoined to marry, the rule of marrying a status equal was conjoined with the conception of legal marriage as a sign of superior status. In other words, the structure was compressed within the confines of the lower class in such a way that a lower-class man could use any status factor, even masculinity itself, as the basis for insisting upon a casual rather than a legally sanctioned union. However, there could be no exact correspondence between status and marriage type within the lower class; the dual forms of marriage became intraclass alternatives, with the superior form sometimes being entered into late in life as the crowning event of a long relationship.

Although I have used language that implies rational choice, the system was not the end-product of a series of individual choices; if anything, it shaped and guided those choices. Outside unions between lower-class women and middle-class men are easy to document for the recent past (see R.T. Smith 1982a for details), but the following case illustrates the continuing relation between hierarchy—including gender hierarchy—and kinship, even when the individuals concerned are of the same economic class.

## The Case of Alice Smith

Alice Smith is a thirty-seven-year-old single mother with six children by four different men.[5] She was born illegitimate in rural Jamaica and, after her mother "walked out on us," as she puts it, she moved to Kingston to live with her mother's father, Conrad Drew, and his wife, Carlotta Drew, whom Alice called "Aunt." Within about a year, her father entered another union with a Miss Parris, who was living near Kingston, in a rural part of St. Andrew, and Alice and one of her brothers stayed with them on and off for two years. Her older sister lived in another rural area, probably as an "adopted" live-in servant. Alice, unable to get along with her stepmother, was brought to stay with a group of people she refers to collectively as "the relatives them." They were a miscellaneous collection of her father's kin living in a rundown area of Kingston on land that had "come down from the old people them." In Jamaica, such land is "family land," on which no member of the kindred can be denied accommodation. There she slept in a big room with her father's sister's daughter, her husband, and all their children.

Alice Smith's first child was born when she was sixteen. When a second child was fathered by the same man, she moved out of that room. However, she still lives on the same family land, in a shack of her own. Like most West Indian women, she has worked all her life, first as a domestic servant and then in a dry-cleaning plant. The father of her first two children lives with the mother of his other children, having contributed virtually nothing to the support of Alice's children. The father of the next two lives with his aunt; like the first, he did not actually live with Alice. The father of the fifth child lives with another woman. Alice's discovery of this relationship hastened the breakup of her arrangement with this man, but they remain on good terms; he visits his daughter, and if Alice needs repairs to the house, he usually does them. The father of her baby had not been around since Alice was eight months pregnant, but during our interviews, he began to visit again. He claimed to have stayed away because one of Alice's children had been rude to him by not saying "goodnight" when he arrived. This exquisite sensibility was only part of the story; it turned out that another woman had just had a child by him—this in addition to his three children in the country and an older daughter at school in town.

Alice Smith is no more resentful of what seems to be blatant sexual and economic exploitation by the fathers of her children than are other informants. One spoke, without regret, of the "upstanding man" who "fall me" as a young girl (R.T. Smith 1982a: 124). Men and women alike will declare that it is in the nature of men to need more than one woman—especially West Indian men—whereas a woman can be satisfied with one man. If women enter multiple unions, they are impelled to do so not out of natural desire but out of practical necessity. It sounds very much like the contrast drawn by Janet Schaw in the eighteenth century between creole white men and women, except that today lower-class women are forced into multiple unions in the search for a stable relationship with an adequate provider.

This case was chosen deliberately because it does not quite fit the received view of matrifocal kinship structure, where the mother-daughter relationship provides a stable domestic core to which men are loosely attached. Alice Smith is not atypical; many children grow up away from their mothers, and not infrequently with female relatives of the father. This does not alter the ideological link between domesticity, female sex roles, and maternity; indeed, Alice Smith's bitter regrets about her own childhood are ample proof of where the cultural stress is placed. Nor is Alice Smith atypical in the number of her unions and "sets" of children. She differs from the middle-class woman who passively accepts male infidelity. Lower-class women are fully aware that a lower-class visiting "boyfriend" who has other relationships is unlikely to be an adequate source of support.

Feminist concern over the plight of lower-class West Indian women is not misplaced, especially concern for those women who have been uprooted from rural communities in which they had the support of networks of kin and are now struggling to make ends meet in the cities and towns. However, that concern should not lead automatically to the conclusion that high illegitimacy rates and multiple unions signify either "disorganization" or "adaptation." Even less should one conclude that mother-focused families, or even families in which the father does not share a household with the children, lead to deficiencies or disabilities in the children. The modern West Indian middle class is well aware of its origin in "irregular" unions (Alexander 1977: 431–32), although it may not recognize equally clearly its own contemporary deviations from a so-called "normal" nuclear family pattern. Nor is it always recognized that many of the most ambitious, creative, and successful West Indians have been the children of outside unions with "irresponsible" fathers and hardworking, dedicated mothers. When those fathers have passed on to their children some advantage—be it wealth, color, education, or preferential treatment in gaining employment—it has not mattered a great deal that the children were illegitimate and brought up in a matrifocal household, and that has been true from the days of slavery to the present. The true disadvantage in the West Indies has been to be black and poor.

## CONCLUSION: FEMINIST ISSUES AND CARIBBEAN DATA

### The Matrifocal Family

The aspect of Caribbean society that has most attracted the attention of feminist theorists has been the matrifocal family, in which women are salient in domestic affairs and men, in the status of husband-father, are marginal to the close bonds between mothers, children, and daughters' children (R.T. Smith 1956). Caribbean mothers, unlike those in the classic matrilineal societies, have not been under the politico-jural domination of brothers and mothers' brothers; therefore the Caribbean data seem to pose new questions about the universality of familial and kinship roles, and the ability of women to sustain viable family units without men in the status of husband-father, or avuncular protector. I have discussed elsewhere the nature of the dual marriage system and its implications for social policy in the contemporary Caribbean; here I will concentrate on its relation to some theoretical issues in feminist writing (R.T. Smith 1982).

### Natural Functions

Much discussion in the feminist literature has focused upon biological givens, upon the apparently irreducible facts of human nature. The matrifocal family is easy to interpret as a reduced, but still natural, form of the nuclear family, a form that continues to fulfill all the functions of the family through the heroic efforts of, in George Lamming's graphic phrase, "my mother who really fathered me" (Lamming 1953: 11).

Feminist theory has moved beyond this point, as is evidenced by numerous recent articles (Collier & Yanagisako 1987). Whatever the irreducible facts of biology may be, they are incorporated into social and cultural systems in ways that are, if not infinitely varied, remarkably diverse. Biology does not determine social and cultural arrangements; attention has been shifted elsewhere, most notably onto an examination of the economic and class factors that combine with gender, kinship, marriage, and family. It is here that the history of interpretation of Caribbean data is valuable in emphasizing the errors of economic determinism.

## Economic Determinants

In New World colonial societies, the social and cultural systems that developed over time were, and are, more than epiphenomena of economic exploitation. Economic activities and economic class position certainly affect kinship, family, and marriage. Just how profoundly they do so is shown by Verena Stolcke's study of immigrant coffee workers in Brazil (1984). Recruited as families from Germany, Switzerland, and Italy, these workers initially were sharecroppers, operating in a system of labor relations which—despite its exploitative features—used families as units, thus reinforcing many aspects of "traditional" family structure such as paternal authority and a sexual division of labor. Today those coffee workers are transformed into a semiurban proletariat selling their labor on a daily contract basis and being trucked to work sites. The demand for female labor and the fragmentation of the old family work teams have changed the internal relations of the family, change reminiscent of industrializing England, where unemployment altered men's traditional role (Engels 1958; Smelser 1959; Anderson 1971).

Chattel slavery in the West Indies was an extreme form of economic exploitation; we have seen that writers from Adam Smith to the present have assumed that it was destructive of family relations. But all labor systems, including slavery, have to be seen in a wider context of social and cultural organization. Stolcke's coffee workers are affected by many things other than their participation in the labor market. Some of the changes that she reports, such as intergenerational conflict, may be due to urbanization and a closer integration into a Brazilian creole way of life. Lancashire cotton operatives, for all the trauma of male unemployment and the demand for female and child labor, did not experience a complete breakdown of family relations. In the Caribbean, despite the disrupting effects of plantation labor, Hindu and Muslim immigrants were not prevented from achieving a new equilibrium in family relations which differs in important ways from that of Afro-Americans (Smith and Jayawardena 1959; Jayawardena 1960; Jayawardena 1962; R.T. Smith 1957a; R.T. Smith 1963). Slavery, and the societies in which it was embedded, were more than systems of labor relations.

## Class Relations

In an article on seamstresses and dressmakers in Turin, Italy, Vanessa Maher has provided us with a penetrating insight into the complexities of establishing and maintaining class differences, and into the relation between work, class, and female roles in a small—though crucial—sector of Italian urban society (Maher 1987). The cultural distinction that she, and her informants, make between the "outside" world of work and public life and the "inside" domain of private, domestic, and essentially feminine activities has always been a feature of West Indian life as well—as we have seen. These cultural distinctions have not altered the fact of women's labor outside the home. There are some interesting parallels between Turin seamstresses and the colored women of eighteenth- and nineteenth-century West Indian society. Like the *sartina* of the Turin atelier, colored housekeepers, personal maids, and seamstresses were given privileged entry to the domestic domain of the higher classes. They too were renowned for their extravagance in dress. Colored women were in great demand at balls, where they partnered white men, and they played a prominent part in masquerades and festivals (Wright 1937: 243–47). However, for the colored woman, be she slave or free, this was not just a liminal phase between childhood and a settled life married to a man of her own class. Colored women, and men, may have been anomalies in a cultural system that posited pure races, but it was precisely because of their kinship connections and color that they were able to establish themselves as the nucleus of a new middle class. The complicating factor of race makes the comparison of Italy and the West Indies particularly interesting. It shows that supposedly universal distinctions of "public" and "private" domains, linked to hypothetical societal functions, fail to capture the complex realities involved; they mean different things in the two cases. As Stolke (1981) has pointed out, the subordination of women in class society is largely derivative of an ideology of natural inequality that persists within the formal egalitarianism of bourgeois society. In societies founded on racist ideas, such as those of the Caribbean, one would expect colored and black women to be doubly subordinate; once on the grounds of race and once because of their femininity. But we have seen how colored women, like the *sartina*, penetrated the class world of the dominant groups. Whereas the Italian woman eventually returned to her natal class and married an equal, the colored woman was the matrix of a new social element capable, once economic and political conditions were right, of emergence as a new class. Those women bore and raised their children in the archetypical matrifocal family, without legal attachment to the fathers of their children and without the social commitment that such attachment implied. But these were the families identified by Higman as being among the elite of the plantation slave and free colored labor force.

## Class and the Dual Marriage System

A double-standard of sexual behavior—freedom for men to have outside affairs while women are obliged to remain faithful—is found in both Europe and the Caribbean. It is tempting to see this double-standard as part of "nature," necessary for the continued operation of any society since men are naturally promiscuous while women must be confined to a stable domestic environment to make social reproduction possible. Not only is the assumption false, but this case shows the importance of the context in which double-standards develop.

Europe and the Caribbean are each affected, in different ways, by the development of capitalist economies and the social relations created by those economies. The prerequisite for a fully developed system of extramarital concubinage is a class system in which women of lower status are available as mistresses, a condition that certainly prevailed in both areas. In Europe, prostitution and concubinage existed alongside concepts of family honor that required sexual restrictions on women; therefore, prostitutes, kept women, and the mothers of illegitimate children were dishonored and socially marginal. Despite Adam Smith's pronouncements (and those of later writers), there were few prostitutes among West Indian women either during slavery or after, although some real prostitution occurred. Honor was closely related to race, and for all the fulminations of people like Edward Long, people of mixed race—illegitimate or not—enjoyed more social honor than their black kin. By the same token, they had less social honor (even if of legitimate birth), than the most ignorant, illiterate white. Once these differing structural principles are understood, comparison is more meaningful.

Social science has measured all kinship against the standard of modern Euro-American bourgeois nuclear family structure. It has been argued, with much plausibility, that this family form—along with its associated concepts of "public" and "private" domains—is produced by capitalism and is reduced to performing the special functions of social reproduction and providing a "haven in a heartless world." The theory of the isolated nuclear family is an accurate representation of the situation of the bourgeoisie in developed capitalist societies.

Although the Caribbean and Latin America have been influenced by developments in North America and Europe, the material base is not the same and the ideology of the nuclear family has played a very different role in dependent and peripheral areas—a role closely linked to the maintenance of a different system of social relations and social hierarchy.

The dual marriage system of the West Indies is not a particular manifestation of European norms and deviance, nor is it the inevitable outcome of economic organization, to be changed solely by improved economic conditions. Its curious tenacity derives from its being embedded in a social formation with its own integrity and its own historical development. It demonstrates the variability of family structure and gender roles, while also showing the importance of ideology as a constituent element in that structure.

# CHAPTER SIX

# Family, Social Change, and Social Policy in the West Indies (1982)

For Europe and North America there is a large literature devoted to the evaluation of social policies; for the Caribbean it is often difficult to find out what the polices are, much less how they are actually implemented.[1] Most social welfare agencies in the Commonwealth West Indies have the shape and direction which they acquired during the colonial period, and in spite of some recent new departures it is to that period we must refer in order to understand the present situation. The last major review of social policy in the West Indies was occasioned by the riots and disturbances of the late 1930s, which led to the appointment of a Royal Commission and the subsequent passage of the Colonial Development and Welfare Acts of 1940 and 1945. Independence from Britain has not generally resulted in a searching examination of social policy—rhetoric to the contrary. The tendency seems to be to try to bring the area into line with a universal "modern" practice, suitable or not, for no politician wishes to appear to be unprogressive.

This chapter is not intended as a review of social policy, even in the restricted area of the family. Others will have to undertake that task. Its more modest aim is to reexamine the premises on which the policies of the terminal phase of colonial rule were based, to ask how they appear in the light of more recent work on the family, and then in the final section, and with the greatest hesitation, to suggest some implications of this work for the formulation of policy bearing on the family.

## COLONIAL DEVELOPMENT AND WELFARE

The first Social Welfare Adviser to the Comptroller for Development and Welfare in the West Indies, a post created in response to the riots of 1938 and the report of the Royal Commission which investigated their causes, was T.S. Simey. An academic sociologist who eventually became Charles Booth Professor of Social Science in the University of Liverpool, he spent the years 1941 to 1945 struggling to understand the nature of West Indian society and devise policies appropriate for it, rather than just importing ready-made schemes from Europe. He believed, ardently, in the possibility of a scientific approach to social engineering.

In the modern history of social policy in this region Simey is a particularly strategic figure. Not only did he play a leading part in implementing the new colonial polices but he also absorbed the social ideas of the most progressive elements of the West Indian middle class, and particularly the Jamaican middle class. He taught the first graduates of the new Welfare Training Courses held at Mona, Jamaica in 1943 and 1944, thus helping to set the pattern for future training. Most importantly he embodied his ideas and his experience in a book which is an indispensable guide to the thought of the period. Internally contradictory in many ways, *Welfare and Planning in the West Indies* raises all the important issues, and he regarded it as "the record of the beginning of a fascinating and supremely important experiment in the planning of society and human relationships" (Simey 1946:30).

Simey is also relevant to our topic in that he regarded the family as a central institution, with a formative influence on personality, and thus on society as a whole. In this he followed the conventional wisdom of his day and foreshadowed many subsequent interpretations which also found "looseness" of family relations to be a major factor making for persistent poverty (M.G. Smith 1966; Moynihan 1965).

The bedrock of Simey's thinking is a series of ideas which are still with us in the 1980s, the simplest being that the West Indies are impoverished economically, disorganized socially, and deficient culturally. "The symptoms of serious disease in the body of modern society are only too obvious in the Colonies in general, and in the West Indies in particular" (Simey 1946:vi). Although his task is to "investigate the causes of the ills which lie behind [the symptoms] and propound a really effective cure" he has decided *a priori* that colonial society is a special kind of problem. "Life in the Colonies is, indeed, lived in a backwater from the main stream of human affairs, at one and the same time in several centuries, the social philosophies, moral values, and customs of which are mingled together in the wildest confusion" (ibid). How this differs from Britain with its ceremonial royalty, vestigial aristocracy, nineteenth-century utilitarian economic ethic, and the beginnings of a twentieth-century welfare state, he does not say.

In the circumstances of the 1940s political independence appeared to be some way off, contingent upon a series of intermediate factors. Self-determination would not be possible without adequate wealth, and that was dependent upon a "social dynamic" powerful enough to drive the economic machine. Modern sociology was to provide both the understanding of the problems and the techniques for solving them; techniques for generating the "social dynamic" that would set the machine of progress in motion. "The work of the academic sociologist is being steadily translated into the language of the administrator, and a new method has been developed whereby social relationships and social problems can be studied objectively" (Simey 1946:viii). These are brave words and upon their promise has grown up a veritable industry of survey research, data banks, training programs in social and political administration, experts, advisers, and consultants. Sociology as an academic discipline would have been better served if it had claimed less and had fewer impossible demands placed upon it. It is a pity that Simey had not been influenced more by Karl Marx and Max Weber who knew, each in their own way, that the naïve positivism of a supposedly value-free social science does not provide a set of blueprints for utopia.

In proper scientific manner Simey begins with infrastructure, a discussion reminiscent of Durkheim. Distances, densities, communications, population characteristics (deploring the lack of adequate statistics), are all dealt with before he turns to the issue of economic production, housing ("the most striking fact about the West Indian peoples, as exemplified in their houses, is their poverty"), income distribution, and nutrition (Simey 1946: 11). And thus we come to the family by way of a direct comparison with Britain and America, in spite of the equal value of all ways of life.

In Great Britain and North America nutrition centres on the family, and it is impossible to arrive at a clear understanding of social conditions in the West Indies without some consideration of the problem of family organization. The wages earned in Barbados, for example, are insufficient to support family life of the type common in Great Britain; in the West Indies all members of a working-class family have to work if the budget is to be balanced (Simey 1946: 14–15).

He goes on to contrast the way in which a common family meal in Britain acts as a prop to family solidarity, whereas in the West Indies, because the working classes do not possess the necessary furniture, this integrating activity is absent. This kind of crude, and simple-minded, determinism crops up again and again, even though in other places he makes many astute observations which totally contradict the idea that poverty determines all. The crux of the matter for Simey is that

> the prevailing type of West Indian family which is encountered over and over again in all the colonies is very loose in organization. It is rarely founded on the ceremony of marriage, and the relationships between its members are often very casual indeed. There is little control over the children, who may receive plenty of maternal affection…but little in the way of careful general upbringing (1946: 15).

It is fateful for the subsequent argument that poverty becomes the prime factor in shaping family relations. Men cannot discharge those obligations which are accepted without question in Britain and North America. But poverty is only part of a wider condition; along with lack of resources and inadequate nutrition there is a more general "weakness in social organization." Only the church "stands out as a rock round which the welter of disorganized human life surges" (Simey 1946: 18). However, the church does not seem to be able to fill the cultural void left by the forcible divorce from African culture and the as yet incomplete possession of the western way of life. Without the binding power of a common culture, and internally divided by racial cleavage, the picture is very like that drawn by J.C. Furnivall for the "plural societies" of the Far East— as we were repeatedly to be reminded by M.G. Smith during the next two decades. Unlike M.G. Smith, both Simey and Furnivall stressed the solvent power of modern capitalism, and both called for cultural renewal or a new form of secular religion, nationalism (See Chapter Seven).

Simey's treatment of religion runs curiously parallel to his discussion of the family. In neither case are African forms suitable for life in the West Indies. Some aspects of African religion persist in the form of superstitions embodied in sects which he dismisses contemptuously as sapping the energies of the people and undermining their economic life. Similarly sexual activity filled a need for self-expression and gratification among slaves, and like superstition it continues to function in the same way in the present. From the baseline of the slave plantation one can follow the functional adaptation of behavior right up to the present. If Haitian peasants have several wives it is because they need them to work their holdings; similarly Jamaican farmers must have the right to chop and change among partners in the interest of keeping up production. Migration within a particular territory, or to find work outside, leads "naturally" to the creation of several families, and the man has to stop sending support payments to the previous partner. So, economic factors account for "the prevalence of the maternal family," but not totally; the patriarchal nature of the "true peasant family" (described in almost the same terms as were used subsequently by Henriques 1953:109), tends to prejudice "the vast majority of young women against marriage as such" (Simey 1946:87). Indeed he recognizes that in the towns, where prosperity is greatest, one finds the least marital stability.

When we have peeled back all the layers of Simey's discussion, we come to a series of ideas about personality which, while not unique to him, have a decided effect upon his policy proposals. Juvenile delinquency is widespread he says—without offering any evidence for the assertion—and he follows this surprising observation with some speculations about child care and discipline. Children grow up without "that close association between father and child" which is taken for granted in Great Britain and North America. Children are allowed to run wild outside but are harshly disciplined at home. Adults, not being "schooled in self-control" cause children to grow up suffering from "excessive anxiety and feelings of insecurity" (Simey 1946: 90). Add on to this the frustration engendered by racial discrimination and what do you get? Aggression, often disguised as unreliability, laziness, sensitivity to insult, and even physical hostility.[2] The middle classes are subject to even more stress than the lower class; efforts to dissociate themselves from the masses, combined with the excessive individualism and competitiveness of modern life, creates hostility, a domineering attitude to the lower class and a "profound spiritual *malaise*" (ibid: 104). This is all the more significant for Simey since middle-class patterns of behavior have to be adopted by the whole society. "There is no going back, no possibility of founding a new culture on working-class society alone" (Simey 1946: 103).

Recognizing that the West Indies cannot divorce itself from the rest of the world, and contending that things are getting worse rather than better, he calls for a total reorientation of administrative thinking. Recruitment of a better type of colonial administrator: efficient, selected by modern methods of psychological testing, open to scientific knowledge, and dependent upon the dispassionate views of sociologists and anthropologists to guide the West Indian peoples toward self-determination via community organization and group therapy. All that nasty aggression, laziness, and sexual self-indulgence must be treated by methods developed for dealing with disturbed ex-prisoners of war. Through group therapy they have been restored to normalcy without any recourse to moralizing. Ultimately Simey's vision is a polity ruled by an elite, a specifically West Indian elite to be sure, guided by cadres of social researchers providing blueprints for middle-class leaders.

> A specifically West Indian plan of action must be adopted, and the preparation of the essential blueprint is the task facing the sociologist (Simey 1946: 239).

> From the West Indian point of view, the future lies with the middle classes. Given a collaboration between them and their friends in Great Britain, progress towards the building up of a mass political movement of which they will become the leaders should be steady and secure (ibid: 258).

And who is to say that it has not been steady and secure? It is true that he regarded Bustamante with apprehension, but he would surely have approved of Sir Alexander Bustamante. The West Indies now have an abundance of planners, blueprint makers, analysts of social ills, and fabricators of new cultural orientations—frequently disguised as discovered "roots." And there is no doubt that things are better in many ways now than they were in 1945. There is more education, better health and nutrition, better housing; people are better clothed; and there are even better public transportation, water supplies, and power. To what extent these things are the result of careful planning and not just a shrewd political response to widespread public demand, a response made possible only because of a period of worldwide economic growth, is an interesting question—which I do not intend to pursue. What is interesting though is that *there seems to have been very little change in family structure.*

Simey had one flash of insight. He failed to follow it up but it does provide me with a convenient lead into the next section, which is an examination of West Indian kinship in the light of some recent research.[3]

## WEST INDIAN KINSHIP AND FAMILY STRUCTURE

The exploitation of the women of the masses by the men of the upper classes has brought with it a general lowering of standards of behaviour which is now a part of a West Indian culture common to people of all races. The upper classes have set a bad example which it will take many generations to efface, and it is by no means certain that as middle-class standards become more widespread in the population the situation will show any tendency towards improvement (Simey 1946: 100–101).

Here we are suddenly spirited away from all that poverty and lack of furniture and absence of a common meal, into a far different realm; a realm of "power" and "exploitation"—words which Simey uses quite rarely. Simey has hit upon a most important truth, though he does not pursue it very far. In order to understand West Indian kinship it must be seen in the context of class, and classes are not discrete, separate groups, each with its own culture and way of life; they are entities in relationship with each other. The fate of one is intimately bound up with the fate of the other. Simey's idea of "a bad example" is silly, as though West Indians were children. This is a system of social relations and a structure of ideological concepts which were in place almost from the beginning of settlement in the West Indies.

### The Establishment of a Structure and its Transformation

The early settlements on St. Christopher, Nevis, Montserrat, Antigua, and Barbados came closest in form to those established on the North American mainland. Richard Dunn (1972: 18) says that "Until the 1640's the Barbadians formed a simple community of peasant farmers."

By 1640 the population of Barbados was about the same as that of Virginia, but its tobacco exports were considered to be inferior to those of the mainland colonies. The tobacco period, from 1627 to about 1640, was one of rapid population increase, but it was not an economically successful period, nor did it produce a family-based society; the settlers were mainly young and there was a chronic shortage of females. The growth of sugar cultivation between 1640 and 1660, accompanied by the importation of African slaves, ensured that Barbados would not follow colonies such as Massachusetts in creating a family system closest to that of the British Isles. Thenceforward slavery impressed its mark upon all social institutions, including kinship and the family, though not quite in the way it has generally been suggested. Barbados was not unique; it was merely a forerunner of developments in all the West Indian territories.

Britons and Africans together created a creole society. The Britons no more preserved their customs than did the Africans; between them, and out of their hatreds, exploitations, copulations, mutual dependencies, and sometimes even love, they created a new social order, an order that has been accorded any social value with only the most grudging reluctance.

The next two centuries saw the growth and spread of plantation agriculture using slave labor, a system which, whatever else it was, represented an advanced form of rational agriculture with careful accounting and calculation at all stages of production, transport, and sale. The slave was property of course, and not all aspects of life were yet "commoditized." Planters made conscious calculations about the relative costs of replacement or reproduction of the labor force. The plantation mode of production had enormous influence upon every aspect of the lives of those involved in it, but it was not the sole, direct determinant of family and kinship relations. Port Royal in the seventeenth century had "yards" with kinship units reminiscent of those of modern

Kingston; Belize and the Bahamas had "West Indian kinship" without plantations. The crucial factor seems to have been the establishment of a hierarchical social order in which racial categorization was fundamental, and in which a dual marriage system was institutionalized. Such systems are not unique to the West Indies, or even unusual, but Caribbean kinship has not yet been placed in a full comparative framework (See R. T. Smith 1982).

Recent historical scholarship on the West Indies and North America has begun to establish a series of propositions which reverse prior thinking about the influence of slavery on family structure. Gutman (1976), Genovese (1972) and Fogel & Engerman (1974), in their various ways, argue that slave families in North America were far more "normal" than previously had been thought. They attribute the "disorganization" of black families more to the conditions, and especially the economic conditions, which faced freedmen after emancipation, especially with the hardening of racial prejudice which locked them out of economic opportunity. For the British West Indies, Craton has summarized the recent revision of the picture of slave families as follows:

> If one took the nuclear two-headed family as the quintessentially modern family form, it was beguilingly easy to propose its different incidence during the registration period as relating to the degree of maturation, creolization, or modernization of each slave unit, and thus to suggest a historical progression from some aboriginal African form of family (Craton 1979: 25).

> The discovery by Higman…that Africans were at least as likely as Creoles to form nuclear families, modified the original model. This revision…led Higman to a second developmental model…the establishment of "elementary nuclear families" was the primary response of the displaced Africans…A second slave generation began to establish extended families based on the formation of virilocal "yards" within single plantations…in subsequent generations, kinship networks expanded as slaves increasingly practiced exogamy.…The process tended toward matrifocality rather than the nuclear family, especially where lack of slave-controlled provision grounds, money, and property deprived slaves of the chance of "marriage strategies" (ibid.: 26–27).

Craton accepts Higman's more differentiated model and elaborates the context of changing plantation organization, increased miscegenation, and the deteriorating quality of slave life. In spite of his tendentious use of such terms as "nuclear family" and his misuse of the concept of matrifocality (he seems to think it means female-headed households), and in spite of his belief in the importance of the "filtering down into the West Indies of evolving concepts of the 'modern family'" (ibid.: 28), he recognizes, more by a kind of feeling than from any real evidence, the importance of continuing African traditions, especially as regards marriage (ibid.: 31).

The general direction of Craton's argument accords with that being presented here, though he appears to underemphasize the importance of creolization. It was not so much the "filtering down" of "concepts of the 'modern' family" as it was the growing involvement of Blacks in the dual marriage system of creole society and in the system of social relationships structured by class and color values. However, he is right to stress the peculiarity of the marriage system of Africans which, to oversimplify, generally makes a sharp separation between sexual relations and the contract of marriage which establishes political rights, rights over the procreative powers of women (regardless of "biology"), and rights of inheritance and succession. Even in some highly patriarchal, patrilineal societies, such as the Nuer, there may be great freedom in making and breaking sexual unions while marriage remains stable. One can speculate that there was a certain compatibility between the freedom to make and break sexual unions, and the developing struc-ture of the dual marriage system of creole, class society. While the two are by no means the same, they could converge. However, speculation is not history, and what is needed is detailed evidence as to the nature of such convergence.

It is proposed here that the different forms of family found in the West Indies are generated by a set of principles which find differential expression in varying social and economic contexts. These principles are not to be found enunciated in oral tradition nor set out in any document; they must be inferred from a wide range of manifestations, both historical and contemporary. Overformalization of these principles eliminates the ambiguity, uncertainty, and contradictions which are an integral part of the system. Unfortunately it is necessary to provide a summary which involves just such overformalization, but it is hoped that case material will go some way toward restoring the uncertainty of real life.

## The System Outlined

The West Indian system of kinship, marriage, and the family consists in a differentiated series of forms generated by

1. A mating system which enjoins marriage with status equals and non-legal unions with women of lower status.

2. A kinship system which places a lower priority of solidary emphasis on conjugal than on con-sanguineal ties.

3. A family system which is matrifocal but not matriarchal.

4. A domestic system which does not confine relations within an easily defined and bounded "household."

5. A system of sex-role differentiation which stresses the segregation of conjugal roles, permits the participation of women in the occupational system, allows men to disperse economic resources, but requires that women concentrate them.

6. Cultural assumptions which assign specific characteristics to "West Indian" sexual and mari-tal patterns.

Unwieldy though this statement is, it has the advantage of bringing together a number of con-troversial issues which have usually been the subject of quite one-sided arguments. We may take these points one by one.[4]

*A mating system which enjoins marriage with status equals and non-legal unions with women of lower status.* Simey apparently appreciated the importance of this dual marriage system when he wrote the statement quoted earlier (page 85), but he quite failed to follow the origin of this system of hypergamous marriage back to "slavery," as will any middle-class West Indian in discussing the origin of the middle class itself. Alexander (1977: 431) has documented what he terms the myth of origin of the Jamaican middle class; their ideas about the descent of the middle class from "a white planter and a black slave." The equation of middle-class status with mixed racial origin is an interesting aspect of the way in which class is conceptualized, but the myth also encapsulates certain generic ideas about the embeddedness of the "inside/outside" distinction in the marriage system. While there is no formal rule sanctioning "outside" unions—indeed extramarital sexual relations are formally condemned—it is clear that non-legal unions, whether co-residential or not, are generally accepted. In private conversation, a Jamaican judge pointed out that adultery is almost never advanced as grounds for divorce in Jamaica. A petitioner will usually cite her husband's taking up with another woman as the beginning of a series of acts of cruelty, or as precipitating desertion. In the case reported in *The Star* on February 10, 1982, the petitioner said that the marriage "went well for the first few years and then they started having very serious problems.... In June 1976 her husband told her that he was seeing a young lady. She spoke to him and told him to break off his relationships with the young lady, but he told her that he had no intention of so doing." Eventually he started living with the other woman while continuing to live with his wife, and she had a child at the end of 1977. However, the petition for divorce was based on numerous assaults and acts of cruelty during the period 1979 to 1981, and not on grounds of adultery.

The origin of the dual marriage system lies in the formative period of West Indian society, when customs common in Europe acquired an intensification and special quality when practiced in a slave-based society. Whatever the origin of the system, contemporary research shows that it is deeply embedded in the fabric of West Indian life (see Austin 1974; De Veer 1979; Alexander 1977; R.T. Smith 1978). Alexander's discussion of the "myth of origin" of the Jamaican middle class, especially the "established" middle class or people born to middle-class status, was referred to earlier. To find the same kind of concept in working-class areas was quite surprising. Diane Austin, on the basis of field research in a working-class neighborhood in Kingston, reports as follows (1979: 500):

> I found that many working-class informants claimed descent from a European, generally a planter, whether or not they could establish the genealogical links. So common was this claim, that where at the outset I had pursued diligently any suggestion of a European relation, I came to treat such claims as fictive. They represented first and foremost a mythic statement of identity in color-class terms.

Austin (1979:500) provides a full discussion of the genealogy of a Mrs. Mills, a "near black" woman from the rural parish of St. Mary, now married to a welder. Mrs. Mills gave this account of her background:

> My father's father, he is an Englishman for the mother of my grandfather was a fair woman, and the father was an Englishman. I know my grandfather pretty well. He has blue eyes and has silky blond hair.... My father is pretty nice looking, Indian looking man.

It turned out that Mrs. Mills is indeed the outside child of an outside child, and does have a whole collection of fair-skinned relatives in high-status occupations—as Austin was able to observe at the funeral of Mrs. Mills's great aunt. Mrs. Mills is unusual only in that she has more contact with these relatives than other working-class informants who have higher-status relatives. However, the point is not that all lower-class West Indians have kinship ties with white, fair, or high-status people—which would be absurd—but that class and status differences are inserted directly into the kinship system by virtue of a dual marriage system which operates at all levels of the society. Nancy Rogers is a hairdresser living in another working-class area in Kingston; she was interviewed as part of the kinship study that I directed, and the following quotations are from the field notes. Previously married, she separated from her husband, who later migrated to England and died there. Born in the country, Mrs. Rogers claimed that her father had been a "planter" and not simply a "cultivator." She proclaimed her ambition over and over again and was much preoccupied with questions of color. In the matter of marriage she proclaimed that

> You have to choose a man who can give you children good color, and make them brighter than you and more upstanding. If you come from black and go married black again, they no going improve. I not saying you must marry for the sake of color alone, for there are plenty good black men—teachers and doctors and so on. They have education, so the children born with more sense and refinement.

She herself had two of her three children before she was married "...when I was sixteen I have Joan.... Is a man name Gordon fall me. He was quite an upstanding man you know." Her special plea to have this man's name omitted from the genealogy, precisely because he was "an upstanding man" is interesting. The name used here is fictitious of course. Mrs. Rogers was very hard on her Aunt Ellie who, she said, was totally lacking in ambition. (Aunt Ellie was actually her maternal grandmother.)

> My granny did have flat mind. She live in the bush there and just like pure black nigger man. So that's why we now don't have better quality. Aunt Ellie did have flat mind man; she just go, go so, with any black man.

Mrs. Rogers, like Austin's informants, has been referred to as "working class." However, the question of whether one has to draw lines within the lower class is a difficult one. Is there a point in the movement down the status scale where the reference points change? Do we reach a point where there is no question of claiming even mythical descent from a European ancestor? A point where a new stability emerges, unaffected by the dynamics of class interaction though perhaps determined by class position? Is Aunt Ellie's "flat mind" characteristic of a much greater body of people who do not care about status, or if they do are so discouraged that they rest tranquil in a different way of life? The evidence is to the contrary.

Austin (1979: 502) goes quite far in suggesting that "through this class principle in kinship...life itself is defined by class, and class is legitimated in the process as a universal principle of social organization—for some families and not others, it is true." She points to the important fact that women constitute almost half the labor force, that forty-two percent of household heads are women—most of them working women—and that female unemployment was running at 35.6 percent in 1976 in Jamaica (ibid.: 502 fn4). However, it is not just economic need that induces women to enter into non-legal unions. Where neither property, status, nor economic need are crucial considerations, the structure is still operative, generating an array of visiting, common-law and legal marriages as alternatives, and sometimes as alternatives which are taken up sequentially by the same couple over a lifetime.

*A kinship system which places a lower priority of solidary emphasis on conjugal than on consanguineal ties.* In view of the preceding discussion it is permissible to ask what is meant by "conjugal ties" in this statement. To which part of the dual marriage system does it refer? By "conjugal ties" is meant the relationships which are found in the whole array of types of union. This aspect of West Indian kinship has been particularly well documented, though information on the middle class (or on the upper class if such can be said to exist), is sparse. The statement on priority of solidary emphasis has been carefully formulated and should not be taken to mean more than it says. It does not say that conjugal bonds are weak (though they might well be); it does not say that marriage in the West Indies is unstable (though that can be measured); it does not say that "love" is not an important element in conjugal relations (Alexander 1978 has documented its ideological importance among the Jamaican middle class). It means precisely what it says; there is a relatively greater emphasis upon consanguineal solidarity than on conjugal ties. More careful research will be needed to establish the range and variability in these relationships, and I would be hard pressed to provide a definition of "solidary" that would permit of easy measurement. However, the results of this relative emphasis can be seen, even in the familial relationships of the stably married. This structural principle articulates very closely with the next two.

*A family system which is matrifocal but not matriarchal.* Men dominate West Indian society. Sex-role differentiation has a definite hierarchical dimension (see pp. 92–95 below). But if men are dominant they are also, in their role as husbands and fathers, apt to be marginal to the cluster of familial relations which focus upon women in their role as mothers. There has been a great deal of misunderstanding of the meaning of "matrifocal," deriving in large part from misuse of the concept (see R.T. Smith 1956; 1973; 1978b). It has nothing to do with female-headed households, or if it has, the two should be treated separately. The matrifocal nature of family relations is a structural principle, which combines with the relative lack of emphasis upon the conjugal relationship to produce a distinctive pattern of feeling and action within the family system. There is a close link between this and the dual marriage system, though the link is at the level of structural principle rather than specific events.

It has been common to think of the matrifocal family as being a lower-class phenomenon produced by poverty, but there is a splendid historical example which shows the importance of power rather than poverty. An almost archetypical case of a matrifocal family is described by Michael Craton in his book *Searching for the Invisible Man* (1978). The following is my summary of Craton's account.

> This family was part of a complex network of kin springing from the various unions of white men and Coloured women in the area of Lluidas Vale, Jamaica, occupied by the Worthy Park plantation. One branch of the family stemmed from the various unions of Dr. John Quier, the famous physician; another from the union of Peter Douglas, owner of Point Hill Estate, and Eleanor Price—originally a mulatto slave, but freed by Peter Douglas in 1789, she bore him ten children and lived as the mistress of his house at Point Hill. Before Eleanor Price became the Kept Mistress of Peter Douglas she bore one child, Lizette. The father was probably a white bookkeeper named Nash. Lizette was a quadroon, being the child of a mulatto mother and a white father, and she caught the eye of Rose Price, great-great-grandson of the founder of Worthy Park Estate who was in Jamaica from about 1792 to 1795 putting the source of the family fortune in order.
>
> When Rose Price, then about 24 years old, first took up with Lizette she was a thirteen year old slave girl. Rose Price arranged for her manumission and she bore two children for him. He returned to England, married a woman with aristocratic connections who bore him fourteen legitimate children and helped him to acquire a baronetcy. Rose Price left Jamaica before the second child, a son, was born, and Lizette went to live with her mother Eleanor Price, in the house of Peter Douglas. All this sounds quite familiar to anyone who has studied modern West Indian kinship. The subsequent development of the family is of great interest.

Rose Price arranged with Peter Douglas that when his outside children reached a suitable age they should travel to Britain for further education. Elizabeth, the daughter, eventually married a Scots clergyman and never returned to Jamaica. John, the son, after studying engineering, returned to Jamaica in 1823 to live with his mother, grandmother, aunts, uncles (the children of Peter Douglas), and his cousins, in what was clearly a matrifocal household even when Peter Douglas was alive. Both his grandmother and his mother lived to a ripe old age, and in a surviving letter which John Price Nash wrote to his sister in Scotland he speaks of them both with affection and respect.

This case embodies the structural principles of the system in a vivid way, and it also shows the process by which legitimate and illegitimate lines diverge, becoming polarized in class terms. Elizabeth and her descendants disappeared into the Scottish population until Craton uncovered the Jamaican connection; John and his descendants became part of the Jamaican middle class but as they were absorbed back into the Jamaican population they became progressively darker when declining material fortune made "good" marriages more difficult to achieve. (See Craton 1978:331–39 for details).

In our contemporary middle-class interview material we find cases where a husband-father is perceived to be "irresponsible" by virtue of his "outside" activities of drinking and womanizing. But we also find cases where faithful, sober, devoted husbands are concerned about their children's regard for them.

Mr. Benton explained at length the tendency for Jamaican children to disparage and belittle their fathers.

> I have found that very often young people tend to have—young people who are progressing toward adulthood, they tend to regard their father as just a convenience...and this kind of general attitude makes it difficult for the father to play his role properly...and it also seems to me this way, that very often, ah women who are grown up in homes where they didn't have a father—I mean they didn't you know receive the care and protection of a father in a definite way—they seem to grow up without understanding the true role of the father in the home and ahm sometimes they tend, I think too, to believe that everything should revolve around them.

Although he and his wife have "worked out a plan" he is always conscious of the tendency toward a matrifocal bias in the internal relationships of the family, a bias which he sees clearly as coming from men ultimately, and their "outside" activities. This is not just the result of Benton's experience; it is an integral part of the culture of the Caribbean, brought to a sharp focus in the consciousness of the upwardly mobile who are striving to live a planned, careful, orderly, clean, religiously informed life as opposed to what our lower-class informants (and Professor Simey), call the "loose," "dirty," "careless," "up-and-down" life of common experience.

*A domestic system which does not confine relations within an easily defined and bounded "household."* This has been discussed in previous publications (R.T. Smith 1973; 1978a; 1978b). Activities such as childcare, the acquisition, cooking, and consumption of food, washing, sleeping, sexual relations, and other activities generally regarded as "domestic," are not neatly confined within the bounds of a single "household." Still less can we assume that the typical household contains a nuclear family, appearances and survey data notwithstanding. These are complex issues and space does not permit their extended discussion. Our case materials remind us over and over again that although people are quite prepared to play the game into which they have been educated by several generations of census and survey takers, and provide a neat list of household members, further investigation quickly dissolves the image of the isolated nuclear family. The following case is from my own field records.

> The family of Mr. and Mrs. Black in the village of August Town, Guyana, was listed in 1953 as living on a particular lot in a particular cluster of wooden buildings—two frame houses and a separate kitchen. Mr. Black, a carpenter, already had several outside children, and he owned a house in another village in which he had installed a lady friend and their son. Two of the Blacks' daughters were living in August Town with spouses, one married and one in a common-law union. As recorded in 1956, these daughters spent a good deal of their time in the family home with their mother and their children (who always called their maternal grandmother "mama"), ate there frequently, played with Mrs. Black's younger children who were about their age, and often slept there. Mr. Black divided his time (somewhat unpredictably) between his two homes. By 1975 things had changed a good deal. Both Mr. and Mrs. Black were dead. The family home, considerably the worse for wear, was now occupied by the youngest daughter and her three children (by three different fathers) and a son—now a police constable. The rates on the land were paid by another daughter living in the United States of America. For periods the policeman would give a weekly allowance to his sister who then cooked and washed his clothes, but at other times he would complain that she was wasting his money and "board" with a married sister in the village—that is, pay her a weekly sum to provide food for him. These married sisters had by now their own grown-up children with whom they maintained close interactive relations that can only be described as "domestic" even though the people involved were apparently distributed over a number of "nuclear family" households. This kind of pattern is not peculiar to rural Guyana. There is no need to belabor the point, but it is necessary to remember that lists of occupants of "households" do not constitute an adequate guide to family and domestic relations.

*A system of sex-role differentiation which stresses the segregation of conjugal roles, permits the participation of women in the occupational system, allows men to disperse economic resources, but requires that women concentrate them.* Until recently the significance of sex-role differentiation as an important component of family structure has been underestimated. Elizabeth Bott (1957; 1968) in her pioneering work on English families, did not at first recognize that her "segregated" and "joint" patterns of conjugal-role activity were but special instances of differences in sex-roles.

Implicit in many historical discussions of the family is these idea that a "normal" family is a nuclear family; this assumption is reflected in the very terminology when reference is made to "denuded" families. Another pervasive assumption is that stable, normal families exist when a male in the position of husband-father is possessed of authority and control over economic resources. In many discussions of the slave family and the transition to free labor, the weakness (or the supposed weakness) of the family, is attributed to the insecurity of the husband father because of his inability to command steady and adequate income. The concept of a "normal" family consisting of a man who is active in the politico-jural and economic domains, a wife who has responsibility for the domestic domain, and their children to whom legitimate status is transmitted by virtue of the parents' marriage, is a concept with far-reaching consequences. It is embedded in all English thinking about welfare policy since the beginning of the seventeenth century, and inevitably it has deeply affected West Indian discussion of these issues.

Unfortunately it bears little relation to the realities of West Indian working-class life, nor to English working-class life for that matter (see Land & Parker 1978).

Thomas Roughley's *The Jamaica Planter's Guide* (1823), a source mined to exhaustion by writers on slavery, has some interesting things to say about work organization. At this period the slave trade had been abolished for some time and planters were concerned about the reproduction of their labor force since that seemed to be the only method of replacement. Roughley had a lot to say about childcare, the treatment of pregnant women, the care of the aged, and the like, and all these discussions are clearly and overtly linked to the problem of running the plantation. The "great gang" is composed of the strongest and most skilled men *and* women, attended by a field cook who is to see that they are fed well and on time. The "second gang" is made up of sickly people, youths, sucking mothers and the aged, attended by nurses who look after the infants while the mother is at work in the fields. Mothers get an occasional break in order to feed their children. (Substitute free labor for slave and a factory for a plantation and all this might sound quite "modern"). The third, or "weeding gang" is composed of children from five to six years and upwards under the direction of a driveress. Roughley appears to be as solicitous of the welfare of these children as any modern social worker. He (1823:104) points out these children are

> drivers, cattlemen, carpenters, coopers, and masons, as it were in embryo.... Even in common life, throughout civilized Europe, the welfare of the child is the grand object of the parent. The owner and the overseer of those valuable shoots should act the part of a parent, fosterer, and protector, looking on them as the future prop and support of the property.

He details the age at which children should be weaned (twelve to fourteen months), the desirability of "inoculation for the cow or smallpock," the daily feeding of weaned children with soup, and the monthly dosing with worm medicine and castor oil. By the age of three they graduate to a group supervised by an old woman who keeps them clean, fed, and busy, each child aided by a "wineglass of acidulated sugar beverage, and a taste of good rum to each, as an enlivener" (Roughley 1823: 122). Surely preferable to the laudanum with which the children of the English working classes were rendered tranquil while their mothers labored in the textile mills of Lancashire.

The old, the sickly, and the incapacitated are not neglected. The old "should be allotted to those kinds of occupations which do not bear hard upon them." But, "something they should always have to do, to keep their minds employed, and their bodies in easy activity." Similarly with the invalids, "Though much cannot be expected of them, yet it is best to keep them at some employment," such as planting and cleaning fences (ibid.: 113–17).

Roughley's experience was on the large Jamaican sugar estates. Such paternal solicitude and precise management was less likely to be found on small properties, and indeed we do not know to what extent it was actually practiced anywhere. We do know that he describes a pattern of labor utilization which was widespread and which continued on plantations using indentured labor after slavery has been abolished. We also know that indentured labor on Guyanese plantations received better medical care, crude though it might have been, than did the free laborers who lived in villages. This is reflected in mortality statistics.

This is not the place to review the wide range of economic circumstances which existed after the abolition of slavery. It was unusual for the ex-slaves to be able to constitute themselves into a stable and prosperous "peasantry." Indeed, few of them tried. What they attempted to do was to alter the conditions under which they sold their labor power, and to remove themselves from the control of the plantations. British Guiana saw the most successful movement of slaves into independent villages, but, as Walter Rodney (1981) has recently reemphasized, they did not become "peasants" (see R.T. Smith 1956, 1962). Like settlements in other parts of the West Indies, they were constituted around a Christian church with its attendant school, and the villagers, far from withdrawing from creole, colonial society, were drawn ever more closely into it. Legal, Christian marriage in the hierarchical system of creole society was a sign of status and it came to be associated with women's cessation from work outside the home. It was a class-defined institution, opposed to other forms of union within a system of unions, and so it remains today. Only in this context does "poverty" make any sense as the precipitating cause of non-legal unions.

Of course, women were out of luck in post-emancipation society. They remained actively involved in occupations outside the home, while at the same time losing whatever services were provided by the plantation; services such as daycare for their children, a cook to provide food at work, free medical services and maternity leave. Now they had to work outside and take on domestic responsibilities at home. In view of the history of the West Indies and of women's labor it is remarkable to what extent the very concept of womanhood continues to be bound up with mothering and with the performance of such domestic activities as cooking, washing, and cleaning.

Erna Brodber (1975), in her study of Kingston yards, has provided some revealing insights into the way in which quite independent women allow men to dominate them. These women rent rooms in yards, into which they admit boyfriends who may or may not contribute significantly to household expenses. They go out of their way to cook attractive food, keep the men's clothes in order, and generally play the role of obedient wife. If there is a TV set it is the man who chooses the program, even if the woman is paying the rent; if the man wants to sleep after lunch the children are chased away. Although middle-class women have "helpers" to do the dirty work, the kitchen and the house remain their domain. One middle-class woman told us that her late husband had never been in the kitchen; with a wife, two daughters, and a maid he never even poured himself a glass of water.

Ideologically there is a close association between the "inside" domain and activities of women and the "outside" life of men. Both Austin (1974) and De Veer (1979), in their work in Kingston and May Pen respectively, have shown how deep-seated and pervasive are these ideas about sex-roles. The aspect to which attention is drawn here is the way in which men tend to use income, be it in cash or in kind, to fulfill obligations which are often dispersed over a number of domestic groups. They may give contributions to their own mothers, the mothers of their children, current girlfriends, and of course to their own wives or common-law wives. Such material as we have on this question shows that lower- or working-class men may have a remarkable number of claims on their income. In a study carried out among lower-class men in Kingston, Anderson Parks (personal communication) describes how a delivery van driver with a steady, but not large, income tends to run up debts for such items as stereo equipment, regularly drops off money to pay the rent of a current girlfriend, passes by to leave a contribution to the support of an outside child, visits his mother with a gift and eventually arrives home to his wife with a considerably reduced pay-packet, some of which will be kept back to meet his entertainment expenses.

There is no reliable measure of the extent to which this pattern is general, or the extent to which it is confined to the lower class. As usual there is a great deal of variability, and one could point to cases where married middle- or working-class couples pool their resources for the purchase of a house or the education of children. However, our women informants are quite articulate about the propensity of men to "wander"; field materials, some of them going back as far as 1951, confirm that it is quite common for men to disperse resources while women concentrate them. It is easy to devise functional explanations for this flow of resources; it avoids the reliance of any one domestic unit upon a sole source of income which is apt to be cut off in an unstable labor market. Like all functionalist explanations, this one fails to explain why this particular solution should have emerged rather than another.

"I feel a woman can control their nature more than a man. I just have that feeling. I mean, a woman will easier be satisfy with one man when a man can't be satisfy with one woman. Right?" (De Veer 1979:108). This statement of a male Jamaican could be regarded as a rationalization of his own behavior, or as special pleading. It couches the argument in universalistic, "natural" terms, against which moral arguments carry little weight. But West Indians also claim special characteristics, as though nature had singled them out from the rest of mankind.

*Cultural assumptions which assign specific characteristics to "West Indian" sexual and marital patterns.* "Jamaicans love a whole lot of woman, you know. Lot of woman, not just one. They don't stick to one, they must have girls outside, that's just the way.... They love sport [laugh]. Married men, unmarried men, it don't matter." (De Veer 1979:150). This happened to be a working-class woman speaking, but much the same sentiment can be found at every level of the society.

West Indians do not have a monopoly on polygynous tendencies, nor is it unusual for men to use positions of power to secure access to women. In Africa many young men seethe with resentment at the monopolization of young women by old men; not necessarily out of sexual frustration, but because access to women is itself a sign of power, prestige, and maturity. Nineteenth-century European society had a well-documented under-life. The male members of the British royal family, or some of them, were renowned for their sexual exploits. Karl Marx fathered a bastard son on his domestic servant and Friedrich Engels had a Kep' Miss from the Lancashire working class; it may have shown a democratic impulse, but of course he did not marry her.

The rising divorce rate and the increase in female-headed households in the United States sometimes appears to indicate that they are following in the wake of the West Indies. The appearance is false. There is no loss of faith in the monogamic ideal in the United States, even among that growing number of people for whom the Census Bureau had to devise a new term, "POSSLQ," or Person of Opposite Sex Sharing Living Quarters. The rate of remarriage is exceedingly high. The West Indies are closer to Victorian England than to the egalitarian customs of the modern youth of North America and Europe with their apparent mastery of the techniques of birth control. Certainly the ideology is different; divorce and remarriage is really a searching for the one, true, right person and is not based upon a notion that monogamic fidelity is impossible.

## POLICY IMPLICATIONS

Social policies which bear directly upon the family are surprisingly uniform in modern bureaucratic societies, and all states, regardless of their level of economic development or the nature of their political system, tend to adopt similar policies (Kamerman & Kahn 1977). Cadres of professional "social workers," "family case workers," "probation officers," and the like are to be found everywhere and are increasing in number. They are an integral, and perhaps inevitable, part of the modern state apparatus; that is, the state apparatus which increasingly regulates the lives of its citizens. Michel Foucault and his associates have shown how recent is this development (Foucault 1965, 1970, 1973, 1978a, 1978b; Donzelot 1979). The invention of modern institutions such as the prison, lunatic asylum, orphanage, and workhouse went hand-in-hand with the growth of that scientific approach to planning which so captivated Simey. Poverty, marital stress, child neglect, bastardy, and unemployment came to be seen as aspects of "social pathology" to be studied, regulated, and (optimistically) cured by rational intervention on the part of paid servants of the state. The ideology of rational intervention continues to motivate social policy in the face of growing skepticism as to its efficacy. Some students regard this bureaucratic apparatus as a part of the regulatory, or police, function of the state, particularly since its clients are the poor and the unruly. Whatever the truth or otherwise of that idea, it is clear that the general trend toward more social intervention in family life is unlikely to diminish, whatever is said here. However, our previous analysis suggests that there are certain aspects of West Indian family structure which are neither pathological nor amenable to cure by concentrating on the poor.

We must agree with Simey (1946: 100–101) in his one flash of insight, that "as middle-class standards become more widespread in the population the situation will [not] show any tendency toward improvement" in the exploitation of women, though in the interest of neutrality we might re-phrase it to read, "will [not] show any tendency to change." Far from the system showing "looseness," "disorganization," or "disintegration," it appears to be very stable. The dual marriage system is intact. Illegitimacy rates have not fallen significantly. Whether one likes the pattern of West Indian kinship or not, one cannot realistically says that it is disorganized. West Indians have extensive kinship ties, and at all levels of the society kin tend to be supportive, loving, and kind—with occasional lapses of course, and allowing for the divisions created by class. It is not that West Indian kinship is weak; it is that it has distinctive patterns which need to be recognized.

These distinctive patterns are not "caused" in any simple way by "poverty." That is not to say that poverty is not a grave social problem in the West Indies; poverty, along with unemployment, underemployment, lack of opportunity, and absence of adequate bases for self-respect, must all be addressed by social policy. But these things are not caused by the family system any more than the family system is caused by them. They are all part of the structure in place, produced by the political economy of the West Indies, by its historical experience, and by the manner in which class has been structured in West Indian society.

In the almost fifty years since Simey wrote *Welfare and Planning in the West Indies* there has been a great deal of change in this region. Most of that change has been in the direction envisaged and advocated by him. The expansion in the size of the middle class, effected by widening educational opportunity and the increase in bureaucratic, service, and sales occupations, has been made possible mainly by increases in the export of bauxite and oil, and by the development of the tourist trade. It would have surprised Simey to see how little of this increased prosperity has come through agriculture, but he would have been gratified by the growth in local industry to substitute for imports and to provide housing. As is widely recognized, these changes have not altered the basic structure of dependence of the region on the industrialized countries. With the possible exception of Cuba, and the very peculiar case of Guyana, all these developments have been based squarely upon the expansion of the middle class, and upon the extension of middle-class aspirations to an ever-widening circle.

It is difficult to imagine any fundamental change in these trends in the immediate future. Social policy seems to incline toward a local form of welfare capitalism. National Insurance schemes for the employed; generous pension, housing, medical, and other perquisites for the upper middle class—be they in business, government service, politics, or the military—and for such of the rest of the middle and working classes as can bargain for these perquisites; and very little left for the growing numbers of the poor. High rates of population growth coupled with the closing off of migration outlets and the apparent impossibility of economic growth outpacing population growth, seem to guarantee high levels of unemployment, crime, and inadequate social services. Under these circumstances it would be unrealistic to expect any drastic change in family structure. For the lower class it is only the mutuality of kinship and community that keeps the very poor afloat at all, and given the continuation, and even the intensification of class relations it does not seem likely that the dual-marriage system will disappear.

It is tempting to attribute present circumstances to "colonialism" or to "slavery" or "the plantation," and a case can be made for each such attribution. An even better case can be made for explaining much of the present difficulty in economic life to the continuing pattern of relations between the developed and underdeveloped parts of the world. But when it comes to family structure the case is somewhat different. When people declare, with some measure of pride, toleration, or amusement that "Jamaica man can't satisfy with one woman" then it does not seem quite fair to blame it all on people like William Montagu, Viscount Mandeville and 5th Duke of Manchester who, as governor of Jamaica from 1808 to 1827, left more than place names behind him. According to Edward Brathwaite he had numerous brown-skinned progeny, and at least five of his illegitimate children were at school in Kingston in the 1830s. (However, his wife, Lady Susan, daughter of the Duke of Gordon, a great beauty and a woman of independent spirit, had run off with one of her footmen even before he left for the West Indies.) Interesting as these historical events undoubtedly are, we must remember that the present-day system is being maintained, being reproduced every day, by the actions of independent West Indians exercising their prerogatives of freedom, privilege, dominance, and submission. It is nonsense to say that West Indians cannot afford to marry, that unstable unions and female-headed households are an adaptation to poverty and economic insecurity (Why that adaptation and not some other and why did East Indians, who were equally poor, not make that adaptation?), and it is nonsense to say that Jamaican men can't satisfy with one woman and must have outside children. All these things are part of the system as it developed and as it is being maintained.

Repeated attempts have been made to try to swing this system into conformity with the so-called "nuclear family pattern" or "the Christian family." More than one hundred and fifty years of intensive persuasion from the pulpits of the churches has had little discernible effect; perhaps the persuasion was directed at the wrong people. Attempts to enforce the bastardy laws have not been conspicuously successful, especially when the fathers were respectable members of the middle class. There is often a great deal of confusion about what is being aimed at when policy is discussed. The churches have been trying to alter behavior by expounding a code of Christian morals, but a great deal of social policy and legislation is aimed at something different.

One common approach is to try to solve some of the problems of poverty and excessive population by forcing men, as it is said, to "live up to their responsibilities." But even the early census reports, cited by Simey, noted that women in stable unions have more children than those in common-law or visiting unions which are short-term, because they are more constantly exposed to the possibility of pregnancy. Population increase will not be checked by getting all women into stable unions, unless there is also an increased use of contraceptives, freely available abortion, or as in India, a policy of paying people to undergo sterilization procedures. India has a family policy in that sense, just as countries which need population increase sometimes pay child allowances.

The problem of poverty will not be solved by getting everyone into nuclear families, unless there is also a vast increase in available income and employment. To get everyone living in nuclear families might well exacerbate the situation—always a risk with any policy. As it is now the working people share a great deal of their income with the really poor in one way or another, though we do not know just how that is accomplished.

In recent years attempts have been made to alter the existing pattern of family structure by legislating away those features deemed undesirable. The new constitution of Guyana has a clause which says that henceforth there shall be no difference between legitimate and illegitimate children. There is as yet no enabling legislation so we do not know just how this is to be accomplished, but Jamaica has laws with the same intention. However, the father has to make proper recognition of an illegitimate child, and even if he does so there is nothing to prevent discrimination against outside children in bequests. Such laws do have limited use in regularizing the position of children in inheritance cases where the father's intention is clear, but they will not change the family system unless they are accompanied by procedures for the establishment of paternity of a degree of severity which seems unlikely to gain acceptance.

Policies which may do most to bring about change in West Indian family life are those that enhance the status and rights of women, to the point where they are not constrained by traditional concepts of their role. Equal pay for equal work, equal job opportunities, adequate day care facilities, freely available abortion under safe and hygienic conditions, and all the things which make it possible for people to choose freely how they will manage their affairs. It is not for the state to dictate how people should behave in their private lives, and one may doubt the degree to which professional intervention should be used in family affairs.

If this long discussion has taught us anything it is that a family system such as that of the West Indies arises in a particular kind of class society with particular kinds of sex roles, and it is unlikely to change until the pattern of class relations changes. Even then there is no guarantee that family and sex roles will immediately be transformed. These are what Ferdinand Braudel calls structures of the *longue durée*. As yet the social sciences have very little idea as to how, and at what rate, they change.

# PART TWO

# Conflict and Difference: Race, Culture, and Politics

# CHAPTER SEVEN

# *Plural Society Theory (1966)*

Over the past ten years or so there has been a growing tendency for writers on Caribbean affairs to use the model of "the plural society" as a guide for the explanation of major social ills. If there is conflict over economic policy as in British Guiana in 1962; over the alleged misdemeanors of elected officials in Grenada; over the difficulties of making a West Indian federation work; over labor legislation in Trinidad; over almost anything in fact, it can be explained in terms of the operation of the "plural society." Dr. Michael G. Smith, a Jamaican now teaching at the University of California, has been the main, though by no means the only, advocate of this way of thinking. Beginning with his essay *A Framework for Caribbean Studies* in 1955 he has published a series of papers which have provoked controversy as well as attracting followers, to the extent that there now exist "schools" of thought on the subject. A collection of these papers has recently been published under the title *The Plural Society in the West Indies*.

In this short essay the aim is to examine the plural society idea, its origins in the discussion of colonial policy, and its influence in shaping both the vision and the reality of a Caribbean future.

The central problem in the discussion of any social situation is whether one should emphasize stability, continuity, and the fact that people observe the "rules," or whether one should stress the fact of conflict, continuous change, deviation from the rules, and indeed the constant revision of the rules themselves. A problem must arise in the sense that while all societies must have some coherence and stability if they are to be thought of as societies at all, none is static and without internal divisions, frictions, and conflicts. All reasonably sophisticated social theorists attempt to take account of these two aspects of social existence—continuity and change—though they may stress factors making for one or the other.

At first glance it would appear that the plural society concept, as used by Dr. M.G. Smith, is designed to deal with political conflict and social change, especially since great stress is laid upon the inadequacies of other theories for the understanding of Caribbean problems. But it soon becomes clear that plural society theory has no real dynamic dimension, is essentially pessimistic, and deals only with a very limited range of conflict situations.

The basic idea is that certain societies, among them those of the Caribbean region, appear to be made up of a number of sub-societies, each of which is an integrated entity with its own culture, while the relations between these sub-societies are established and maintained solely by political dominance and force. Thus Jamaica is to be thought of as a series of social and cultural sections, basically defined as black, brown, and white, held in fixed relations by force. No peaceful change in the social system is possible because the sections have nothing in common except involvement in economic and political relations which are essentially antagonistic.

The superficial resemblance to Marxist theory is misleading. Marxism sees conflict rooted in class interest as part of an historical process leading to higher levels of integration and to an eventual resolution of the conflict, whereas plural society theory can predict nothing beyond the fact that conflict is always likely between groups which define themselves in terms of kinship and race.

In the preface to his collection of reprinted essays, Dr. M.G. Smith tells us clearly for the first time that he has sought to "develop and apply the work of J.S. Furnivall." Furnivall was one of the first twentieth-century writers to deal extensively with the problems inherent in multiracial societies created by colonialism. He also introduced the term plural society into the literature, but there is very little resemblance between Furnivall's overall analysis and that of more recent writers such as M.G. Smith. It is not always profitable to trace ideas to their source but in this case the original seems to provide rather more insight than its derivatives.

Furnivall's main work is *Colonial Policy and Practice: A Comparative Study of Burma and Netherlands India.* Most of the inspiration for recent work on pluralism seems to come from pages 303–312, where the concept of The Plural Society is discussed. These nine pages contain an attack upon laissez-faire economics, and many of the ideas stated there were expressed by Furnivall as long ago as 1910 in an article in *The Economic Journal.* The argument is straightforward; in tropical countries which have been subjected to European colonization, the free play of economic forces has resulted in the creation of multiracial societies which have no overall common standards or culture save that of animal existence on the one hand and economic competition on the other. In developing this idea further, Furnivall puts forward two contradictory assertions.[1] He says on the one hand that each racial section "holds by its own religion, its own culture and language, its own ideas and ways," and although they mingle in the marketplace, they do not combine.

Dr. M.G. Smith has taken up this casual observation and developed the view that in the plural society each section practices its own separate "institutions." However, the whole argument of *Colonial Policy and Practice* is that laissez-faire economics and colonial rule combine to produce a situation in which market forces bring together racially diverse populations; these forces then act as a "solvent" of traditional culture and values, creating conditions of social atomization in which a highly individualistic society is held together by the twin forces of market relations and colonial domination, the withdrawal of which would lead to anarchy. To quote Furnivall himself:

> On looking at a plural society in its political aspect one can distinguish three characteristic features: the society as a whole comprises separate racial sections: each section is an aggregate of individuals rather than a corporate or organic whole; and as individuals their social life is incomplete (p. 306).

Only in India is the situation held to be rather different because "...British India has been protected against the solvent influence of economic forces by the shield of caste" (p. 538).

Furnivall's major concern in the second half of the book is to examine post-war colonial policies and to assess their shortcomings and probable effects. It is here that he differs so profoundly from what Gordon Lewis has rightly called the pessimism of the plural society point of view in Caribbean Studies. He argues that all colonial powers have come to recognize the corrosive effects of laissez-faire economics, and imbued with ideas of progress, efficiency, and social justice, they have fashioned various new policies to promote colonial development and welfare. Basic to these new policies is the idea—shared by Conservatives and Socialists alike—that economic development is the basic prerequisite for colonial welfare and for the transition to independence. Furnivall tries to show that such a scale of priorities solves no problems and may actually aggravate them. It is worth quoting at length on this point:

> Modern colonial policy promulgates welfare measures to counteract the ill-effects of economic development, but looks to pay for these measures by injecting capital to expedite development....

Colonial powers feel even more virtuous when they contribute to the cost of colonial development and welfare, incidentally subsidizing home capital and labor.... These things may be good business for the British taxpayer (so far as the money is not wasted), for we all have a finger in the colonial pie. But they are not altruistic. They serve merely to speed up the development of the colonial estate and enhance its value as a business concern to the colonial power. Once again, as so often in past colonial history, we seem to hear Little Jack Horner exclaiming "What a good boy am I" as he pulls out a few more plums (p. 541–42).

Sponsored economic development is likely to aggravate rather than cure the condition of "anomie" (normlessness) which was originally produced by economic forces. How then can welfare be achieved?

[P]rogress is not a condition of welfare, but welfare is a condition of progress; the problem is human, not mechanical, and compulsory progress bears fruit in disaffection and unrest. If we are to reconcile progress and welfare in the tropics we must organize a demand for welfare among the people.

Now if tropical peoples are to be enabled to promote their own welfare, it is necessary to create an environment in which they enjoy the requisite status, a sufficient motive and adequate means to do so. The promotion of welfare is possible only in an autonomous society (p. 542).

He goes on to point out that just as economic freedom leads to "economic bondage to the moneylender or employer" so the introduction of Western political institutions such as parliamentary democracy prove unworkable, so that:

We now impose conditions on political advancement, postponing autonomy until some remote future when by welfare measures the people shall have been endowed with the qualities requisite for working western institutions.

But in the plural society of the tropics the problem is not to create political institutions which will express the common will; such a thing does not exist. The problem is to *create a common will* and this is a task which requires something analogous to religion. Furnivall argues that Nationalism is the "religion" on which reintegration is built.

Nationalism must indeed figure largely in any project of reintegration, for the object of reintegration is the framing of a national society capable of independence, so far as any minor (or even major) power is capable of independence in the modern world (p. 547).

I have dealt at some length with Furnivall because it is important to show that the notion of plural society as it appears in his work is but a small part of his overall conception of the nature of "tropical society." It is also contradictory to the general trend of his analysis, since he lays great emphasis upon the dissolution of traditional society by the operation of a "pure capitalist" order. That dissolution is well documented, there is merit in some of the prescriptions advanced for reintegration, but the weakest part of the discussion is that dealing with the nature of colonial society itself.

In the Caribbean we can see much more clearly than could Furnivall (who dealt almost exclusively with Southeast Asia) that colonial societies create their own peculiar institutions. In the interregnum between the dissolution of traditional values and culture of the constituent groups, and the hoped-for future of revolutionary national reintegration, what is it that holds the society together? Furnivall sees this as a period of laissez-faire individualism in which law and order is ensured only by economic self-interest and colonial police activity.

M.G. Smith seems to agree that there is an absence of moral cohesion among the different sections, though *within* each section there is a definite institutional integration. The structural cleavages based on racial/cultural differences are fundamental, and any change in the distribution of political power will involve conflict between these sections—a conflict which will probably be violent and intense. One's objection to such a prediction is not that violent conflict is unlikely, but that the prediction is based upon an oversimplified and distorted view of the present situation and explains away all conflict as being rooted in differences of primordial identity.

West Indian colonial societies were held together by force, but obviously not by force alone. After 1840 the emphasis laid upon Christianity, upon education, respect for the law, "good" as opposed to "bad" behavior and language, and upon the idea of "moral upliftment" indicates that there was a clear and deliberate attempt to create a set of common values (or an imposed ideology if one wishes to call it that) for the whole society. In practice this meant a common recognition not only of the *de facto* power position of the Europeans but also of the superiority of English culture. This has been remarked upon by almost all observers of the West Indies and has been described as a "white bias" in the whole social life of the colonies.

To say that West Indian society was integrated around the recognition and acceptance of the idea of the superiority of English culture does not imply that these societies were either culturally or socially homogeneous. It does not mean that there was not resentment against British rule and some active opposition to it. It does not mean that there was not an active opposition to injustice, poverty, and exploitation. It does not mean that there were not active, living sub-cultures that were definitely not "English," nor that there was not from time to time active attempts to rejuvenate "African" or "Indian" or other cultures. It means no more than it says—that things in these societies tended to be judged in terms of a comparison with English culture and English standards and that the whole structure of the society including the ranking system tended to acquire a "legitimacy" in terms of these standards and values. "African" and "Indian" and "Chinese" and other subcultures existed and still exist, but they have always been evaluated in a general context by comparison with an ideal which was formally "English," just as particular physical characteristics have been evaluated by reference to a European model. One is aware of all the difficulties that are raised by speaking of the "legitimacy" of a social order which assigned such radically different social statuses to whole ethnic groups, especially if it is assumed that all members of the society passively accepted this ranking system and agreed with it. But it is not necessary to assume that there was a complete consensus of opinion; all that is important really is to recognize that there was sufficient acceptance of the idea of English superiority to stabilize the system, and to lead to a particular kind of social integration.

This process of integration through some degree of commitment to common values should not be thought of as a process of "anglicization." Although it involved the idea of the superiority of things English and based the ranking system upon that idea, it was not a simple matter of "acculturation" to English culture for everyone in the system. The present writer and Chandra Jayawardena have referred to the process as being one of "creolization" but since this term is used rather loosely it perhaps needs some explanation. Creolization involved two major processes; in the first place it involved the creation of some area of common culture corresponding to the social relations in which people of varying ethnic group were involved. Thus some form of English came to be the normal method of communication by all Guianese, to take one case, and eventually there has been an increasing spread of common educational standards through formal schooling. On the other hand *it was an integral part of the process of creolizaton to stress the differences between groups identified as "racial" groups.*

Thus creole culture, while encouraging some level of common cultural participation, also emphasized cultural differences and resulted in the precipitation of socially exclusive groups at every level of the society. This resulted form the very fact that the value standards for the whole society were "English" or "white people's"; that is, defined in terms of race as well as culture. Non-whites could become "English" only in a very limited sense, no matter how well they commanded the culture of the "mother country." This is why the term "Afro-Saxon" is ironical.

So the argument advanced here is that creolizaton did involve societal integration and did involve a fundamental change in the culture and social structure of the constituent ethnic groups, but it did not lead to the creation of a unified society. On the contrary it was basic to creole colonial society to maintain an image of a divided society. The "plural society" model is in fact a very close approximation to the kind of cultural image necessary for the maintenance of a divided creole society; all it needs grafted onto it is the idea of the basic superiority of one of the segments.

The values and the ranking system we have been discussing did not exist in a vacuum. In the British West Indies, Englishmen controlled both the economy and the polity, but other groups and individuals in creole society struggled for a greater share of wealth, more power, and higher status. These struggles were rooted in self and group interest but their general nature and mode of expression show how deeply internalized the notion of the superiority of English culture had become. Colored and Negro and Chinese and Portuguese and Jewish and East Indian professionals, merchants, and intellectuals proudly proclaimed their "culture" and "refinement" and education and hotly contested their exclusion from political office and the charmed circle of Government House "society." Even racially based organizations aimed more at the "moral upliftment," "progress," and general "advancement" of their members than at communal segregation or the glorification of ethnic culture.

The bulk of the population was preoccupied with its day-to-day suffering and frustrations. Ill-health, poor diet, long hours of work, poor wages, social degradation, and constant humiliation all produced either an aggressiveness which was mostly turned inward upon the local community, or a profound yearning for salvation which found expression in magic and religion. Sporadic outbreaks of violence against estate overseers, Chinese or Portuguese shopkeepers, against fellow workers of different race, expressed some of the cleavages—the "pluralism"—of colonial society, but they also indicated the extent of mass discontent which was rooted in conditions of perceived hardship rather than in racial differences.

The significance of the concept of "social class" for the understanding of Caribbean social structure depends to a large extent upon the definition of class that is adopted, but even if it is taken to mean simply a division of the society into groups with differential access to wealth and spending power it throws some light on aspects of the social scene neglected by "plural society" theory.

These Caribbean societies have similar histories of plantation agriculture overlaid by the uneven development of other economic sectors, but everywhere there is a tendency for a common pattern of class structure to develop. This is due in large part to the similar relation these territories now have to Britain, the United States of America, and Canada, but whatever the reason, the similarity of pattern is clear. At the bottom of the social hierarchy is a mass of low-income earners, unemployed and semiemployed who are beginning to feel progressively more deprived as the media of mass communication pour forth a steady stream of "market information" originally designed for high-consumption societies. Above this group and separated from it by an income gap which varies from one territory to another is that amorphous group often known as the "middle class" but which in this context it is better to refer to as the high-income sector. (Its income is not high in relation to its aspirations but is high enough to permit of a socially conspicuous consumption level.)

This group derives its income from a variety of activities which we can ignore for the moment. More importantly for the present discussion is the fact that it spends its income in a generally similar way, thus establishing a similar "style of life." A family in this group aims to own a car, a refrigerator, washing machine, cooker, radiogram, television set, a standard group of household furnishings such as settee, chairs, dining table and chairs, coffee tables, glasses, crockery, cutlery, ice-containers, a suitable stock of drinks, and proper clothing for its members. The "backstage" areas of bedrooms, bathroom, and so forth will also be properly equipped and careful attention will be given to the house itself and its surrounding garden no matter how small. The important point to make here is that although people of this income/consumption group may be divided in all sorts of ways into cliques, clubs, ethnic groups, and so on they are all very much alike; they can and do visit each other's homes and know how to behave, they talk about very much the same things and think in much the same way.

On the employment side they are also fairly easily interchangeable since they all receive much the same sort of formal education (their children even more so) and while there may be some tendency toward ethnic specialization in economic activity this is rapidly breaking down or changing in character.

The interesting thing about this situation is that there is a sharply increasing demand for an approximation to some of these consumption patterns on the part of all the members of the society, a demand which has been stimulated by both political changes and increased awareness of mass consumption patterns in other countries. However, these demands are expressed through the framework of the old society and are often modified into a set of dependency relationships rather than leading to any real creative innovations.

A class analysis provides politicians and social reformers with a jumping-off point for action designed to bring about change, and at the same time permits a repudiation of the old colonial rulers and of white dominance in terms which are not expressly "racial." Of course the ideological terms in which it does this are borrowed form outside the society, and they can become the vehicle for the expression of a narrow elite interest or even of ethnic group interests, or alternatively they can result in the development of a new dependency relationship with a new "mother country." A great deal depends upon the honesty with which local problems are analyzed and tackled. It does appear that structural change must involve a repudiation of the colonial relationship at the political level, and then the creation of a basis for the evaluation of status which repudiates the old emphasis upon "refinement" and command of "English" culture. Both these repudiations are difficult, since the first creates problems of international relations and the second creates problems in the judging of competence. Innovation must meet with a good deal of emotional opposition and create anxiety.

What we are witnessing in British Guiana and other similar places is a transitional stage in which an attempt has to be made not simply to create a common will out of near-chaos, as Furnivall suggests, nor to reshuffle the sections in a "plural" society, but to transcend the limitations of the structure imposed by creole colonial society and to swing the whole system in a new direction. Plural society theory of either the Furnivall or M.G. Smith variety seems to suggest that there is no existing basis for such a shift, though Furnivall appears to be much more hopeful about the possibilities of "Nationalism."

It is perfectly true, as both A. Singham and L. Best have pointed out in *New World Quarterly*, that "cuckoo politics" and the "neocolonial model" can serve to hide, behind a facade of spurious activity, a basic reluctance to abandon the old social structure, its values and its dependence upon outside approval, sponsorship, guidance, and aid. What are the alternatives and to what extent are they determined by "pluralism?"

The current conception of nationalism in most West Indian territories is a projection of the status yearnings of the old colonial élites who through a long period of struggle became the spokesmen expressing the frustrations and sufferings of the whole society. Having succeeded the old colonial authorities they now seek to consolidate their position by replacing loyalty to the British by loyalty to a new ruling group (which is very closely modelled upon the old despite any appearance of radicalism), and to its own symbols of office (not markedly different from those that have passed on).

After the usual spectacle of the independence celebrations, the bulk of the population does not appear to feel any great involvement in the new "nation" for the simple reason that their position is not appreciably different. The élan that was produced in the early days of the struggle against colonial rule or economic hardship—in the 1940s in Jamaica, by the PNM in Trinidad, and in 1953 in British Guiana—is soon dissipated. But even if there is no revolutionary transformation of the system, is it justifiable to say that nothing has changed? Or to say that there has merely been a substitution of one segment for another at the top of the political hierarchy? In all the territories the new political élites have come into office on the basis of popular votes and their policies have been committed to reform and economic development and national reconstruction. Education at all levels has been steadily increasing in volume and improving in quality and content; some degree of industrialization, however small, has taken place; and, as we have noted already, there has been a steadily rising level of consumption expectation.

It could be argued that these things will in themselves have a cumulative effect in time and will lead to a progressive change in values and in structural relations. Insofar as they shift the societal emphasis toward achievement and rationality, create new occupational structures and a new uniformity in consumption patterns and leisure activity, so they will minimize the structural significance of ethnic differences, even if these continue to be perceived to be important.

The dangers of such a relatively slow evolutionary process have been pointed out; not least by politicians who have noted the widening gap between the "haves" and the "have-nots" produced by the uneven growth of different economic sectors and the consequent disparities in consumption levels. These difficulties stem partly from the slowness of economic growth, but also from the timidity of politicians, and sometimes from their sheer laziness. Politicians can make a big show of apparent activity simply by inviting or accepting all the standard international programs, by passing incentive legislation to lure foreign investors, and then hoping for the best. "Experts" appear in large numbers and there is a considerable increase in the activities of merchants, insurance companies, banks, and import agencies, which cream off any increased wealth put into circulation by aid programs or by developments in productive activity.

More importantly perhaps, the adoption of this sort of dependent posture is closely associated with a political program which lays maximum stress upon the right of individuals to earn high wages or salaries and the right to spend freely, and which gives undue advantage to traditional elites as well as introducing new enclaves of high-income foreigners. The alternative course of austerity, accumulation of capital, and government initiative in developing the economy inevitably runs into political difficulties, irrespective of whether it is desirable or not. Thus the whole question of strategies for economic development and for social reconstruction becomes inextricably bound up with the "communist" versus "anti-communist" debate and with external alignments.

It must be remembered that adopting an austerity program may not avoid the problem of creating high-consumption elites and even enclaves of conspicuously favored foreigners. It is not the purpose of this article to discuss the relative merits of different strategies for economic development but to raise again the question posed by Furnivall as to whether economic development presents an opportunity or an obstacle for social change and national integration. It seems clear from the examples of other countries that the demand for welfare *can* become a major societal goal and the mobilization of national resources *can* provide a means of creating new structures cutting across ethnic alignments. This is not simply a matter of creating new market relations which leave the "plural" nature of culture and society intact. It involves the creation of entirely different modes of social relationship which counterbalance those of ethnicity—without destroying them completely of course—but such a path of economic development must involve a large cross-section of the population in creative tasks.

It seems therefore that real conflicts within these societies are going to arise over class interests on the one hand and over competition for power on the other and are likely to involve alignment with outside forces. While ethnicity may be invoked and even perceived as the major cleavage, it may be an expression of quite different bases of conflict.

British Guiana's experience over the past ten years highlights some of these problems of interpretation very clearly. The tragic events of this period are easily construed as an inevitable clash between sections of a plural society consequent upon a change, or impending change, in the relations between these sections. The element of truth in this interpretation is very obvious, especially to Guianese who have experienced the full bitterness of racial hatred, but it is an inadequate and incomplete explanation and is misleading if it is taken as a measure of future possibilities. To interpret what has happened in the past as an expression of a fundamental social division between "African" and "Indian" sections is to ignore the conflicts of interest over economic questions and the effect of alignment with outside forces and interests.

It also ignores the role played by other elements in the society which are interested in maintaining some of the basic structural features of creole society. The fact that political party loyalties have been allowed and even encouraged to crystallize along racial lines represents a regression to the normative order of colonial creole society, and under these circumstances it is quite fitting that the Queen of England should remain as head of state of the new nation of Guyana. But the other structural realities remain and will have to be faced.

After the independence spree what then? Will meaningful goals be established for the whole society and will there be marked changes in the relations arising from the economic system? Or will independence mean simply a change in the composition of the élite, leaving the basic structure of the society unchanged? Grave problems must arise in trying to satisfy the aspirations of a rapidly increasing population, and there is bound to be a growing reservoir of resentment and frustration just as there is in most new nations. At the same time that those problems are being faced, there is the problem of trying to overcome the limitations of colonial creole society at the cultural and symbolic level. This issue may be evaded of course and some variant of the popular slogan of "out of many, one people" used as a means of trying to erase ethnic differences.

But before ethnic identity can be transcended it must be *asserted* in order to ensure the stature, participation and self-respect of everyone in the local community; not because race is a necessary basis of social identity but because it has been made so in creole society. This is not a situation peculiar to the Caribbean; it exists in the United States of America, which Dr. M.G. Smith considers not to be a plural society at all!

All these forces, economic, political, cultural, and racial, combine to create the climate in which Guyanese society has to develop. The problem is to face up to the reality of the situation and *to find a sense of belonging in the fact of living together and building something new*. Politicians need be neither administrators of the colonial estate, mere creatures of the plural society, nor abject sycophants of the great powers. They cannot create something out of nothing in a sterile environment, but neither are they wholly determined in their course by the forces of the past. Men create their own history out of the materials that are at hand, and although the materials are not very lavish they have to be used. It is rather foolish to talk about the Caribbean showing the rest of the world how to live. This is mere posturing in order to obtain a nod of approval from the "people who count." Nobody will learn anything from the way in which Caribbean peoples create their own history; it is the living and the creating that matter, not the demonstration. The dangers of parochialism and "narrow nationalism" are greatly exaggerated; no small country can avoid involvement in the wider world, but it needs to value itself and its peculiarities and find significance in its own experience at the same time.

Guyana faces independence in a dangerously divided condition and it would be an optimistic person who did not foresee a long period of strain within the new nation, aggravated by the unfortunate domination of politics by personalities, rather than principles. The élan of 1953 has evaporated but the past thirteen years will not have been wasted if they have taught Guianese something about themselves. They have measured the depth of the things which divide Indians from Africans; what they have not yet done is to measure their ability to create something together.

# CHAPTER EIGHT

# Caste and Social Status Among the Indians of Guyana (1967)

More than half the population of Guyana is descended from immigrants from India; the rest is made up of persons of African, Chinese,[1] Portuguese, and Amerindian descent, and a large number of persons of racially mixed origin.[2] The East Indians (henceforth referred to as Indians) recognize themselves, and are recognized, as a differentiated group within the society of Guyana. They retain a considerable amount of Indian culture, including religious belief and practice, but absorption into a new social system marked by sharp ethnic differentiation has profoundly changed the meaning and content of "Indian Culture" in the new setting.

One of the most striking features of this process has been the disintegration of the caste system. Changes in this institution have been so extensive that the caste system as it is known in India cannot be said to persist even in a modified form. Castes are no longer endogamous units defined in terms of meaningful functions—ritual, economic or political.

The problem of "What should we mean by caste?" has been set out adequately by Leach (1960). The main problem is to decide whether the term shall be used solely to refer to the social institution peculiar to Hindu India, or whether we may use it to indicate any extreme form of social stratification. Leach prefers to retain the term as a descriptive label for aspects of Indian society, while other contributors to his symposium favor a wider use of the term. It is not part of our task to settle this terminological question, although the question of what is a variant and what is a different form becomes particularly acute when discussing the social institutions of overseas Indians.

It is our argument that, whichever criteria of caste are accepted, it is doubtful whether the phenomena discussed here could be usefully thought of as castes or as a caste system. However, in order not to prejudge the issue, we retain the term until the data have been presented.

Although the caste system was not recreated in the colony of British Guiana, some elements of it retain a place in Hindu social life; but their meaning and functions have changed radically. One object of this paper is to show that caste survives as an ascribed attribute of individuals which is relevant only within a limited set of activities and contexts. Even such limited significance shows that there is some continuity of cultural values from India; it would be surprising if there were not, considering the fact that the majority of Guyanese Indians are Hindus. But in the operative system of social stratification and differentiation, factors such as income, education and occupation, or of ethnicity are far more important than Hindu castes. Within the Indian community castes do not form operative groups comparable to *jati* groups. Many writers have suggested that systems of sharp ethnic differentiation constitute caste systems. The colonial society of British Guiana certainly had many castelike features, but to call these "caste" confuses the issue and obscures important differences at the level of culture, including values.

## PATTERNS OF SETTLEMENT

The Indians were imported as laborers for the plantations, all of which are situated on the narrow, low-lying coastal strip. Since the early part of the last century these plantations have concentrated on sugar production; they have grown in size and diminished in number; and their ownership has been consolidated. All are now controlled by two companies. This process has been dictated mainly by the demands of efficiency and economy, but the result is that in Guyana cane is grown on large plantations with hired labor; unlike Fiji and Mauritius, Guyana has hardly any small farmers. Therefore, even after the indenture system was abolished, Indians in the sugar industry remained wage workers. Today almost 20 percent of the total population of Guyana reside in plantations, and the great majority of these are Indians. Most tasks in cane cultivation are carried out manually, although considerable progress has been made in mechanization and in the application of modern scientific methods. Schemes of technical training have been organized and sugar workers have been encouraged to build their own houses through loans and grants. But the sugar worker still is an employee in a large industrial-agricultural concern, and even when he grows some rice on a plot provided by management or obtained through his own initiative he is primarily a member of the rural proletariat rather than a peasant.[3]

Since the first decade of the twentieth century, the majority of Indians have lived outside the plantations. Indentured immigration was started partly to make good the loss of labor resulting from the partial withdrawal of the emancipated Negro slave from plantation labor and partly to defeat the Negroes' demands for higher wages. After emancipation most of the Negroes had gone to live in the villages where they grew crops such as cassava, plantains, and other vegetables for their own use and for sale, and from where they could work for wages on the plantation if they so desired. The indentured laborers provided a core labor force which could be depended on to carry out the essential tasks, and which could be paid very low wages. The planters were not anxious to see the immigrants return to India after the trouble and expense of importing them. So they encouraged those who had completed their indentures to settle in villages close to the plantations, where their labor would still be available. Some Indians settled quite independently, becoming farmers, shopkeepers, or hucksters. Official land-settlement schemes were not very successful before the early twentieth century, mainly because they were not economically remunerative (Nath 1950). There was no movement of Indians from plantations to economically independent villages comparable to that which had been made by Negroes. The Negro villages were established as communities focused upon a church, and with the positive intention of escape from the plantations. Indians rarely established villages in this way. Indian villages either developed out of collections of rice farmers (rice became profitable with the growth of an export market during the first twenty years of this century), or they were the residue of abandoned sugar plantations.[4] There was rarely any conscious attempt to recreate a specifically Indian mode of village life on the Guyanese Coast. Sometimes Muslims congregated in small settlements in an informal way, but even this practice was not a marked feature. A few settlements grew upon land bought by individual landlords and rented to rice farmers. The most famous of these settlements was McDoom village on the east bank of the Demerara river, where the proprietor, Mr. McDoom, made strenuous efforts to create a model village community on his lands.

Since 1900, rice cultivation has come to be the basic economic activity in the villages. Negroes as well as Indians are engaged in rice cultivation although rice is often spoken of as an "Indian" crop.[5] Rice is a small-farmer's crop, average holdings being between five and ten acres. A good deal of machinery is now being used even by small farmers (Smith 1957; O'Loughlin 1958). Whatever type of community Indian farmers live in, they share a basically similar pattern of life which arises partly because of economic similarities and partly out of the "Indian" mode of life they have developed. The term "Indian" is used here to distinguish this mode of life from that of other Guyanese rather than to refer to a pattern of life identical with that of a villager in India.

Although it is possible to refer to "Negro" or "Indian" villages, there were, until recently, very few communities which were not ethnically mixed. In a few, the numbers of Indians and Negroes were almost equal. The extent of interpenetration of ethnic groups was demonstrated rather tragically during the first half of 1964 when political conflict resulted in killing, beating, rape, and arson. Indians living in predominantly Negro villages and Negroes in Indian villages in the affected areas tended to move out, so that there was considerable displacement and virtual segregation for the first time in Guyanese history. Not all the country was affected, and in some mixed villages Negroes and Indians joined to form vigilante committees to prevent violence.

The extent of urban migration and social mobility among the Indians should be mentioned here, although these will be dealt with more fully below. The urbanization of Indians began during the nineteenth century. There was first a drift to town of Indian beggars, hucksters, and unskilled laborers. At the other end of the scale a small number, who were usually the children of drivers, interpreters, priests, and house servants of white planters, managed to acquire a higher education and move into prestigious occupations such as dispensing, medicine, or law. Their number was very small until well into the twentieth century. In between these two extremes, an increasing number of moderately well-to-do Indians, who had made their money in such diverse ways as farming, shopkeeping, moneylending, or clerical occupations, began to buy houses or open shops in Georgetown. Since 1945 the movement of Indians to Georgetown has grown as more have acquired higher education and are entering urban occupations. At the census of 1960, Indians constituted 22 percent of the total population of Greater Georgetown.

## THE PERIOD OF IMMIGRATION

The Indians who came to British Guiana were almost all brought to work as indentured laborers on the sugar plantations. They were recruited from a wide area of India, and before embarkation the recruits were registered; their personal characteristics, including caste affiliation, were recorded.

An analysis of a random sample from immigration registers shows that the great majority of immigrants were from northeastern India: Uttar Pradesh, 70.3 percent; Bihar, 15.3 percent; and Bengal, 1.4 percent. Most of the remainder came from Rajputana, 3.1 percent; and south India, 4.4 percent (Smith 1959). The sample, which records ninety-five castes, shows that most of the larger castes of northeastern India were represented. However, this representation was not proportionate: several factors influenced the selection of recruits.

One was official policy. The original policy was to import the "hill coolies" of northern India, who had the reputation of being hardy and docile agricultural laborers (Nath 1950). But these were difficult to obtain and recruiters were therefore instructed to enlist emigrants from the "agricultural castes" because agricultural experience was mistakenly equated with agricultural caste. There was therefore a bias against those whose caste occupations were not agricultural. Castes whose occupations were cultivation and herding thus comprised about 36 percent of the Hindu immigrants, while Brahmin and trading castes were each less than 2 percent and artisan castes were 8.7 percent. However, about 11 percent were Kshatriya, Thakur, and Rajput.

Another factor was the likelihood that low castes found in emigration an escape from their depressed situation. Thus 22.6 percent of the immigrants consisted of menial castes, of which three-quarters were Chamar, Dusad, and Pasi. The proportion of these castes among the immigrants was several times their proportion in northeastern India (Crooke 1896 I:cxlvii). Further, nearly half the artisans were weavers (Kori), who were frequently outcastes and were, in India, beginning to be thrown out of work by machine-made imports.

For the purposes of studying change, one can assume that the emigrants were the carriers of an "Indian culture," bearing in mind the major caste, religious, and regional differences. All had been involved in "caste society," and had some contact with the central elements of Hinduism or Islam.[6] Many of them had been displaced from a traditional way of life by the advent of British economic enterprise and administration. Others were misfits in their villages, and had signed indentures as a convenient means of escape. In some sense the Indians who embarked upon the immigrant ships may have been among the first products of the breakdown of the traditional caste system in India itself.

## INFLUENCE OF PLANTATION LIFE

Without going into details of the history of Indian immigration into the West Indies, it is important to mention certain general features of the historical experience of Indians in the colony of British Guiana. Throughout Guyanese history, the plantation has been a basic social as well as economic complex. In the first days of coastal settlement, plantations were almost self-contained units and, although a wider society grew up around them, they continued to be relatively self-sufficient and socially isolated. Apart from the British and the Amerindians, every ethnic group in Guyana has passed through a phase of plantation labor, so that the plantation has stamped its imprint upon all Guyanese. From the middle of the eighteenth century until 1917, the plantations received recruits from Africa, from the West Indian islands, from Madeira, from China, and from India. They even received a few from Germany, Ireland, England, and Malta in the 1830s.

Techniques of induction were developed which corresponded very closely to those described by Goffman (1961) as being typical of "total institutions." The Indians who arrived in British Guiana had already begun their induction process: they had been numbered, issued with standard clothing, and had their eating habits reorganized in accordance with administrative requirements. Their prior social experience, including caste, was largely ignored.

Immigration and the indenture system destroyed the demographic basis of caste group structure. Some castes were represented in too small numbers to persist as endogamous units. In addition, there was a severe imbalance in the sex ratio which was only partly restored in later decades by the imposition of a quota of females on every shipload. The following figures indicate the acute shortage of women during the indenture period (Nath 1950: 208–209):

*Women per 100 males among immigrants and on plantations*

| Among Immigrants | | Among Plantation Residents | |
|---|---|---|---|
| Year | Women | Year | Women |
| 1838 | 3 | 1875 | 45 |
| 1848 | 25 | 1885 | 54 |
| 1858 | 38 | 1895 | 59 |
| 1868 | 38 | 1905 | 67 |
|  |  | 1915 | 69 |

Scarcity of women resulted in intense competition for the few available and made the maintenance of caste endogamy most difficult. Marriage was very brittle and both men and women generally married several times. It was common for a unit of mother and children to pass successively through the households of two or three males before the children were adult.

During this period there were many intercaste marriages, the children of such unions being ascribed to the father's caste. According to a contemporary observer (Bronkhurst 1883: 286–287):

> A woman of low caste may be taken in a kind of marriage by a high caste Hindu, but a high caste or respectable woman will not be given in marriage to a man who is a Chamar (cobbler) or any other inferior caste. All such temporary marriages hold good whilst they are in Demerara, but when they arrive in India there is an end to such marriages. The woman goes one way and the man another.

Intercaste marriages among those who did not return became the established pattern. Judging from present evidence, in time, hypogamy became as frequent as hypergamy.

Conditions in the ships during the long voyage to the West Indies had made caste avoidances impossible. Absence of segregation was perpetuated in the plantations, where the laborers were housed in barracks partitioned into rooms, one to a family. Here members of different castes lived in close proximity, sharing the same water supply, latrines, and sometimes even kitchens.

If these traumatic, but temporary, experiences were the only ones, it is conceivable that the caste system could have been reconstituted at a later period when conditions were more propitious. However, there were other less direct but more pervasive and persistent influences which destroyed the caste system beyond reconstitution. Officials of the Government of India, sent out to report on the conditions of the Indians, noted these changes. In 1893 Comins noted (p. 79):

> Caste is not only modified, but its laws and restrictions are practically ignored after the immigrants leave Calcutta.

In 1925 K. M. Singh commented (p. 13):

> Indian customs undergo considerable change in the Colonies. For instance, among Hindus in British Guiana there are no depressed classes, caste restrictions in terms of marriage as well as food are practically non-existent, and there is no purdah.

The deeper influences underlying this change were connected with the fact that the expectations, rights, and duties of the new world in which the immigrants found themselves were quite alien to those of the way of life in which caste was a dominant factor.

For instance, the division of labor in the plantation was based on economic and technological practices which belonged to a culture quite foreign to that in which caste was embedded (Jayawardena 1963: 29–36). It was administered by managers who were not concerned with the preservation of traditional Indian ways. The assignment of immigrants to jobs in the factory and the field bore no relation to their caste statuses, taboos, and specializations. The type of occupational specialization which was the economic basis of the Indian caste system was not found in the plantation. Men of different castes performed the same jobs, worked in the same gangs under the direction of an overseer, and were paid at the same rate. Consumer goods required by laborers were purchased at the plantation store. There was no place for *jajman* (personal service) relations in the economic organization of the plantation.

Similarly, the political system of the plantation bore no relation to the caste system. Decisions were made by a European manager and executed by European overseers, each of whom was assisted by one or more drivers selected by management from among the laborers. These decisions had to be obeyed by all laborers, regardless of caste. The laborers had no authority to make any important decisions even in nonlabor activities. Most plantations had courts presided over by management officials, where policies concerning social life were laid down and enforced, and where public and private disputes between laborers were settled. Matters handled by the manager's court ranged from disputes between Hindus and Muslims to complaints of wives against husbands, and the composition of households. Laborers were not permitted to form associations to regulate any important matters relating to their economic and political interests. Although there was sporadic community-wide organization of action (strongly disapproved by managements) in the fields of religion and labor disputes, there were no *panchayats* or caste councils. In later decades managers permitted and helped in the formation of religious associations which they closely supervised.

The plantation managers' interest in controlling all aspects of caste derived from this major concern. Some managers regarded the lower castes as better laborers. Comins reported such a classification which distinguished Kurmi, Ahir, Chamar, Dusad, and Dom as "best laborers"; Kshatriya, Jat, and Kahar as "good laborers"; and Brahmin, Bania, and Sonar as "worthless." High-caste coolies were suspected of being ringleaders in strikes, and their influence was regarded as "pernicious" (Comins 1893: 79).

The caste hierarchy received no support from the structure of authority of the plantation. Managers dispensed rewards, privileges, and favors in accordance with work, loyalty, and obedience, irrespective of caste. They had little sympathy for, and enough power to destroy, a parallel hierarchy of power and prestige which could interfere with their freedom to deploy the labor force, or which could cause friction among the laborers. Authority based on caste had little prospect of persisting outside the sphere of labor either, since managers could and did intervene in any matter which directly or indirectly affected discipline. Thus a laborer who resented the attempts of high castes to assert their superiority could complain to management of provocation and annoyance.

Managers were, in principle, indifferent to the preservation of traditional Indian institutions. Yet, although their main guide as to whether to permit a given practice was its effect on labor discipline, there was often a latitude of decision where their own cultural attitudes came into play. If the attitudes of senior and experienced managers of the 1950s may be taken as indications of those of their predecessors, it is possible to indicate some aspects of the culture of the immigrants, against which nonconformists could win managerial sympathy. Spirit possession ("playing jumby") and sorcery ("obeah") were strongly disapproved. To a lesser degree the complete authority of husband over wife, and of mother-in-law over resident daughter-in-law were disfavored by managers. Similarly, managers regarded claims of caste superiority with suspicion and skepticism. While there was some appreciation of the "martial" Kshatriya, there was also a sentiment that an individual's rewards should depend on his worth in this life as a hardworking, obedient, and thrifty laborer. Although most managers were tolerant of religious customs and treated Brahmin priests with some deference, they were also inclined to suspect an element of charlatanry in the Brahmin's invocations and predictions.

At the same time, managers may have been influenced by caste in selecting drivers. Since one of the main qualifications of candidates for this office was ability to discipline the gang, there was a bias in favor of Kshatriya and Brahmin. On the other hand, the derivation of leadership qualities from caste was only a presumption which was likely to be overridden by such considerations as personality, efficiency, and reliability. Among the famous and powerful drivers recalled by older men, Brahmins and Kshatriya figure prominently; but there were also Kurmi, Lohar, Kewat, and Teli. At present, drivers are derived from all castes, including Chamar, Bhar, and Dusad.

In short, the immigrants were resocialized into the role system of the plantation. This change did not mean that they lost all memory of Indian culture and of the roles appropriate to life in an Indian village, any more than the inmates of a prison or mental hospital or a concentration camp forget what life is like on the outside. Many indentured laborers returned to India upon completion of their period of service and were absorbed back into Indian society; some took back considerable sums of money which they had saved.[7] Those who stayed in British Guiana were not "completely stripped of their culture"—a phrase which has caused some difficulty and given rise to bitter argument when applied to the New World Negro. They continued to practice many customs that they had brought from India, and since their numbers were being constantly augmented by new arrivals, Indian languages continued to be used by many. But they were involved in a different social system and their culture had to be adapted accordingly.

At the level of colonial political structure, officials often felt that the Indians ought to be left alone and not assimilated into Guianese society lest they become "spoilt" like the Negroes. By the end of the nineteenth century the Negroes, the Portuguese, and the colored intelligentsia secured constitutional reforms which gave them control over the legislature after more than three decades of struggle against planter domination. The Governor and the planting interest retained control of the Executive Council, and the idea was very generally prevalent that the Indians regarded the British administration and the planters as their guardians and protectors against Negro domination. Contrariwise, it was also pointed out to the intelligentsia that demands for a widened franchise would lead to the "uncivilized" Indians obtaining a large measure of control. It therefore suited the planters to encourage Indians to retain or revive such elements of Indian culture as did not interfere with the running of the plantation. This attitude was not uniform; some planters encouraged Christian missions working with the Indians and tried to persuade laborers to send their children to school; but the majority seem to have preferred to keep their laborers illiterate and tractable by discouraging assimilation to creole ways.

## CHALLENGES TO THE LEGITIMACY OF CASTE

The norms of the caste system were also undermined by doubts concerning the legitimacy of claims to high-caste status. These arose partly through the realization that the high castes, who had already transgressed by crossing the seas, were also not observing the prescribed taboos, and partly out of the practice of changing caste.

## Passing

It is believed that some immigrants assumed high-caste status when they arrived in British Guiana. The phrases "ship Brahmin" and "ship Kshatriya" express this skepticism. Since the immigrants arrived as individuals rather than as kin groups or village sections, local communities in British Guiana were composed of immigrants from different districts of India. There was no reliable means of ascertaining claims to high caste. Passing sometimes took the form of assuming surnames such as Sharma or Tiwari (Brahmin) and Singh (Kshatriya). Those who dared do so, even if their contemporaries disbelieved them, had only to weather some sneering and gossip, which decreased with the passage of time. There was no organization with the authority to sift claims, nor was there a consensus on such matters so that spurious claims could be concertedly ignored. Some argued that they, or their parents, assumed a low caste in order to be accepted as immigrants. A high rate of residential mobility among plantation laborers enabled some to establish their claims. Eventually, whatever doubts were entertained in one generation were forgotten in the next.

Doubts concerning caste also arose from the instability of marriage and family life. Children were often brought up by step-parents or maternal kin. Many adults of today know little about their parents, not to mention their castes. Others have assumed the castes of those who fostered them. Family instability produced a background of genealogical uncertainty in the histories of many individuals who could, if they wished, change their castes. The relatively large number of Brahmins and Kshatriya today tempts one to stress the fact of passing. On the other hand, it should be noted that the actual proportion of Kshatriya among the immigrants was larger than might be expected from immigration policy. Furthermore, it is possible that, during the period of the scarcity of women, Brahmins and Kshatriya had better chances of obtaining wives, and so of procreating their kind, than did lower castes.

It is unlikely that passing occurs to any significant extent today, if only for the reason that little is to be gained from it. Though many prominent leaders in national organizations are of high caste, it is reasonable to suppose that the first Indians to obtain higher education were the children of drivers, interpreters, and Brahmin priests, so that a selective factor has been at work. There is also the probability that persons who were of higher caste felt greater self-confidence and were more oriented toward social success and the performance of leadership roles.

But, whatever the speculations about the past, the actual extent to which these factors prevailed cannot be accurately assessed today. What is important is that they are believed to have occurred. This undermines the legitimacy of the claim to superiority of the local high castes, for such doubts can be raised to question their status. Thus it is sometimes said, "There are no 'real' Brahmins (or Kshatriya) in Guyana today."

## Religious Influence

The majority of Indians in Guyana claim to be orthodox Hindus. In 1960 there were 187,432 Hindus out of a total Indian population of 267,840. A small number of these belong to Hindu reform movements such as the American Aryan League. These movements are influential but do not have a large membership. Muslims numbered 49,297, and although this group includes a handful of Negroes and other non-Indians, it is remarkable that in Guyana Islam is thought of as an "Indian" religion. The conversion of Indian immigrants to Christianity was begun during the nineteenth century but was never very successful.

Merely to enumerate the religious affiliation of Indians, without examining what these categories mean, can be very misleading. It is particularly so in the case of Hinduism, which in India was a congeries of various beliefs and practices tied to a whole way of life. Reform Hinduism such as that represented by the Arya Samaj, or the American Aryan League as it is called in Guyana, is more easily definable since it has become an open church with a formal doctrine. Although it incorporates many elements of the Indian religious tradition, it is imbued with values which derive more from Europe than from ancient India. "Orthodox" Hinduism in Guyana is partly a collection of bits of traditional belief and rite, and partly a formal organization which came into being in response to attacks by reform Hindus. As in India itself, a Sanatan Dharm Maha Sabha was formed in self-defense against attacks from the Arya Samaj and, as in the case of the parent organization, the doctrines of this body represent a retreat from some orthodox outposts to more defensible positions. In Guyana these are relatively recent developments, dating from the late twenties and early thirties of this century.[8]

These various religious developments have reinforced challenges to the legitimacy of caste. The ritual distinctions which formed a basis of the caste system were totally discarded. Caste rites were dismissed as superstition, and there are no more caste priests. Life-cycle rites have been standardized, and all castes perform the same marriage and funeral ceremonies, which are conducted by Brahmin priests regardless of the castes of their clients. Brahmin priests do not serve only the twice-born castes. The investiture of the sacred thread (*janeu*) is a relatively rare ceremony, and is held mainly in Brahmin families. All castes participate freely in *puja* (sacrifices), holy readings, services in the temple, and public festivals.

The only expression of caste in orthodox religious activities is the privileged position of Brahmins, who alone have the right to perform the main rites. The Guyana Pandits' Council, which is closely allied to the Guyana Sanatan Dharm Maha Sabha, recommends priests to the Government for appointment as marriage officers. The Pandits' Council will never recommend anyone but a Brahmin priest, nor would any Sanatan branch appoint a non-Brahmin as a priest to a community temple.

Brahmins who do not practice as priests are, for the most part, classed as other laymen, although on occasion they too may receive *dakshina* as a token "feeding of Brahmins." In *yag* (reading and exposition of the scriptures by several pandits) there is a special enclosure for Brahmins. But this area is occupied by practicing priests, and a Brahmin who did not consider himself adept in ritual and scripture would hesitate to join them.

Guyanese Hindus have been receptive to reformist ideas which reject the caste system. While actual converts to Arya Samaj are relatively few, its views on caste and Brahmins have gained wide currency. In Guyana the American Aryan League attacks the whole concept of hereditary priestly status, accuses the Brahmins of fraud, and condemns such things as idol worship. According to the reformists, the four *varna* were meant to indicate levels of spiritual achievement attained by an individual during his lifetime. Their views are aptly summarized by the slogan, "One is a Brahmin not by birth but by deeds." The Arya Samaj argue that any member of the Samaj with the requisite piety and technical knowledge can act as a priest. The Government recognizes priests of this sect so that in the society at large they are not distinguished from orthodox Brahmin priests.

Even within the Sanatan movement there are dissidents such as the Bharat Sevashram Sangh who sympathize with Arya Samaj views about the privileges of Brahmins. A case in point is that of a dispute which arose in a village temple in 1956. A small group of men (who were influential in the village and relatively prosperous) started a branch of the Bharat Sevashram Sangh. At first they obtained permission to carry out their special ceremonies in the temple in the absence of the Brahmin priest, but were later denied the concession. Consequently they acquired a small "church" of their own in which they carried out rituals, sometimes inviting a friendly Brahmin priest from a neighboring village, but managing quite well on their own most of the time.

### Attitudes to Caste

The majority of Hindus are able to tell an inquirer which caste they belong to. But this dimension of their social personality is very small, and is of relatively little significance in most cases. In the local idiom the usual word for caste is "nation," a term which also means race, tribe, or ethnic group: thus, black nation (Negroes), white nation, Indian nation, Fula nation (Muslims). Brahmins are "high nation" and Chamars are "low nation," and in the idea system of Guyanese Indians these two groups represent the poles of the caste hierarchy.

Attitudes toward caste vary little among the different sections of the Indian population. Some high-caste families may seek to preserve their exclusiveness in various ways, but the common attitude is expressed in such comments as "Nation is ol' time story," or "Nation dead-out now." This view is in part an assessment of the significance of caste in social life and in part a condemnation of caste as a reactionary and disruptive force. Many assert that "Nation cause the downfall of the India people," meaning that disunity bred by caste led to the foreign domination of India.

In 1958, for example, a visiting dignitary from India was widely applauded for his forthright condemnation of caste as the cause of India's "backwardness," even though his pronouncements drew a mild protest from the Pandits' Council. Insistence on caste rank is regarded as a kind of snobbishness derived from an outmoded past. Most people feel that caste consciousness contradicts the progressiveness and modernity felt to be necessary if Indians are to prosper in modern Guyana.

### Caste Hierarchy

With their absorption into Guyanese society, Indians have adopted Guyanese criteria for the evaluation of social status. In comparison with income, occupation, education, race, and style of life, caste is recognized to be irrelevant in the many important fields where Hindus interact with other groups. In such fields, performance determines the social career of the individual Hindu, as it does those of individuals of other ethnic or religious groups; Hindus are accorded a high social status if they possess the qualities and achievements valued in the wider multiethnic society. Non-Indians have little knowledge of Indian cultural traditions and are insensitive to gradations of caste.

High-caste individuals may speak in private of the unethical and boorish manners of the low castes. They may refer to the past, when their forefathers refused to treat low castes as equals. The sons of high-caste families may be invested with the sacred thread, especially if the father is religious. But the holding of such a ceremony depends on whether the father is wealthy enough or cares enough about the added prestige it will bring him. The incentive to publicize high ritual status in this way is limited by the fact that, although being twice-born in itself has value, alone it does not confer a special status on the individual. Outside the sphere of influence of Indian tradition, there is no appreciation of this dimension of the Hindu's social personality, for here the important characteristics are, as we mentioned earlier, race, occupation, and education.

Furthermore, in the plantations the caste hierarchy is contrary to the egalitarian ethic which informs most social relations between laborers (Jayawardena 1963). A person who parades his caste superiority offends notions of proper conduct. In a typical reaction, a man who boasted "Me a Kshatriya; me got warrior blood," was knocked into a ditch by an Ahir who taunted him with the query, "Where you warrior blood now?" Much of this attitude also prevails in the villages, though there is more room for differentiation based on individual ownership of property.

Brahmin priests themselves are aware that they work in a milieu unfavorable to claims of superiority. Criticism of their alleged venality and chicanery is not uncommon; they are said to have "fooled the people" in the past, kept them in ignorance, and battened on *dakshina*. Brahmin priests restrict their expectations to ritual contexts and, when they finish a ceremony, rejoin the other guests to eat and smoke as equal members of the fraternity of Indians. The honorific title of *Maraj* is accorded only to those Brahmins who lead a respectable life, especially to priests. Addressed to a Brahmin who patently does not do so, the title carries ironic connotations. Conversely, it may be said of a pious man that although he is not a Brahmin, "he lead the life of Brahmin." The traditional respect due to a Brahmin is awarded mainly to those who regularly or occasionally act as priests.

The behavior of the Hindus of Guyana has become Sanskritized by processes similar to those that have occurred in India, and has been described by such writers as Srinivas (1952) and Cohn (1955). As the status divisions between *jati* groups had no significance in the context of Guyana, so cultural and ritual differences between people of different castes lost their meaning, and gradually the concept of a Hindu status hierarchy came to be polarized in terms of a contrast between Brahminical or Sanskritic patterns on the one hand, and Untouchable patterns on the other. The Brahmin and the Chamar came to represent two ends of a scale of status valid only within the Indian subgroup of Guyanese society, and even then not to all its members, particularly the growing number of Muslims. With the abandonment by low castes of distinctive rites and the standardization of ceremonies, the Untouchable end of the ritual scale has also lost all significance and differences are marked only by degrees of Sanskritization.

The upwardly mobile Indian will often adopt a more Sanskritic mode of life or become a Christian or Muslim and so leave the Hindu system of status evaluation altogether. The upwardly mobile person of Brahmin or Kshatriya origin may begin to lay more stress upon his ritual standing and become more orthodox. But, if the upward movement continues, eventually every Indian also becomes more creolized. This does not mean that he ceases to stress his "Indianness," but he enters a new social domain where it takes on new significance and where caste has little meaning. Of course, the coincidence of high secular (class) status and high ritual status may be valuable in claiming representational roles, but neither is necessarily linked to the other. Indians may attribute to a high-ranking person the characteristics of Brahminical behavior, whatever his caste. Thus Dr. Jagan is often said to be a "pure *sannyasi*" because, according to Indian villagers, he neither drinks nor smokes and eats only vegetable food.

## Pollution

The notion of pollution has become so restricted that, with a few gradually disappearing exceptions, it no longer serves to classify castes. The only concepts of pollution which are important are those involving lifecycle events such as birth and death. The avoidances and ablutions prescribed for these periods are carried out by all but the nominal Hindus.

Although the Chamars are regarded as being at the other end of the scale from the Brahmin, from the point of view of behavior they can hardly be distinguished form other non-Brahmins. People say that in the past Chamar families reared pigs and conducted pig sacrifices. However, pigs were gradually replaced by goats and, in time, all animal sacrifice was abandoned under the mounting criticism that such practices were barbarous and superstitious. A very few families still rear pigs for sale, and they are said to be Chamar, but the vast majority of Chamars have long since abandoned this practice.

In general, the same views on what is clean and what is polluting are accepted and adhered to by all castes. Pollution is a matter not of what a given caste may or may not do, but of what a "good Hindu" may or may not do. All Hindus are inclined to avoid such occupations as shoemaking, clothes washing, or butchering. Eating pork and beef is forbidden to all, and this taboo is generally obeyed in rural areas, although it is said that some break it surreptitiously. "Taking life" (as in hunting and fishing) and eating meat are avoided only by "good Hindus," and are engaged in by all castes without loss of caste prestige. With the exception of Brahmin priests, and those "leading the *sadhu* life," all castes drink alcohol; and a Brahmin who owns a rum shop suffers no loss of esteem.

## Commensality

There are no restrictions on commensality on public occasions. At weddings and religious ceremonies guests sit down together at meals prepared by their host regardless of his caste. Persons of higher *class* are often fed separately, and Brahmin priests may be included with them. Attendance at such gatherings, especially in plantations, is an obligatory public affirmation of ties of kinship, neighborhood, or friendship with the host. A refusal to participate is an unfriendly, snobbish act likely to provoke a quarrel at some later date. In such quarrels, arising out of behavior suspected of asserting superiority, the insult, "You dirty Chamar bitch!" may be heard. But this has no reference to the caste of the person abused, who may be a Chamar, a Brahmin, or of any other caste.

Although there are no restrictions in public, occasionally restrictions operate in private. While the latitude of choice in inviting guests to a public feast, or in attending one, is limited, individuals are relatively free to decide whom they will invite to private dinners in their homes, or with whom to share food if visiting at mealtimes. In this respect there are a few well-to-do high-caste families who express a reluctance to entertain low castes. But, although this avoidance refers to the caste system, it is an expression of status snobbery rather than caste avoidance in the traditional sense. Brahmin priests, who may depend for a living on the three or four ceremonies they perform each week, eat at the homes of clients, regardless of caste. They, as well as individuals in respected positions, such as professionals, overseers, drivers, teachers, and clerks, both high-caste and low, are prized as guests by humble laborers and farmers. The notables do not usually reciprocate by inviting their lower-class hosts.

This phenomenon is not a persistence of caste restrictions on commensality, for in the traditional situation the high castes offer food to the lower but refrain from accepting it. The situation described is a reversal of orthodox caste practice, and represents the exclusiveness and gains of a high status which is not of the caste type.[9] In the cases observed, such discrimination was practiced when low caste was compounded by low status on other grounds, and not when low caste was associated with high socioeconomic status. The appeal to caste provides a justification for maintaining social distance in a different type of social stratification.

Restrictions on commensality resembling those of caste occur sporadically, not between castes but between Hindus and Muslims when they choose to emphasize religious differences concerning food taboos. Hindus may object that the utensils used for cooking mutton have been previously used for beef; and Muslims may avoid eating at Hindu homes because the animal has not been killed in the prescribed manner. However, these restrictions are almost never practiced by whole groups and are not usually emphasized even by the orthodox. When invoked, such objections are counters in disputes of wider dimensions which have little relation to differences of religious belief.

## Endogamy

There is no prohibition of marriage between castes and intermarriage occurs more often than not. Children are ascribed the father's caste. However, caste may be taken into account and balanced against other factors such as income and education when a spouse is chosen. High-caste parents who prefer high-caste spouses for their children are particularly likely to do so.

One factor which governs the realization of this preference is the availability of spouses of the appropriate caste. Young people of a marriageable age, and of the right caste, may not be available in the district or within the network of contacts through which marriages are arranged. Scarcity is partly solved by selecting someone of similar or approximate caste rank. A Brahmin father, for example, may choose a Kshatriya husband for his daughter and feel satisfied that he has kept up his prestige. This practice may also be found among castes which are numerically small.

The education and occupation of the bridegroom and the financial circumstances and social standing of his family are as important as caste (Smith and Jayawardena 1959). A high-caste father may prefer a low-caste bridegroom with good prospects to a high-caste one with no future. A Brahmin priest thus married his daughter to a Chamar. Conversely, Brahmin youths make economically advantageous marriages with low-caste girls.

High-caste status thus can be exchanged for other types of reward and prestige. Where these other benefits are not pronounced, marriages tend to be contracted within the caste or between castes of approximate rank. What is avoided, if feasible, is not marriage outside the caste but too great a disparity between castes. However, marriages of high castes with low castes occur even when there are no social advantages, when romantic attachment and personal choice figure prominently in the selection of a spouse.

## Caste in the Plantations

The fact that caste is not a basic determinant of social status within the Indian community can be illustrated with reference to the internal organization of local communities. In this section we present quantitative data showing the relation of caste to other social characteristics of the Hindu population of two plantation communities: Blairmont, West Coast Berbice; and Port Mourant,

Corentyne, both in the country of Berbice. We do not have corresponding figures for the villages, but consider that they would be similar in essential respects to those presented here, except that there would be a higher proportion of persons professing ignorance of caste origin. In the succeeding section we discuss some aspects of a rice-growing village in order to show the way in which a local elite is related to the system of social stratification in the country as a whole. Social stratification in plantations has been analyzed elsewhere (Jayawardena 1963: chapter 3).

The statistics presented here were collected in the course of a general social survey by asking the heads of households to name their castes and those of their dependents.[10] Where possible, information was also collected about the castes of the mothers and of the spouses of married siblings and spouses. It is, however, unwise to place too much reliance on these figures, and the following words of caution are in order.

Because caste influences an individual's position in the community only marginally, there was little public consensus concerning caste status that would enable a check to be made on personal statements. It is unlikely that more than a few lied grossly about their castes, but minor mistakes and distortions may have passed unnoticed.

Nearly a quarter of the household heads in Blairmont, and a smaller proportion in Port Mourant, stated that they did not know what their caste was. These numbers were reduced after consultation with Brahmin priests who had conducted many of the marriages in the locality, with old men who knew the histories of many of the families in their neighborhood, and with kinsmen.[11] Judging from these indirect sources of information, the proportion of people who did not know what their caste was, and who were reputed to be low caste, was not markedly high. Those whose caste was ascertained indirectly represented the whole range, excluding Brahmin and Kshatriya. In the following tables they are classified according to the castes attributed them by reliable sources. There is no means of deciding whether claimed lack of knowledge was due to ignorance, principles, or deliberate concealment.[12] To the extent that it was the first, it should be remembered that the categories in which some are classified are meaningless to them.

Except among the high castes, the usual attitude was that questions concerning caste raked up aspects of tradition which were better buried and forgotten. In some cases there was doubt and speculation and replies were informed guesses. Some interpreted their caste according to present circumstances, evaluating field labor as "Vaisya." There were a few who derived their castes from affinal connections. The son of a Chamar priest of the Siva Narayani sect gave his caste as Gossai because of his father's profession. Where such inaccuracies were perceived (and there can be no assurance that they always were), further questions were asked in order to arrive at the ancestral caste.

Of some importance in this connection are the two castes, "Bengali" and "Madras," which indicate regional origin. The "caste system" of the Guyanese Indians is derived from Uttar Pradesh, and Indians from other regions seem to have been regarded as undifferentiated "nations." Persons of the "Madras nation" recognize that they were traditionally divided into castes, but very few know what these are, and other Indians do not care. Yet the Madras Indians retain some cultural peculiarities which set them off from the North Indians. By contrast, those who call themselves "Bengali" are completely identified with the North Indians, and their separate "nation" is revealed only in answer to specific questions concerning caste.

In the survey of Blairmont, thirty-four caste names were collected and in Port Mourant, twenty-five. The number of married persons in each caste is listed in Appendix A. For convenience of tabulation the castes are classified into five categories:

I. High Castes (comprising Brahmin and Kshatriya)

II. Middle Castes (comprising Gossai, Ahir, Kurmi, Bania, Mali, Gadariya, Teli, Boojwa, Halwai, Murau, Nonia, Sonar, Lodh, Lala, Kalpa, Nao, as well as "Vaisya" and "Bengali")

III. Low Castes (comprising Chamar, Kahar, Kewat, Bhar, Pasi, Dusad, Kori, Dhobi, Bhuiyar, Musahar, Dom, Kalwar, Katik, as well as "Sudra"

IV. "Madras"

V. "Do Not Know"

The rank order of the first three is derived from the views of knowledgeable residents. There were a few discrepancies concerning the place of Nao, Kahar, and Kewat; in these cases the more general view is followed. The Madras are regarded as a different sort of Indian people and are not included in the same hierarchy as the others.

Tables Ia and Ib compare caste with occupational status, which is the basis of social stratification in the plantation. Junior Staff (clerks, drivers, and foremen), Skilled Laborers (electricians, mechanics, welders, panboilers, tractor operators, and the like), and Unskilled Laborers (cane-cutters, shovelmen, forkmen, weeders, mule boys, and the like) may be arranged in a descending order of income and prestige. In Blairmont (Table Ia) a proportionately greater number from the High Castes is found among the Junior Staff, probably because of the tendency in the past to select drivers from the higher castes. Yet there is no consistent pattern of association between caste rank and occupational status. For example, while the percentage from the Low Castes among the Junior Staff is lower than that from the Middle Castes, it is also lower among the Unskilled Laborers. The highest percentages of Skilled Laborers are found in the categories "Madras" and "Do Not Know." The absence of any association between the occupational hierarchy and caste is more marked in Port Mourant (Table Ib), where the Low Castes have the highest percentage of Skilled Laborers. The distribution of frequencies in each table is not statistically significant.

**TABLE IA.** *Caste and occupational status: Blairmont\**

| Caste | | Junior Staff | Skilled Laborers | Unskilled Laborers | Total |
|---|---|---|---|---|---|
| High | No. | 13 | 12 | 38 | 63 |
| | % | 20.63 | 19.05 | 60.32 | 100.00 |
| Middle | No. | 15 | 12 | 90 | 117 |
| | % | 12.82 | 10.26 | 76.92 | 100.00 |
| Low | No. | 9 | 14 | 62 | 85 |
| | % | 10.59 | 16.47 | 72.94 | 100.00 |
| "Madras" | No. | 1 | 3 | 5 | 9 |
| | % | 11.11 | 33.33 | 55.56 | 100.00 |
| Do Not Know | No. | 4 | 10 | 23 | 37 |
| | % | 10.81 | 27.03 | 62.16 | 100.00 |
| | No. | 42 | 51 | 218 | 311 |
| | % | 13.50 | 16.40 | 70.10 | 100.00 |

*Total* $\chi^2$ = 9.54; d.f. = 8; $p > 0.20$
\*Excluding those not employed in the plantation, and those under 21 years.

**TABLE IB.** *Caste and occupational status: Port Mourant\**

| Caste | | Junior Staff | Skilled Laborers | Unskilled Laborers | Total |
|---|---|---|---|---|---|
| High | No. | 1 | 3 | 22 | 26 |
| | % | 3.85 | 11.54 | 84.62 | 100.00 |
| Middle | No. | 0 | 3 | 65 | 68 |
| | % | 0.00 | 4.41 | 95.59 | 100.00 |
| Low | No. | 2 | 11 | 65 | 78 |
| | % | 2.56 | 14.10 | 83.33 | 99.99 |
| "Madras" | No. | 3 | 2 | 23 | 28 |
| | % | 10.71 | 7.14 | 82.14 | 100.00 |
| Do Not Know | No. | 1 | 1 | 14 | 16 |
| | % | 6.25 | 6.25 | 87.50 | 100.00 |
| | No. | 7 | 20 | 189 | 216 |
| | % | 3.24 | 9.26 | 87.50 | 100.00 |

*Total* $\chi^2$ = 7.38; d.f. = 8; $p$ > 0.30
\*Excluding those not employed in the plantation, and those under 21 years.

Tables IIa and IIb compare caste with degree of education. In Blairmont, the High Castes have a higher percentage of persons with more than five years schooling than do the Low Castes. While this difference may reflect a greater readiness among members of the High Castes to avail themselves of educational facilities, again there is no consistent association between caste rank and education. The percentage of those without education is higher among the High Castes than among the Middle Castes or "Do Not Know." The last show the highest ratio of those with more than five years of school. A greater percentage of Low Castes than of Middle Castes have been to secondary school. The slight tendency of High Castes to be better represented in the higher

**TABLE IIA.** *Caste and education: Blairmont\**

| Caste | | No Education | 1-4 Years | 5-6 Years | Secondary School | Totals |
|---|---|---|---|---|---|---|
| High | No. | 15 | 25 | 22 | 6 | 68 |
| | % | 22.06 | 36.76 | 32.35 | 8.82 | 100.00 |
| Middle | No. | 23 | 64 | 29 | 3 | 119 |
| | % | 19.33 | 53.78 | 24.37 | 2.52 | 100.00 |
| Low | No. | 28 | 37 | 18 | 3 | 86 |
| | % | 32.56 | 43.02 | 20.93 | 3.49 | 100.00 |
| "Madras" | No. | 4 | 1 | 5 | 1 | 11 |
| | % | 36.36 | 9.09 | 45.45 | 9.09 | 100.00 |
| Do Not Know | No. | 6 | 15 | 15 | 1 | 37 |
| | % | 16.22 | 40.54 | 40.54 | 2.70 | 100.00 |
| | No. | 76 | 142 | 89 | 14 | 321 |
| | % | 23.68 | 44.24 | 27.73 | 4.36 | 100.00 |

*Total* $\chi^2$ = 16.34; d.f. = 12; $p$ > 0.10
\*Excluding those under 21 years.

**TABLE IIB.** *Caste and education: Port Mourant*

| Caste | | No Education | 1-4 Years | 5-6 Years | Secondary School | Totals |
|---|---|---|---|---|---|---|
| High | No. | 7 | 19 | 8 | 1 | 35 |
| | % | 20.00 | 54.29 | 22.86 | 2.86 | 100.00 |
| Middle | No. | 24 | 36 | 27 | 0 | 87 |
| | % | 27.59 | 41.38 | 31.03 | 0.00 | 100.00 |
| Low | No. | 24 | 42 | 24 | 2 | 92 |
| | % | 26.09 | 45.65 | 26.09 | 2.17 | 100.00 |
| "Madras" | No. | 10 | 12 | 7 | 2 | 31 |
| | % | 32.26 | 38.71 | 22.58 | 6.45 | 100.00 |
| Do Not Know | No. | 4 | 5 | 10 | 1 | 20 |
| | % | 20.00 | 25.00 | 50.00 | 5.00 | 100.00 |
| | No. | 69 | 114 | 76 | 6 | 265 |
| | % | 26.04 | 43.02 | 28.68 | 2.26 | 100.00 |

*Total* $\chi^2$ = 7.75; d.f. = 12; $p > 0.80$
*Excluding those under 21 years.

**TABLE IIIA.** *Caste and place of birth: Blairmont**

| Caste | | Born in Plantation | Born within Radius of Ten Miles | Born beyond Radius of Ten Miles | Totals |
|---|---|---|---|---|---|
| High | No. | 30 | 19 | 18 | 67 |
| | % | 44.78 | 28.36 | 26.87 | 100.00 |
| Others | No. | 169 | 38 | 38 | 245 |
| | % | 68.98 | 15.51 | 15.51 | 100.00 |
| | No. | 199 | 57 | 56 | 312 |
| | % | 63.78 | 18.27 | 17.95 | 100.00 |

*Total* $\chi^2$ = 11.71; d.f. = 2; $p < 0.01$
*Excluding those under 21 years and those born in India.

**TABLE IIIb.** *Caste and place of birth: Port Mourant**

| Caste | | Born in Plantation | Born within Radius of Ten Miles | Born beyond Radius of Ten Miles | Totals |
|---|---|---|---|---|---|
| High | No. | 26 | 1 | 6 | 33 |
| | % | 78.79 | 3.03 | 18.18 | 100.00 |
| Others | No. | 201 | 13 | 9 | 223 |
| | % | 90.13 | 5.83 | 4.04 | 100.00 |
| | No. | 227 | 14 | 15 | 256 |
| | % | 88.67 | 5.47 | 5.86 | 100.00 |

*Total* $\chi^2$ = 7.86; d.f. = 2; $p < 0.05$
*Excluding those under 21 years and those born in India.

occupations may reflect the correlation between education and occupation. Yet the overall inconsistency between caste rank and educational attainment shows that, at least in recent times, Low Castes have also used educational facilities. This trend is illustrated clearly in Port Mourant (Table IIb), where the percentage of those with more than five years of school is higher among the Low Castes than among the High Castes. The degree of association between caste and education is, if at all, extremely low in Blairmont, and none in Port Mourant.

Tables IIIa and IIIb throw some light on the discussion of passing. They show that a relatively high percentage of High Castes were born beyond a ten-mile radius of the plantation: in Blairmont 26.86 percent of the High Castes as compared with 15.51 percent of the others and, in Port Mourant, 18.18 percent as compared with 4.03 percent. This contrast suggests the possibility that several of those who migrated from one district to another successfully claimed a high caste. In the past (before about 1939), communications were poor, so that a ten-mile radius

**TABLE IV.** *Percent of marriages intracaste*

| Caste | Total Married Males | Percent of Marriages Intracaste |
|---|---|---|
| BLAIRMONT: | | |
| Kshatriya | 36 | 27.77 |
| Ahir | 34 | 32.35 |
| Chamar | 32 | 21.87 |
| Brahmin | 25 | 36.00 |
| Bengali | 21 | 9.52 |
| Kahar | 14 | 0.00 |
| Kurmi | 12 | 0.00 |
| Kewat | 11 | 0.00 |
| Bhar | 10 | 20.00 |
| Madras | 8 | 25.00 |
| Lohar | 6 | 0.00 |
| Gossai | 5 | 0.00 |
| Gadariya | 5 | 0.00 |
| Teli | 5 | 20.00 |
| *All* | 224 | 22.01 |
| PORT MOURANT: | | |
| Chamar | 49 | 38.77 |
| Madras | 26 | 23.07 |
| Kshatriya | 22 | 18.18 |
| Ahir | 22 | 27.27 |
| Gadariya | 12 | 0.00 |
| Kurmi | 11 | 27.27 |
| Bhar | 10 | 10.00 |
| Brahmin | 9 | 55.55 |
| Kahar | 7 | 14.28 |
| Nao | 6 | 16.66 |
| Nonia | 5 | 40.00 |
| *All* | 179 | 31.92 |

defined the area within which the plantation community could maintain regular contacts with other plantation and village communities. It would have been difficult to verify the castes of strangers coming from beyond this range.

Although caste influences marriage, the frequency of marriage within the caste is very low. This supports the view that "nation is ol' time story." In Table IV the castes with five or more married males are listed, and the percentage of intracaste marriage is indicated. The figures for females are comparable.

These figures suggest that the degree of intracaste marriage is partly associated with caste rank; thus the higher frequencies tend to be associated with the top (Brahmin and Kshatriya) and bottom (Chamar) of the hierarchy. On the other hand, the size of each caste also appears to be relevant, in that such castes as Ahir and Madras have relatively high rates of intracaste marriage. Whatever the reasons for variations between the castes, it is clear that neither statistically nor normatively is caste among the Guianese Indians an endogamous unit.

Nevertheless, despite the absence of sanctions against intercaste marriage, as well as the fact that most members of each caste marry outside it, caste rank influences the selection of spouses indirectly. Since the small numbers in many castes make in impracticable for them to practice endogamy, in Tables Va and Vb the data on the castes of husbands and their wives are arranged according to the five categories described above. This procedure takes into account the possibility that numerically small castes may regard some others as acceptable alternatives.[13] These two tables show that, excluding the category "Do Not Know," most marriages in both plantations occur outside the caste categories. On the other hand, the selection of spouses in relation to these categories is not random. There is a statistically significant tendency toward marriage within the category, even though it does not represent the majority of marriages. The figures support the observation that, although caste is not usually a key factor in the choice of a spouse, an attempt

**TABLE Va.** *Caste and marriage: Blairmont\**

| Husband Caste | | Wife Caste | | | | | Totals |
|---|---|---|---|---|---|---|---|
| | | High | Middle | Low | Madras | Do Not Know | |
| High | No. | 31 | 15 | 9 | 0 | 5 | 60 |
| | % | 51.67 | 25.00 | 15.00 | 0.00 | 8.33 | 100.00 |
| Middle | No. | 23 | 35 | 23 | 4 | 16 | 101 |
| | % | 22.77 | 34.65 | 22.77 | 3.96 | 15.84 | 100.00 |
| Low | No. | 18 | 18 | 23 | 5 | 16 | 80 |
| | % | 22.50 | 22.50 | 28.75 | 6.25 | 20.00 | 100.00 |
| Madras | No. | 0 | 2 | 1 | 2 | 1 | 6 |
| | % | 0.00 | 33.33 | 16.67 | 33.33 | 16.67 | 100.00 |
| Do Not Know | No. | 4 | 3 | 1 | 0 | 14 | 22 |
| | % | 18.18 | 13.64 | 4.54 | 0.00 | 63.64 | 100.00 |
| | No. | 76 | 73 | 57 | 11 | 52 | 269 |
| | % | 28.25 | 27.14 | 21.19 | 4.09 | 19.33 | 100.00 |

*Total* $\chi^2$ = 54.73; d.f. = 16; $p < 0.001$

\*The following categories of persons are excluded: those widowed or separated at the time of survey; those Hindus whose spouse's father was not a Hindu; Christians who gave "Christian" as their caste.

**TABLE Vb.**  *Caste and marriage: Port Morant**

| Husband Caste | | High | Middle | Low | Madras | Do Not Know | Totals |
|---|---|---|---|---|---|---|---|
| | | | | | | **Wife Caste** | |
| High | No. | 11 | 6 | 6 | 4 | 3 | 30 |
| | % | 36.67 | 20.00 | 20.00 | 13.33 | 10.00 | 100.00 |
| Middle | No. | 14 | 30 | 13 | 6 | 5 | 68 |
| | % | 20.59 | 44.12 | 19.12 | 8.82 | 7.35 | 100.00 |
| Low | No. | 5 | 14 | 33 | 6 | 17 | 75 |
| | % | 6.67 | 18.67 | 44.00 | 8.00 | 22.67 | 100.00 |
| Madras | No. | 2 | 5 | 5 | 6 | 6 | 24 |
| | % | 8.33 | 20.83 | 20.83 | 25.00 | 25.00 | 100.00 |
| Do Not | No. | 0 | 2 | 2 | 4 | 7 | 15 |
| Know | % | 0.00 | 13.33 | 13.33 | 26.67 | 46.67 | 100.00 |
| | No. | 32 | 57 | 59 | 26 | 38 | 212 |
| | % | 15.09 | 26.89 | 27.83 | 12.26 | 17.92 | 100.00 |

*Total* $\chi^2$ = 47.93; d.f. = 16; $p < 0.001$

*The following categories of persons are excluded: those widowed or separated at the time of survey; those Hindus whose spouse's father was not a Hindu; Christians who gave "Christian" as their caste.

is made to avoid great disparities of caste rank.

Tables VI, VIIa, VIIb, VIIIa, and VIIIb throw light on factors that influence the tendency to marry within the caste or with castes of approximate rank. While Table VI shows that there is a similar tendency in both plantations, Tables VIIa and VIIb and Tables VIIIa and VIIIb suggest that the factors influencing it differ. Table VIIa shows that in Blairmont marriage within the category is associated with the first marriage and, conversely, marriage outside the category is associated with subsequent marriages.

Among the rural Hindus, a girl's first marriage is normally to a bachelor. The agreement to marry is made between the parents or guardians of the bride and groom, and the wedding is conducted by a Brahmin priest according to customary Hindu rites (Smith and Jayawardena 1958)—"under the bamboo," to use the creole expression. In this elaborate and costly ceremony, which is one of the main public events in the life of rural Indians, large numbers of guests from the local communities of both fathers are feasted, first in the home of one and then in the

**TABLE VI.**  *Caste category and marriage in the two plantations*

| | | Blairmont | Port Mourant | Totals |
|---|---|---|---|---|
| Marriage within | No. | 91 | 80 | 171 |
| Caste Category | % | 43.54 | 48.19 | 45.60 |
| Marriage outside | No. | 118 | 86 | 204 |
| Caste Category | % | 56.46 | 51.81 | 54.40 |
| | No. | 209 | 166 | 375 |
| | % | 100.00 | 100.00 | 100.00 |

*Total* $\chi^2$ = 0.63; d.f. = 1; $p > 0.30$

home of the other. Wedding ceremonies are the most prominent expression of Indian cultural distinctiveness in the multiethnic society. They provide a means whereby an individual demonstrates his membership and prestige within the local Indian community. It is in this exhibition of "Indian culture" that most surviving minutiae of the traditional culture, many of them meaningless and slightly incongruous to the performers, are preserved and reenacted. The tendency to avoid marked disparities is linked to such wedding customs. The concern to do things the customary way entails some attention to traditional avoidances. The influence of caste on marriage thus persists as a peripheral part of the complex of "Indian culture" of which the bamboo wedding is a central item. But the persistence takes the form of avoiding great disparities of caste rather than of caste endogamy. And even this, as the figures attest, is a dispensable part of the cultural tradition.

According to Hindu custom, a woman marrying a second time is not entitled to a traditional ceremony; a man may, but usually does not, go through one a second time.[14] Second and subsequent marriages are therefore informal, and any ceremonial recognition is marked by a private *puja*. In contrast to the first marriage, which is a transaction made in public between the parents and expresses their social position and interest, a second marriage is an individual decision made by the contracting persons in private, even though friends and relatives may have arranged the introduction. Individuals are relatively free to choose their second spouses on the basis of personal likes and assessments; they are not influenced by considerations of caste.

The frequency of caste-ignored marriage is therefore related to the frequency of remarriage.

**TABLE VIIa.** *Caste category and order of marriage: Blairmont – females*

|  |  | First Marriage | Subsequent Marriage | Totals |
|---|---|---|---|---|
| Marriage within | No. | 78 | 13 | 91 |
| Caste Category | % | 49.68 | 25.00 | 43.54 |
| Marriage outside | No. | 79 | 39 | 118 |
| Caste Category | % | 50.32 | 75.00 | 56.46 |
|  | No. | 157 | 52 | 209 |
|  | % | 100.00 | 100.00 | 100.00 |

**TABLE VIIb.** *Caste category and order of marriage: Port Mourant – females*

|  |  | First Marriage | Subsequent Marriage | Totals |
|---|---|---|---|---|
| Marriage within | No. | 73 | 7 | 80 |
| Caste Category | % | 48.67 | 43.75 | 48.19 |
| Marriage outside | No. | 77 | 9 | 86 |
| Caste Category | % | 51.33 | 56.25 | 51.81 |
|  | No. | 150 | 16 | 166 |
|  | % | 100.00 | 100.00 | 100.00 |

Total $\chi^2$ = 0.00; d.f. = 1; p > 0.99

**TABLE VIIIa.** *Education and marriage according to caste category: Blairmont – males*

|  |  | Marriage within Caste Category | Marriage outside Caste Category | Totals |
|---|---|---|---|---|
| No Education | No. | 21 | 31 | 52 |
|  | % | 40.38 | 59.62 | 100.00 |
| 1-4 Years | No. | 42 | 62 | 104 |
|  | % | 40.38 | 59.62 | 100.00 |
| Over 4 Years | No. | 28 | 25 | 53 |
|  | % | 52.83 | 47.17 | 100.00 |
|  | No. | 91 | 118 | 209 |
|  | % | 43.54 | 56.46 | 100.00 |

Total $\chi^2$ = 1.90; d.f. = 2; p > 0.30

**TABLE VIIIb.** *Education and marriage according to caste category: Port Mourant – males*

|  |  | Marriage within Caste Category | Marriage outside Caste Category | Totals |
|---|---|---|---|---|
| No Education | No. | 32 | 13 | 45 |
|  | % | 71.11 | 28.89 | 100.00 |
| 1-4 Years | No. | 34 | 43 | 77 |
|  | % | 44.16 | 55.84 | 100.00 |
| Over 4 Years | No. | 13 | 31 | 44 |
|  | % | 29.55 | 70.45 | 100.00 |
|  | No. | 79 | 87 | 166 |
|  | % | 47.59 | 52.41 | 100.00 |

Total $\chi^2$ = 14.34; d.f. = 2; p < 0.01

In Port Mourant, however, although marriages are bedeviled by the same tensions as in Blairmont, there are processes of mediation and resolution, lacking in the other plantation, which result in a lower incidence of separation and remarriage (Jayawardena 1960). The question then arises as to what factors operate in Port Mourant to produce a similar proportion of marriage outside the caste categories, despite the lower incidence of remarriage.

Tables VIIb and VIIIb illustrate the situation in Port Mourant. The first shows that the frequency of marriage outside the caste categories is not related to remarriage. The second shows that the degree of education of the husband covaries with disregard for caste in the choice of a spouse. Thus the majority of those without education have married within the caste category, while the majority of those with five or more years of education have married outside it. By contrast, in Blairmont, degree of education is not significantly associated with marriage outside the caste category.

The difference between the plantations may be explained partly by the more creolized and prosperous character of Port Mourant and of the Corentyne district in general.[15] In comparison with the Indians of Port Mourant, those of Blairmont may be described as relatively more conservative and closer to the immigrant coolies of the indenture period. The Indians of

Blairmont praise Port Mourant as a "bright," progressive, and modern place. Trends of change incipient in Blairmont may be observed at a later stage in Port Mourant. Parental choice of a spouse is more limited by the wishes of children in Port Mourant. In Blairmont, where deference to tradition is greater, customary avoidance, as marked by the absence of free intermarriage, exercises a stronger influence. Other factors such as wealth and occupation being equal, traditional distinctions receive more attention in Blairmont, so that marriage regardless of caste occurs mostly in second marriages, which are made away from the glare of ceremonial publicity.

In both plantations, however, traditional restraints are strong enough to make marriage outside the Hindu community (with the exception of marriage with Indian Christians) relatively rare, though the incidence of this is somewhat higher in Port Mourant. Such marriages follow a pattern similar to intercaste marriages in Blairmont: they are mainly subsequent marriages which are transactions occurring outside the arena of Indian public celebrations. In Blairmont, out of nine marriages of Hindus with Muslims or Negroes, six are subsequent marriages, and in Port Mourant eight out of twelve are subsequent marriages. Out of the first marriages of this type in both plantations, five followed elopements.

## CASTE AND SOCIAL STRATIFICATION IN THE VILLAGES

The village on which this section is based has a population of about 2,700 people, is administered as a Land Settlement by the central government, and is less than ten miles from the capital, Georgetown. It is therefore not a "typical" village, and is probably less conservatively "Indian" than some other predominantly Indian communities of rice farmers. On the other hand, it is known as a center of organizations concerned with the expression of Indian identity and culture in the context of Guyanese society as a whole. There is no strongly corporate community identity expressed through a local government organ which could provide a vehicle for local leadership. The government of the community is paternalistic, being formally in the hands of the Land Settlement Department. There is a locally elected Advisory Committee, and membership of that committee is carefully arranged by the residents to include all the major racial and religious groups: Negroes, Muslims, orthodox Hindus, and reform Hindus.

Within the community, division is a more marked feature than unity. The community developed directly out of abandoned sugar plantations between 1908 and 1912, after which resident laborers gradually changed over to rice cultivation and stock raising. Some cane is still grown for sale to nearby factories but it is of minor importance. There are divisions within the community in terms of geographical section, in terms of wealth and education, and in terms of factional division. There were approximately 150 Negroes in the village in 1956, many of them descendants of Barbadian immigrants who had been resident laborers in the days of sugar. Relations between Negroes and Indians were very good at that time, with no sign of conflict, despite the fact that the Negroes tended to keep to themselves and looked to nearby Negro communities for most of their social life. Negro teachers at the local government-run primary school mostly lived outside the community or on its periphery and were not involved in community affairs outside the school. All the village children attended school, where they were taught in accordance with standard Guyanese curricula by both Negro and Indian teachers.

This particular village had the largest number of Muslims of any Guyanese rural community—approximately 700. All constituted one Jamaat of the orthodox Sunnatwal sect, which was a closely knit body with a full complement of officers, a mosque, and a small school where Urdu and Arabic were taught outside normal school hours. Muslims are not residentially segregated, and while their local community is closely knit, Muslims participate in many local organizations which cut across religious affiliation, while in the country as a whole they identify themselves as Indians vis-á-vis other ethnic groups. This identification was clearly shown in the general election of December 1964, when a party was formed to appeal to the collective feelings of Muslims and to win their votes away from the dominant People's Progressive Party. That new party received only 1,194 votes, while the total number of Muslim voters was probably near 20,000.

The Hindus are divided into three groups: the Arya Samaj, the Bharat Sevashram Sangh, and the residue of persons claiming to be orthodox Sanatanists. The most active Hindu group is the Arya Samaj, whose members use religion as a positive weapon in the fight for respectability and prestige. All three Hindu groups have some measure of organization similar to that described for the Muslims. That is, all have committees of management, and all run schools for instructing children in Hindi and religion outside normal school hours. The Sanatan group also has a temple and an official Brahmin priest, while the two reform groups tend to take on additional tasks for the benefit of their members: some own collections of cooking utensils, plates, and cups which can be used at weddings or on other ritual occasions; some have burial funds; the Muslims run a Scout troop. We may regard these organizations as vertical segmental divisions of the village population since they contain members of varying status. They are in no way ranked in prestige, nor does every villager belong to one of them. The Sanatan group is the least organized, since any Hindu who is not a member of one of the reform groups will claim to be a Sanatanist, even if he hardly practices his religion. A few Indians are Christians—either members of churches outside the village or attending one of the two very small churches within it—though being Christian does not mean that they are not also Hindu.

So far as the horizontal status divisions within the community are concerned, one can distinguish at least four levels. At the bottom are the majority of villagers who are small farmers and who sometimes work for wages in the plantations or the Public Works Department. Most of the Negroes are casual workers rather than farmers, while a few are skilled tradesmen. Among Indian villagers there are some skilled workers such as carpenters, tinsmiths, and tailors, but almost all grow rice as well. Rising just above the ordinary level, but not yet distinguished in any clear way from it, are farmers who have rather bigger acreages and therefore more income, men who have small shops or run a taxi, perhaps a goldsmith or a man who has a herd of cattle or goats. These men are apt to speak with a more authoritative voice in village or religious-group affairs; many of them are found as faction leaders in religious groups, and many get elected to committees of various kinds. Above them are the men of more than average wealth, such as large storekeepers, rice-mill owners and farmers, or men with secondary education who have been absorbed back into the village economy, usually through the inheritance of a family business. There is, finally, a group of residents who are quite different. In 1956 this stratum was composed of individuals who were more highly educated and who held positions outside the village, such as civil servants, teachers, lawyers' clerks, salesmen, plantation technicians, agricultural officers, and so on. This stratum is particularly important because it constitutes a link between the village and the wider society of a kind that would not be found in many smaller Indian villages.

There is no direct correlation between caste origin and any of the status divisions mentioned here. The socioeconomic system of the village is thus not made up of a collection of *jati* groups between which there is both separation and interdependence. There are hardly any traditional occupations which are of significance, except those of barber and priest, and a few specialized trades such as goldsmith.

Within the three lower strata, religion and Indian custom tend to be very important. For the lowest status group, religion is full of magical elements. Its members carry out domestic rituals to achieve good luck or wealth or health, or to give thanks for good fortune. In the case of Hindus, their religious beliefs and ideas are taken from oral tradition and from popular Hindu works such as the *Ramayana*, and even Muslims of this stratum manage to inject many magical features into Islam. In addition to formal religious beliefs and practice, use is made of obeah men, or of special healing practitioners who use magical means; some Brahmin priests provide such services as a sideline. Life-cycle rites are also observed, together with the magical precautions associated with them. Members of the Hindu reform movements are drawn mainly from the next two higher levels. Here there is generally a much greater awareness of religious doctrine and a tendency to be dissatisfied with orthodox Brahminicial teaching based on popular sources. Since these persons are generally oriented to achievement of some kind, even if it is only within the social-status system of the local community, they either seek to adhere more closely to Sanskritic norms within the Sanatan group, or become actively opposed to orthodox Hinduism through the reform movements. If they are of higher caste origin, then it is likely that they will stay within the Sanatan body. Among this group, religion becomes quite literally a means of arguing about status and prestige, and the reform movements tend to be divided into factions for this very reason.

The highest status group in the village is not directly involved in these activities and conflicts. Although its members are bound to the village through ties of kinship and neighborhood, and may patronize local religious and other organizations, their main ties of social intercourse are either with people of similar status within the village or with friends outside. More choices are open to such individuals in expressing their social standing, though some features are obligatory. For example, all these persons will be distinguished in terms of dress and speech. Whereas the majority of villagers normally wear open-necked shirts and trousers only, or perhaps the distinctive Indian smock worn over the trousers, the village elite will normally wear in addition ties and jackets when they go to work. Similarly, they will speak "better English." Almost all will adopt a more "creole" style of life in such things as home furnishings, eating habits, drinking, and entertaining. But beyond this, they may react to higher status in various ways. Some tend to drop Indian ways altogether, may marry non-Indians and move to Georgetown. If one does marry an Indian, she is usually of similar social status, and the couple may acquire non-Indian friends, go to dances, and engage in other "creole" ways. Alternatively, such persons may become quite involved in religious organizations at a wider level than the village. They may acquire positions in the urban Hindu or Muslim organizations and, while they become more "creole" in many aspects of their daily lives, they may simultaneously become more militantly "Indian." Or they may drift away from religion, while at the same time remaining self-consciously Indian, and perhaps become involved in Indian social and political organizations. But whatever happens, these individuals tend to move into a world which is multiracial, where there is opportunity to become more creolized, but also more opportunity to ascribe the jealousies, frustrations, and failures of a competitive world to race and racial discrimination. This aspect is discussed more fully below.

We have seen that the domain within which religion and adherence to traditional Indian customs is most important is that of the village. But at the same time, the members of the higher status groups in the village achieve their position not on account of caste origin, but because of their economic or educational standing. The position of Brahmin priests is interesting in this respect. Most are of lower-class origin and have little formal education, so that they are unable to acquire the kind of status in the wider society that most Christian ministers acquire. There is no regular training procedure for Hindu priests, and their sons rarely become priests themselves if they have been to secondary school. The result is that Brahmin priests have prestige of a very limited kind. Most are no match for an educated and vocal person of low-caste origin when it comes to decision making, even within the religious organizations. Many Brahmin priests manage to rise within the local hierarchy to at least the second and third level because many manage to acquire more land. But they cannot become part of the village elite without the formal education and occupational prestige that are basic to its membership.

## INDIAN ORGANIZATIONS AT THE NATIONAL LEVEL

It has already been indicated that there are national organizations of one kind or another that are specifically Indian. The Guyana Sanatan Dharm Maha Sabha is one such organization, as is its affiliate the Guyana Pandits' Council. Apart from these religious organizations, there is the Guyana East Indian Association, which was formed in 1919 with more specifically political aims. Leadership in many of these organizations has often devolved on persons of high caste, and this tendency may be taken as an indication of the persistence of caste prestige. Yet, though we do not wish to minimize the relevance of caste as one factor in the selection of leaders in these organizations, it needs to be pointed out that in the vast majority of cases the persons concerned are also of high status on the occupational scale. Furthermore, the educated elite of Indians has assumed positions of leadership whatever their castes and, it may be added, irrespective of religion. Prominent Indians have been Muslims and Christians as well as Hindus. It is also a striking fact that the Hindu religious organizations have not become vehicles for the expression of political ambition, even though attempts have been made to make them such. Dr. Jagan, for instance, is the acknowledged leader of the vast majority of Indians in Guyana. He has no formal religious affiliation, is not of high-caste birth, and is married to a white American.

## CASTE IN THE TOTAL SOCIETY

The discussion so far has showed that "caste" is not a useful concept for understanding the internal organization of the Indian community in Guyana. We have seen that Indians are involved in a wider system of social relations which is multiracial and multicultural, and that this involvement affects every aspect of their lives. What are the main features of that wider system, and does it present any features which are castelike? One of the difficulties of analysis here is that the system has been constantly undergoing rapid change, partly because of the changing composition of the population since about 1840. In order to simplify matters, it is convenient to present a rather static model of what we term the "colonial society," and then indicate what processes modified that system.

Colonial society, as defined here, grew up around the plantation, and at first included only the planters, a few free persons of color, and some white artisans. After emancipation the old nonslave society was extended to incorporate the ex-slaves as peaceful citizens. The focus of these new developments was upon integration and law and order and they were based upon the common recognition of the superiority of British culture and of the dominant position in the society of British people. While there was no ordering of the society into legally defined ethnic groups, there was an implicit assumption that the various groups in the society were different in recognizable ways. The basic units of the system were initially the British, the Africans (as they are still often termed), and the intermediate group of Colored. As immigration proceeded after 1840, the Indians, Portuguese, and Chinese were added.[16] The Amerindians were always peripheral, being regarded as childlike creatures of the forest, even though they had previously been used for the unchildlike task of capturing or killing runaway slaves.

As in the case of the Hindu caste system, these groups came to be integrated into one social system, through their common recognition of the differences between themselves, and their common recognition of the superiority of the white group and its style of life. Just as Hindus in India recognized the superiority of the Sanskritic culture practiced by the Brahmins, so Guyanese came to accept the idea of the superiority of English culture. In traditional India there was a common recognition of certain key elements of the religious tradition, despite the separation of castes and their divergent styles of life. Similarly, in Guyana, all groups accepted a basic minimum of English culture. Language came to be universally English, despite class variations in dialect; the progressive adoption of a creole culture was also an integrating factor. However, so far as the model of "colonial society" is concerned, the really significant basis of integration was that all groups accepted the value of whiteness, even though they recognized that they were not white and could not be white themselves. In making such an assertion we do not mean to neglect the fact that the British as the dominant political and economic group ensured compliance partly by coercion. Coercion often took the form of naked force, especially in the plantations. But even in the latter communities there were mechanisms at work leading to the passive acceptance of a subordinate role by the slaves and indentured laborers: mechanisms analogous to those found in concentration camps, for example (Cohen 1953). Both slaves and indentured laborers fought back, and Guyanese historiography is punctuated by investigations into riots and disturbances in plantations. But these protests were sporadic and uncoordinated until the middle of this century.

The ranking of ethnic groups in the social system of colonial society was by reference to whiteness; but whiteness had two dimensions. Color and physical characteristics were one important dimension of the definition of whiteness, and on this basis Indians tended to rank higher than Negroes because of their lighter color, straight hair, and more "European" features, as did the Portuguese and the Chinese. The other dimension of whiteness was cultural, and on this basis the Negroes ranked higher than Indians because they were Christian, more educated as a group, with a larger proportion of their number in white-collar occupations, and in general more anglicized in their style of life. While it is broadly true that both Negroes and Indians accepted the superiority of the English, each looked down on the other. The Indian looked down on the Negro because he was black, and the Negro looked down on the Indian because he was "uncivilized," each judging the other in terms of one aspect of "whiteness."

To some extent this system of social relations has remained operative, but other developments have modified it. The most important have been the emergence of what we call—for lack of a better term—a national "middle class," and the development of lower-class organizations which transcended ethnic divisions. A creole intelligentsia emerged during the nineteenth century, composed of persons who had moved into prestigious occupations through education. With the growth of colonial society, there was an increase in the number of positions available for teachers, lawyers, clergymen, doctors, and civil servants. At first these positions were filled by Englishmen (as the managerial positions in plantations continue to be filled), but it became increasingly difficult to persuade Englishmen to come out to the colony to fill the lower ranks. Consequently a limited degree of social mobility developed for educated local people. Teachers were recruited through the pupil-teacher system, and civil servants through the few secondary schools originally started for Europeans but which gradually broadened their intake. Other semi-professional occupations, such as dispensing, soon became open to persons of lower class.

By the end of the nineteenth century there were enough persons of Portuguese, Negro, Colored, Chinese, and even a few of Indian origin to constitute a radical political group, its members expressing their dissatisfaction with planter domination and demanding a greater share in the political life of the country on the grounds of their cultural qualifications. Although the urban middle class remained to a large extent fragmented into ethnic associational divisions of one kind or another, and while color remained almost as important a determinant of status as occupation or education, there was at least the overt recognition of values laying stress upon achievement, although achievement was still measured and expressed in terms of anglicization. Nonetheless, a break had been made away from development toward a "caste system" in which each group has special rights and in which endogamy is enforced. The white group continued to be mainly endogamous, but intermarriage between other groups became common.

We accept as a useful means of distinguishing caste from other types of stratification Leach's argument that

> For me, caste *as distinct from either social class or caste grade* manifests itself in the external relations between caste groupings. These relations stem from the fact that *every* caste, not merely the upper elite, has special "privileges." Furthermore, these external relations have a very special quality since, ideally, they exclude kinship links of all kinds (Leach 1960:7).

Empirically, a caste system of this type has never been found in Guyana, although the formal features of the ideal type of colonial society bore some resemblances to it. To a limited extent it was accepted that each ethnic group had special occupational characteristics: Europeans were top administrators and managers; Africans were civil servants, teachers, policemen, nurses, and part-time cane cutters; Indians were resident plantation laborers and rice farmers; Portuguese were shopkeepers, spirit merchants, and salesmen; Chinese were storekeepers and traders; the colored were civil servants, clerks, and professionals. However, this occupational expectation was never more than a rough conception of the social system. There was never any formal allocation of privileges or of hereditary rights to such positions, and certain key avenues of social mobility such as teaching, law, medicine, and dentistry remained wide open to anyone who could acquire the qualifications. The civil service too remained formally open to appointment on the basis of merit, and commerce to individual initiative. During the nineteenth century it was the Portuguese who availed themselves of these opportunities and were the most important radical element which led the assault upon the whole conception of the Englishman's exclusive rights.

At the lower-class level, the development of solidarities cutting across racial divisions was much less evident. We have already remarked upon cooperation and multiethnic representation at the local community level. Despite the tendency for local communities to be predominantly either Indian or Negro by reason of the histories of their establishment, there was never any residential segregation. Intermarriage between Indians and other races has been infrequent though not unknown by any means; it has been common between Negroes, Portuguese, and Chinese. Trade-union development in the early 1920s united Indians and Negroes in a common struggle for better wages and working conditions. But unionism decayed subsequently and, in the 1930s, tended to be replaced by the development of ethnic movements such as the League of Coloured Peoples and the East Indian Association. Even the unions, though formally representing all races, tended to organize mainly within racial divisions: for example, the British Guiana Labor Union among the Negroes and the Man Power Citizens' Association among the Indians. After the reforms introduced on the recommendations of the West India Royal Commission of 1938, there was a fresh growth of political parties and trade unions. The first election to be held under universal adult suffrage in 1953 produced the remarkable victory of the Peoples' Progressive Party, which was at that time the vehicle for both Negro and Indian radical sentiments, and focused a good deal of middle-class resentment against British domination. The subsequent disintegration of that party into two sections, based on separate Negro and Indian electoral support, is a complex matter than cannot be discussed here.

From one point of view, recent politics in Guyana represent a revival of some features of the colonial-society model. With the British vacating political power, the question of succession has arisen. If the old P.P.P., with its broad multiracial electoral base, had been permitted to inherit that power smoothly instead of being expelled from office on charges of "communist subversion," then it is possible that it could have built up an institutional framework which transcended race at the political level. But at present, although the two parties that have emerged from the old P.P.P. have each maintained a multiracial leadership, the average voter regards them as vehicles for the expression of racial solidarity. However, it is significant that both parties profess to represent national rather than racial interests and are, therefore, committed to programs, and policies which they claim will advance the welfare of all sections. Whether they will have this actual outcome is another question.

## CONCLUSIONS

It may be argued that the definition of "caste" adopted here is unduly narrow, and that this narrow definition permits the conclusion that caste is not found in Guyana. Perhaps a great deal depends upon one's initial approach: those who start with a primary interest in the structure of society, rather than in culture, are led toward the analysis of economic, political, and juridical relations. In Guyana, it is clear that such relations within the Indian community are not structured along caste lines. Nor do we consider it justified to suggest that a caste system exists within the total society in which the Indians constitute one caste. The similarities between a multiethnic society and a caste society are only partial; they are suggestive but can be misleading.

The "caste system" among the Hindus of Guyana is not a set of groups "which are at once specialized, heirarchized and separated (in matters of marriage, food, physical contact) in relation to each other" (Dumont 1961). The "castes" are not parts of a system of interdependent relationships, political, economic or ritual (Leach 1960). They cannot even be described as social groups.

Culturally speaking, it is clear that some of the idiom of caste has persisted. In any Guyanese village where there are Indians caste is discussed. Most are able to provide some sort of answer if asked the question, "What is your caste?" When marriages are arranged, caste may become pertinent. But when these bits of consciousness of Indian tradition are translated into action they amount to very little. If they were crucial, it would not be possible for the castes of many to be unknown to others. In the village described above, the majority of people dismissed any discussion of an individual's caste as being unimportant, though it was recognized that a Brahmin would prefer a Brahmin for a son-in-law, and oppose the marriage of his daughter to a *poor* person of low caste.

Caste is no longer a principle of social structure but a source of prestige on which some individuals can draw in limited areas of social life. This statement applies especially to Brahmins, who can still claim their traditional monopoly of priestcraft and the respect attached to it. For laymen, caste becomes a factor to be considered in arranging a traditional Hindu marriage, and even in this it is only one of several considerations.

Outside the context of traditional ceremonies, caste is ancillary to such major determinants of social status as occupation, wealth, and style of life, which are as much the basis of prestige in the Indian subgroup as they are in the wider society. There is, of course, an aura of prestige about being born of a high caste, analogous to the English concept of "gentle birth"; and similarly, a low caste carries connotations of humble origins. While the high caste alone means little, it can add to the prestige achieved in other fields. Thus a Brahmin teacher, clerk, or driver may be treated with more respect than a Chamar in those positions. However, this bonus of esteem, unlike the case of "gentle birth," is not derived from observed characteristics of the individual such as speech or deportment, nor from personality traits, but from the historical association of Brahmins with holiness and Kshatriya with imperiousness.

One point which emerges from this discussion is that items of culture change their meaning in situations which are quite different from those in which they developed. We are familiar with the contemporary relics of feudal culture in modern Britain, for example, but no one would make the mistake of equating a modern baron or knight with his medieval counterpart. Similarly, although some Indians may clothe their leaders in traditional dignity, and refer to the late Dr. J. B. Singh as an "Indian prince" because of his Kshatriya origin or refer to Dr. Jagan as a "pure Sanyasi" because of his supposed behavior, it is clearly understood that these are symbolic statements about the positions and respect these men had in Guyanese society, positions which they achieved through education and their performance as leaders in the national political scene.

**APPENDIX A.** *Caste composition of the married population**

| Caste | Blairmont | | | Port Mourant | | |
|---|---|---|---|---|---|---|
| | *Males* | *Females* | *Total* | *Males* | *Females* | *Total* |
| Brahmin | 27 | 38 | 65 | 9 | 15 | 24 |
| Kshatriya | 38 | 48 | 86 | 23 | 23 | 46 |
| Gossai | 6 | 5 | 11 | 3 | 3 | 6 |
| Ahir | 37 | 47 | 84 | 23 | 26 | 49 |
| Kurmi | 13 | 8 | 21 | 11 | 11 | 22 |
| Bania | 3 | 4 | 7 | 4 | 2 | 6 |
| Mali | 4 | 2 | 6 | 2 | 2 | 4 |
| Gadariya | 5 | 1 | 6 | 13 | 5 | 18 |
| Teli | 5 | 7 | 12 | 3 | 5 | 8 |
| Boojwa | 2 | 0 | 2 | 0 | 0 | 0 |
| Halwai | 1 | 0 | 1 | 0 | 0 | 0 |
| Lohar | 7 | 1 | 8 | 0 | 1 | 1 |
| Lodh | 0 | 0 | 0 | 0 | 1 | 1 |
| Murau | 2 | 4 | 6 | 3 | 2 | 5 |
| Nonia | 1 | 3 | 4 | 7 | 7 | 14 |
| Sonar | 2 | 1 | 3 | 4 | 1 | 5 |
| Kalpa | 0 | 0 | 0 | 1 | 0 | 1 |
| Lala | 1 | 0 | 1 | 0 | 0 | 0 |
| Nao | 0 | 1 | 1 | 6 | 1 | 7 |
| "Vaisya" | 2 | 2 | 4 | 0 | 0 | 0 |
| "Bengali" | 23 | 12 | 35 | 0 | 0 | 0 |
| Chamar | 35 | 36 | 71 | 54 | 49 | 103 |
| Kahar | 14 | 9 | 23 | 7 | 6 | 13 |
| Kewat | 11 | 9 | 20 | 0 | 0 | 0 |
| Bhar | 11 | 8 | 19 | 10 | 5 | 15 |
| Pasi | 3 | 3 | 6 | 5 | 6 | 11 |
| Bhuiyar | 2 | 1 | 3 | 0 | 0 | 0 |
| Dusad | 3 | 2 | 5 | 4 | 7 | 11 |
| Kori | 1 | 2 | 3 | 2 | 2 | 4 |
| Musahar | 1 | 4 | 5 | 0 | 0 | 0 |
| Dhobi | 3 | 1 | 4 | 1 | 1 | 2 |
| Dom | 0 | 2 | 2 | 0 | 0 | 0 |
| Kalwar | 0 | 1 | 1 | 0 | 0 | 0 |
| Katik | 0 | 2 | 2 | 0 | 0 | 0 |
| "Sudra" | 1 | 0 | 1 | 1 | 2 | 3 |
| "Madras" | 9 | 12 | 21 | 28 | 39 | 67 |
| Do Not Know | 22 | 61 | 83 | 16 | 38 | 54 |
| *Total* | 295 | 337 | 632 | 240 | 260 | 500 |

*Including those divorced, separated, and widowed.

# CHAPTER NINE

# Race and Class in the Post-Emancipation Caribbean (1982)

The abolition of slavery in New World societies is usually seen as a momentous event which resulted in a complete social transformation. Although the abolition of the legal status of slave required a rearrangement of social relations, the diverse social practices which constituted slavery did not all disappear overnight. In this chapter, I shall examine the continuities in structure which have shaped Caribbean societies through long periods of apparent change. My central argument will be that liberal ideologies developed in the post-emancipation period, ideologies which stressed individual achievement as the basis of social status, were systematically transformed by underlying assumptions about race and that this affected social practice in significant ways.

One can make a convincing case that "social stratification" in the Caribbean grew directly out of the calculated self-interest of an economically and politically dominant class of unscrupulous planters and merchants. There is much evidence that the dominant class joined with missionaries and administrators to try to transform the ex-slaves into a stable, obedient, docile and hard-working class of wage-laborers; that is, to try to preserve the basic structure of relations of production by deploying ideological, rather than physical, means of coercion. More direct means of coercion continued to be exercised. Racism, and the continued exploitation of labor by any means available, including the tying of blacks to estates by rent policies, denying them access to land for independent cultivation, or importing indentured labor in order to drive down wages, all seem explicable as the expression of the economic and class interests of the planters. I want to stress at the outset that there is no doubt as to the manipulative, oppressive, and racist nature of the actions of the planter class in the nineteenth century, and much of the twentieth. However, there are many aspects of Caribbean social development that cannot be explained as the result of self-interested manipulation. I intend to focus on these aspects, but in doing so I do not wish to be misinterpreted as ignoring major features of the class system. The influence of economic and political factors upon social development has been adequately discussed elsewhere.

## RELATIONS OF PRODUCTION, DEVELOPMENT POTENTIAL, AND IDEOLOGY

In 1840, just after the ending of slavery in the British territories on which this chapter will concentrate, the Caribbean comprised many different societies which exhibited features usually associated with more developed, industrial social structures. A disciplined and differentiated labor force; the factory processing of cane into sugar, rum, and molasses; a reasonably well-developed transport system; a wide range of trades and crafts; relatively advanced systems of medical care; and a widespread interest in upward social mobility. There is no need to get involved in the debate over where plantation slavery fits in the development of modern capitalism, but it would be difficult to disagree with Mintz's careful statement that

> the history of Caribbean plantations does not show a clear break between a slave mode of production
> and a capitalist mode of production, but something quite different. The succession of different mixes
> of forms of labor exaction in specific instances reveals clearly how the plantation systems of different
> Caribbean societies developed as parts of a worldwide capitalism, each particular case indicating how
> variant means were employed to provide adequate labor, some successful and some not, all within an
> international division of labor transformed by capitalism, and to satisfy an international market cre-
> ated by that same capitalist system (Mintz 1978: 87).

Although slaves received no wages and therefore are generally reckoned to lie outside the system
of commodity exchange, it is well known that West Indian slaves produced vegetables and small
stock for sale in local markets (Mintz & Hall, 1960), and by the nineteenth century when ownership of small gangs of jobbing slaves was widespread, many were virtually working for wages
and paying a fixed weekly or monthly fee to their owners (Higman 1976: 42).

Slavery was abolished in the British West Indies in 1838 after a four-year period during which
slaves had been paid wages. A flood of activities was unleashed, all designed to transform slaves
into citizens and to promote the development of the colonies. A system of primary education was
established that was in some respects ahead of that in Britain; secondary education was expanded; local development banks were established as new capital became available from the payment
of compensation money to slave-holders; there was a good deal of experimentation with machinery and improved methods of agriculture; and there was rapid dissemination of ideas of
"progress," "upliftment," and economic betterment. Arthur Lewis, speculating as to the reasons
for Jamaica's failure to undergo significant economic development between 1838 and 1945,
wrote the following:

> [By 1870] The sugar industry was reasonably prosperous, and the first shipments of bananas had been
> made. The old unstable political system had been swept away, leaving power in the hands of a series
> of relatively able Governors. The island was a part of the modern world; as much so as Argentina or
> Australia; more so than Japan or Russia. Why did it get left behind? (Lewis 1961: xvi).

In one way or another every answer to this frequently asked question points to the inhibiting
effects of a rigid system of hierarchical differentiation in which race and class are intimately related. Sometimes "culture" is introduced as an additional factor though it is most frequently treated as an integral part of one or other of the major variables. Of course, one need not accept
Lewis's appraisal of the situation. The Caribbean territories were, and are, small with limited populations and very small internal markets. While they were ideally suited to be plantation colonies
generating great wealth during the eighteenth century, they have few mineral resources (bauxite
and oil were not developed until the twentieth century) and they experienced a large emigration
of the most skilled workers at the crucial period when a free society was created. However, if
Jamaica did not have the potential of Japan or Russia, surely it had as much potential as
Tasmania, and certainly the system of social stratification had an inhibiting effect upon further
development.

## EXPLANATIONS OF CARIBBEAN STRATIFICATION

The most frequent assumption is that racism arises as a rationalization of exploitation in general and plantation slavery in particular. Patterson, for example, inclines towards the view that the structure of West Indian societies can adequately be explained by the material requirements of plantation agriculture, and insofar as racism is an integral part of that structure it is a by-product of the situation which equated Negro with slave (Patterson 1967). He is by no means alone in assuming that racial differentiation grew out of the experience of slave-trading and slavery. For example, Curtin implies that racist ideas are either pre-judgments, subject to correction through experience, or the product of a nineteenth-century "scientific" racism which happened to coincide in its promulgation with the beginnings of segregation in the post-emancipation United States and with the beginning of European conquest in Africa (Curtin 1974: 19). Curtin is careful not to say that racism is a rationalization of domination but his discussion inclines in that direction. In his earlier work on Jamaica, he recognizes the complexity of the situation, rejects what he calls a "Marxist claim that the ideas of any society grow only from the relations of classes and the mode of production," but he stresses the close relation between "social status [and] the economic order of the plantation system" (Curtin 1955: 42) and the fact that

> Hiding behind every aspect of the failure to attain the cultural and social assimilation of the two Jamaicas [European and African] was the background of racial distinctions and racial consciousness. The question of race was beneath the surface of every Jamaican problem, intermingling with other issues, and making all solutions more difficult. As time passed, it became increasingly serious, since many conflicts and unsolved problems could be translated into racial terms and so arise again at the next stage as a bar to mutual understanding (Curtin 1955: 172–73).

In spite of this insight, he never comes to grips with the question of the role of racial ideas because he interprets racial discrimination as a product of such things as lack of understanding of "African" ways, the minority position of the whites or the prejudice of an increased number of white women in Jamaica after 1840.

In what is perhaps the most sensitive discussion of Jamaican slave society to have appeared so far, Brathwaite lays great stress upon the development of a creole society and culture in which Africans and Europeans influenced each other, and, through a creative social praxis, produced a specifically Jamaican culture. Reacting to the negative image of eighteenth-century Jamaica favored by writers such as Patterson, Brathwaite enumerates those things that had indeed been created in spite of the inhibiting effects of slavery and he shows their value and their potential. He argues that the process of creolization would have been carried forward into the second half of the nineteenth century had it not been for the racial fears of the whites. "Blinded by the need to justify slavery, white Jamaicans refused to recognize their black labourers as human beings, thus cutting themselves off from the one demographic alliance that might have contributed to the island's economic and (possibly) political independence" (Brathwaite 1971: 307). Again it appears that slavery and the system of relations involved in plantation agriculture is the real root of those influences which shape the society, including its beliefs about racial differences.

Lloyd Braithwaite's pioneering study of social stratification in Trinidad focuses upon the relative importance of ascriptive as opposed to achievement criteria in the values governing stratification (Braithwaite 1953). While this study is extremely sophisticated in its recognition of the interplay of values in different spheres of social system functioning (it uses Talcott Parsons's pattern variable scheme), it adopts a linear view of development from slave society, where the values of particularism-ascription governing the system integrative sphere were dominant, to a hypothetical state where the values of universalism-achievement appropriate to the adaptive sphere will be paramount. For Braithwaite it is precisely the introduction of such things as British common law, ideas of economic development, education, and a rational bureaucracy that involve the reordering of values, and thus he is led to argue that Trinidad's position as a part of the British Empire laid the foundations for its transformation to a structure antithetical to colonialism. He is certainly not unaware of the contradictions which inhere in the system during its supposedly transitional stage, as is clear from his discussion of the characteristics of the middle class, but his theoretical framework assumes an inherent tendency of the system to move in the direction of universalism-achievement.

Although Braithwaite does not derive the initial structure of Trinidad's social stratification directly from slavery, there is no doubt that he considers the legal definition of slave status a considerable buttress to the dominance of particularistic-ascription values, and there is a sense in which any persistence of those values is a continuation of the structure of slave society. Hoetink has reacted sharply against the assumption that social differentiation in post-emancipation society is a continuation of certain elements of slavery:

> Wherever in Afro-American societies both a multiracial system and a slavery system coexisted together for a protracted period and contained the above mentioned similarities [of being horizontally layered structures], which caused each to crudely reflect the other, the continuation of the multi-racial *Herrschaftsüberlagerung* after the abolition of slavery was considered a prolongation of the structural elements of slavery—the sociological causes of the contemporary socioracial structure were sought in that vanished institution (Hoetink 1979: 48).

He argues, correctly, that socioracial stratification has existed independently of slavery, in the slave societies of the Caribbean such stratification occurred in the free sectors of society. Hoetink proposes an analytical separation of socioracial and socioeconomic stratification as a necessary prerequisite for understanding their interrelation. The correspondence between these two orders has always been less than perfect, causing grave difficulties for theories of economic determinism, but these difficulties have tended to be ignored. Emancipation in the Caribbean certainly involved a reordering of some aspects of labor organization, but one may question whether it involved any change in the structure of socioracial stratification.

Hoetink is correct to stress the independent existence of socioracial structures, but he neglects the interaction of these structures with others at the same level of generalization. Economic stratification is not merely actual; like socioracial stratification it proceeds from cultural premises and enshrines values. Hoetink believes that the ultimate source of differences in socioracial stratification systems is a difference in "somatic norm image" deriving ultimately from differences in appearance. This is neither a useful nor a convincing extension of the theory (see Hoetink 1967).

In discussing the contrast between Hindu caste society and European individualism, Louis Dumont has used the concept of "encompassed" and "encompassing" values and structures. He points out that while India recognizes the principle of equality, it is contained within the encompassing principle of hierarchy (Dumont 1970: chap 11). As Dumont is the first to acknowledge, his formulation bears a strong resemblance to Talcott Parsons's conception of a value hierarchy. In what follows, I shall explore the relevance of some of these concepts in asking to what extent we can isolate a "socioracial stratification," and how it is related to class, whether in Hoetink's words "the socioracial stratification 'prevails' over the socioeconomic one," and how the values of individualism and equality relate to concepts of racial difference and are, or are not, encompassed by them.

## CONCEPTS OF RACIAL DIFFERENCE

At the beginning of the last decade of the eighteenth century, a prominent Jamaican planter and writer, Bryan Edwards, gave a detailed account of the population of the British West Indies. He saw fit to phrase the initial description in terms of "four great classes": "The whole inhabitants therefore may be properly divided into four great classes. 1. European Whites; 2. Creole or Native Whites; 3. Creoles of mixed blood and free native Blacks; 4. Negroes in a state of slavery" (Edwards 1793: vol. 2, p. 2). Jews and emigrants from North America were not covered by these categories, but Edwards points out that the Jews of Jamaica "enjoy almost every privilege possessed by the Christian Whites" apart from the right to vote and hold public office.

Edwards is fascinating because he is the most enlightened colonial writer to discuss slavery. He clearly detests the institution and is fully aware of the manner in which it degrades both master and slave. He is a perceptive observer of colonial society, a sharp commentator on issues of colonial politics, and he fully understand the weakness of the colonial economy. He wants to modify slavery to the point where blacks will have a sense of worth with an attachment to the land on which they live and work, but he cannot envisage any radical change without the risk of civil war.

It is tempting to use Edwards's writing to show that concepts of racial difference grow naturally out of the functional requirements of a particular mode of economic production. This is mistaken. In spite of his preoccupation with economics, he is more concerned about the future development of Jamaica as a society. It is no accident that the first step in his discussion of the population divides it into "classes" which reflect underlying assumptions about innate qualities deriving either from "blood" or the combined effects of climate and breeding. It is these concepts that provide the broadest framework of his thought, and it is into that framework he fits the more detailed discussion of occupations. In this sense, Edwards expresses certain deep structural conceptions that were to persist beyond the formal abolition of slavery, and which continue to affect Caribbean societies today. Let us look briefly at the way he describes his classes before taking up again this question of cultural concepts and their place in social action.

Edwards describes the Europeans as including lawyers, doctors, and clergy, army and navy personnel, merchants and their employees, tradesmen such as millwrights, carpenters, masons, and coppersmiths, and finally the large body of plantation owners, managers, overseers, and bookkeepers. Far from arranging these Europeans into a hierarchy of occupational status, he is at some pains to explain that their most prominent characteristic is their "independent spirit, and a display of conscious equality, throughout all ranks and conditions. The poorest White person seems to consider himself nearly on a level with the richest, and, emboldened by this idea, approaches his employer with extended hand, and a freedom, which, in the countries of Europe, is seldom displayed by men in the lower orders of life toward their superiors." Most commentators have agreed with Edwards that "it arises without doubt, from the pre-eminence and distinction which are necessarily attached to the complexion of a White Man, in a country where the complexion, generally speaking, distinguishes freedom from slavery." (Edwards 1793: v.2, p. 7).

Despite the plausibility of Edwards's explanation, it should be remembered that egalitarian ideologies were already being disseminated in Europe and fast gaining currency in the New World. Many Jamaican whites applauded the principles of the American Revolution and shared the concepts on which the Constitution was built. Elsa Goveia points out that, as early as 1774, Edward Long based his arguments against the right of the Crown to delegate authority upon the same source as the American colonists—the political theories of John Locke (Goveia 1956: 58). Also like the Americans, Long and others after him reconciled their political theories with the existence of slavery by arguing that political liberty was only for free men. Long went much farther and characterized Africans as being less than human. It is interesting that Goveia, full of admiration for Long as an historian and theorist of colonial political rights, but equally appalled by his racism, should attribute the latter to the shaping power of a desire to maintain the social order: "His great work is more than a description of the society in which he lived. It is a monument, commemorating the power of all societies to mould, and often to warp, the minds and hearts of individuals that the social order may be preserved" (Goveia 1956: 62). But of course it would be equally true to say that it was the ideas of popular sovereignty, individualism, and egalitarianism espoused by Long that were distorting and warping the very foundations upon which the society had been built. As time went by, these ideas came to permeate the whole social fabric and it is their coexistence with racist concepts that makes post-emancipation society so fascinating.

Edwards was not a racist in the same sense as Long. His view of Africa and Africans is more enlightened and more accurate. He shows knowledge of the different African nations from which the slaves are drawn, and details their different qualities and characteristics. The "similitude of manners and a uniformity of character throughout the whole body" of the slaves is produced by the institution of slavery itself and the conditions under which the slaves are forced to live (Edwards 1793: v.2, p.78). But in spite of the importance which Edwards attaches to social environment, it is clear that he thinks in terms of a basic racial character which is capable of only limited modification. For this reason he dismisses the free blacks as being but little different from "their brethren in bonds" since they have no Christian blood in their veins (ibid: 26). The most they can expect is an amelioration of their condition and a transformation into a body of people with an attachment to the place where they live and work. As we shall see, such ideas remained important throughout the nineteenth century.

It is in discussions of the population of mixed descent, the colored, that one can see the structure of these idea in high relief, and it is here too that the contradictions in the conceptual structure come most closely into conjunction with contradictions in the social structure. The colored were the offspring of white men and black women or, more frequently as time went by, of white men and colored women. Edwards begins his discussion of the Free People of Colour (not all colored people were free of course) by noting the many different "varieties," and by noting that while the Spanish make a multitude of fine distinctions, the British distinguish only sambos, mulattos, quadroons, and mestizos. It is not necessary to describe these categories since the classifications are well known; the important thing from the point of view of this discussion is that the class of colored are defined by descent; by the variable proportions of black and white blood which they are believed to have inherited.

It is often remarked that in North America such distinctions were not made and that colored and black were all classed together as being Negro. This is not true; distinctions based upon the supposed degree of mixture of blood have always been recognized. What has varied is the significance attached to them. In Jamaica prior to 1761 there were few restrictions upon the rights of white fathers to free their colored children and to will property to them, but in that year an act was passed restricting the value of such bequests to 2,000 pounds. In spite of their formally free status, coloreds had few civil rights, but they were used to fill many necessary roles which would otherwise have been filled by whites. It is easy to assume that it was the shortage of whites that led to the custom of freeing colored people in the first place, but this is as erroneous as the argument that white men were forced to mate with black women because of the shortage of white women. A new, creole system of marriage was created in the Caribbean in which non-legal unions were an integral feature, separate from and contrasted to legal unions between whites (see R. T. Smith 1978a). Similarly, the existence of coloreds as a separate category with supposedly special aptitudes preceded their allocation within the occupational structure. Whether considering slaves or work cattle, the planter believed that white, or partly white, slaves or animals were weak and unsuited to hard physical labor. Similarly it was believed that aptitude for skilled labor was proportional to the amount of "white blood." Higman has shown that the number of births of colored persons increased sharply after the abolition of the slave trade in 1807, particularly in relation to the number of births of blacks, and this at a time when high mortality and the cessation of the flow of new slaves was leading to marked labor shortages. In spite of the financial loss which it entailed, colored slaves continued to be allocated to occupations which did not involve field labor. Sambo slaves, because of their less than half-white origin, were more frequently retained in low-status field labor and this was a growing source of dissatisfaction among them. In fact, Higman believes that the frustration felt by colored slaves as more of them began to compete for fewer high-status occupations my have been one of the factors in the slave rebellion of 1831 (Higman 1976: chap.11). It would be ludicrous to suggest that planters were wholly constrained in their treatment of colored people by their beliefs in the effect of racial mixture, but it is equally mistaken to suppose that sheer calculation or economic necessity determined the allocation process. Furthermore, the basic structure of concepts of racial difference have remained quite stable even after their divorce from legal and economic distinctions. Black and white were conceived as being fundamentally different in nature and the calculus of color status was set in terms of "mixture."

In a recent study of cultural conceptions of race among middle-class Jamaicans, a study which was a by-product of a more extensive study of kinship in the Caribbean, Alexander has shown that informants identify race with "blood" in much the same way as their eighteenth-century forbears. He shows that the vast array of terms which are used to refer to persons of African, European, and mixed descent are an elaboration of a basic structure of five categories which opposes black to white, produces a middle category of brown, and then opposes each end to the middle to produce dark and fair. The system of categories is in all essentials the same as black, white, mulatto, sambo, and quadroon as described by writers such as Edwards and Long (Alexander 1877: 420). Even more interesting is the fact that race, as a fundamental property of each individual reflected in such features as hair, facial structure, and complexion, is believed to be referable to an historic past in which race and class coincided and in which the complexity of Jamaica's present racial situation is believed to have had its origin in the sexual union of a "slave" and a "plantation owner." As Alexander explains, this has the classic symmetry of an origin myth which "relates events that have taken place in the past and are yet still in the present, not simply as past causes of present conditions, but actually present" (Alexander 1977: 432). It is worth quoting further on this since he lays out some of the issues with which we shall deal later:

Race…establishes the historical rootedness of the society and its members' place in it. It does so in a way that locates this historical rootedness directly in the experience of the persons' bodies and thus to a certain extent fuses the continuity of the person with the continuity of the society. Every time a person experiences inconsistency among race, physical appearance, status, and class, he is referring the present to a past in which there were two original groups—one English, white, civilized, master, and solidary, the other African, black, uncivilized, slave, and solidary—that mixed without amalgamating. Every time a person perceives himself or someone else in terms of race, he commits himself to a view that sees the present as the result of a long process of mixture in which the two elements are always kept track of because they have never really joined together (ibid: 432–33).

While the basic conceptual structure has persisted without perceptible change, there have been changes in the class distribution of Jamaicans and in the manner in which racial differences are evaluated and operate in social practice. Nor should we expect to find a consensus among Jamaicans in their judgments as to the significance and entailments of color differences. The inconsistency between race, physical appearance, status, and class to which Alexander refers can be produced not only by the peculiarities of genetic inheritance and by the movement of blacks into higher-status positions; it can also be produced by the invocation of counter-ideologies of equality which challenge the validity of the historic paradigm. Alexander is correct to emphasize the fact that, whenever perception is based on concepts of race, then a certain structure is motivated. The question now is: how did such perceptions constrain action? To what extent are they subordinated to other perceptions based on concepts of ability, occupational achievement, and the like? How do such structures operate in the process of social life?

In order to answer such questions, it is necessary to turn to a description of the class structure as it emerged during the second half of the nineteenth century, and in so doing to assess the implications of the continuing distinction between black and white that lies at the heart of Alexander's "myth of origin."

## THE CLASS SYSTEM

When the British colonies were forced to abandon slavery in 1838, they were, for the most part, well into a long-term economic decline that had started early in the century. The reasons for this decline are manifold and the debates surrounding it need not concern us here. The plantation cultivation of tropical produce for the metropolitan market is correctly perceived to have been the most important reason for the ascendance of these islands during the eighteenth century and a formative influence in determining their class structure. It was also a major reason for their economic decline when metropolitan markets no longer accorded preference or monopoly. But the importance of the plantation system should not blind us to the diversity of colonial economies or the complexity of their occupational structure.

Higman, by a complex series of calculations, arrives at the conclusion that in Jamaica in 1832, on the eve of emancipation, there were 670 estates producing sugar and that less than half the total slave population was employed on those estates—less than 155,000 out of a total slave population of 312,876 (Higman 1976: 14). The rest of the slaves were located on coffee, pimento, and mixed-crops estates or in such urban occupations as wharf-laborer, skilled trades, or even as prostitutes. Higman's estimate of the distribution of the slave population in 1832 is shown in Table 1 (ibid: 16).

**TABLE 1.** *Higman's estimate of the distribution of the Jamaican slave population in 1832*

| | | |
|---|---|---|
| Sugar | 155,000 | 49.5% |
| Coffee | 45,000 | 14.4 |
| Livestock-pens | 40,000 | 12.8 |
| Urban | 25,000 | 8.0 |
| Minor-staples estates | 20,000 | 6.4 |
| Jobbing gangs | 20,000 | 6.4 |
| Pimento | 3,000 | 0.9 |
| Wharves | 1,000 | 0.3 |
| Other | 4,000 | 1.3 |
| Total | 313,000 | 100.0 |

The figures shown do not include occupations filled by free persons. Apart from the estate owners, attorneys, managers, and other supervisory staff, most of whom were white, there was a considerable labor force of skilled tradesmen, people engaged in commerce and trade, and domestic servants of various kinds. Internal trade in foodstuffs, a limited sector of craft trades and construction were by no means negligible even though agriculture continued to dominate the economies of all the Caribbean territories throughout the nineteenth century. It is possible that many craft trades such as cabinetmaking, leather-working, saddle-making, printing, cigar-making, and tailoring were more important in the eighteenth and early nineteenth centuries than they were after cheap manufactures began to be imported in larger quantities. Although importation has always been a characteristic of these economies, and the distribution of imported goods has been a major source of economic opportunity for upwardly mobile elements, the *idea* of import substitution and of developing local industries has been a constant preoccupation. However, very few industries apart from those which processed local agricultural products—such as the manufacture of rum, cigarettes and cigars—managed to get stated until after World War II.

No total census of Jamaica was undertaken before 1844, but Eisner estimates the racial distribution in 1834 as shown in Table 2 (Eisner 1961: 127). The white population had declined steadily from its peak of 34,152 in 1824 and, although it maintained its numbers between the mid-nineteenth century and the 1920s at about 14,000, it declined as a proportion on the total population from about 4 percent to less than 2 percent. By contrast, the colored population increased both absolutely and proportionally from 40,000 (10.8 percent) in 1834 to 68,500 (18.1 percent) in 1844 to 100,300 (18.8 percent) in 1871. The big jump between 1834 and 1844 is probably due to the fact that many people, especially children, who had been classified as "black slaves" in 1834 were reclassified as "colored" after emancipation.

The size and proportions of the various racial elements are of less interest than their

**TABLE 2.** *Eisner's estimate of the racial distribution in Jamaica in 1834*

| | | |
|---|---|---|
| Whites | 15,000 | 4.0% |
| Free Coloured | 40,000 | 10.8 |
| Free Black | 5,000 | 1.3 |
| Black slaves | 311,070 | 83.9 |
| Total | 371,070 | 100.0 |

**Table 3.** *Distribution of labor by industry in Jamaica*

| Industry | 1844 | | 1871 | | 1891 | | 1921 | |
|---|---|---|---|---|---|---|---|---|
| | '000 | % | '000 | % | '000 | % | '000 | % |
| Agriculture | 116.0 | 71.5 | 147.0 | 68.0 | 172.5 | 62.8 | 192.0 | 55.3 |
| Industry and construction | 18.5 | 11.4 | 36.6 | 16.9 | 47.2 | 17.2 | 61.1 | 17.6 |
| Commerce | 4.9 | 3.0 | 6.3 | 2.9 | 10.9 | 4.0 | 20.6 | 5.9 |
| Professions | 2.0 | 1.3 | 4.4 | 2.0 | 7.0 | 2.5 | 11.4 | 3.3 |
| Domestic service | 20.8 | 12.8 | 22.1 | 10.2 | 37.1 | 13.5 | 62.2 | 17.9 |
| Totals | 162.2 | 100.0 | 216.4 | 100.0 | 274.7 | 100.0 | 347.3 | 100.0 |

distribution through the occupational system, for although race has been an independent mark-er of status, we are dealing with societies in which occupations are ranked, and the possibility of occupational status mobility has always been a social fact. Table 3 gives a schematic outline of the general disposition of the labor force by industrial category (Eisner 1961: 162). In the following discussion, I shall try to provide a summary of the changing configuration of class boundaries during the nineteenth century as new social and economic factors enter the picture. Although we have seen that writers on the Caribbean generally employ a tripartite class image, usually embodying the idea of racial differentiation (white upper class, colored middle class, black lower class), I shall try to describe groupings which seemed to emerge as identifiable elements either in the system of production, distribution, and exchange or as politically conscious elements.

## THE UPPER CLASS

Despite the formal independence of most contemporary Caribbean societies, one could argue plausibly that their upper class is now, and always has been, foreign. During the colonial period, it was the owners of major economic enterprises, be they plantations, shipping lines, lumber mills or large mercantile houses, and secondarily the administrative and military agents of the imper-ial power who constituted the upper class. Today, with native governors, prime ministers and gen-erals, it is less easy to see how foreigners could constitute an upper class. It is no accident, how-ever, that a great deal of social life revolves around the foreign embassies and the large hotels where foreigners stay, and that the mass media continue to project an image of the outside world that is infinitely more desirable to most people than the local reality.

After emancipation, there was a rapid decline in the number of whites in Jamaica and in other colonies. Their domination of the economy also diminished, particularly if Jews are not counted as being "white." By 1826, when they achieved full civil rights, Jewish merchants were already a prosperous and numerous element in the capital city. In the 1830s, they forged an alliance with the articulate leadership of the colored population, challenging the domination of the Assembly by the planter class. By 1840, one can identify the four major elements that would dominate the politics of the late nineteenth and early twentieth centuries: the Governor, the colored and Jewish elite, the planters, and the mass of black labor. The Governor represented Britain and imperial interests, and in the 1830s Britain was intent upon pushing through the abolition of slavery against the strenuous opposition of the planter class—"the Proprietary of the Island" as Governor Metcalfe called them. One of the reasons that the Jewish and colored populations had been accorded full civil rights (in 1826 and 1832, respectively) was to enlist them against the planters in favor of abolition. Metcalfe was perceptive enough to see that once the blacks were free, the Assembly would change from a forum for the discussion of planter interest to one where the interests of the "masses" would be articulated by colored men—and even by blacks themselves in time. He realized that when that time came, the planters—"the Proprietary"—would be only too anxious to have the Crown, through the Governor, use its power to check the Assembly. As Hall points out (Hall 1959: 7–8), the alliance of Jewish merchants and colored professionals, jour-nalists and the like did come to constitute an increasingly assertive "Town Party" opposed to the planters, but this group did not press vigorously for the further transformation of the society and in 1865, after a minor outbreak of violence in a country parish in which a body of outraged laborers attacked what they considered to be a corrupt and oppressive alliance of local officials and planters, the Assembly voted itself out of existence, leaving the way open for direct British rule. The black masses, augmented by imported indentured labor, remained largely inarticulate, except for protest riots and demonstrations, until well into the twentieth century. This fourth element thus remained outside the formal arena of politics but its presence was felt in many ways.

The advent of Crown Colony Government not only strengthened the power of the Governor and his officials, but it coincided with the transformation of the ownership of the sugar industry from individual to corporate. Robotham has argued that it was the repossession of marginal lands by companies, which were buying up abandoned and inefficient estates through the new instrument of the Encumbered Estates Act, that set off a rash of protests similar to the one in Morant Bay that precipitated the abolition of the constitution in 1865 (Robotham 1977). The upper class was thenceforward to be composed of the English official class, the survivors of the old planter families and the top representatives of the new corporate owners. Also hanging on as marginal members of the charmed circle around King's House (the new symbolic center of the society) were some less wealthy survivors of the old upper class, an increasing proportion of which began to migrate to North America or to sink imperceptibly into the colored middle class. Other elements managed to push their way up, particularly from among the Jewish population, as their fortunes prospered.

In a recent article which indicates what could be done with more extensive research, Stanley Reid argues that Jamaica's present-day corporate economy is controlled effectively by twenty-one families of creole whites, Jews, Syrians, and a few Chinese. These families are extensively intermarried and are represented in 125 directorships of banks, trading companies, construction, shipping, manufacturing, and other firms. Names such as Ashenheim, De Cordova, Hart, Henriques, Brandon, and Nunes go far back in Jamaica's history and indicate the continuing importance of the business elite formed in the immediate post-emancipation period. How they got to their present position is the story of the rise of the middle class (Reid 1977).

## THE MIDDLE CLASSES

The middle classes are the most interesting element in the period with which we are dealing, for they were created by the conditions of colonial society and in them lay the major dynamic of the society. The alliance of colored and Jewish elites was the forerunner of similar alliances elsewhere in the Caribbean between merchants and intelligentsia. Trade and education were the mechanisms through which these classes were formed. New patterns of trade created alliances between produce dealers and growers, but the expansion of education made a sharp separation between the small output of the secondary schools and the products of primary education. The effect of both trade and education was to create a two-tiered "middle class" with divisions within each tier, and the whole system provided complex bridging elements between the upper and lower classes.

### Trade

Even during slavery there had been an active trade between Jamaica and the Gulf ports, both Spanish and American, mediated by Jewish and colored merchants who exported the products of smaller properties growing "minor" crops such as ginger, pimento, arrowroot, and coconuts, and who imported food, lumber, and other goods. This trade expanded after emancipation, but it was the development of banana cultivation in the 1870s that both enhanced the position of the local produce merchants and consolidated the growth of a black rural farmer middle class.

In Guyana, there was a parallel alliance of local merchants and North American business interests in the late nineteenth century, but here the "minor industries" were products of the interior, such as gold, diamonds, and wild rubber. Extraction was financed mainly by Portuguese and Chinese businessmen and carried out by black prospectors. Thus we see that different racial groups responded to similar economic opportunities, even though entrepreneurship remained encapsulated in racially defined groups.

Trade was not all one-way, and one should not underestimate the importance of importation as the major component of entrepreneurial activity. The major income of merchants has come from importing cheap goods from Europe and North America (more recently from India and other Eastern countries), and external linkages with foreign exporters have been crucial in forming the political views of this class. They have been represented in whatever limited local manufacturing industry developed (mostly the processing of agricultural products), but their dominant orientation has been to foreign trade.

## Education

The earliest schools in the colonies were private or endowed schools for the children of those whites who could not afford to send them to England. Since many free colored were the children of whites, it became common for them to be admitted to these schools; few were educated in England. Badly run for the most part, they taught gentility to girls and gave boys a grounding in the classics, fitting them either for entry to the professions or the rank of gentleman. After emancipation, such schools came to constitute the core of the secondary school system. The largest in Jamaica was Wolmer's Free School (which took fee-paying students). In 1814 it had an enrollment of eighty-seven students, all of whom were white. By 1820 it had 116 white children, and seventy-eight colored, but by 1830 the balance had changed completely so that eighty-eight white children were outnumbered by 194 colored. In the next four years the colored enrollment increased to 420 while the white decreased slightly to eighty-one. In spite of this upsurge of colored enrollment, secondary education remained highly restrictive until after 1950. In Jamaica in 1929 there were only twenty-five secondary schools with a total enrollment of 2,677 students, or one in fifty of the school-age population of 133,850.

Graduates of the secondary school system became white-collar workers in the expanding government and business bureaucracies and came to think of themselves as members of an "intelligentsia," literate in English and in command of English manners, sharply distinguished from the mass of uncultured ex-slaves and indentured immigrants. I have argued elsewhere that the reason for the emergence of a Caribbean intelligentsia was the need to create a new basis for the integration of society once slavery had been abolished. This need translated itself into the creation not only of police forces and the deployment of military and judicial power, but also into the formulation and dissemination of ideologies through which commitment to colonial values could be secured.

> The very forces that were used to integrate creole society—religion, education, the law, medicine, journalism, the civil service—resulted in the creation of a creole elite which, by the end of the nineteenth century, was referring to itself as "the intelligentsia." This group owed its position within the society to achievement in the sense that it filled valued occupational roles and commanded and

manipulated "English" culture, but it is evident that its members came to believe themselves to be qualitatively different from the other non-Europeans by virtue of their "refinement" (R. T. Smith 1967: 237).

I would now agree with Edward Brathwaite that one should make a distinction between creole society, which he defines as the integration of all races around the development of local culture and local values as happened in Jamaica prior to 1865, and colonial society, which integrated local society around the dominance of metropolitan culture. There was no indirect rule here.

The system of elementary education was aimed at the lower class of ex-slaves, but it found its principal support among the more prosperous small and medium-sized farmers engaged in the production of "minor," that is non-plantation, crops. Its existence also led to the creation of a lower middle class of primary schoolteachers who became an important reservoir of black leaders. The system started in the period immediately before emancipation and the big initial development was over by 1845. Between 1820 and 1834 there were forty-seven new schools opened in Jamaica and, of this number, forty were intended for the use of slaves and were financed by the mission churches. In 1837 the British Government started to make grants for the building of schools and this gave impetus to the expansion. By 1836 there were already 307 schools with a student body of 16,592 or about one in five of the population aged 5–15 years. In addition there were 139 Sunday schools and ninety-five evening schools attended mainly by adults. The intention of this massive educational effort was to ensure that the slaves would take their place as free men—quiet, obedient, and hard working.

The problem of providing enough teachers was a serious obstacle to expansion. Mico College was opened in 1836 and Calabar College in 1842 to train Jamaican teachers and catechists, but there was a continuing shortage of both. Eventually most teachers were produced by the Pupil Teacher system—a form of on-the-job training. Whatever its shortcomings, elementary-school teaching was almost the only means by which poor blacks could escape from manual labor. The primary-school teacher was very poorly paid and there was almost no opportunity to rise into higher-status occupations. However, in the rural communities where church and school were most effective, particularly among the middle farmers who could make enough money to maintain a respectable style of life, the schoolteachers were the local elite. The clergy ranked higher but each minister had to serve many different communities, while the headmaster of the school was always there, as lay preacher, adviser, local politician, and leading figure in all voluntary organizations, including the Jamaica Agricultural Society. In Guyana the situation was the same, and there schoolteachers played a leading role in the Local Government System (see R. T. Smith 1956).

A few primary-school teachers managed to get their children into secondary schools and then into the professions or the civil service, but such upward mobility for Africans was very limited, especially in Jamaica. As late as 1922, when there were at least a few elected members of the Legislative Council and the Governor had nominated the first black man ever to be a non-elected member of that body, it was possible for Frank Cundall, Secretary of the Jamaica Institute, to publish the following in a semi-official handbook explaining Jamaica to intending settlers and visitors: "The negro race has at present gone but a short way on the path of civilization. The individuals are still as children, childlike in belief and faith. Once gain their confidence and they will trust you implicitly. A cynic might add, as long as it suits them to do so" (Cundall 1922: 44). He goes on in this vein for several pages and includes a statement that "African languages consist to a large extent in gesture," a partial explanation for the fact that lack of understanding "is often due to a limited vocabulary rather than a lack of sense" (ibid: 46). Cundall was one of the most enlightened Englishmen in the country at the time, but it is surprising that there does not seem to have been any objection to writing of this kind. Exactly the same passages were printed year after year. One must suppose that the few blacks who had managed to attain professional or higher middle class status were in such a minority, and in such a precarious social position, that they considered it useless to object. It is possible that some of them shared the opinions of the whites about the mass of uneducated blacks. However, there had always been some members of the middle class who had a deeper understanding of the culture and aspirations of the lower class and who were to provide leadership. Although the lower class lacked any kind of formal organization prior to the 1930s, it was certainly not quiescent.

## THE LOWER CLASS

Throughout the West Indies the "lower class" has been divided into at least four identifiable sectors, and the interplay between race and class is no less complex here than at higher levels of the occupational status system. These were: a class of resident wage-laborers or marginal cultivators mainly dependent on wages; a more prosperous middle farmer group with enough land to live on and perhaps employ casual laborers; a regularly employed urban working class; and a marginal urban underclass existing on casual labor or a host of illegal activities ranging from prostitution to theft or begging.

It is sometimes argued that emancipation was followed by the creation, or recreation, of "peasantries," but this term can be misleading. Eisner shows that in Jamaica the slaves were not anxious to leave established settlements on the estates, but they wanted adequate wages in order to buy food, shelter, clothing, and to participate in education and church life. In Guyana the ex-slaves established independent villages very quickly, but they appreciated the difficulty of selling cash crops in a declining market and they were reconciled to continuing as wage-laborers at a reasonable wage. Even though wages were not reasonable, they split their time between estate work, growing cash and subsistence crops and working in the interior. In Jamaica there were relatively few church-based villages; most ex-slaves were forced into a tenant relationship in which house spots and provision lands (which had been provided free prior to 1838) often were calculated in terms of so many days of work. The abandonment of estates was accelerated by the passage of the Sugar Duties Act by Britain in 1846. Jamaican sugar estates declined in number from 670 in 1936 to 300 in 1865 to 111 in 1900 to only thirty-nine in 1930. Some of this decline was due to consolidation of estates as corporate capital began to move into sugar production and practice economies of scale. In Guyana the same process took place as sugar estates diminished from 230 in 1820 to only nineteen in 1958. Sugar continued to provide employment for most wage-laborers, but in Jamaica by the turn of the century bananas had overshadowed it as the most profitable crop.

The reason that students of West Indian societies are able to talk about "reconstituted peasantries" is that plantations developed a new form of relationship to their labor force after emancipation—a relationship in which the worker regarded himself as a "small farmer" who worked occasionally for wages. A core labor force of resident workers was retained on the estates, usually by the importation of indentured workers. In Jamaica the majority of black cultivators continued with the same kind of mixed-crop and small-livestock production they had practiced during slavery, and they supplied the internal marketing system that has so graphically been described for all parts of the Caribbean (Mintz 1955; Mintz & Hall 1960; Katzin 1959; Spence 1964; Ostrowski 1969; Romalis 1969). Most plots were too small to keep one person working full time, and income from the sale of produce was supplementary to wage-labor. Migration overseas was particularly important, and Jamaicans migrated to Central America to work on railway construction, on the Panama Canal, and on the banana plantations of the United Fruit Company. They also migrated to Cuba as sugar-workers and more recently to Britain, Canada, and the United States. Afro-Guyanese provided the labor for gold- and diamond-mining, the collection of wild rubber and for bauxite-mining.

It was noted earlier that elementary education and church participation was most effective among the middle farmers in Jamaica (see p. 156 above). They became the backbone of the respectable churches, ambitious for their children's education and pushing them as far as they could go into the lower levels of the middle class: into teaching, nursing, the police, and the lower levels of the clerical branches of the civil service. In Guyana the whole of the Afro-Guyanese population congregated into church-based communities, becoming imbued with the values of respectability and "English culture," which they used to differentiate themselves from the Indian indentured sugar-workers.

Elementary education was different both in aim and in content from that provided through the secondary schools. In 1847 the Colonial Office circulated a dispatch in which four broad types of subject-matter were recommended for elementary schools. The first was religious instruction, the second the English language "as the most important agent of civilization for the colored population," third was a brief reference to the importance of teaching the peasant how to calculate and enter into agreements (though they did not specify how this should be done), and finally they stressed the need to "teach the mutual interests of the mother country and her dependencies; the rational basis of their connection, and the domestic and social duties of the colored races."

In some colonies, such as Guyana and Barbados, elementary education was very successful in providing instruction in the values of colonialism and Christianity. In Jamaica, a smaller part of the ex-slave population was reached. Partly because of the hilly terrain and the scattered location of the population, the Jamaican schools were less effective in reaching marginal laborers and small farmers. But there was also a growing disillusionment among the ex-slaves as social conditions for most of them failed to improve after the initial period of post-emancipation euphoria. Elementary education had little success among those who felt themselves to be confined at the very bottom of the social hierarchy, and it is for this reason that the East Indian population in Guyana and Trinidad remained largely uneducated until after World War II.

Indentured workers from Europe, Portuguese Madeira, India, and China began arriving before the slaves were emancipated. The motive for their importation was a continuing supply of cheap and easily disciplined labor. While Indian immigration was confined to only a few areas in Jamaica, the production of sugar in Guyana and Trinidad was totally dependent upon immigrants. All immigrants entered the society at the bottom, replacing the lowest-status workers, and most have remained there. Whether they escaped from plantation labor or not, immigrant groups continued to be identified primarily by race and this has introduced complications into the class system. Most importantly it has militated against the creation of broad class movements, but the manner in which race was associated with upward mobility is also of the greatest interest.

The first immigrants to move out of plantation labor were the Portuguese in Guyana. Between 1840 and 1850, Portuguese immigrants to Guyana exchanged their place as sugar-workers for a near-monopoly of the retail trade. It is not easy to explain why they should have been able to do this. Certainly white importers gave credit preference to the Portuguese, mainly because they believed that they were unsuitable for field labor. But one of the reasons they were unsuitable for field labor was that they drank too much—hardly the best reference for a high credit rating. During the slavery period, free colored hucksters handled retail trade by traveling round the estates selling cloth and other imported goods to slaves. These people were driven out of business in a very short time. It is sometimes argued that the Portuguese and other similar marginal groups succeed in business enterprises of this kind because they have no close kinship ties with their customers. Others point out that Portuguese, Chinese, Indians, and Syrians come from societies with long traditions of literacy, trade, and accounting, or that, being strangers, they are able to seize upon opportunities not perceived by established elements. None of these explanations is very convincing, but the fact remains that many occupational specializations quickly became structured along racial lines. There is just enough truth in Naipaul's story of the Trinidad baker to make it worth repeating here. The story is quoted by Sidney Mintz from Naipaul's book *A Flag on the Island.* The hero is a black baker who, having learned his trade from a Chinese, opens his own shop only to find that nobody busy from him. He explains why:

> When black people in Trinidad go to a restaurant they don't like to see black people meddling with their food. And then I see that though Trinidad have every race and every colour, every race have to do special things. But look, man. If you want to buy a snowball [flavored ice], who you buying it from? You wouldn't buy it from an Indian or a Chinee or a Potogee. You would buy it from a black man. And I myself, when I was getting my place in Arouca fix up, I didn't employ Indian carpenters or masons. If an Indian in Trinidad decide to go into the carpentering business the man would starve. Who ever see an Indian carpenter?.... And look at the laundries. If a black man open a laundry, you would take clothes to it? I wouldn't take my clothes there.... And then all sorts of things fit into place. You remember that the Chinee people didn't let me serve bread across the counter? I used to think that it was because they didn't trust me with the rush. But it wasn't that. It was that, if they did let me serve, they would have no rush at all. You ever see anybody buying their bread off a black man? (Mintz 1974: 48).

The hero solves his problem by putting his Chinese wife to serve behind the counter.

One should not exaggerate the continuing monopolization of "occupational niches" by racial groups; most of it was due to the erection of barriers by groups already established in a particular occupation, barriers which took their form from an existing system of racial differentiation which then became further rationalized by attributing special aptitudes to already defined races. But even when these barriers to occupational mobility have been weakened or broken down, racial identification continues to cut across class and to distort incipient class solidarities. This is most clearly evident in Guyana, where the rural population is no longer specialized in economic activities by race, but race is still the major line of cleavage in the society as a whole.

An urban sector of the lower class has always existed and has become much more important in the twentieth century. Urban occupations have included domestic service (which merits extended treatment in its own right and has recently begun to receive more attention (Higman 1978; Rubbo & Taussing 1977), general laboring in transport including dock labor, construction and a very limited manufacturing sector. The urban laboring class has always been swollen by large numbers of unemployed and underemployed persons, though never to the extent one finds today.

A skilled working class was required from the earliest days of plantation cultivation and we have already seen how free colored came to replace whites as carpenters, masons, coopers, coppersmiths and the like. As the colored seized upon education as the means of entry to white-collar occupations, blacks took their place in the skilled occupations. Although many Indians are in skilled trades, they have tended to specialize in shopkeeping or in occupations such as taxi-driving which involve self-employment.

We have seen that the lower class had virtually no political representation during the nineteenth century, it was the theory of Crown Colony Government that the Governor would represent the interests of the unrepresented classes—by which was meant the laboring population. In practice, workers made their views known by whatever means were available to them: by riots, strikes, the beating of estate overseers, and by the widespread stealing of growing crops. The highlights of such activities are well-known—the Morant Bay rebellion of 1865 in Jamaica or the 1938 riots which swept through the whole of the West Indies. But there was a steady day-by-day conflict between plantation workers and management which is usually ignored. It took a very long time for these conflicts to become structured through collective bargaining, and when trade unions were organized in the early twentieth century, they tended to be closely intertwined with movements of racial solidarity. Their leadership was almost invariably assumed by members of the intelligentsia of lawyers, doctors, dentists, journalists, and the like, a development which was partly due to the nature of the political system in which incipient parties seized upon trade unions as a useful vehicle for political mobilization, and partly due to the existence of racial solidarities cutting across class lines. However, the term "racial solidarities" conceals a great deal of difference in the meaning attributed to race by the different class elements. Whereas the middle-class elites saw themselves as being in all respects as "cultured" and educated as the English whom they wished to join or supplant at the apex of the society, at the very bottom of the status hierarchy groups retained a much stronger identification with African or East Indian culture. The poorer section of the Jamaican lower class developed its own forms of fundamental Christianity interlaced with elements of African-derived liturgy. Pocomania, and later Rastafarianism, flourished in Jamaica while in Guyana the East Indian population never abandoned Hinduism and Islam. The more politically organized forms of "cultural nationalism" began after World War I. Marcus Garvey is the best-known Jamaican of this period and his Universal Negro Improvement Association, despite its emphasis on racial pride and a return to Africa, was deeply imbued with the culture and symbolism of colonial society. It represented the ultimate frustration of blacks operating within an ostensibly universalistic achievement system which nevertheless defined achievement in terms of an impossible total Anglicization. In that respect, it was typical of all the racial organizations such as the East Indian Association and the League of Coloured Peoples. There is a sense in which the only way to break out of the confines of the colonial value system was to assert black or Indian racial solidarity in opposition to white domination; in Guyana and Trinidad the aftermath of that necessary assertion has been tragic in dividing blacks and Indians against each other.

## CONCLUSION

Although it can be shown that there has been relatively little change in the structure of concepts of race in Caribbean societies, it is necessary to distinguish between cultural conceptions of the kind referred to here, and "values." Cultural conceptions are the elements which "define the nature and components of the world, the units of which it is made up, and the meaning of those units" (Schneider & Smith 1978: 6). Although such conceptions can be analyzed as if they existed outside time, they are never entirely divorced from valuation in their use in social practice. However, the valuation of racial differences seems capable of considerable variation without altering the fundamental structure of assumptions about the existence of race itself. Perhaps a contrasting case will make clear what I mean.

The island of Lamu is situated in the Indian Ocean just off the coast of Kenya; its social history is described in a book by Abdul Hamid el Zein, *The Sacred Meadows*. The book is an extremely complex analysis of religion and ritual practice in the context of social relations and I cannot do more than mention a few details here (El Zein 1974).

The history of Lamu is told in different ways by different groups. The first settlers were from Arabia and came in several different waves, which came to constitute a ranked hierarchy of intermarrying classes. An intrinsic part of that ranking was Islamic ritual. The people of Lamu began to expand to the mainland late in the eighteenth century and they bought slaves to cultivate rice for the India-Arabia trade. The slaves were of course Africans, and the *Wangwana*, the ruling class of Lamu, considered it a waste of time to try to give them anything but the rudiments of Islam since they were the accursed descendants of Ham. As in the Caribbean, slaves were divided into grades and one class of slaves was assigned to domestic service. Also as in the Caribbean, the ruling class took slave concubines and produced a new category of people. However, here the theory of conception was different from that in the Caribbean and posed a somewhat different ideological problem. According to the Lamu theory of conception, children are formed wholly from male substance and women are merely the vessel in which the substance develops. The ideological problem was—should the son of a man by a concubine be equal to sons born of free wives? In social practice they were not equal because they lived in the slave-quarters, ate inferior food, and so on. Human ingenuity soon came up with an amendment to the theory of conception to accommodate these facts. The *souriya* (concubines) were hot like a fire and anything put into them came out burned. Thus the offspring became "tarnished" in the terms used by West Indians such as Long. However, it was a somewhat different kind of "tarnish" and the ideology had different developmental possibilities. The son of a slave woman by a free man inherited his father's name and he was considered to be a patrilineal relative of his father's kin. The female child of a slave woman always inherited her mother's slave status and remained a slave with no complications of paternal descent. Usually she was married off to a high-status slave.

As one might expect, over time the male offspring of slave women and high-ranking men increased, and their increased numbers coincided with a decline in the economic ascendancy of the ruling class. I will not go into the details of Lamu history except to say that things were complicated by the entry into Lamu of a group of Arab immigrants who were *sharif*—that is, claimed direct descent from the Prophet by virtue of which they possessed *baraka*. Being low in the stratification system they took slave wives, or wives of low social status, but because of their emphasis upon descent they claimed that *any* son of a *sharif*, irrespective of maternity, was "light" in terms of spiritual quality. There is no need to go into the complications of the possible interaction of these various theories of descent, but the interesting comparative implication is that here we have a complex system of social differentiation involving slave status, race, and religious purity, and a marriage system which generates anomalous classes. What gives distinction to Zein's work is the manner in which he explores in great detail the interaction in social practice between different ideologies and their use in political and economic relations. Lamu has remained an extremely conservative Islamic community and a center of Islamic learning. Therefore the secular struggles of different status groups have been worked out mainly in terms of religious controversy. While the old aristocracy might still believe that only people of Arab origin are civilized, it is clear that the theories of conception and the cultural concepts of race do not permit a clear-cut distinction between "racially" pure Arabs and others. In fact, race is not part of the language of ritual, political, and economic status; the operative terms are religious charisma, or "light," and purity of descent from the Prophet. The latter does not in any way divide "Arabs" from "Africans" and there is no concept of "mixed blood" (see El Zein 1974 for further discussion).

This case demonstrates not only the importance of examining the whole context in which cultural constructions are used, but also the need for careful analysis of the constructs themselves. Lamu's people did not have the concept of race that West Indians share and this made a difference in the way in which the struggle between classes and status groups was conducted. Lamu has done its best to resist "modernization" and this is one reason for the continuing importance of religious and kinship values. The Caribbean is very different, not merely in its culture but also in its relation to European expansion and European capitalism.

John Rex once suggested that the Caribbean, because of the absence of modern industry, lacks the "tight political and economic framework" found in industrial societies and is, therefore, less amenable to class analysis than a society such as South Africa (Rex 1971: 401). He may be forgiven for accepting too much of M.G. Smith's arguments at face value, but I hope that I have made a sufficiently strong case in this paper for the applicability of class analysis, and for the fact that slavery was the first stage of a most complete absorption of these societies into a capitalist mode of production. Certainly by the last quarter of the nineteenth century there was a very tight political and economic framework; the marginality of the landless or semi-landless classes was an integral part of the system.

One of the most interesting features of the Caribbean is the way in which concepts of achievement have been assimilated to the idea of race. In the paper on Trinidad by Lloyd Braithwaite to which I referred earlier (1953), the assumption is made that the society is moving from a state where the values of particularism-ascription are dominant to one in which the adaptive sphere and its associated values of universalism-achievement have primacy. In Braithwaite's view, this movement has been impelled by the transmission of these values from Britain through the instrumentality of imperialism and its agents—the British Colonial Office appointees. Once having established schools and an open civil service, then no amount of nepotism in the appointment process could effectively hold back the tide of colored and black persons who claimed the right to admission on the basis of ability. This is a peculiarly favorable view of the effects of Crown Colony Government, and it neglects the extent to which "achievement" was predicated upon assimilation to a very particularistic model of status, a model which was indeed that of the British official class. There is something to be said for Edward Brathwaite's idea that, left to themselves, the West Indies (or Jamaica at least) would have been able to develop further into a truly creole society. (It is interesting that Brathwaite is a Barbadian, for Barbados is the only ex-British colony which had an unbroken history of operating under its own constitution without the imposition of Crown Colony Government. Its sugar industry was not radically transformed, it retained a resident white upper class, and although it is generally characterized as having had a "color bar," it is the one country that developed a deep sense of national unity and a common "culture"—even if it appeared abjectly pro-British at times.) It is possible that, with representative institutions and the development of trade with North America, the local elites may have become more responsive to the interests of the lower class—not because of any superior moral sense, but because they would have been bound together by economic relations of a quite different kind and would have further developed a local culture. When Crown Colony Government inserted British paternalism as the guardian of the interests of the "unrepresented" classes, it created a local middle class concerned only with itself, clamoring to be recognized as "English" (Afro-Saxon in more recent terminology) on account of its "cultural" attainments. It also coincided with the penetration into the West Indies of a quite different form of capitalist enterprise which transformed the sugar industry into a corporately owned and British-managed sector of the economy. Absentee ownership had been common enough before the middle of the nineteenth century, but some Englishmen had put down roots, shallow though they might have been. The English who ran Jamaica after 1865 had no roots in the country, no relatives among the colored population, and no respect for West Indians whatever their ability as cricketers, classical scholars, or barristers. What post-emancipation governor would have had five of his bastard children at school in Kingston, as did the Duke of Manchester in the first decades of the century?

The colored middle class played the pivotal role in post-emancipation society, from the point of view of societal integration at least. Although it defined itself in racial terms as being quite different from the blacks, the system permitted some limited mobility by blacks into the higher reaches of the status order, though this was hardly noticeable before the 1920s. Far from being a reflection of values stressing open achievement, this was a form of "sponsored" mobility in Turner's sense (Turner 1964), and the favored few were expected to undergo a process of "whitening" akin to that discussed by writers on Brazil (Degler 1971: 193). The logic of such a system of integration is the total disappearance of the Africans as a recognizably separate group—physically through intermarriage with lighter-colored people and culturally through, in this case, Anglicization.

Under these circumstances it is not surprising that, after the British departed, the emphasis of the independent states upon the equality of all racial groups in the building of the new nation soon came to be seen as a device to ensure the continued hegemony of the Anglicized elite, and the economically privileged position of the local capitalist classes formed out of the light-colored or white minorities. As I have shown, the spontaneous protests of the lower class and the labor movements, which partially contained them during the twentieth century, had always incorporated a racial element which was a reflection of the existential reality of the plight of African and Indian workers. But there is nothing more racist in the ideologies of Black Power or East Indian cultural nationalism than there is in the ideology of a multiracial state which makes that ideology the vehicle for the domination of society by a particular class. The legacy of post-emancipation society was a liberal ideology which embodied racial concepts within its very structure.

## ACKNOWLEDGMENT

I am grateful to the participants in the Leiden workshop in Racism and Colonialism, and to Professor William J. Wilson and his students, for comments on this paper. I regret that I have been unable to take Professor Wilson's advice to be more rigorous in my use of the term "racism," but I trust that the reader will have enough information to be able to distinguish between the various uses to which ideas of race difference have been put in Caribbean societies.

# CHAPTER TEN

# *Living in the Gun Mouth: Race, Class, and Political Violence in Guyana (1995)*

[T]he history which became part of the fund of knowledge or the ideology of the nation, state or movement is not what has actually been preserved in popular memory, but what has been selected, written, pictured, popularized and institutionalized by those whose function it is to do so.... [A]ll historians, whatever else their objectives, are engaged in this process inasmuch as they contribute, consciously or not, to the creation, dismantling and restructuring of images of the past which belong not only to the world of specialist investigation but to the public sphere of man as a political being.

—Eric Hobsbawm, "Introduction: Inventing Traditions," in Eric Hobsbawm and Terence Ranger (eds.), *The Invention of Tradition.*

## INTRODUCTION

Early in 1975 I visited a village in Guyana where I had lived for the whole of 1956. As I walked along what is rather grandly named "Main Street," an old man greeted me and we exchanged a few words before I moved on. The incident was hardly noteworthy, but one phrase, repeated several times—half anguished and half defiant—has remained clearly in my mind. He said, "Doc, we are living in the gun mouth here; living in the gun mouth." The phrase conjured up images of cannon and seige, even perhaps a war of attrition carried on by armies arrayed against each other and securely dug in for the long haul. But there was no visible warfare; no cannons; no smell of cordite or landscape of ruin. This apparently peaceful village of rice farmers showed definite signs of increased prosperity compared to 1956, with some splendid new houses and a vast proliferation of tractors and agricultural machinery.[1] However, it was very noticeable that almost all of the 250 Afro-Guyanese who had lived peacefully in this predominantly East Indian village for many, many years were gone. Both the dramatic image of living "in the gun mouth," and the disappearance of the Africans, had their origin in the events of the 1960s during a period of what is usually called "racial violence."

In a piece of inspired anticipation, Brackette Williams begins her 1991 book on Guyana with a long reference to the problems of Serb-Croat relations in Yugoslavia (Williams 1991). At the time she chose that opening there was little indication that the state of Yugoslavia was likely to disintegrate in the immediate future, nor of the eventual virulence of the "ethnic cleansing" that has accompanied that disintegration. Nor, I am sure, did she intend her discussion of Serbs and Croats to suggest any such radical dénouement for Guyana. However, Guyana experienced something of that particular sickness for a short time in the early 1960s; there was expulsion of minorities from rural communities, beatings and killings, and even proposals for dismantling the state and creating two "ethnic nations," African and East Indian. What began as a vague suggestion by some members of the Afro-Guyanese elite in the early 1960s was taken up and formalized as a proposal of *The Society for Racial Equality* and is still discussed by Guyanese inside and outside the country.[2]

In 1953 the then colony of British Guiana had its first elections under a new constitution intended as a first step toward independence. A socialist party, the People's Progressive Party, led by Dr. Cheddi Jagan, an Indian dentist, and Forbes Burnham, an African barrister, won handily and took office. One hundred and thirty-three days later the British Government announced that the constitution was suspended because of "communist subversion." In 1955 the party split into two factions, and in 1957 Mr. Burnham formed the People's National Congress, leaving Dr. Jagan as leader of a depleted People's Progressive Party. After 1957 the contest between these two parties was increasingly couched in terms of a struggle between Africans, represented by Mr. Burnham and the P.N.C., and Indians, represented by Dr. Jagan and the P.P.P. This was the background to the "racial violence" to which I referred earlier. From December 1964 to October of 1992, Guyana was governed by the People's National Congress as a virtual, and occasionally as a nominal, one-party state, effectively containing, but not eradicating, the conflicts and resentments that had been expressed during those years of violent confrontation between Indians and Africans. Now that the People's Progressive Party is back in office after the first reasonably free elections in twenty-eight years the configuration of forces appears to be remarkably similar to that in the 1960s.

The People's Progressive Party continues to find its main electoral support among Indo-Guyanese voters, and the People's National Congress is still regarded as the vehicle of Afro-Guyanese interests. If the cause of the violence of 1962, 1963, and 1964 was an upsurge of racial antipathy rooted in primordial identities and expressing itself in the struggle over political power, then it is logical to assume that the very same racism will assert itself once again. We have grown used to assuming that racial and ethnic conflict is inevitable—even natural—and in the worldwide scale of violent conflicts Guyana is hardly worth more than a passing mention. In this essay I argue that whatever racial antipathies exist in Guyana today are not the same as those of the 1960s; that the recasting of the politics of the 1960s in terms of racial antagonism was not an automatic reversion to "primordial identities," or even the reassertion of colonial hegemonic values, but a complex process in which many elements were involved, and in which even social scientists played a part. As such it raises interesting questions about how we choose to interpret political conflicts, about the images we adopt when we formulate research problems, and the way in which research becomes entangled in political processes.

Questions of race, ethnicity, and cultural pluralism are already the stuff of academic analyses of Guyana's ills, and those analyses are—and have long been—themselves a part of the political process in that unfortunate country, contributing not a little to the shape it has taken. Practically all of those writing about Guyana, and I include myself, invoke history, more or less explicitly, to enable understanding of the events with which we deal. Unfortunately the "history" is often of the most general kind, purporting to establish the root causes of present-day divisions and antagonisms in the society. Thus C.Y. Thomas has identified "racial disunity" as hampering the "objective unity" of the Guyanese working class; he attributes it to the introduction of indentured immigrants after the abolition of slavery and the process that "created a functional basis in the division of labor among the two ethnic groups of sugar workers [Africans in the factory and Indians in the field], and later generated two distinct areas of settlement near to each estate: the so-called African and Indian villages" (Thomas 1984: 83).[3]

Brackette Williams has shown in convincing detail how the contradictory ideologies of egalitarianism and hierarchy operate in social practice in the daily life of Guyanese, and I cannot praise too highly the quality of her analysis and the depth of her understanding of the process of cultural struggle in the everyday life of that country. However, her discussion of the way in which the various "racial/ethnic groups" were incorporated into the hierarchical structure of colonial society refers once again to a generally familiar image of historical development.[4] How did the hierarchy of apparently specialized positions come to be accepted by all the participants? She contends that

> ...formal policies and informal practices of both the dominating Anglo-European elite and the subordinated diverse elements of the non-elite population combines to form a framework of objective and ideological constraints within which the racial/ethnic groups developed different adaptive strategies for subsistence and social mobility (1991: 148).

This is a familiar argument, used to explain how the image of the "Land of Six Peoples," each with their special functions to fulfill, came to exist in the first place, as well as the supposed actual distribution of "races" through the occupational system. Demurring slightly from Drummond's argument that the stereotypes of "racial/ethnic" types become detached from any specific material processes (Drummond 1974: 51), Williams contends that this break is possible only because the stereotypes themselves were originally "tightly tied to the production of groups, of group identities, and of patterns of conduct among members of these groups" (1991: 152); subsequently the stereotypes were explained in terms of "blood," or race itself. I do not contest the accuracy of her historical material, but does it follow, as she asserts, that the relations among the subordinated non-European groups during the establishment of Anglo-European dominance "set the terms of the politics of cultural struggle in contemporary Guyana" (1991: 154), implying that the politics of cultural struggle have been shaped by those very terms over a long period of time?

Finally, it has been the constant refrain of so-called plural society theorists that Guyana is made up of sections that differ fundamentally in culture, and that whatever fragile unity exists is made possible only by the dominance of one superordinate section. Thus M.G. Smith contends that the unified independence movement of the early 1950s inevitably disintegrated,

> ...since, in addition to differences of race, colour, ecology, social organization, historical experience, religion and the like, the two segments (Creole and East Indian) were anchored in very different cultures and kinds of social structure, and accordingly differed profoundly in their economic needs and interests, even though their members seemed superficially to belong to such common inclusive classes as the "peasantry" or "proletariat." In other words, the unity forged by Jagan and Burnham in 1953 was more superficial and illusory than it seemed; and so were the prospects of Indian assimilation, Guyanese integration and modernization" (M.G. Smith 1984: 110–111).

The implication of all these invocations of Guyana's past is that it would take a major revolution to render that past neutral—or at least less potent—in shaping the present. Without conceding the potency of that imagined past, I want to argue, as I have previously, that a revolution of sorts was in process of being made. As Clifford Geertz observed some years ago, "The men who raised this challenge (of creating a proper "nationality" in the modern manner), the nationalist intellectuals, were...launching a revolution as much cultural, even epistemological, as it was political"

(Geertz 1971: 362). In British Guiana that revolution was stopped dead in its tracks by outside agents working upon the very forces that nationalism was striving to overcome. Discussion of this period cannot be divorced from questions of value and of international politics, nor can it ignore the important part played by the nationalist intellectuals and the manner in which they shaped and trimmed the ideologies through which the struggle for power was conducted. However, I do not suppose that one can attain a complete understanding of the process of social transformation by concentrating solely upon the macro-structures of the state and its articulation with Cold War politics. Although I begin with a brief recounting of the background to, and the nature of, the so-called racial violence of the 1960s, it is important to ask how and why the general populace responded in that particular way to the actions of national leaders and their patrons in London or in Washington, Havana or Moscow, and how social scientists have chosen to interpret those events.

## BACKGROUND TO "RACIAL VIOLENCE"

When I arrived in British Guiana in May of 1951, I entered a society where Anglo-European hegemony was not yet ghostly, to use Brackette Williams's image, but very much alive. Queen Victoria's birthday was still celebrated as "Empire Day" on May 24th with a school holiday, free cakes and drinks for schoolchildren, a message from the monarch, and a parade in the capital, led by the Governor and Colonial Secretary on horseback. These ritual spectacles of Empire did not neutralize the pervasive discontent and opposition to colonial rule that had been growing for many years and had been given additional impetus by other theatrical events over the previous decade.

The visits of a series of investigators and royal commissions appointed to make recommendations for alleviating economic distress and countering the violent protests that had swept through the region during the late 1930s were the occasion of intense public interest: in January and February of 1939, the West India Royal Commission led by Lord Moyne held public hearings in Georgetown. The proceedings were relayed from the hearing chamber to a large public gathering on Bourda Green. Both the sugar industry and the British administration were harshly criticized by a stream of witnesses ranging from clergymen (most of them either British or Canadian) to trade unionists, professionals of all kinds, politicians, leaders of voluntary associations, and representatives of both the East Indian Association and the Negro Progress Convention. The memoranda submitted to the Commission by the various bodies are a rich source of information on discontent, and also on the nature of racial stereotypes. Thus, the East Indian Association stated unequivocally that East Indians did not wish to lose their racial and religious identity, preferring to retain contact with Mother India, though willing to work with others for the social and economic betterment of the country. The Sugar Producer's Association (the focal point of white economic power) submitted a memorandum that described the African Guyanese sugar worker as "essentially a gay, emotional person, fatalistic in his attitude to life, and as a rule taking no thought for tomorrow. His main requirements," they said, "are food, shelter, bright and attractive clothing, a little spare money for rum and gambling, and the opportunity for easy love making" (Chase 1964: 94). A young journalist who covered the hearings wrote subsequently, "it all added up to laying bare in all its nakedness the social history and present plight of a deprived people" (Drayton n.d.: 21). Sir Walter Citrine, the British trade unionist who was a member of the Commission, felt it necessary to try to neutralize the frequent allegations that disturbances and discontent stemmed from "communist subversion," a formula that was to play a crucial part in the events of 1953. The recommendations of the West India Commission were radical and far-reaching, at least within the possibilities of a colonial order as exploitative as that of Britain, and a whole apparatus of "development and welfare" was set up.

Political theatrics continued in British Guiana with the visit of the Constitutional Commission that arrived in December of 1950 and departed in mid-February 1951, bringing political issues into the forefront of social consciousness once more. There was another parade of witnesses in a series of public hearings, and once again the opportunity existed for the airing of racist sentiments. Such sentiments were rarely expressed, but the Commission was moved to observe that while the Indian population had previously been inclined to "resist assimilation" it now had come to a "realisation of their permanent place in Guianese life and to a demand for equal participation in it," a challenge that "has stimulated the other races into closing their ranks" (British Guiana Constitutional Commission 1951: 14). They continued:

> Race is a patent difference and is a powerful slogan ready to the hand of unscrupulous men who can use it as a stepping stone to political power.... We do not, however, wish it to be thought that life in British Guiana is dominated by racial tension, or that there are not many heartening signs of the development of a genuine Guianese outlook.... We were...impressed by the amity with which peoples of all races live side by side in the villages, where mutual dependence is, of necessity, recognised. It was reassuring to find that racialism spoke with a hesitant voice in public, and that virtually no proposals for communal representation were made to us (1951: 14–15).

The Commission recommended a constitution for British Guiana that established universal adult suffrage to elect a legislature from which a majority of the executive would be drawn. The details of the constitutional arrangements are not important (details may be found in the report of Constitutional Commission, or in R.T. Smith 1980); suffice it to say that these reports, along with the rising tide of expectations throughout the British colonies, stimulated an enormous interest in the coming elections scheduled for the spring of 1953.

In the period immediately before the elections of 1953 there was considerable dissension within the People's Progressive Party over the wisdom of adopting an extremely radical left-wing posture. The local newspapers, and particularly the *Daily Argosy* (a vehicle for official and big-business interests), maintained a persistent barrage of criticism against the communist leanings of the People's Progressive Party. Several of the early supporters of the party left because of their embarrassment over the tone of the party newspaper, *Thunder,* and it so happened that the majority of them were Afro-Guyanese. This does not mean that all the party "radicals" were Indo-Guyanese; among the most militant were Africans, Chinese, and persons who would have been classified as "Mixed" or "Coloured." However, Burnham had the largest popular following, especially in Georgetown, where he was an active trade union organizer. Although he was urged by many of his friends to leave the party, he refused because, as he frequently said, it was important to maintain the party as a genuinely multiracial vehicle for political reform. The most vociferous opponents of the P.P.P. were actually Indo-Guyanese, and Dr. Jagan has provided a very full, and generally reliable, account of the configuration of parties and factions, including their use of racial appeals, during the campaign leading up to the elections of 1953 (Jagan 1966: Chapter 7). He has also described the week of crisis following the electoral victory of the P.P.P., a week during which there was intense rivalry between Jagan and Burnham over the distribution of ministries and nominations for the positions of State Councillor (Jagan 1966: 137–39). Unfortunately there is no comparable written account by Burnham.

During the 133 days that the original People's Progressive Party held office, there is no record of conflict among the party leadership, which is not to say that conflict did not exist. The parliamentary group provided a common front against the governor, Sir Alfred Savage, and in favor of a number of measures that were later referred to as evidence of a communist plot to subvert the constitution (see British Guiana Constitutional Commission 1954; R.T. Smith 1980; Henfrey 1972; Jagan 1966). When the constitution was suspended on October 9, 1953, Burnham and Jagan went together to London to brief the Parliamentary Labour Party leaders, just as a collection of Guianese opponents of the P.P.P. rushed off to consult with the British government, then led by the Conservative Party under Winston Churchill. They subsequently went on an extended tour of Europe and India together, but without winning the enthusiastic support of the Indian government. In the editorial Introduction to a collection of Burnham's speeches, clearly written with Burnham's approval, the editors say:

> Before the restrictions, Burnham travelled to England with Jagan to protest the British decision (to suspend the constitution). He knew, however, that Jagan's devotion to the communist cause transcended his commitment to his own country. As a nationalist, Burnham was already questioning in his own mind the wisdom of continuing his alliance with Jagan…. By the time they had returned to Guiana, Burnham had made up his mind to part company with Jagan unless the latter was prepared to put Guianese nationalism above posturing as an international communist (Burnham 1970: xix).

Whatever the historical accuracy of this statement it is clear that Burnham carefully positioned himself as a moderate against Jagan's radicalism, and the 1954 commission reporting on the causes of the suspension of the constitution identified Burnham as "the leader of the socialists in the Party" as against Dr. Jagan and five others who were "enthusiastic supporters of the policies and practices of modern communist movements and were contemptuous of the European social democratic parties, including the British Labour Party" (quoted in Jagan 1966: 199–200). The events of the period between the elections of 1953 and the attainment of independence in 1966 have been detailed in a number of publications so that I shall present here only the most schematic account (see R.T. Smith 1971, 1976, 1980; Newman 1964; Reno 1964; Jagan 1966; Despres 1967; Glasgow 1970; Lutchman 1974; Henfrey 1972; Danns 1982).

In 1955 Burnham attempted to seize control of the People's Progressive Party from Jagan but merely succeeded in splitting the party leadership into two factions. Burnham's editors laconically report that "Burnham defeated Jagan for the party's leadership at internal party elections" (Burnham 1970: xx), whereas Jagan has a complex ten-page discussion of the events, claiming that Burnham had engineered an illegal party congress, packed with his supporters. Jagan and his supporters walked out of the meeting, which proceeded to replace Jagan with Burnham as leader of the party and to demote the most militant of Jagan's supporters to minor positions in the leadership. The details are not particularly relevant to an understanding of the fact that these maneuvers were designed to reduce the influence of the "extremists" and enhance Burnham's position in the eyes of the British and the United States. They paralleled the 1952 expulsion of the "radicals" from the Jamaican People's National Party. Burnham was perfectly well aware that the split in the party could encourage racial polarization, and in that respect the situation was quite different from Jamaica. Indeed he warned against such a development in an article published in his faction's edition of *Thunder,* the organ of the People's Progressive Party (Burnham 1970: 7–8).

The first election to be held under a revised constitution, with limited powers assigned to the elected representatives, was held in August of 1957; both factions of the P.P.P. contested the elections, along with a number of smaller parties. When the results were announced the Jagan faction had won nine of the fourteen seats, the Burnham faction three seats, and two other, anticommunist parties, one seat each. Following these elections Burnham absorbed the more conservative, and predominantly African, United Democratic Party, forming a new party under the name People's National Congress. This could be interpreted as a further move to the right on Burnham's part, but it also consolidated the racial basis of his support. The next step forward in the resumption of progress toward political independence for British Guiana came with the elections of August 1961 that were widely accepted to be the prelude to the negotiation of independence. Political forces had been concentrated by this time into just three significant parties. Apart from the P.N.C. and the P.P.P., a new party had appeared under the label United Force. Under the leadership of a successful Guianese businessman, Peter D'Aguiar, it absorbed most of the extreme anticommunist forces. By this time there was a general recognition that a coalition government would be best for the country, since the support of the principal parties was now divided along lines that coincided with both urban-rural divisions and race, but all attempts to effect a reconciliation between Jagan and Burnham failed. For all the declarations of the various leaders, they increasingly had to cater to the interests of constituencies that were perceived to be racial. However, the rhetoric of the campaigns concentrated on other issues, with the United Force taking a strongly anticommunist line against the People's Progressive Party, and Burnham attacking the P.P.P. as extremist, in the hope that the fear of communism would sway the rural Indian farmers, rice millers, and shopkeepers. In the event the P.P.P. won twenty of the thirty-five seats, while the P.N.C. won eleven and the United Force, four. Jagan was named premier and the stage seemed set for a rapid move to independence, especially as Burnham had been vociferous in declaring that he would press for immediate independence no matter which party won a majority of seats. In fact, the victory of the P.P.P. in the 1961 elections was the prelude to a prolonged campaign of destabilization aimed at removing Jagan and the P.P.P. from control of the country.

Large sums of money were poured into the country from the United States to support activities aimed at toppling Jagan's government, activities ranging from the financing of religious, newspaper, and magazine campaigns to the organizing of strikes and disturbances. In a speech delivered on November 5, 1961 to the Annual Congress of the P.N.C., Burnham outlined his strategy for political action in the wake of the P.P.P. victory. He began by making a case for proportional representation on the grounds that the P.P.P. had won twenty seats in the Legislative Assembly with 93,000 votes, or 42.6 percent of the votes cast, while the P.N.C. with 89,000, or 41 percent, had gained only eleven seats, and the United Force with 16.3 percent of the votes cast had won only four seats. He observed that "the P.P.P., regardless of what its leaders may say or think, represents to its adherents and supporters as well as to their opponents an Indian racial victory" (Burnham 1970: 15), and went on to say that "the People's Progressive Party is not to be retained, but contained and repelled" by the People's National Congress.

Joining increasingly with D'Aguiar and the United Force, Burnham launched an unrelenting attack on every proposal made by the P.P.P. government, fomenting demonstrations and strikes that led to arson, violence, and various forms of civil disobedience. Unable to contain the unrest with the police resources available, Jagan was forced to ask the British to send troops to restore order. At the same time, he attempted to break the strikes by depending upon Cuba to supply gasoline and to provide a market for Guyana's rice. There is no doubt that Jagan moved closer to the U.S.S.R. and its satellites as the United States and Britain became firmer in their resolve to remove him. And they saw the opportunity in the imposition of proportional representation that permitted a coalition of the P.N.C. and the U.F. to assume office following the 1964 general election. Treating the whole country as one constituency, the P.P.P. secured 109,332 votes, the P.N.C. 96,567, the U.F. 26,612, and four minor parties gained only 2,929 among them. The P.P.P. was awarded twenty-four seats, the P.N.C. twenty-two, and the U.F. seven seats, giving the P.N.C.–U.F. coalition a majority of five, enough to justify the British Governor in asking them to form a government. From that point forward the United States threw its support behind Burnham, who quickly cast off his dependence on the United Force, seized control of the state apparatus, and ensured that future elections would produce favorable results for him and his party (see Jagan 1966; R.T. Smith 1971, 1976; Reno 1964; Despres 1967; Glasgow 1970; Lutchman 1974; Henfrey 1972; Danns 1982 for detailed accounts of events leading up to this election). As Arthur Schlesinger wrote in his account of the Kennedy administration, "With much unhappiness and turbulence British Guiana seemed to have passed safely out of the communist orbit" (1967: 713).

The struggles of these political leaders over control of the state and its organs has to be seen in the context of global forces of economic and political domination. They shaped their ideologies, strategies, and tactics in accordance with their perception of what was possible in the world arena. But what enabled them to carry along their supporters? The White Paper published by the United Kingdom Government on October 20, 1953, setting out the reasons for the suspension of the constitution, included among its allegations the charge that the original People's Progressive Party had attempted to impose a totalitarian form of government that included the "organization of small cells for recruitment and indoctrination" (British Guiana Suspension of the Constitution 1953: 11) If this had been true it would have been an extremely interesting development, but when one looks at the situation from the bottom up, so to speak, the perspective is quite different.

## LOCAL AND NATIONAL HIERARCHIES

Such a "bottom-up" perspective is suggested by a number of different developments in anthropology. The growing influence of Foucault (already on the wane in some places); the appeal of Gramsci's writings on ideology and the importance of the hegemonic force of civil society as opposed to direct domination by the state and its coercive power (Gramsci 1971: 12); and the burgeoning literature on resistance and subaltern studies all direct attention to the articulation of power that is diffused throughout the lower levels of complex societies. In a recent paper, Diane Austin-Broos has suggested that the tendency to identify the "political...in terms of nationalist or class-based movements responsive to colonialism or neo-colonialism, and (to use) the 'cultural'...to denote all those other modes of practice and imagery that are not especially concerned with the domain of the state" is a mistake that neglects the importance of a "politics of moral order" that is in no way subservient "to the logic of a politics of state" (Austin-Broos 1992:

294–95). Her specific analysis of Jamaican Pentecostalism has limited application to Guyana, but it converges nicely with Brackette Williams' admonition that

> Rather than insisting on class analysis, if our interest is in disclosing how inequalities stemming from objective conditions are exacerbated or left unremedied by nationalist ideologies and ethnic reactions, we must provide detailed accounts of how ideological fields operate to sustain the pragmatic subordination and the divisive intents of a diverse population (Williams 1991: 29).

And by the same token those detailed accounts will show how politics are carried forward in diverse domains. Instead of asking how a society-wide system of classes is represented at the level of local communities one can ask more profitably how systems of power are represented or contested there, and how they articulate with class and status groups in a wider structure of inequality.

Paying attention to the micro-processes of status contestation fits with a reconsideration of Max Weber's work on class, status, and power. The standard interpretation of Weber is that he took Marx's concept of class and decomposed it into class, status, and power. Every sociology student learns the simple definitions of these concepts, derived, usually, from the inadequate translations by Gerth and Mills (Weber 1946). To reduce economic, prestige, and power considerations to "variables" not only does violence to Weber's intentions, but fails to grasp the complex interpenetration of these abstracted elements. Weber used a number of different concepts that are usually all translated as "social stratification." His preferred term was *Gliederung*, meaning articulation or structure, with articulation being much closer to Weber's intention than stratification, and more useful as an image of class/status distribution. I rely here upon Daniel Wolk's recent reconsideration of Weber's work that has uncovered shortcomings in the translations of Weber's texts, leading to serious distortions of his intentions (Wolk 1994). Weber's concepts of class situation and status situation are still most useful for mapping the terrain of structures of inequality; that is, the pattern of distribution of class and status that defines a structure or order of inequality. However, they demand consideration "from the bottom up."

The patterns of distribution of the material and symbolic conditions of life among groups, and categories of individuals, define their situations of both class and *Stand,* or status group. Social scientists have generally interpreted Weber to mean that social class and social honor can be measured as the attributes of individuals which can then be aggregated to reveal the structures of inequality. This oversimplifies a complex and subtle argument, as Wolk so ably demonstrates.

Weber regarded *Stand*—honor or prestige—as the decisive distributive element in a social order, but he recognised that it applies to groups, and not to individuals. This is why style of life *(Lebensführung)* is such an important element in the self-characterization of groups; these styles of life are in competition with one another, so that it is the *relations among groups,* not individual characteristics, that are at stake. To attempt to score individual prestige on a uniform scale of ranking is quite useless (and impossible in practice as Shils so convincingly argued in 1968) since each status group asserts the value of its style of life without necessarily conceding a position of inferiority in a status order. Therefore, one has to study and record the oppositional characterizations of groups. At their simplest these may involve statements such as "those people are ignorant" in contrast to us, who are educated (a commonly heard sentiment in Guyana); or those people have disorganized families, as opposed to us who really value families; but the contrasts may be much more complex and subtle. The increase in the number of villagers building personal

Hindu shrines in the 1970s seemed to have a great deal to do with racial polarization stemming from the 1960s that had deflected Indians from expressing status through "creolization." Not that such a process had been halted; many, perhaps most, Indians living in Georgetown continued to be conspicuous consumers of imported goods. One wondered just what was being said by the rice farmer on the West Coast Demerara district who, in the 1950s, displayed his American car in a glass garage.

Class situation is different from status situation in that it applies to individuals who specifically do *not* form a group. But class situation is not merely possession or non-possession of goods. People become a class when they are subject to the same market conditions where the life-chances, as Weber puts it, depend upon the control of material property, which in turn permits the conversion of mere wealth into capital, facilitating the monopolization of the "opportunities for making profit through exchange." Class situation in this sense is *not* just a matter of income distribution, but takes into account the influence on life-chances of being able to dispose of marketable objects. Although these are "material" objects, Weber uses the word *sachlich* (material) in such a way that it can include all kinds of impersonal things such as bookkeeping systems, expert ways of doing things as disparate as business dealings, political lobbying, or controlling material objects. When seen in this light, Weber's concept of class is quite close to that of Marx, but broadens somewhat the concept of "control of the means of production."

Unlike Marx, Weber regarded the persistence of status groups in modern complex societies to be one of their most fundamental features. Groups based on kinship, race, religion, or other "primordial" characteristics are joined by others that are the very products of the apparently rational-legal and bureaucratic processes of modern society. Among the most important of these are the products of modern educational institutions that claim the right to distribute certificates, degrees, and diplomas, thus controlling the admission of individuals to the charmed circles of the "educated." In modern economies, the market is a mechanism for the balancing of interests in a purely impersonal and non-subjective manner that makes it the ideal-typical case of pure economic order, in which "pure class situation, nakedly and unambiguously, visibly to everyone, looms as the power that determines everybody's destiny" (Weber 1968: 953). Even so, a new kind of *Ständliche* development takes place as bureaucrats create new status groups based on education or certification, limiting entry to their ranks on the basis of possessing degrees, certificates, or diplomas. Within the organizations that produce "qualified" individuals, status distinctions based on the most trivial activities appear, such as those among different fraternities, sororities, or sporting activities. It is not difficult to see the relevance of this for the modern Caribbean. Bourdieu has shown how the actual designation of groups by occupation really serves to mask the true basis of their recruitment and membership.

> The members of groups based on co-option…(doctors, architects, professors, engineers, etc.) always have something else in common beyond the characteristics explicitly demanded. The common image of the professions…is less abstract than that presented by statisticians; it takes into account not only the nature of the job and the income, but those secondary characteristics which are often the basis of their social value (prestige or discredit) and which, though absent from the official job description, function as tacit requirements, such as age, sex, social or ethnic origin, overtly or implicitly guiding co-option choices…so that members of the corps who lack these traits are excluded or marginalized (Bourdieu 1984: 102–103).

For all the reasons outlined here, it is more useful to follow Weber (and Wolk's reconsiderations of his work) and refer to "structures of inequality" than to use the dubious concept of "social stratification," and to view such structures as the articulation of a complex series of status groups. Class and status groups are inextricably intertwined, each conditioning the other rather than being separate "variables" in a calculable matrix.

If we now return to Guyana, following Diane Austin's advice to consider the way in which power is concentrated within various status groups rather than asking how class and race segment the society as a totality, we may be able to attain a better understanding of the course taken by violence in the 1960s. It would be unrealistic to expect that concepts of race, steretotypes, or whatever we want to call the residues of Anglo-European hegemony, will simply fade away.[5] Discussions of "integration" that assume it to mean complete homogeneity, as opposed to "pluralism," are hardly worth consideration. The discussion of Caribbean societies has been imprisoned in the straightjacket of the plural society debate for far too long; any reasonable discussion of post-colonial society must take into account the conflict and contestation that inevitably accompanies any process of nation building or state formation. As Bourdieu points out, at the level of professional organization, various forms of social origin, including putative race, will long continue to be a part of the process of group formation, even in those groups that are supposedly rational-bureaucratic. The question is not whether cultural constructions of race continue to exist in the modern world—they do—but under what conditions does "race" or "ethnicity" come to be a major fault line in the society, making for violence of the kind that was seen in British Guiana in the 1960s. What does ethnography tell us about the way in which race and cultural differences infused the quotidian experience of rural Guyanese and their status considerations?

## AFRICAN GUYANESE AND THE VEHICLES OF THEIR RELATION TO COLONIAL SOCIETY

I first went to British Guiana with the express intention of studying a "Negro village." That fact is, in itself, an interesting commentary on the manner in which anthropological problems were formulated in the early 1950s. Without going into the details of the manner in which colonial interests shaped anthropological research, suffice it to say that both official and academic forces inclined anthropologists working in the British colonies to focus upon the study of supposedly coherent entities within colonial societies. Thus, contemporaries going to Africa formulated projects for the study of this or that "tribe," while work in the Caribbean was focused upon this or that "racial/class group." Lloyd Braithwaite did his first study in the village of Blanchisseuse, considered to be a remote "Negro" village in Trinidad, not far from Melville and Frances Herskovits's field site of Toco, and he followed it up with the study of a predominantly East Indian community near Port-of-Spain. However, both Braithwaite and I attempted to locate our studies in a wider context of colonial society, and this was already the period when Fernando Henriques was writing about the color/class system of Jamaica, and Julian Steward and his students were attempting a portrait of Puerto Rican society as a whole. Still, even those efforts worked through the medium of the community study and with a particular vision of the totality within which the community was embedded.

After a few weeks of surveying I found what was widely recognized to be a "very African" village in the West Coast Berbice district. This designation was used by the villagers, who had a lively sense of the founding of the two original sections of the village by groups of ex-slaves who pooled their resources and purchased title to the land. As I explained in my first book on British Guiana (1956), that land had been passed down to the present inhabitants with a strong presumption that it should not be alienated to "strangers" in general and to East Indians in particular. Just to the west of August Town (a fictitious name), lay one of the largest East Indian villages in the country, the village that has been described in detail by Marilyn Silverman under the name of Rajgahr (Silverman 1980). Maintaining these fictitious names, once an anthropological convention, is a waste of time. Anyone in Guyana can easily recognise which villages are being written about, and indeed Marilyn Silverman provides a map of her area with the correct name of "August Town" (which is Hopetown) clearly marked, just as I referred to her "Rajgahr" by its correct name in various places. Nonetheless, in order to avoid confusion I will continue to use the fictitious names here. The farmers of Rajghar were desperately short of rice land and cattle pasture, while August Town residents had large amounts of uncultivated land that they were unwilling to sell, or even to rent. The generalized fear of losing land had been formalized in a village council resolution during the 1930s, asserting that title to village land would not be granted to any person not born there—including immigrant spouses, regardless of race.

In spite of this, relations between August Town and Rajgahr were, while not exactly close, at least cordial in 1951. Rajgahr men frequently stopped off in August Town rum shops on their way home from the sugar estate at Bath; Rajgahr women regularly sold vegetables in August Town at the early morning market (see Plate I in Smith 1956, facing p. 32); the East Indian headmaster of the Rajgahr Lachmansingh Memorial Canadian Mission (Presbyterian) School lived in a rented house in August Town; some August Town people regularly went to weddings in Rajgahr, especially since they had kin there through intermarriages among Africans, Chinese, and East Indians that had taken place over many years; and some August Town rice farmers had their padi milled by Rajgahr millers. An August Town African had been an elected member, and even elected Chairman, of the Rajgahr Village District Council (Silverman 1980: 54–63). August Town proper was bordered on the east by a private estate owned by a family of East Indians who were very much a part of what I referred to as the August Town elite. That family sold the estate after I left, but when I returned for a further three months fieldwork in 1975, the estate was owned by yet another East Indian who had greatly improved the estate house and was successfully growing rice on a large scale. The old store in the middle of the village that had been owned by a Portuguese family was now splendidly improved but owned by an East Indian popularly known as "Nutcake," not because of any presumed mental peculiarities, but because he had started out some years earlier as a vendor of coconut cake and had gradually increased his fortune to the point where he was able to buy and improve the old store and purchase a hire car in which he made a daily run to Georgetown and back.

I could go on to detail the ways in which the tissue of everyday relations involved individuals severally identified as African, East Indian, Chinese, Portuguese, and so forth, relations that were largely blanked out by the decision to study "an African village," and showed complicity in the ideological vision of British Guiana as a "Land of Six Peoples." However, I also want to stress the fact that the processes of "cultural struggle" described by Brackette Williams involved few elements deriving from Indian/African relations, partly because of the relative segregation of August Town and Rajgahr, but also because Anglo-European hegemony was all too real and had not yet become ghostly. The August Town elite—head teachers, the Portuguese storekeeper, the wealthy

Indian family—and its extensions in the district including the District Commissioner, the Police Inspector, the Medical Officer, and the English manager of the nearby sugar plantation, all ordered their status striving in relation to the signs and symbols of British domination. The headmaster of the August Town Congregational School, who was very much a local African person, had a photograph of himself prominently displayed on the wall of his house flanked by photographs of the current King and Queen of England, while on the opposite wall were prints of "The Artful Dodger," "Oliver Twist," "Duty Calls," and "The Hero's Return." Individuals like this mixed freely with persons of other "races," as when they played bridge or attended each other's parties, and they represented to the village population the mode of their articulation with the colonial society.

When the report of the Constitutional Commission was published in October 1951, it aroused very little interest in August Town. Many people thought that universal adult suffrage was a mistake since it would inevitably result in large-scale bribery and corruption, and insofar as anyone had an opinion on the matter it was just as likely to prefer that British Guiana continue to be run by outsiders, as that it should be independent. Among the more politically aware, the major struggle was perceived to be a struggle against the poverty and backwardness imposed by an exploitative economic system represented by "King Sugar" in particular and colonialism in general. As the campaign for the 1953 elections gathered momentum, this relative apathy dissipated and August Town, like other rural areas of British Guiana, became caught up in the excitement of a new beginning. However, the rising fortunes of the People's Progressive Party did not result in the creation of new status groups in August Town; traditional elites and the general populace divided their support among a number of parties and individuals, and insofar as they rallied to the P.P.P., they were attracted by Forbes Burnham's accomplishments as an orator, as a Guyana scholar, a barrister, and all the other marks of mastery of English culture.

Although August Town was—and is—a poor village, it had long been closely articulated with many aspects of colonial society. I have described elsewhere the remarkable absence from Guyana of syncretistic African Christian churches, especially when compared to Jamaica (R.T. Smith 1976). African villages in Guyana have generally been tightly integrated into churches controlled from the capital, Georgetown, and ultimately from Britain or, in the case of the Catholic Church, more recently from the United States. August Town's Anglican and Congregational Churches claimed the allegiance of the vast majority of villagers, while only a minuscule number of people belonged to small chapters of the Jehovah's Witnesses. At the same time there was a lively, but generally clandestine, participation in various forms of African-derived religious practices ranging from spiritual healing to witch-finding to "Cumfa" rituals (see R.T. Smith 1976: 327–32). In an ideal-typical way they could be said to be comparable to Jamaican Pentecostalism in that the participants were predominantly women even though the controlling agents, such as drummers and ritual specialists, were frequently men, and that they gave women some sense of empowerment in situations of general subjugation. During the nineteenth century there was an upsurge of African religiosity, but it seems not to have consolidated into syncretistic churches, probably because the Christian church schools provided the means for status "upliftment" and for some limited occupational mobility into urban trades and into teaching, nursing, and the police (see Rodney 1981: Chapter 4). The Christian churches in the African villages were centers of social empowerment at the same time that they were instruments of hegemonic domination by the colonial state. They developed their own hierarchies of clergy, lay clergy, schoolteachers, and

other officials that reflected both class differences and male domination, but most of these people were tied by kinship to a wide range of people in the villages. Schoolteachers constituted the
main body of the village elite and connected it directly with the colonial society through their
membership in various local government bodies, and in the case of one individual, through his
nominated membership of the Legislative Council.

## THE "PROBLEM" OF EAST INDIAN "ASSIMILATION"

As I pointed out above, the recourse to history, or to cultural differences, to explain the contemporary situation in Guyana tends to shift into a focus on the "problem" of East Indian "assimilation" to some hypothetically homogenous national culture. Even so fanatical a proponent of the
plural society view of Guyana as M.G. Smith eventually saw Guyana as a two-segment society:
Creoles and East Indians (M.G. Smith 1984: 110). It is, then, worth asking how rural Indian
communities have articulated with colonial society since the 1950s. So long as discussion revolves
around a supposed opposition between "plural society" and "common culture" or "common values," it is likely to degenerate into the listing of similarities and differences that are held to add
up to identical, or disparate, institutions and norms. A similar problem arises if a sharp and exclusive distinction is made between "class" and other forms of social identifications based on "race,"
"religion," or "culture." The communities formed by East Indians differed in several significant
ways from those formed by African ex-slaves. We can leave aside the sugar plantations where the
plantation management exercised considerable control, even over the establishment of religious
organizations of one kind or another (see Jayawardena 1963), until, first, organs of the central
government, and then organized trade unions came to be vehicles for the articulation of plantation workers' interests. I shall concentrate on the rice-growing village of Windsor Forest that I
studied in 1956 and again in 1975, and the village studied by Silverman in 1969–70 to which
she gave the fictitious name "Rajgahr." Space does not permit a detailed analysis and comparison
of these two villages but certain aspects of their contrasted experience are revealing.

Rajgahr was founded in 1902 as a government land settlement for former indentured immigrants in lieu of return passages to India. By 1911 there were 623 residents, though it is likely
that laborers resident at Plantation Bath worked some of the land which they had been allotted
without moving into the village. Rice was grown both as a subsistence crop and for sale though
many inhabitants continued to work on the sugar estate. Although Rajgahr was a government
land settlement, it was incorporated as a Country District with a council of seven members
appointed by the central Local Government Board. The one church in British Guiana that had
been active among East Indian immigrants was the Canadian Mission Church, (thus indicating
yet again the manner in which colonial social institutions segmented the population); its head,
the Reverend Cropper, had been the resident minister at Plantation Bath where most of the
Rajgahr residents had formerly lived. When the village council was formed, Reverend Cropper
was appointed as a member along with a series of other prominent persons who were both literate in English and, for the most part, Christians. Silverman provides a wealth of detail on the
manner in which Rajgahr's internal politics developed over the years from the founding of the
village until 1970, when she left the field. Because it was a village district with its own council,
the politics of the local community was focused in that arena. This is very different from Windsor
Forest (see R.T. Smith 1957; Smith and Jayawardena 1958, 1959, 1967; and Hanley 1975, 1979
for fuller discussions of Windsor Forest).

At the beginning of the twentieth century Windsor Forest was an active sugar estate but the company that owned it failed to maintain proper sea defences, probably due to financial problems consequent on falling sugar prices. Repeated inundation by the sea further reduced profitability and eventually the company abandoned the plantation, leaving the resident laboring population of East Indians, Africans, and Chinese to fend for themselves. A few pieces of land were sold or given to the residents, and eventually the colonial government acquired the estate at execution sale in order to protect its interest in outstanding debts. The residents gradually converted the sugar lands to cattle pasture and rice land, the factory was broken up and sold to help pay the cost of repair to the sea wall, and eventually the government decided to convert the estate, and its neighbour La Jalousie, into government land settlements. The colonial government made the fateful error of offering plots of land to the residents on ninety-nine-year leases at a fixed rental of $6.00 per acre per annum (one British West Indian dollar equaled approximately fifty-five cents U.S. in 1956; in 1995 one Guyana dollar is worth less than one cent U.S.). In return for this rent, the government undertook to provide all maintenance of the estate, including sea defense and water control costs. The administration of the village was effectively vested in the regional superintendent of "Government Estates: West Demerara." Although a locally elected Advisory Council had been instituted it had little power and was not a forum for local political and factional conflict as in Rajgahr. However, this does not mean that such conflicts were absent. On the contrary: Windsor Forest's development as a rice-growing community closely paralleled that of Rajgahr, with the same growth of internal differentation as millers and shopkeepers emerged as a new village elite. However, in Windsor Forest the vehicle for status striving was not the mobilization of factional support for village council office, but religious organizations.

The three major religious organizations in 1956 were the Muslims, who operated a mosque, a school for teaching Urdu and Arabic, and a boy scout troop; the Arya Samaj, a Hindu reform group that owned a small meeting place and a school for teaching Hindi; the Sanatan Dharm Maha Sabha, the orthodox Hindu group that operates a temple complete with salaried priest and a small Hindi school. The Bharat Sevashram Sangh, a Hindu splinter group commonly known as "the Bengalis," was relatively new and relatively small. These organizations each had a full complement of officers, such as President, Secretary, Treasurer, and committees of management, providing ample scope for the working out of factional politics. The articulation of status groups within the village was expressed through complex arguments and discussions of religious doctrine. Individuals aspiring to leadership roles within the various organizations would pore over sacred books and secondary works so as to be able to make impressive and informed speeches on various public occasions. There can be no doubting the sincere interest of many of these individuals in the details of religious doctrine, but at the same time the language of religious dispute was also the language of factional conflict. The most influential men were those with an ample economic base, either as store keepers, rice millers, or large farmers; religious knowledge and piety were additional qualifications for status group leadership.

When the election campaigns gathered momentum prior to the 1953 elections there were numerous independent candidates and small parties that appealed with varying degrees of indirectness to Indian voters. Silverman has shown that the formation of the People's Progressive Party provided the basis for the formation of a new faction in Rajgahr (Silverman 1980: 115–30). In Windsor Forest, there was a tendency for the religious groups to align with national parties. The Muslims were generally sympathetic to parties that opposed the People's Progressive Party, while the Arya Samajists were the most receptive to radical reform. In both communities the development of racial polarization in the early 1960s led to a consolidation of electoral support behind the P.P.P., but there was no automatic alignment of all Indians with that party. In Rajgahr at least one prominent leader became a member of the People's National Congress when it was formed by Forbes Burnham, and in Windsor Forest there continued to be strong opposition to the perceived "communism" of the People's Progressive Party. More importantly, the struggle between the parties at the national level did not remove the importance of local status groups nor did it totally permeate them.

## CONCLUSION

A more careful analysis of the internal structure of apparently segregated rural communities than I have been able to make here would show how schematic are the depictions of the fundamental social and cultural separation of the African and Indian "communities" as they are so often called. There is nothing in their internal structure to suggest such a fundamental separation. In the early 1950s there were fundamental divisions among both Africans and Indians over the issues of "communism" and "capitalism," divisions that led to varying levels of alignment with political parties committed to these ideologies. However, Silverman's detailed analysis of the internal politics of Rajgahr shows clearly that it was never simple primordial identity or deep cultural divisions that produced political alignments. Economic and status interests determined the alignments of local factions within a complex articulation of contesting status groups.

In the period of intense conflict designed to remove or retain Jagan and the P.P.P. as the controllers of the state apparatus, a period that lasted for only a few years, from 1961 to 1965, racial confrontation dwarfed the status defining significance of local groups, and that struggle has certainly affected social relations at the most mundane levels in the period since then. However, at the risk of being labelled optimistic, not to say naïve, I am uneasy with theories that assume either the inevitability of that very conflict, or the equal inevitability of its consequence in the future. In 1994 it is important not to allow the historical imagination to become settled upon the idea that disabling racial conflict was, and therefore is, inevitable. The most pessimistic, and also exaggerated, account of Guyana's ills that I have seen recently is a paper written by Ralph R. Premdas of the University of the West Indies, Trinidad, entitled "Ethnic Conflict and Development: The Case of Guyana." There is an almost apocalyptic tone to the paper, detailing the pervavsive "ethnicization" of politics since the 1950s, and arguing that the hostility between Africans and Indians has even divided overseas Guyanese communities. Yet his arguments are not too far removed from those I have set out above. He traces the situation at the beginning of 1992 to the odd concatenation of circumstances that occurred in the 1950s as the original People's Progressive Party fell apart from a combination of external interference and failure of leadership on the part of Burnham and Jagan. However, he also assumes a preexisting "pluralism" in the population of British Guiana exhibited in residential and occupational segregation, with a concomitant segregation of voluntary associations such as trade unions, religious organizations, and so forth. As with most models of the society constructed in terms of a macro-image of social relations, this one ignores or minimizes the many areas of social life where relations did not conform to the assumed determination of race or "ethnicity," but Premdas is too good an observer of social reality to completely overlook data that do not conform to this image.

Brackette Williams's work was carried out in Guyana during the most repressive period of P.N.C. domination, when Burnham attempted to convert himself from a client of the United States into the leader of a Third World socialist state, thus preempting Jagan's claim to be the authentic leader of an authentic socialist party.[6] She viewed this situation as one where

> …ethnic groups in Guyana stress cultural traits, interpret their experiences, and organize the functions of ethnic culture with one eye on preventing the other groups from taking over particular material opportunities that they believe should belong to their group, and with the other eye on the future construction of putative homogeneity and its institutionalization in civil society as they struggle over who should inherit the power relinquished by the Anglo-Europeans at the end of the colonial era (Williams 1989: 438–39).

And she strikes a somber note as she generalizes her insights to say that *ethnicity* labels the politics of cultural struggle in the nexus of territorial and cultural nationalism that characterizes all putatively homogeneous nation states," implying, and not without reason, that all nation-states, because of the very basis of their construction, must marginalize "peripheral categorical units" (1989: 439).

However realistic a conclusion this may be, it seems to short-circuit the consideration of bases of status group formation other than race, and to overstress the importance of the putatively homogeneous nation state as the only significant reference for constructing a transformist hegemony, perhaps because of the very tendency of any discussion of "ethnicity" to lead toward that outcome identified by Max Weber when he wrote of the "disutility of the notion of 'Ethnic Group'."

> [T]he notion of "ethnically" determined social action subsumes phenomena that a rigorous sociological analysis…would have to distinguish carefully: the actual subjective effects of those customs conditioned by heredity and those determined by tradition; the differential impact of the varying content of custom; the influence of common language, religion, and political action, past and present, upon the formation of customs; the extent to which such factors create attraction and repulsion, and especially the belief in affinity or disaffinity of blood; the consequences of this belief for social action in general, and specifically for action on the basis of shared custom or blood relationship for diverse sexual relations, etc.—all of this would have to be studied in detail. It is certain that in this process the collective term "ethnic" would be abandoned, for it is unsuitable for a really rigorous analysis (Weber 1968: 394–95).

Premdas has half acknowledged that by the early 1950s "something of a shared locally derived 'creole culture' had emerged" in British Guiana, but that the years of intensifying polarized conflict "practically destroyed all these shared institutions and practices" (Premdas 1992: 25). But is this true? The state apparatus may have been dominated by the People's National Congress embodied as an African party, but it surely embraced a large number of Indians, especially in local government bodies, and the party itself succeeded, no matter how cynically, in recruiting Indian membership. By the early 1980s, the P.N.C. had deployed enough patronage at the local level in the rural areas to persuade many Indians to offer at least nominal allegiance, and some offered a great deal more. One day when I was talking to another anthropologist in a Georgetown bar, in the company of a very old friend of mine from Windsor Forest, I asked him what was involved in his job as a local party organizer in the village. He answered that it was largely to take note of subversive talk such as he had just heard from us, and report it to "the authorities." He was only half joking.

One other aspect of the Guyana case is important. Daniel Miller, in a study of Trinidad, has been impressed by the dualism of attitudes toward the nation-state:

> ...on the one hand, a passionate nationalism, and a sincere concern with the history, and achieve-
> ments of the country including its symbolic elements such as the national anthem. At the same time
> I heard politicians bemoan the lack of these concerns, and found in other contexts...quite the oppo-
> site sense of self-denigration and antipathy to the idea of being Trinidadian (Miller n.d.: 7).[7]

The same is certainly true of Guyana and the Guyanese. Both Guyana and Trinidad are now, and always have been, creatures of modern capitalist expansion, and although it is justifiable to consider their internal dynamics, and even their attempts to create nations out of the remnants of colonial states, one cannot ignore the continuing reality of dependence, in all senses of that term, nor the incorporation of a wider hegemony into their very constitution. The ideology of the People's Progressive Party of the 1950s was socialist, universalistic, and full of bluster about creating a completely new society. It has been remarked frequently that Dr. Jagan's socialism was also peculiarly American, but however that may be, it was certainly egalitarian, universalistic, and individualist. Now that his party is back in office he has embraced the idea of building a market economy and encouraging outside investment. But apart from such economic development strategies, the Guyanese people are now, and always have been, deeply affected by what has been called globalization.

I suggested at the beginning of this chapter that "history" has been used by social scientists studying political conflict in Guyana in such a way that it has directed attention away from the complexity of the conflicts, and onto the stereotyped images of how Guyana was created and what continues to be its real underlying structure. Is this a denial of the relevance of history for anthropological analysis? Of course not. Rather it is a call for what Sydel Silverman called the "responsible use of historical material...a collaboration (of anthropology and history) in which the work of each discipline can nourish that of the other" (Silverman 1979: 433). Unfortunately the overwhelming interest of students of Guyana, whether historians or social scientists, has been in the roots of recent social conflict, to the extent that one historian has shaped his investigation of nineteenth-century Guyanese history around the dubious project of "testing" the plural society versus stratification theories (Moore 1987). However, I have been primarily concerned with the recourse to more distant history as a means of supporting analyses of recent events, a procedure fraught with problems of its own, as Orlando Patterson pointed out some years ago (Patterson 1982). Daniel Miller, in a novel but creative way, has employed a very generalized history in his study of Trinidad (1994). Arguing that Trinidad is a salient example of the problems of modernity, he contends that

> ...from its inception Trinidad has been the creation of the global economy, and continues to have lit-
> tle protection from the buffeting of larger economic trends.... The Caribbean was itself the creation
> of a modernist scheme established with unusual clarity and completeness by Europeans, and today
> the IMF and World Bank continue to exert this peculiar rationality of economics, if in less extreme
> fashion (Miller 1994: 24).

Building upon his previous work on mass consumption, work informed by an unusually broad understanding of both philosophy and anthropological theory, Miller recognizes the diversity of the origins of Trinidad's population and the salience of ethnicity in self-representation. However, he also perceives a generalized sense of oppression deriving from the experience of colonial domination that has "created a culture of disparagement of the powerless and emulation of the powerful" (1994: 22), a culture that has been vividly depicted in the various writings of V.S. Naipaul. Even more significant are the conclusions derived from a careful examination of material culture, where he found that "ethnic distinctions were of minimal importance to the selection of objects and their juxtaposition in home design" so that there were "evident discrepancies between what people expressed in language and what they seemed to value in action" (1994: 10).

Guyana is not Trinidad of course, but certain aspects of their development and present condition are similar. In both cases local people are working to create systems of value with materials, both real and ideal, that derive not only from their immediate environment and their historic experience, but also from within a global system that is just as important to them. There is no reason to believe that the "nationalist intellectuals" of today are any less creative than those to whom Clifford Geertz referred, and much reason to hope that they are a good deal wiser. The deeply pessimistic Ralph Premdas writes that Guyana has passed "the collective insanity threshold" that produces crippled personalities, and is seeking psychological redemption through communal parties, led by apocalyptic personalities, that are no longer the means of aggregating political interests but are more like psychiatric clinics (Premdas 1992: 26). But where does he publish this analysis? In a discussion paper for the United Nations Research Institute for Social Development. So that in the midst of despair there is hope.

# On the Disutility of the Notion of "Ethnic Group" for Understanding Status Struggles in the Modern World (1995)

Ethnicity seems to be a new term. In the sense we use it—the character or quality of an ethnic group—it does not appear in the 1933 edition of the *Oxford English Dictionary*, but it makes its appearance in the 1972 *Supplement*... It [made] the 1973 edition of the *American Heritage Dictionary*, where it is defined as "1. The condition of belonging to a particular ethnic group; 2. Ethnic pride." One senses a term still on the move.... Any such categorization taken up and given currency by sociologists suffers from a certain presumption of disutility.... Does it make for greater precision in describing the world, or does it merely compound the confusion, fuzz further the fuzziness? Is it the result of insight, or the resort of bewilderment? Nathan Glazer and Daniel P. Moynihan (eds.) *Ethnicity: Theory and Experience.*

## INTRODUCTION

Ethnicity is like "family" or "marriage:" everybody knows what it means but nobody can define it adequately. The terms "ethnicity," "ethnic group," and now "ethnic cleansing" scream at us from newspaper headlines, radio and television, and—unhappily—from the writings of social scientists, many of whom use them as though they referred to some real, tangible phenomena and processes the existence of which is self-evident. Although the possibility of rolling back the tide of this particular usage is virtually nil, it is worthwhile, I think, to try to make clear some objections to it. In 1981 Anthony D. Smith began the introduction of his book *The Ethnic Revival* with an attack on liberals and rationalists (closely related to the equally misguided cosmopolitans and socialists) who have dreamt, he said, of "The dissolution of ethnicity. The transcendence of nationalism. The internationalisation of culture....(only to be)...confounded and disappointed...(as) ethnic ties and national loyalties have become stronger and more deep-rooted than ever" (p. 1). John Comaroff ended his 1987 paper "Of Totemism and Ethnicity" with the observation that "it (ethnicity) refuses to vanish—notwithstanding the once commonplace tendency to predict its imminent demise" (Comaroff 1992: 66). The epigraph at the head of this chapter was a prelude to a resounding declaration by Glazer and Moynihan that "ethnicity" is not just an attempt to wrap up a series of old problems in a new word, problems that would be more adequately considered in all their diversity, but refers to a newly emergent phenomenon, a category "as significant for the understanding of the present-day world as that of social class itself" (2–3). Whereas in the past, they say, ethnic group was a label applied to minorities exhibiting characteristics that were survivals from an earlier age, the term is now applied to "all the groups of a society characterized by a distinct sense of difference owing to culture and descent," even to old Americans designated by "the odd term WASP" (4). It was hardly a coincidence that this discovery of "a sense of difference owing to culture and descent" in the United States followed swiftly upon the early successes of the civil rights movement and the racist counterattack against it, and it is interesting that they saw fit not to include power as a dimension of their newly discovered ethnic groups. The civil rights movement was about political representation, equal opportunity for employment, education, housing, and such mundane things, and not about dashikis, haircuts, tastes in music, or what name you would go by, though it was easier to focus on "culture" than on jobs. In one of the more interesting articles in the Glazer and Moynihan volume, Daniel Bell reviews the whole arc of circumstances under which the term "ethnicity" has been pressed into service, before concluding that "the term *ethnicity* is clearly a confusing one... Though there is an obvious difficulty in using the term *ethnic* in any consistent way, that common designation for a culturally defined 'communal group' is too pervasive to escape, and by and large, it will have to serve" (156–57). For what it will have to serve is not clear, but in the course of his paper Bell makes explicit the extent to which this supposedly new "ethnicity" is really plural society theory in thin disguise. Anthony Smith's disclosure of "the ethnic revival" was prompted by his observation of nationalist political movements and conflicts within modern states ranging from Afghanistan to Zimbabwe, and in large measure echoes the ideas set out by Edward Shils and Clifford Geertz in *Old Societies and New States: The Quest for Modernity in Asia and Africa* (Geertz 1963). Brackette Williams has provided us with an excellent survey of the remarkable efflorescence of the concept of ethnicity in the work of anthropologists in the 1970s and 1980s as they used it to try to solve theoretical and methodological problems created for their discipline by the profound changes in international political and economic relations (Williams 1989).

Another statement on this subject appeared in print just too late for Professor Williams's review, though it shares many of the characteristics and concerns of the publications with which she dealt so fully. John Comaroff's above-quoted paper "Of Totemism and Ethnicity" appeared originally in 1987 (though he says that it was "drafted first in 1982"), and the author considered it important and timely enough to reprint in a collection published in 1992 (Comaroff and Comaroff 1992). Comaroff believes that ethnicity is a substantial, even a "primordial," thing that "has its origins in the asymmetric incorporation of structurally dissimilar groupings into a single political economy" (Comaroff 1992: 54). Such a conception is reminiscent of Lucy Mair's 1938 attempt to define a "zero point of social change" (Mair 1938), especially when he writes of "segmentary ethnicity" as a hierarchy of identities, "of 'tribe,' 'nation' and 'race,' each a particular refraction of ethnicity" (58–59). Erroneously equating something he calls "the Weberian tradition" (consisting mainly of writings by Shils and Geertz) with Weber's own ideas on this subject (derived not from Weber himself but from Hechter's misreading of Weber), Comaroff dismisses the idea that "primordialism" is the stubborn residue of traditional culture to be erased by modernization, but then reinvents it as a general need for societies to create categories. Totemism and ethnicity, he argues, are modes of social classification and consciousness, each produced as a specific historical structure. Totemism "emerges with the establishment of symmetrical relations between structurally similar groupings" while ethnicity is the incorporation of structurally *dissimilar* groupings into a single political economy. Just how "structurally dissimilar" differs from "culturally different" is not clear, but it appears that in locating ethnicity in the historical moment of incorporation of dissimilar groups into "a single political economy" Comaroff has achieved precisely that essentializing of the concept that he criticized in the "Weberian tradition" and falsely attributed to Weber himself.

But to return to Professor Williams's review; by the end of it she had not quite rejected the use of the term ethnicity but had certainly thrown considerable doubt upon its usefulness. As she put it

> [E]thnicity labels the politics of cultural struggle in the nexus of territorial and cultural nationalism that characterizes all putatively homogeneous nation-states. As a label it may sound better than tribe, race, or barbarian, but with respect to political consequences,…it still identifies those who are at the borders of the empire…an ideologically produced boundary between "mainstream" and peripheral categorical units of this kind of "imagined" social order (439).

So conceived, the label is recognized to be precisely what it was when W. Lloyd Warner reported its application by the dominant groups in Yankee City in the 1930s; that is, a derogatory designation for low status immigrants and their descendants (Warner & Lunt 1941). However, she is also correct in her contention that lay persons have taken up the label in their struggles for status, especially in the societies of Europe and North America.

In this paper I concentrate on material collected in Chicago as part of a wider study of the effects of poverty on what were defined as four "ethnic groups"; African Americans, Mexicans, Puerto Ricans, and whites. This designation immediately raises questions of the most complex kind.

## CLASS, RACE, AND "ETHNICITY" IN CHICAGO

I am concerned here with use of the term "ethnicity" to discuss problems of poverty and inequality in the United States, rather than with the nationalist conflicts that have come to be categorized as "ethnic struggles," though the phenomena are not entirely unrelated. I want to reaffirm the value of the concepts of class, status, and style of life, deriving ultimately from the work of Max Weber, and to argue that they are much more sensitive analytical tools for the explication of structures of inequality and the struggles that inevitably accompany them. Those struggles certainly find expression through images of "primordial identity" and invented traditions, but to afford those images an undue salience by using the term ethnicity distracts attention from the continuing power of racism, and trivializes more complex processes of nationalism.

The people studied in Chicago in the late 1980s were at the very bottom of the status hierarchy and for most of them their class and status situations converged to create an overwhelming sense of being "poor." The material on which this discussion is based was collected as part of a project officially called the University of Chicago Urban Poverty and Family Life Survey, but more familiarly known to insiders as The Poverty Project.[1] It originated as part of a continuing debate started in the 1960s following the publication of the notorious Moynihan report on poverty in the United States. Daniel Patrick Moynihan was then a senior official in the Department of Labor; although the report was supposed to discuss the question of why, in spite of the enactment of civil rights legislation, the material circumstances of the African-American population in the United States had deteriorated rather than improved, it was—surprisingly— entitled, *The Negro Family: The Case for National Action* (see Rainwater and Yancey 1967 for a full reprint of this report). That is, the explanation of why such a high proportion of African Americans remained poor, in spite of the removal of the formal barriers of racial discrimination, focussed not on discrimination or unemployment but on the family life of poor black people as the putative cause of their problems. Moynihan wrote:

The fundamental problem, in which this is most clearly the case, is that of family structure. The evidence—not final but powerfully persuasive—is that the Negro family in the urban ghettoes is crumbling. A middle-class group has managed to save itself, but for vast numbers of the unskilled, poorly educated city working class, the fabric of conventional social relationships has all but disintegrated. There are indications that the situation may have been arrested in the past few years, but the general post-war trend is unmistakeable. So long as this situation persists, the cycle of poverty and disadvantage will continue to repeat itself (U.S. Department of Labor 1965, reprinted in Rainwater and Yancey 1967: 43).

Therefore, it was argued, an entirely new approach is needed that will aim at the establishment of a stable Negro family structure, and this would be the means—the only available means—of solving the American Dilemma. This refers of course to the dilemma of persistent racism in a country formally committed to equality, a dilemma identified by Gunnar Myrdal in his massive study of race relations in the United States (Myrdal 1944).

The criticisms of the Moynihan Report were swift and vociferous; many of them are reprinted and discussed in the volume edited by Rainwater and Yancey referred to above (1967). However, certain assumptions about the relation between family structure and social life are common to Moynihan and most of his critics. He says: "The role of the family in shaping character and ability is so pervasive as to be easily overlooked. The family is the basic social unit of American life; it is the basic socializing unit. By and large, adult conduct in society is learned as a child" ( 51). This widely accepted social science notion is linked to the further observation that there is a standard family system in the U.S.A.; deviations from this standard are survivals from the age of European migrations, and they actually *account for* the differences in the progress and assimilation of various ethnic (that is, national) and religious groups. Those groups *with stronger traditional family bonds* have progressed faster than others. The report does not elaborate on this, telling us neither which groups are being referred to nor the way in which their family bonds spurred them on to success, or even what the content of those bonds might have been, but we can easily recognize this as a piece of folk wisdom closely linked to Moynihan's discovery in the 1970s of "ethnicity" as the great new force in the world. In the 1967 paper the rudimentary notions of ethnicity have profound implications:

> But there is one truly great discontinuity in family structure in the United States at the present time: that between the white world in general and that of the Negro American. ...The white family has achieved a high degree of stability and is maintaining that stability....**By contrast the family structure of lower class Negroes is highly unstable, and in many urban centers is approaching complete breakdown** (Rainwater & Yancey 1967: 51, emphasis in original).

A note points out that a section of the Negro community *has* attained a stable middle-class (white?) pattern, but there is no parallel note to the effect that a section of "the white community" has achieved an "unstable" pattern. The significance of this report lies in its attempt to construct for African Americans an "ethnic culture," the major characteristic of which is its "disorganization," "breakdown," and unstable families.

Space precludes extensive discussion of the Moynihan Report, and it is introduced here only because the University of Chicago Urban Poverty and Family Life Project started out where Moynihan left off, so to speak, and carried forward many of the Glazer and Moynihan ideas about ethnicity. How was this project conceived and what did it aim to do?

In 1985 Professor William Julius Wilson of the Department of Sociology at the University of Chicago was successful in interesting the Ford Foundation, The Children's Bureau, and many other agencies in a big new study of poverty and the continued decline of the African American family. The proposed study was expanded, partly at the insistence of some of the granting agencies, to include four so-called "ethnic" groups in Chicago—blacks, Mexicans, Puerto Ricans, and whites. In what sense these are "ethnic groups" was not discussed since their existence was taken for granted. The centerpiece of the study, and by far the most expensive part, was a stratified, random, multistage probability sample survey of 2,490 respondents selected from the low-income areas of Chicago, with the most impoverished areas being oversampled to increase the pool of "underclass individuals and families." The original idea was to get 800 black individuals, 400 Mexican Americans, 400 Puerto Ricans and 400 whites, all of whom were parents and between the ages of eighteen and forty-four years. (In the event completed interviews were obtained from 1,184 individuals classified as being black, 365 white, 488 Mexican, and 453 Puerto Rican). The details of this survey will not be discussed here.

A small group of people involved in the project (including myself) became increasingly concerned that the sample survey omitted large areas of concern, as well as being deeply flawed in its basic assumptions. Therefore we planned a small study designed to get at cultural concepts (rather than individual "attitudes," "opinions," or "views") concerning class and shared perceptions of the social and physical environment; this survey of a subsample of individuals who had been interviewed in the main survey came to be known as *The Social Opportunity Survey*. Resources were sufficient to interview only 168 individuals. Carried out during the summer of 1987, this small survey was constructed as a series of open-ended questions to guide the graduate student interviewers, who in turn encouraged respondents to provide a free-flowing discourse. The interviews, which were tape-recorded and typed up verbatim by the interviewer immediately afterwards, produced a rich account of the ideas of people who live in the so-called urban ghettos of Chicago. The Social Opportunity Survey data are drawn upon here, as are data from an extensive series of life histories compiled on the basis of repeated interviews with the same informant over a period of several months.[2]

## CONCEPTS OF STATUS AND PERCEPTIONS OF SOCIAL OPPORTUNITY IN CHICAGO'S LOW-INCOME AREAS

Historically Chicago has been a mosaic of neighborhoods into which a succession of national groups migrated; there were Irish neighborhoods, Polish, Lithuanian, Scandinavian, Jewish, Bohemian, African American, and more recently Mexican, Puerto Rican, Indian (from India), Korean, Vietnamese, Arab, and less well known groups such as Assyrians. In the past many of these neighborhoods built their own religious centers, had their own-language newspapers, and were organized by the Democratic Party political machine through a complex system of ward organizations. Today the neighborhoods are much less clearly defined or politically organized, there is a good deal of mixing of poor people from different backgrounds, and a process of simplification of the categories corresponds to the realities of city politics, which is organized in terms of black, white, and Hispanic blocs, with something called the lake-front liberals constituting an unpredictable swing vote. The population group that is most markedly segregated in

Chicago is variously designated as black or African American, and the degree of that segregation has nothing to do with "ethnicity" and everything to do with racism and poverty. Immigrants from Mexico and Puerto Rico have tended to accumulate in particular areas of the city, but there are many low-income areas where immigrants and African Americans live side by side. One can quickly appreciate the complexity of actual living experiences, and the way in which categories of social classification are shaped by wider political forces, when listening to informants discuss such issues as whether there are different groups in Chicago, who belongs to them, where they stand in relation to each other, and which of them have more or less opportunity to get ahead.

## Residence and Segregation

In spite of the image, and to some extent the reality, of segregation by race and national origin there is a general perception among many poor people that they live in "mixed" areas. For example, Gloria Nunez is a Mexican immigrant living in Pilsen, the most concentrated area of Mexican immigrants in the city. When asked what kinds of people live in the area she said: "We have a little bit of everything. We have more Hispanics than anything, especially now. But there are blacks. Before there were just Americans, Italians, and Poles. Now we are mostly Latino. Now we are mostly Mexican whereas before it was mostly white. But we still have a few of everything." Carmen Diaz, a twenty-six-year-old divorced woman whose parents migrated from Puerto Rico, lives in an area that was described by the interviewer as "residential with a mixture of black, Latino, and poor white." Susan Lynn Jones, is a twenty-nine-year-old white woman who came to Chicago from North Carolina in the late 1970s and now lives in a public housing project. Her perception of the area where she lives is: "Well there's Puerto Ricans who have their problems, blacks, the whites, the Germans, the Pollaks—Polish rather. It's like everybody in their own minority. Except in here, like the part that I live in is predominantly Puerto Rican. There's more Puerto Ricans in this block than at the other end. At the other end they are mostly white and hillbilly. But it is like we are our own little U.N., national union, whatever that place is called. We've got Puerto Ricans, Mexicans, we've got Gypsies, we got white, we got hillbilly, we got black, we've got Jewish, we've got the German. It's like the U.N. and we all help each other. But you go outside of this area it's like a war zone." She went on to describe the gangs and the guns that are an integral part of life in Chicago's poor neighborhoods. Maria Gonzalez was born in Chicago of Mexican American parents. She too stressed the diversity of the neighborhood where she lives. "Yes, we have a lot of different nationalities here and all. They all have different job occupations here. There is a nurse across the street and the lady next door was one of the Jews in the Holocaust. She tried to burn the number on her arm and just listening to her is amazing."

African Americans were less likely to remark on the mixed nature of their neighborhoods for the simple reason that they are the most markedly segregated, but there are many racially mixed areas around the edges of the predominantly black neighborhoods. Although race is a certainly a prime factor in segregation, for the really poor, being able to find a place that you can afford is also a major consideration. For example, the thirty-three-year-old Mexican immigrant, Jesus Calzada, who has lived in Chicago for eight years and is married to an African-American woman, lives in a three-story brick building with about twelve apartment units in it, with his wife and five children. The apartments were in a terrible state of repair with worn and rickety stairs, wooden floors that were worn and splintered, walls with cracked plaster and chipped and peeling paint. All the residents of this building are, according to him, "Latino," even though the neighborhood is predominantly black. They do not live there because his wife is black, but because eight years ago it was the only place they could find that was affordable.

As in the poverty areas of most cities in the United States, excessive numbers of people occupy a rundown housing stock vacated by upwardly mobile groups that have moved, usually to the suburbs. In Pilsen, the area of greatest concentration of Mexican immigrants in Chicago, many, if not most, of the modest, single-family homes have been converted into apartments, and Fred Sanchez's house is no exception. The interviewer who developed this case and wrote up the extensive tape-recorded interviews described the apartment in her introductory notes as follows:

> House is a two flat at least—maybe three. They live in the first floor front and I can't tell if there is a rear apartment or not. It is a two story frame house. A high-ceilinged large front room looks from the outside as if it were once a store. They have two old couches in there one of which his wife stays on round the clock (she has terminal cancer). There are two TV's—a small black and white and a large color. There is a stand-up wardrobe in one corner of the living room, and a table over in another corner with flowers from friends and a framed picture of the unmarried daughter with her two kids. There are other trinkets and religious things like a crucifix and picture of Christ. The room is sparsely furnished and seems spacious because there is little in it. A gas space heater from which the exhaust pipe has fallen off. Behind the living room is a fair-sized kitchen with a washer hooked up to the sink, but no dryer. There is a stove, refrigerator, and table to eat at. The bathroom is off the kitchen. A short staircase takes you up half a floor to the bedrooms of which there are three for five kids and two adults. The bedrooms are uniformly small with room for just one single bed in each. I don't know where everybody sleeps. The electricity goes out if too many things are going at once—e.g. the TV, washer, and small electric fan. It is an old building with no windows to the front. The battered door has carpet pad material nailed around it to prevent drafts.

These are not atypical living conditions for people in the low-income areas of Chicago, and the cleanliness of the apartments varies a good deal according to the diligence of the occupants and the number of persons living there.

## Egalitarianism

Chicagoans use a complex array of categories and terms to map their social world. We saw that Maria Gonzalez refers to "nationalities" and "job occupations" as major indicators, but without any implication of their being bounded and separate groups. The first preoccupation of the poor is with the stigmatizing effect of poverty, with issues of fairness and respect. Race is certainly a crucial distinction in this city but is not always in the foreground of the preoccupations of the poor. The following extracts from recorded field interviews are interspersed with my editorial comments. The names are fictitious and some details of the cases have been altered to ensure confidentiality.

Elise Graber is a thirty-one-year-old white woman living in an area that is now heavily Mexican and African American with a residual white population of about 10 percent.[3] Married with four children, she is on welfare and food stamps but works illegally for a dry-cleaner as a presser. After she made some disparaging remarks about Mexicans, she was asked to say which of the classes that she had identified is higher, or lower, than the others.

> "I don't spend much time thinking about things like this. I would say that the lower class is better than the middle and the upper class. 'Cause they got to struggle more to get what they want. And

then the middle class is behind 'em. And the upper class just out and out stink. They were born with silver spoons in their mouth, they think their shit don't stink. It's the only way I can put it....There's a big difference between the upper and lower. The middle you can just forget about it because they don't know which way to go, they're just making it... The ones that got money thinks they are better than anybody so they don't care about you. The low class, they got to struggle for what they got and what they want, I just think they're better than the other ones." And then with penetrating insight into the relational nature of these categories she said, "Each class thinks they're better than the other ones." After all that she identified herself as being, "Right now, the middle class. I mean I don't have a lot of money but I'm not poor either."

This kind of explicit egalitarianism was quite common among poor whites and usually coexisted with a marked racism. Douglas Perkins, a poor, divorced white man, living with a woman in a residential hotel in Uptown, a predominantly low-income white area, said of the people there: "They all drink, they're all looking for a job. Ain't none of em can get one. I'm one of the lucky ones. I've had a job for three years." When asked whether people in Chicago differ from each other and whether everybody in Chicago is equal, his answer was concise: "No. I don't really think they're different, some people get treated wronger than others is all." And on the question of whether there are classes in the city he was equally direct: "I can say blacks, whites, and Puerto Ricans and Mexicans, they ought to be all in the same class. If it wasn't for the governor and the president and the mayor everybody would be in the same class." He thought that all of them ought to be equal but if compelled to rank them, "I'd down the Puerto Ricans. They probably wouldn't be down if they had a job. Mexicans and blacks are pretty well equal. I'm not going to tell you no lie. (At this point the interviewer asked, *So the blacks and Mexicans are over the Puerto Ricans?*) Yeah. (*And where are the whites?*) Over. I can't say all of them 'cause there's assholes in every crowd. I can't tell you whites are over everybody else. You got these hillbillies down here, they like to fight all the goddam time." In another interview one black woman put the matter of difference very concisely: "There's them that have and them that have not. 'Cause when you're poor, color doesn't make any difference." And elsewhere a Mexican woman said:

> Here, where we are, let's say you have a black. There are some destructive ones because they don't know how to act. But if they are going to be destructive, they go far away to another place and they don't bother you. So we say they are good because if they don't hurt you personally, you say they are good. And there are some Puerto Ricans but as long as we don't have problems we say they are good too.

### Race

Although the class situation of our respondents was a primary preoccupation, race is a pervasive and inescapable dimension of social categorization in the United States. We have already seen that many respondents perceive the major divisions in the city to be precisely those identified by the scholars who set up the Urban Poverty and Family Life Project—black, white, Mexican, and Puerto Rican or, more simply, black, white, and Hispanic. But others have a more complex array of categories and terms to map their social world. Maria Gonzalez refers to "nationalities" and "job occupations" as major indicators, but without any implication of their being bounded and separate groups. Fred Sanchez, a forty-three-year-old Mexican American who was born in Texas of immigrant parents, presented a much more complex and sophisticated picture of life in Chicago over the course of a long series of interviews. Most interviews with Hispanics were conducted in Spanish and subsequently translated unless, like Fred Sanchez, the respondent was fluent in English. Fred Sanchez worked at his grandfather's trucking company in Texas from the time he dropped out of school until he came North around 1965, and now lives in Pilsen. In responding to questions about whether he believes that everybody in Chicago is equal, and if not, in what ways they differ, he vacillated a good deal but had his own ideas about what categories are socially significant. The interviewer's questions are in italics.

> *(How do you think they are different?)* In a lot of ways. We don't have the opportunities that a lot of people get here. White people get more opportunities than any other race. And that's a fact. *(What about the other groups?)* That's it. They get the best and what's left over the other people get. Blacks, Hispanics. There are only three groups. White, black, and Hispanic, that's all. *(Blacks and Hispanics get the same thing?)* About the same thing. And sometimes blacks get more. *(Why?)* Because they speak English. See, Hispanics that have an education and blacks that have an education, they have about the same chances as white kids. But if you take three people, a Mexican, a black and a white, and they have the same education and they apply for the same job, who do you think is going to get the job? The white is going to get the job. *(Even if they have the same background?)* Same qualities, same every-thing. *(It doesn't depend whether the employer is white, black, or Hispanic?)* Well, no, if the employer is black, the black might get it. It depends who you're talking to. Now who's hiring, like you said, that makes a difference. If the black person is hiring he might say now lets see who is really the best. I fig-ure that a black and a Hispanic, they give you a chance. They give you a better chance, all three of them. *(They are more fair?)* They are more fair, yeah, I believe that.

It is clear from our interview materials that the overwhelming preoccupation of the poor is with the stigmatizing effect of poverty and with "fairness." Like many of the respondents in this survey, Fred Sanchez did not use the *a priori* categories adopted by sociologists. He referred to Hispanics as a generic category and although he was born in Texas he was not peculiar in this— many Mexican-born individuals also referred to Hispanics. However, black, or African American (a term hardly used among the poor), is also a solid reference group in the United States social system. The usual way of thinking about the cultural basis of hierarchy is to assume that certain ideas about rank are "hegemonic." Thus, in the Caribbean it is customary to think in terms of "whites" or Europeans (or specifically British, French, Spanish, or Dutch) imposing cultural val-ues upon a subaltern population, an imposition that parallels what Gramsci refers to as direct domination by the state (Gramsci 1971: 12). However, "blackness" assumes a negative polarity. This is particularly clear in the United States, but also has assumed a much wider significance in the modern world. There is a sense in which "blackness" has become the prime negative refer-ence point for status groups trying to assert or improve their position. In practice the situation is not absolutely clear-cut; the real world never is. But one can see within the Mexican interview material from Chicago the emergence of just such a discourse; less than uniform as yet, but clearly emergent.

When Fred Sanchez was asked further about the way in which Chicago is divided into groups or classes, he settled for rich, poor, and maybe the "medium class." But when asked about how these classes stand in relation to each other, he went on.

> Whites on top. And then maybe Mexicans and Hispanics in the ...I mean I don't know how many blacks and Mexicans in Chicago. I mean you have two groups here that when they have opportunities

they live pretty well off. I think black neighborhoods are pretty well off. And Mexicans they want to live close to the whites. I don't know why they do that, but when they have the means they do. But other than that they stay around the same areas as the poor. *(So how would you say racial groups are ranked in the city as a whole? If you had to put the three groups in order?)* Blacks and Hispanics are equal in opportunity, but in living together I don't think so. I don't think Mexicans like blacks too much. They do because they're in the same boat. They get along, but not because they want to. Only because they're in the same way. *(But blacks, whites, and Hispanics, if they all had the same money, would they all have the same opportunities?)* Now yes. Before, I don't think so. I don't think it makes too much difference now if you have the same standards to live by the same class. Nowadays, I don't think it makes any difference if you have the money. Well, it depends what state you come from, but you're talking about Chicago, right? *(Right.)* Because in the South, it's still the same thing over there with the blacks and white, ain't it? They still got the guys dress up in white pajamas?

When he started to talk about how the various classes and groups in Chicago get along, some of the complexity of his ideas about race, class, and status began to appear.

Not too well. They are pretty far apart. *(You don't think people of one class get along well with those of another?)* No. Not socially. Maybe for business. You mean for being neighbors and all that kind of stuff? I don't think so. The rich guy don't want to talk to the poor guy. Like the poor people, they got no choice, you understand? So they can socialize with everybody because they ain't got anything to lose. But the person that got something. I don't want to live close to the person that got nothing, that might, you know that I don't feel secure with. But if I had a chance I move out of there so I won't be living like, say in this neighborhood. People here, they don't mind living close to blacks. I mean, they do mind, but they won't be stealing from one another, killing one another because they're in the same boat. Now if I had a little money I would be scared to live around here.

Gloria Perez was equally tolerant of blacks, but equally prone to equate blackness with low status. A forty-year-old immigrant from Mexico, she had been living in an area of Chicago that has a fairly large black population for over seven years, and when asked whether living in a particular neighborhood was likely to affect one's chance of success she said,

Yes. Because many people who live up North and other places look at this neighborhood and say how ugly, how poor and lots of blacks live there and I don't know what all. They think that because there are many blacks here there are only problems. But we don't think that. We have had problems recently but it isn't really because of the neighborhood. We have been very content here. But it does matter a lot where you live because some places you can't even sit outside because of the fights they have. Here we don't have those problems so much because we face the park. That way we have fewer neighbors. With more neighbors facing right on you, you have more fights and more problems.

In the section of the interview dealing with the identification of different groups in Chicago, she was quite indeterminate, preferring to talk about the rich and the poor without any complications. However, when pressed she conceded that there are groups with different customs. When asked how one could tell what group or class a person belonged to she became somewhat more voluble and her discussion was reminiscent of Brackette Williams's discussion of "getting a shock" or "ethnicity and status disjunction" in her book on Guyana (Williams 1991: 177ff). Gloria Perez said,

Well, if they are black you see that they are black. But between the Puerto Ricans and the blacks, they are so crossed that you can't distinguish between them. I have been mistaken. There are persons in my son's school who are black, black, black—very dark. And I would say they were black. But they aren't black, they are crossed, they are Puerto Ricans. The school that my son Jose is in. He had all white teachers, just one Mexican. And we are talking about like nine teachers that he has every day. And I had to go pick up his report card. And I said, in Spanish, "Why do they stick me with this black person" [prieto—also can be used like "nigger"]. And when it was my turn how surprised do you think I was when he greeted me in Spanish. I almost had an attack. Because I was waiting only three or four people back in line and he was watching me but I paid no attention. I kept talking in Spanish. And he told me he had heard what I had said. And I stood there without saying a word, I was so embarrassed. How was I to know that someone so dark could speak Spanish. It seemed his father was Puerto Riqueno and his mother was Mexican or something. I said please forgive me, sir, but I thought you were black because you have that look. So you can't tell very well from sight. Sometimes you confound Mexicans with Texans. Only by listening to them speak can you tell. By their accent. *(So Texans aren't the same as Mexicans?)* For me we each have our own ways. We all speak differently and have our own customs. *(So everyone who speaks Spanish isn't the same?)* We all have something different. Texans are different, Puerto Ricans are different. The way we dress and our customs are different. *(So if you had people who were white, black, Puerto Rican and Mexican, but they were all rich, would they be in the same social class?)* Well, you can't tell about that either because some people look poor and you discover they are rich. I know a man who looks like he has nothing. And he earns thousands of dollars a day. Every day. He is rotting in money. If you saw his bed, it is so old and soiled the sheets are rotten. His sheets look like they are hundreds of years old. I asked him what his money served him if he were going to rot? I told him these things and he said nobody else had ever said that to me.

Negative racial attitudes were more likely to be expressed in the more extended case studies that were collected over a series of interviews than in the single interviews of The Social Opportunity Survey. For example, Linda Gutierrez, a Mexican immigrant who has lived in Humbolt Park for eight years after moving from Guadalajara to Acapulco to Cuernavaca to Mexico City to Chicago, became much more outspoken in her dislike of African Americans after many hours of interviewing. A married woman aged thirty-nine, she has eleven children with her husband, ten of whom live with their parents in the house they have bought. Linda has made few concessions to life in the United States. She speaks no English, and her husband, who works as a carpenter, speaks only a few words. They have both become enthusiastic members of a nearby Pentecostal church which seems to absorb a good deal of their time and energy, and to reinforce her conservative opinions. In spite of her own tangled genealogy, and her own experience of her husband's infidelity, she has developed the idea that her deep dislike of African Americans derives from the fact that black women are insufficiently respectful of their husbands' authority. Although a considerable proportion of the Mexicans and Puerto Ricans we interviewed experienced divorce and separation, men with multiple unions, and women with premarital pregnancies, they generally believed that Hispanics have a more stable family system than African Americans. This is the thin end of the wedge of "family values" that plays such a crucial part in the construction of the negative image of African Americans and leads to the perception that they are *really* different.

## CLASS AND THE SYMBOLIC STRUCTURE
## OF STATUS DIFFERENCES

In recent discussions of ethnicity, the idea of group solidarity, arising out of shared cultural origins or "primordial identity," is muted in favor of a stress on the struggle for position in a complex economy and state organization. This owes a great deal to Barth's 1969 essays on boundary maintenance processes, in which he shifted the focus from the essential qualities of "ethnic groups" onto the political and economic competition taking place at the boundaries of such groups (Barth 1969). However, as Comaroff has emphasized, in modern state structures we are dealing with the hierarchical ordering of status groups, whatever criteria are used in their definition. If "ethnicity" is an unsatisfactory category, imposing a spurious unity on widely disparate phenomena and still carrying the residue of its essentialist origins, is there an alternative? Clearly there is no single specific alternative concept that would not be open to the same objections, but at the same time the term itself will not go away since its very indeterminacy makes it attractive. The only reasonable procedure is to be precise in discussing the components of each particular situation. However, "status" and "class" are much more useful concepts than ethnicity for discussing structures of social inequality, once they are purged of some of their spurious meanings.

The problems posed by the complexities of various bases of inequality in modern society are not new. In the late nineteenth and early twentieth centuries, Max Weber addressed most of them, devising a complex scheme of analytic categories and ideal types that have been widely adopted by recent scholars, and widely misinterpreted and misused. Daniel Wolk, of the University of Chicago, has recently undertaken a detailed examination of Weber's work in this area, uncovering crucial shortcomings in the translations of Weber's texts leading to gross distortions of his intentions, as well as showing more accurately where Weber's own ideas are inadequate (Wolk 1994). Reference was made to this work in chapter ten above, but the analysis is also relevant here. The key issues revolve around Weber's treatment of "honor," "prestige," and "reputation," all concepts that bear directly on the analysis of class, and what has come to be called "ethnicity."

### Weber and the Concept of Status Group

The standard interpretation of Weber's work is that he took Marx's concept of class and decomposed it into class, status, and power. In spite of this vulgarization, Weber's concepts of class situation and status situation remain the most useful concepts for delineating structures of inequality (see Chapter Ten for a discussion of Wolk's reconsideration of Weber's concepts). Social mobility is best thought of not as a process through which socially disembodied individuals rise or fall in an abstract rank order, but as involving a change from one combination of class and status situations to another. In the Social Opportunity Survey and the case studies we attempted to record the oppositional characterizations of groups. It is evident from the few comments set out above that African Americans and Mexican immigrants have elaborate conceptions of difference, but they are not yet as critical for conflict as each group's struggle to gain recognition in a white-dominated milieu.

Weber's concept of "class situation" is different from "status" in that it applies to individuals who specifically do *not* form a group. However, even in his formal definition of class, Weber indicates the complexity of the relations involved:

We would like to speak of a "class" when 1. a plurality of people share a specific causal component of their life-chances *(Lebenschancen)*, insofar as 2. this component is reflected solely in economic interests in the possession of goods and in earnings, that is 3. (this component applies) under the conditions of the market of goods or the labor market ("class situation"). (Weber 1968: 927, retranslated by D. Wolk).

Class situation in this sense is not just a matter of possession of the means of production, or even of "wealth" in a more general sense, but can include skills and even managerial authority.

It is not difficult to see the relevance of Weber's distinctions for the United States, and perhaps even more so for developing countries. In a recent article, Arjun Appadurai cites the curious case of "other backward castes," or OBC, in North India, a putatively primordial status group created out of the bureaucratic distinctions established by the Census of India, but which has now engaged in riots in defence of entitlements to government jobs (Appadurai 1993: 415). In the so-called new nations, a great deal of "ethnic" conflict, as it is called, originates in attempts to monopolize bureaucratic posts or political power by deploying a combination of status claims and class struggle.

The conclusion, then, is that structures of inequality are better understood as the articulation of a complex series of status groups. The processes by which individuals and families move through such a system of articulated groups is much more complex than a mere progression through a series of occupations, or a progressive assimilation to a "mainstream" culture; the purpose of research should be to map the complexities of the terrain through which such movement takes place. In that mapping, Weber's observation that "the notion of 'ethnically' determined social action subsumes phenomena that a rigorous sociological analysis...would have to distinguish carefully" certainly needs to be noted (Weber 1968, Vol. 1: 394–95).

## CLASS SITUATION AND STATUS SITUATION IN CHICAGO'S INNER CITY

How, then, can one apply these principles to the understanding of the social life of Chicago's inner city poor? Or, indeed, to any other social situation? It is, I think, evident that any really good ethnography explores the intersecting and overlapping dimensions of class and status in much the way that Weber actually analysed them, recognizing that class is symbolically constituted just as status groups emerge and find expression through material interests. The belief in primordialism is pervasive in the modern world, and even the liberals and rationalists, cosmopolitans and socialists of this world (to recall Anthony D. Smith's strictures) recognize that it is not merely a survival from some primitive past, but is created and recreated in the most rational bureaucratic societies, usually as a vehicle for status striving and/or material advantage. Therefore, the task for anthropology is to analyze the complexities of the dynamics of class and status, rather than to enumerate cultural characteristics (or supposed characteristics).

This is not the place for such an analysis, but one of the most striking results of our study was to show the extent to which the urban poor are vividly aware of the technical nature of their class situation even as they demonstrate the extent of their internalization of the ideology of opportunity and individual responsibility. The very first question that interviewers were instructed to ask for the Social Opportunity Survey was: *Since this is a study about how conditions affect peoples' lives, perhaps I could begin by asking whether you agree or disagree that America is a land of opportunity where anybody can get ahead, and that everybody gets pretty much what they deserve?* The answers to that question were remarkably positive, though it has to be remembered that this was an opening question so that a negative answer would require a respondent to set a particular kind of tone for the rest of the interview. In fact, as the interviews progressed a great many reservations were expressed about the extent of equality of opportunity, the prevalence of discrimination, and the structural possibility of upward social mobility. Respondent Fred Sanchez (whom we have encountered previously as a participant in the multiple-interview case studies but who also was interviewed for the Social Opportunity Survey) displayed a remarkable understanding of the way in which manufacturing industry has been leaving the city, resulting in fewer jobs being available; of the way in which the Reagan administration appeared to break the power of the unions; and the way in which immigrants from Mexico are willing to work for much lower wages than native-born Americans. He explains that he himself had a good job; "I was making twenty or twenty-two thousand dollars a year there. You know, with overtime. And we had a lot of good benefits there." But then his plant closed down: "The plant had been there a hundred years. It changed names, but it had been there a hundred years doing the same thing. So how are you going to think something like that is going to happen." In spite of his understanding of these structural factors he blamed himself for his present predicament.

> I didn't have a bad life. I made it bad, but I didn't have it bad. I had a lot of opportunities, a lot of opportunities to do something. But I just took it for granted that everything wasn't going to change and it did. I never thought the damn plant was going to close. And look what happened. *(What opportunities do you think you passed up?)* I could have saved a lot of money. I could have done a lot of things. I had the opportunity to advance with their plant. I didn't take the chance. I had the offers and I didn't do it. I didn't want the responsibility. See, because the plant before it closed, all the young supervisors they gave them a chance to go to another plant. And probably I could be still working for the same company but a different plant. That's what happened. But not only that, at the beginning I missed a lot of opportunities. Like when I was working with my brother and my uncle, remember I told you they were mechanics? And I just could have learned it right there and then free and I passed that up. And things like that. I had an opportunity to drive a truck here and get other jobs and I passed them up on account of I had a job where I was working there and I was secure there. And that's what happened. I thought that was it. I thought I was going to retire from there.

There is absolutely no evidence that being of Mexican origin is the overwhelming basis of Fred Sanchez's social identification. The things that matter to him are being poor and being uneducated, and he see the latter as the most important factor in determining social status in late-twentieth-century America.

However, more recent immigrants from Mexico are often preoccupied with their legal status and with their inability to speak English. This latter is not only a technical impediment to getting steady and lucrative jobs, but it also becomes an integral part of status definition. A forty-year-old immigrant from Mexico who has lived in Chicago for seven years had this to say about one of her childhood friends:

> There is a woman, well we aren't talking about a lot of money, but this happened to me. Here in Chicago. She is my *comadre* because when we were girls, we had some big dolls and we baptized them

as though they were real children. We dressed them like real babies. Someone dressed up like the priest and we had a dance and everything. This woman came here when she was 18 or 19, or maybe 20 or 25. She was always intelligent and she got into school here. She became a supervisor in a factory. I ran into her here in Chicago in a store and I greeted her and asked her how she was and how she had been. And she asked me who I was and said she didn't know me. I said, "What! Now you don't know me and I said you are so and so and I am so and so" and I told her all the things that had happened when we were kids. But she pretended she didn't speak Spanish any more. I said "you are so and so and your parents are so and so." And I left her there staring at me in the store. And when I see her now I ask where this American has come from? And other people will do that too. They learn a little English and then they claim they don't speak or understand Spanish. They are presumptuous. Do you think that if I learned a little English I would pretend not to understand when you spoke to me in Spanish? No! These are very hard people… We were brought up together, we are of the same race and now she doesn't know me! Very ugly this. When we were in Mexico she was a little above because her parents were some of the well-off ones and we were of the poorest. But it didn't matter then. We all got together rich and poor alike. We helped each other. But here no. People come here and get big and they don't know Spanish or know you any more. No. That is why I tell you that people change a great deal in a new country, those who want to change. But they change for the worse as often as for the better and that is the problem.

One final bit of ethnography will serve to illustrate the concrete way in which the inhabitants of the low-income areas of Chicago manipulate the signs and symbols of status. Mabel Woods is a thirty-seven-year-old African-American woman who, despite the fact that she is on General Assistance and lives from hand-to-mouth on food stamps, has a bachelors degree and serves from time to time as a substitute teacher in the Chicago Public Schools. The interview, with a person from the University of Chicago, took on a special importance reflected in the fact that she had actually secured permission to conduct the interview in a room belonging to the owner of the apartment in which Mabel Woods rented just one room. The multiple and cross-cutting bases of status were reflected in both the person of the respondent and the furnishings of the room. A summary of the interviewer's description is as follows:

The respondent looked older that her 37 years and had made a special effort to dress-up for this interview. She wore a nice navy print polyester dress with some hot pink in it, a watch which was also hot pink, and her nails were hot pink. She wore bright red lipstick and some dress sandals and sat very primly for the entire two hours and ten minutes of the interview. The room was rented in an apartment on the second floor of a two-story brownstone, reached by very steep stairs and the living room where Mabel had sought special permission for us to sit was much more elaborate than the rest of the building. It had a very nice burgundy carpet and matching drapes, a sofa and matching chair of wood and earth colored velvet, two more nice upholstered chairs with coordinated flowers. There were several handmade satin pillows on the sofa, these and all of the furniture had plastic covers. There was a wooden coffee table with plants on it, a fire-place with very old family pictures, two fancy dolls, one white and one black, resting on the mantle. There was a little rocking chair with a white china doll sitting in it. There was a large picture of a white Jesus above the mantle. There was a wall display which included a clock above the sofa. It was all very, very tidy and there was a handmade screen door which kept the cat from coming into this room. Also, when I went into this room, the lady of the house apologized for not having dusted yet today. The Respondent went about and dusted the seat off for me with a kleenex as well as her seat and the footstool upon which I placed the recorder, although none of these were dusty.

The struggle to maintain respectability and status under conditions of urban decay and economic privation is rarely waged as successfully as this, but even in the most degraded and poverty-stricken living spaces in inner city Chicago, you will find many of these attempts to maintain and assert respectability. We have not done the kind of detailed study of material culture that Daniel Miller has done in Trinidad (Miller 1994), but I am sure that one would find that pictures of Jesus, artificial flowers and throw pillows are universally regarded as important components of a decent apartment no matter what "ethnic group" is involved, while new upholstered furniture kept in its plastic wrappings is another sure sign of status protection.

## CONTEMPORARY NATIONALISM IN THE UNITED STATES

Although respondents among the urban poor in Chicago were remarkably positive about the United States as a land of opportunity where anyone can succeed if they work hard enough, the old image of the melting pot is in obvious need of revision. Arjun Appadurai has recently drawn attention to what he calls an emerging *post-nationalism* that is particularly conspicuous in the United States (Appadurai 1993). In the new wave of post-everything, it was perhaps inevitable that we should have post-nationalism, but as he points out:

> The politics of ethnic identity in the United States is inseparably linked to the global spread of originally local national identities. For every nation-state that has exported significant numbers of its populations to the United States as refugees, tourists, or students, there is now a delocalized transnation, which retains a special ideological link to a putative place of origin but is otherwise a thoroughly diasporic collectivity. No existing conception of Americanness can contain this large variety of transnations (Appadurai 1993: 424).

And, one might add, to use the term "ethnic group" to designate such emergent transnational phenomena adds even more confusion to that already surrounding the term. The *New York Times* of July 25, 1993 cites figures from the United States Immigration and Naturalization Service that show that only 37 percent of eligible Resident Aliens now apply to become United States citizens, preferring to remain attached to their original nation state while enjoying such benefits as accrue from residence in the United States. In the case of some countries the proportion seeking citizenship is even less; in the case of Ecuador it is only 20 percent. This is an enormous change from the classic pattern of immigration and certainly supports Appadurai's argument that the concept of "Americanness" is undergoing profound change. Looked at more closely, the situation is even more complex. Leaving aside the issue of whether "politics of ethnic identity" adequately describes the phenomena under consideration, and overlooking the fact that "refugees, tourists, or students" hardly constitutes an exhaustive list of the types of immigrants holding "green cards," (immigrant visas), there is a multifarious interaction between national origin and local categorizations that produces overlapping and interlocking affiliations of the most entangled kind.

## CONCLUSION

Seeking to limit the use of the term "ethnic" is unlikely to be successful and one can have no illusions about its continued proliferation. We began by saying that ethnicity is like "family" and "marriage" in the sense that these familiar terms seem to need no explication, until we begin to realize that their unexamined meanings distort the observations we are trying to make. One way to avoid such distortion is by the simple expedient of always paying attention to the native categories before imposing our own ideas about what is natural, universal, and self-evident. In some contexts labelling groups or behavior as "ethnic" has more serious consequences than in others. For example, Ralph Premdas has recently published an interesting paper on politics in Trinidad and Tobago in which he uses "ethnic" instead of "racial" (Premdas 1992). However, his discussion is perfectly clear; he is concerned with the racial legacy of colonialism and the need for what he calls "consociational" politics that would accommodate the felt interests and representation of Trinidad's racial groups—East Indians and Creoles. Premdas is careful not to reify these groups into primordial entities, and to restrict his discussion to the need for "proportionality" in the political process. Such moves are a necessary first step in societies like Guyana, Trinidad, Fiji, Sri Lanka, and many others, though only a first step since the more difficult problem consists in actually governing such states.

The establishment of consociational politics will not eliminate structures of inequality, nor can it easily establish the mechanisms through which changes in class or status are achieved. As Premdas points out for Trinidad, there were (and presumably still are) vast discrepancies in the numbers of Indians and Creoles in the civil service, with further discrepancies between Muslims and Hindus. The politics of consociation must lead directly to contention over the process of social mobility comparable to that in the United States. How is equality of opportunity converted into equality of results except by affirmative action? And so we come full circle; labelling political conflict and the social struggle for dignity and respect "ethnic" tells us nothing at all about the real processes involved or about the value commitments that underlie various courses of political action in the modern world.

# NOTES

**CHAPTER TWO**  *Hypotheses and the Problem of Explanation*

1. This term is used in the sense defined by Nadel (1951: 45–47).

2. At this point I have omitted further discussion of the Herskovits's work, a review of previous studies by other scholars, and a brief comparative analysis of material from other parts of the world. The original material may be found at pages 230–51 in chapter nine of *The Negro Family in British Guiana.*

**CHAPTER THREE**  *Culture and Social Structure in the Caribbean*

1. Among recent studies the following deal with family structure and mating: R.T. Smith & C. Jayawardena, "Hindu Marriage Customs in British Guiana." *Social and Economic Studies,* Vol. 7, No. 2 (1958); R.T. Smith & C. Jayawardena, "Marriage and the Family Amongst East Indians in British Guiana," *Social and Economic Studies,* Vol. 8, No. 4 (1959); Chandra Jayawardena, "Marital Stability in Two Guianese Sugar Estate Communities," *Social and Economic Studies,* Vol. 9, No. 1 (1960); Morton Klass, *East Indians in Trinidad: A Study of Cultural Persistence* (Columbia University Press, New York & London, 1961); G.W. Roberts & L. Braithwaite, "Mating Among East Indian and Non-Indian Women in Trinidad," *Social and Economic Studies,* Vol. 11, No. 3 (1962); Chandra Jayawardena, "Family Organization in Plantations in British Guiana," *International Journal of Comparative Sociology,* Vol. 3, No. 1 (1962).

2. These summaries are contained in the "Introduction" and "Final Note" in the volume *Working Papers in Caribbean Social Organization* edited by Mintz and Davenport, and referred to previously.

3. This view is most clearly expressed in T. Parsons & R. Bales, Family, *Socialization and Interaction Process* (Free Press, Glencoe, Illinois, 1955).

4. One of the reasons why East Indians in British Guiana are reluctant to accept automatic registration of customary marriages is that it would then be difficult to dissolve the union if the couple prove to be incompatible.

5. There was a significant jump in the marriage rate immediately following the earthquake in Jamaica in 1907. See Roberts 1957: 287–88.

**CHAPTER FOUR**  *The Matrifocal Family*

1. For example, Fortes reports that 40 percent of household heads at Asokore and 47 percent at Agogo are women; for the three Guyanese villages the percentages are 35.5 percent, 17 percent and 34.5 percent. The proportion for the contemporary United States is roughly 20 percent if one includes females living alone; the proportion among those who are classified as non-white is much higher and comparable to that for Guyana—33.4 percent in 1969.

2. Barnes (1971: 194–226) has noted the same difficulty over Fortes's varying definition of "norms."

3. While I can accept the criticism that the analysis placed too little emphasis upon the distinction between familial and domestic relations, I cannot accept the idea that this was due to some failure to distinguish between them at a definitional level. A careful reading of the book will show that the decision to treat the household as the most important locus of family relations was deliberate and not due to mistaken identity.

4. She says for example, "R.T. Smith has used the term 'matrifocal' to identify the type, thereby emphasizing the role played by the female" (González 1969: 5) To dispel any uncertainty as to whether she equates my use of the term "matrifocal" with her "consanguineal form" she specifically states that "the report [Smith's] lacks details on the actual relationships existing between various members of the family, which makes it difficult to ascertain the nature of the consanguineal household (called 'matrifocal family' by Smith)." "...we are never certain from his description just what the matrifocal family is, other than that it is 'woman-headed' " (González 1969: 128).

5. Thus in a recent book by Farber (1972) we find an extended discussion of matrifocality based on Kunstadter's article.

6. It is gratifying to see that in her most recent article (González 1970), she has extricated herself from some of these difficulties and returned to a point of view remarkably similar to that set out in my earlier work (Smith, R.T. 1956 and 1957). For example she rejects the simple identification of matrifocal with either female-headed households or consanguineal families, and she recognizes that the matrifocal quality of relationship patterns only appears because of the peculiarity of male roles.

7. The study was supported by a grant from the National Science Foundation (NSF–GS–1709) for which grateful acknowledgement is made. I am also indebted to David M. Schneider for many of the ideas used in this study both at the stage of data collection and analysis.

8. That there may be a problem in deciding just what to include or exclude from that domain will be evident if one reads Schneider's paper "What is Kinship All About?" (Schneider 1972).

9. See R.T. Smith 1970 for a fuller discussion of the distinction between cultural, normative, and behavioral aspects of kinship.

10. Since there is considerable, and growing, interest in the whole issue of continuities in culture from Africa to the New World, I should make it clear that my argument in this paper does not preclude the importance of such continuities. I have myself reported knowledge of Ashanti day-names and survivals of totemic beliefs, witchcraft concepts, and ritual activities clearly of African origin among Guyanese villagers of African descent (Smith, R.T. 1956: 131, 158, 164–67). However, it is also crucial to recognize the manner in which these items of cultural material are incorporated in contemporary conceptual systems and the way in which they are used in the process of social life in the modern West Indian context.

11. Spiro's letter to the editor of *Man* (Spiro 1972), correcting Montague's misconceptions about the ideology of "virgin birth," explains very clearly the issues involved here and sets straight the question of what degree of understanding of reproductive processes is involved.

12. The use of the expression "bye-family" among the West Indian lower class may be an

example of the survival of old English terms, or the creation of terms out of English words. The term "bye" in English means secondary, or subsidiary, which is precisely the meaning it has when combined with "family" in the West Indies. The term is also used in cricket (which is the West Indies national sport) to mean a run scored without actually hitting the ball; again a suitable parallel. However, there is also a possibility that it derives from a Hindi word such as Bhai (brother).

13. The idea of a hierarchy of solidary emphasis within the close family relationship complex is dealt with in a preliminary way in Schneider & Smith 1973.

14. Freilich and Coser in a recent paper comment on the similarity between different types of union in Trinidad and suggest that the terms legal marriage, common-law marriage, etc. are all structurally and functionally the same so far as Trinidadian peasants are concerned (1972: 6). I think that this is true, except for the prestige factor.

**CHAPTER FIVE** *Hierarchy and the Dual Marriage System in West Indian Society*

1. Publications based on these studies include Alexander 1976, Alexander 1977, Alexander 1978; Austin 1974, Austin 1979, Austin 1984; DeVeer 1979; Fischer 1974; Foner 1973; Graham and Gordon 1977; R. Smith 1973, R. Smith 1978a, R. Smith 1978b, R. Smith 1982a, R. Smith 1982b.

2. Little attention has been paid to the precise structure of colonial law and its effects upon marriage and inheritance. Pioneering work was carried out by Linda Lewin in Brazil (unpublished manuscript), and more recently Mindie Lazarus-Black has made a detailed study of the relation between legal statute, the judicial process, and family structure in Antigua, West Indies.

3. Isolated cases of marriage between colored men and white women (they were extremely rare) are interesting precisely because they indicate the extent to which property and class could override racial barriers. This was always a latent possibility, reflecting the contradiction between class and color values, and its existence called forth much racist rhetoric (see Brathwaite 1971 and Long 1774).

4. It is interesting that there was a sudden increase in the reported number of colored people in Jamaica from 40,000 (10.8 per cent of the total population) in 1834 to 68,000 (18.1 per cent of the population) in 1844. This remarkable increase is almost certainly due to the reclassification of people previously reported to be "slaves" (see Smith 1982b: 104).

5. The ethnographic present is 1969 when the interviews took place.

**CHAPTER SIX** *Family, Social Change, and Social Policy in the West Indies*

1. A much shorter version of this chapter was presented as a lecture in memory of Professor Chandra Jayawardena, delivered at the University of the West Indies, Mona, Jamaica on March 15th, 1982. Although it does not deal with the joint work we carried out, I am happy to acknowledge how much of my thinking on these matters was influenced by him. I am also grateful to those who attended the lecture for their comments, and to Mrs. D. Powell and the members of the staff of the Department of Sociology, and to Dr. Vaughan Lewis, Director of the Institute of Social and Economic Research, for their kind hospitality.

2. These are all ideas which have surfaced in one way or another in the discussion of poverty

in the United States. See for example the remarkable paper by Walter Miller (1958) which purports to locate the causes of gang activity and crime in the specifics of a lower-class culture made possible by personality characteristics very similar to those described by Simey.

3. Most of the material cited in this section is drawn from the results of a series of studies carried out during the late 1960s and the 1970s under the direction of the author, and involving the collaboration of the University of the West Indies and the University of Chicago. I am grateful to the National Science Foundation and to the Lichtstern Research Fund for the financial support which made most of these studies possible. Fuller accounts of this work will be found in R.T. Smith 1973, 1978a, 1978b; Alexander 1973, 1976, 1977; Austin 1974, 1979; De Veer 1979; Fischer 1974.

4. The material on which the following analysis is based consists not only of the by now voluminous body of census and survey materials, but also of many painstakingly collected genealogies and case studies—family histories really. My assumption is that one can only understand family life if one studies what kinship means to people, and if one is able to comprehend the whole range of individuals' experience. In this research the same individual was interviewed many times, sometimes for as much as one hundred hours stretching over many months. Quick surveys have their uses but they yield data very different from those reported here. For each person interviewed we constructed a genealogy; some of them are enormous, containing as many as 800 to 1000 individuals. See R.T. Smith 1978a, 1978b, and Alexander 1976 for further details.

**CHAPTER SEVEN**   *Plural Society Theory*

1. This was pointed out some years ago by John Rex in "The Plural Society in Sociological Theory," *British Journal of Sociology,* Vol. X, No. 2, 1959.

**CHAPTER EIGHT**   *Caste and Social Status Among the Indians of Guyana*

1. This paper is based mainly on fieldwork carried out between 1956 and 1958 by Smith in a rice-growing village in Demerara and in Georgetown, and by Jayawardena in two plantations in Berbice. Since then Smith has revisited Guyana several times.

2. At the census of 1960 the population was enumerated as follows: East Indian—267,840 (48 percent); African—183,980 (33 percent); Amerindian— 25,450 (4.5 percent); Mixed— 67,189 (12 percent); Chinese—4,074 (0.7 percent); White—3,218 (0.6 percent); Other (mainly Portuguese)—8,348 (1.5 percent); Syrian and Lebanese—69; Not Stated—238. Total— 569,406.

3. For an account of plantation life, see Jayawardena 1963.

4. An abandoned sugar plantation which had been converted into a Government Land Settlement at the end of the First World War was studied by Smith in 1956. Some features of that community are described in Smith and Jayawardena (1959).

5. See Smith 1956 for a discussion of rice farming in Negro communities.

6. We are not concerned with Muslims as a special group here, although they have become an important element in present-day Guyana, and will be mentioned where appropriate.

7. Out of the 238,960 persons who came to British Guiana from India between 1838 and

1917, the majority remained in the colony or died there. Between 1843 and 1949 official repatriation schemes returned 75,547 persons to India. It should be noted that many repatriates found it extremely difficult to readjust to life in India and reengaged for work in the sugar colonies.

8. For an account of developments in Hinduism in British Guiana, see Jayawardena 1966.

9. Leach 1960 and Gould 1964 emphasize the fact that advantages and disabilities in a caste system are characteristically balanced between the component units of the system.

10. The statistics presented here were obtained through a survey which, in Blairmont, aimed at a total coverage but succeeded in covering 94 percent of the Indian households; the rest consists of incompleted schedules, those absent during the period of the survey, and two refusals. The statistics for Port Mourant are based on a sample of 205 households which constitutes about a fifth of the households in the plantation. For various reasons it was not practicable to obtain a random sample. However, the sample was stratified according to area of residence, religion, race, and occupation, the proportions of which were ascertained from records and inquiries.

11. It was more difficult to obtain indirect information about the castes of married women since most of them came from outside the plantation.

12. A few Arya Samajists maintained that since caste was "wrong," questions about it deserved no answer.

13. Although this is not a generally expressed opinion, a couple of informants suggested this.

14. Second marriages can only occur when the first has been dissolved by death, divorce or separation.

15. The two plantations are compared along these lines in Smith and Jayawardena 1959, and Jayawardena 1963.

16. The recognized divisions in the society varied from time to time, and sometimes according to the interests of the observer. For example, one writer distinguished between "Creoles, Barbadians, and Orientals" as constituent parts of the labor force on plantations.

**CHAPTER TEN** *Living in the Gun Mouth: Race, Class, and Political Violence in Guyana*

1. See Hanley 1979 for an account of technological change in this village.

2. Guyana is one of the three "Guyanas"—British, Dutch and French—lying on the northeast shoulder of South America between Venezuela and Brazil. The country is mainly forest and savannah, but a low-lying fertile coastal strip was reclaimed from the sea by the Dutch in the mid-eighteenth century and quickly became a major sugar plantation area worked by African slaves. Acquired by the British in the early nineteenth century, the colony's sugar industry survived the abolition of slavery by instituting schemes of importation of indentured labour from Portuguese Madeira, China, but most notably from India. Portuguese and Chinese immigration was limited, but large numbers of Indians were introduced between 1848 and 1917 so that their descendants are now the largest single racial group. The population was classified in the 1946 census as follows:

| | | |
|---|---|---|
| East Indian | 163,434 | 43.5% |
| African | 143,385 | 38.2% |
| Mixed | 37,685 | 10.0% |
| Amerindian | 16,322 | 4.4% |
| Portuguese | 8,543 | 2.3% |
| Chinese | 3,567 | 1.0% |
| European | 2,480 | 0.7% |
| Asiatic (mainly Syrian) | 236 | 0.1% |
| Not Stated | 49 | |
| Totals | 375,701 | 100.0% |

The population increased rapidly and the East Indian population increased faster than any other. By 1964 the population was listed as follows in the Guyana Year Book.

| | | |
|---|---|---|
| East Indian | 320,070 | 50.1% |
| African | 199,830 | 31.3% |
| Mixed | 75,990 | 11.9% |
| Amerindian | 29,430 | 04.6% |
| Portuguese | 6,830 | 01.1% |
| Chinese | 3,910 | 00 .6% |
| European | 2,420 | 0.4% |
| Totals | 638,480 | 100.0% |

No census figures have been published recently and racial classifications are no longer given in official statistics. However, massive migrations during the 1970s and 1980s—to Canada, Britain, and the USA mainly but also to neighbouring countries in the West Indies and Suriname—have probably offset any natural increase. See chapter one for a recent estimate of the 1994 population.

3. This argument was used by Dr. Jagan, the leader of the P.P.P. (Jagan 1966: Chapter XVI).

4. I do not mean to imply that her discussion of historical developments is simplistic. In fact she has some very interesting and detailed discussions of the Amerindian and Portuguese groups that go far beyond the usual narrative.

5. They may not be residues of Anglo-European hegemony of course; the modern world system is sufficiently saturated with racist stereotypes, and reports of such stereotypes, that it can quickly replenish any fading images.

6. The bitterest blow of all for Jagan was being asked (instructed?) by the Russians and Cubans to cooperate with Burnham (R.T. Smith 1976: 222–23).

7. This passage is quoted with permission from the manuscript draft of Miller 1994, but I have been unable to find it in the published version.

**CHAPTER ELEVEN** *On the Disutility of the Notion of "Ethnic Group" for Understanding Status Struggles in the Modern World.*

1. This project was supported by funds from The Ford Foundation, the Carnegie Foundation, the U.S. Department of Health and Human Services, the Lloyd A. Fry Foundation, The

Rockefeller Foundation, the Institute for Research on Poverty, the Spencer Foundation, the William T. Grant Foundation, the Joyce Foundation, and the Woods Charitable Trust, to all of which grateful acknowledgment is made.

2. In some cases informants chosen for case studies turned out to be unsuitable after one or two interviews, but occasionally those initial interviews provided valuable information that has been used here.

3. One of the preoccupations of the Urban Poverty and Family Life Project was "concentration effects," that is the effect of having poor people concentrated in particular areas, often referred to as "ghettos." However, there was a marked tendency to think of these areas of concentration as being racially homogeneous. Thus considerable concern was expressed at the fact that it proved impossible to find census tracts that contained a predominance of poor whites to compare to similar tracts containing concentrations of poor blacks, Mexicans, and Puerto Ricans. The more significant fact is that the poor, regardless of race or supposed "ethnicity," are concentrated in run-down neighborhoods, as is shown by this case.

# REFERENCES

Alexander, Jack 1976. A Study of the Cultural Domain of Relatives. *American Ethnologist* 3: 17–38

Alexander, Jack 1977. The Culture of Race in Middle-Class Kingston, Jamaica. *American Ethnologist* 4: 413–35.

Alexander, Jack 1978. The Cultural Domain of Marriage. *American Ethnologist* 5: 5–14.

Alexander, Jack 1984. Love, Race, Slavery, and Sexuality in Jamaican Images of the Family. In *Kinship Ideology and Practice in Latin America*, edited by Raymond T. Smith. (Chapel Hill: University of North Carolina Press.)

Anderson, Michael 1971. *Family Structure in Nineteenth Century Lancashire.* (Cambridge: Cambridge University Press.)

Andrews, Evangeline W. and C.M. Andrews (eds.) 1923. *Journal of a Lady of Quality: Being the Narrative of a Journey from Scotland to the West Indies, North Carolina, and Portugal in the Years 1774 to 1776.* (New Haven: Yale University Press.)

Anonymous 1828. *Marly, or A Planter's Life in Jamaica.* (Glasgow.)

Appadurai, Arjun 1993. Patriotism and its Futures. *Public Culture* 5: 411–429.

Ashcroft, Michael n.d. Robert Charles Dallas. *Jamaica Journal* 44: 94–101.

Austin, Diane J. 1974. *Symbols and Ideologies of Class in Urban Jamaica: A Cultural Analysis of Classes.* (Chicago: University of Chicago Ph.D. Dissertation.)

Austin, Diane J. 1979. History and Symbols in Ideology: a Jamaican Example. *Man* (N.S.) 14: 497–514.

Austin, Diane J. 1984. *Urban Life in Kingston, Jamaica: The Culture and Class Ideology of Two Neighborhoods.* (New York: Gordon and Breach.)

Austin-Broos, Diane J. 1992. Redefining the Moral Order: Interpretations of Christianity in Post-Emancipation Jamaica. In *The Meaning of Freedom: Economics, Politics, and Culture After Slavery*, edited by Frank McGlynn and Seymour Drescher, pp. 221–43. (Pittsburgh and London: University of Pittsburgh Press.)

Avineri, Shlomo 1970. *The Social and Political Thought of Karl Marx.* (Cambridge: Cambridge University Press.)

Bahmueller, Charles F. 1981. *The National Charity Company: Jeremy Bentham's Silent Revolution.* (Berkeley: University of California Press.)

Barnes, John A. 1971. *Three Styles in the Study of Kinship.* (Berkeley and Los Angeles: University of California Press.)

Barth, Fredrik 1969. Introduction. In *Ethnic Groups and Boundaries: The Social Organization of Culture Difference*, edited by Fredrik Barth. (London: George Allen and Unwin.)

Bell, Daniel 1975. Ethnicity and Social Change. In *Ethnicity: Theory and Experience*, edited by Nathan Glazer and Daniel P. Moynihan, pp. 141–74. (Cambridge, Mass. and London: Harvard University Press.)

Best, Lloyd 1992. The Contribution of George Beckford. *Social and Economic Studies*, 41: 5–23.

Blake, Judith 1961. *Family Structure in Jamaica.* (New York: Free Press of Glencoe Inc.)

Bolingbroke, Henry 1809. *A Voyage to the Demerary, Containing a Statistical Account of the Settlements There, and of Those on the Essequebo, the Berbice, and Other Contiguous Rivers of Guyana.* (London.)

Bott, Elizabeth 1968 [1957]. *Family and Social Network.* Second edition with new material. (London: Tavistock Publications Ltd.)

Bourdieu, Pierre 1984. *Distinction: A Social Critique of the Judgement of Taste.* Translated by Richard Nice. (Cambridge, MA: Harvard University Press.)

Bourguignon, Erika et al. 1980. *A World of Women: Anthropological Studies of Women in the Societies of the World.* (New York: Praeger.)

Boyer, Ruth 1964. The Matrifocal Family Among the Mescalero: Additional Data. *American Anthropologist* 66: 595–604.

Braithwaite, Lloyd 1953. Social Stratification in Trinidad. *Social and Economic Studies* 2: 5–175.

Brathwaite, Edward 1971. *The Development of Creole Society in Jamaica 1770–820.* (Oxford: The Clarendon Press.)

Braudel, Fernand 1975. *The Mediterranean and the Mediterranean World in the Age of Philip II.* 2 Vols. (New York: Harper Torchbooks.)

British Guiana Constitutional Commission, 1950–51. *Report and Despatch from the Secretary of State for the Colonies to the Governor of British Guiana, 6th October 1951.* Colonial No. 280. (London: His Majesty's Stationery Office.)

British Guiana Constitutional Commission, 1954. *Report.* Cmnd. 9274. (London: Her Majesty's Stationery Office.)

British Guiana: *Suspension of the Constitution 1953.* Cmnd. 8980. Presented by the Secretary of State for the Colonies to Parliament by Command of Her Majesty. (London: Her Majesty's Stationery Office.)

BRO. Bristol Record Office. Microfilm AC/WO 16[17]e; 16[37]. (Bristol, England.)

Brodber, Erna 1975. *A Study of Yards in the City of Kingston.* (Mona, Jamaica: Institute of Social and Economic Research, Working Papers No. 9.)

Brodber, Erna 1982. *Perception of Caribbean Women: Towards a Documentation of Stereotypes.* Women in the Caribbean Project, Vol. 4. (Barbados: University of the West Indies.)

Bronkhurst, H.V.P. 1883. *The Colony of British Guiana and its Labouring Population.* (London: T. Woolmer.)

Buisseret, David 1980. *Historic Architecture of the Caribbean.* (London: Heinemann.)

Burn, W.L. 1937. *Emancipation and Apprenticeship in the West Indies.* (London: Jonathan Cape.)

Burnham, Forbes 1970. *A Destiny to Mould: Selected Discourses by the Prime Minister of Guyana,* Compiled by C.A. Nascimento and R.A. Burrowes. (Trinidad and Jamaica: Longman Caribbean.)

Campbell, Mavis C. 1976. *The Dynamics of Change in a Slave Society: A Sociopolitical History of the Free Coloreds of Jamaica, 1800–1865.* (Rutherford, NJ: Fairleigh Dickenson University Press.)

Chase, Ashton 1964. *A History of Trade Unionism in Guyana 1900 to 1961, With An Epilogue to 1964*. (Ruimveldt, Demerara, Guyana: New Guyana Company Ltd.)

Clarke, Edith 1957. *My Mother Who Fathered Me*. (London: George Allen and Unwin.)

Cohen, E.A. 1953. *Human Behavior in the Concentration Camp*. (New York: W.W. Norton and Co.)

Cohn, Bernard S. 1955. The Changing Status of a Depressed Caste. In *Village India*, edited by McKim Marriott. (Chicago: University of Chicago Press.)

Comaroff, John 1992. Of Totemism and Ethnicity. In *Ethnography and the Historical Imagination*, edited by John Comaroff and Jean Comaroff, pp. 49–67. (Boulder: Westview Press.)

Comins, D.W.D. 1893. *Notes on Emigration from India to British Guiana*. (Calcutta: Bengal Secretariat Press.)

Cousins, W.M. 1935. Slave Family Life in the British Colonies 1800–34. *Sociological Review* Vol. 27.

Craton, Michael 1978. *Searching for the Invisible Man: Slaves and Plantation Life in Jamaica*. (Cambridge, MA: Harvard University Press.)

Craton, Michael 1979. Changing Patterns of Slave Families in the British West Indies. *Journal of Interdisciplinary History* 10: 1–35.

Crooke, W. 1896. *The Tribes and Castes of the North-Western Provinces and Oudh*. 4 Vols. (Calcutta: Office of the Superintendent of Government Printing.)

Cumper, G. E. 1958. The Jamaican Family: Village and Estate. *Social and Economic Studies* 7: 76–108.

Cumper, G. E. 1961. Household and Occupation in Barbados. In *Working Papers in Caribbean Social Organization*, edited by Sidney W. Mintz and William Davenport, pp. 386–419. (Special number of *Social and Economic Studies*, Vol. 10.)

Cundall, Frank 1922. *Jamaica in 1922: A Handbook of Information for Intending Settlers and Visitors with Some Account of the Island's History*. (Kingston, Jamaica: The Institute of Jamaica.)

Curtin, Philip D. 1955. *Two Jamaicas: The Role of Ideas in a Tropical Colony 1830–1865*. (Cambridge, Mass.: Harvard University Press.)

Curtin, Philip D. 1974. The Black Experience of Colonialism and Imperialism, in *Slavery, Colonialism, and Racism*, edited by Sidney W. Mintz. (New York: W.W. Norton.)

Dalton, H.G. 1855. *The History of British Guiana*. (London: Longman, Brown, Green, and Longmans.)

Danns, George K. 1982. *Domination and Power in Guyana: A Study of the Police in a Third World Context*. (New Brunswick and London: Transaction Books.)

Davenport, W. 1961. The Family System of Jamaica. In *Working Papers in Caribbean Social Organization*, edited by Sidney W. Mintz and W. Davenport, pp. 420–54. (Special number of *Social and Economic Studies* 10)

Degler, Carl N. 1971. *Neither Black nor White: Slavery and Race Relations in Brazil and the United States.* (New York: Macmillan.)

Despres, Leo 1967. *Cultural Pluralism and Nationalist Politics in British Guiana.* (Chicago: Rand McNally.)

DeVeer, Henrietta 1979. *Sex Roles and Social Stratification in a Rapidly Growing Urban Area— May Pen, Jamaica.* (Chicago: University of Chicago Ph.D. Dissertation.)

Donzelot, Jacques 1979. *The Policing of Families.* (New York: Pantheon Books.)

Douglass, Lisa 1992. *The Power of Sentiment: Love, Hierarchy and the Jamaican Family Elite.* (Boulder, CO: Westview Press.)

Drake, St. Claire and Cayton, Horace R. 1962. *Black Metropolis: a Study of Negro Life in a Northern City.* 2 Vols. (New York: Harper & Row.)

Drayton, Evan n.d., *The Comrades.* (Unpublished Manuscript.)

Drummond, Lee 1974. *The Outskirts of the Earth: A Study of Amerindian Ethnicity on the Pomeroon River, Guyana.* (Chicago: University of Chicago Ph.D. Dissertation.)

Dumont, Lee. 1961. Caste, Racism and Stratification. Reflections of a Social Anthropologist. *Contributions to Indian Sociology* 5: 20–43.

Dumont, Louis 1980 [1970]. *Homo Hierarchicus: The Caste System and its Implications.* trans. Mark Sainsbury, Louis Dumont, and Basia Gulati. 2nd Edition. (Chicago: University of Chicago Press.)

Dunn, Richard S. 1972. *Sugar and Slaves: The Rise of the Planter Class in the English West Indies, 1624–1713.* (Chapel Hill, NC: University of North Carolina Press.)

Edwards, Bryan 1793. *The History, Civil and Commercial, of the British Colonies in the West Indies.* 2 Vols. (London: John Stockdale.)

Eggan, Fred 1949. The Hopi and the Lineage Principle. In *Social Structure: Studies Presented to A. R. Radcliffe-Brown,* edited by Meyer Fortes. (Oxford: The Clarendon Press.)

Eisner, Gisela 1961. *Jamaica 1830–1930: A Study in Economic Growth.* (Manchester: Manchester University Press.)

El Zein, Abdul Hamid Mohammed 1974. *The Sacred Meadows: A Structural Analysis of Religious Symbolism in an East African Town.* (Evanston: Northwestern University Press.)

Engels, Friedrich 1958. *The Condition of the Working Class in England.* Translated and edited by W. O. Henderson and W. H. Chaloner. (Stanford: Stanford University Press.)

Farber, Bernard 1972. *Guardians of Virtue: Salem Families in 1800.* (New York: Basic Books.)

Firth, Raymond (ed.) 1956. *Two Studies of Kinship in London.* (London School of Economics Monographs on Social Anthropology, no. 15.)

Firth, Raymond, Hubert, J. and Forge, A. 1970. *Families and Their Relatives.* (London: Routledge and Kegan Paul.)

Fischer, Michael 1974. Value Assertion and Stratification: Religion and Marriage in Rural Jamaica. *Caribbean Studies* 14(1): 7–37; 14(3): 7–35.

Fogel, Robert W. and Stanley L. Engerman 1974. *Time on the Cross: the Economics of American Negro Slavery.* (Boston: Little, Brown and Company.)

Foner, Nancy 1973. *Status and Power in Rural Jamaica: A Study of Educational and Political Change.* (New York: Teacher's College Press.)

Fortes, Meyer 1949a. *The Web of Kinship Among the Tallensi.* (Oxford: The Clarendon Press.)

Fortes, Meyer 1949b. Time and Social Structure: An Ashanti Case Study. In *Social Structure: Studies Presented to A. R. Radcliffe-Brown,* edited by Meyer Fortes. (Oxford: The Clarendon Press.)

Fortes, Meyer 1953. Preface. In Fernando Henriques, *Family and Colour in Jamaica.* (London: Eyre and Spottiswoode.)

Fortes, Meyer 1956. Foreword. In Raymond T. Smith, *The Negro Family in British Guiana.* (London: Routledge and Kegan Paul.)

Fortes, Meyer 1958. Introduction. In *The Developmental Cycle in Domestic Groups,* edited by Jack Goody. Cambridge Papers in Social Anthropology, no. 1. (Cambridge: Cambridge University Press.)

Fortes, Meyer 1969. *Kinship and the Social Order: The Legacy of Lewis Henry Morgan.* (Chicago: Aldine Publishing Company.)

Fortes, Meyer 1978. An Anthropologist's Apprenticeship. *Annual Review of Anthropology* 7: 1–30.

Fortes, M. and Evans-Pritchard, E.E. (eds.) 1940. *African Political Systems.* (London: Oxford University Press.)

Foucault, Michel 1965. *Madness and Civilization.* (New York: Pantheon Books.)

Foucault, Michel 1970. *The Order of Things: An Archaeology of the Human Sciences.* (New York: Pantheon Books.)

Foucault, Michel 1973. *The Birth of the Clinic: An Archaeology of Medical Perception.* (New York: Pantheon Books.)

Foucault, Michel 1978a. *Discipline and Punish: The Birth of the Prison.* (New York: Pantheon Books.)

Foucault, Michel 1978b. *The History of Sexuality. Volume I: An Introduction.* (New York: Pantheon Books.)

Frazier, Franklin 1939. *The Negro Family in the United States.* (Chicago: University of Chicago Press.)

Freilich, M. and Coser, L.A. 1972. Structured Imbalances of Gratification: The Case of the Caribbean Mating System. *The British Journal of Sociology* 23: 1–19.

Furnivall, J.S. 1948. *Colonial Policy and Practice: A Comparative Study of Burma and Netherlands India.* (London: Cambridge University Press.)

Geertz, Clifford (ed.) 1963. *Old Societies and New States: The Quest for Modernity in Asia and Africa.* (New York: The Free Press.)

Geertz, Clifford 1971. After the Revolution: The Fate of Nationalism in the New States. In *Stability and Social Change,* edited by Bernard Barber and Alex Inkeles. (New York: Little, Brown and Company Inc.)

Geertz, Hildred 1961. *The Javanese Family: A Study of Kinship and Socialization.* (New York: The Free Press.)

Genovese, Eugene D. 1972. *Roll, Jordan, Roll: The World the Slaves Made*. (New York: Pantheon Books.)

Gillin, John 1945. *Moche: A Peruvian Coastal Community*. (Washington, DC: Smithsonian Institution, Institute of Anthropology, Publication No. 3.)

Glasgow, Roy A. 1970. *Guyana: Race and Politics Among Africans and East Indians*. (The Hague: Martinus Nijhof.)

Glazer, Nathan and Moynihan, Daniel P. (eds.) 1975. *Ethnicity: Theory and Experience*. (Cambridge, MA and London: Harvard University Press.)

Goffman, Erving 1961. *Asylums*. (New York: Doubleday.)

González, N.L. Solien 1969. *Black Carib Household Structure: A Study of Migration and Modernization*. (Seattle: University of Washington Press.)

González, N.L. Solien 1970. Toward a Definition of Matrifocality. In *Afro-American Anthropology, Contemporary Perspectives*, edited by N.E. Whitten Jr. and J.F. Szwed. (New York: The Free Press.)

Gonzalez, Virginia Durant 1982. The Realm of Female Familial Responsibility. In *Women and the Family: Women in the Caribbean Project*, Vol. 2. (Barbados: University of the West Indies.)

Goode, William J. 1961. Illegitimacy, Anomie and Cultural Penetration. *American Sociological Review*, Vol. 26, No. 6.

Goody, Jack 1972. The Evolution of the Family. In *Household and Family in Past Time*, edited by Peter Laslett. (London: Cambridge University Press.)

Gough, Kathleen 1952. Changing Kinship Usages in the Setting of Political and Economic Change Among the Nayars of Malabar. *Journal of the Royal Anthropological Institute*, Vol. LXXXII.

Gould, H.A. 1964. A Jajmani System of North India: Its Structure, Magnitude, and Meaning. *Ethnology* 3: 12–41.

Goveia, Elsa V. 1980 [1956]. *A Study on the Historiography of the British West Indies to the End of the Nineteenth Century*. (Washington, DC: Howard University Press.) [Mexico: Instituto Panamericano de Geografia y Historia.]

Graham, Sara and Derek Gordon 1977. *The Stratification System and Occupational Mobility in Guyana*. (Mona, Jamaica: Institute of Social and Economic Research.)

Gramsci, Antonio 1971. *Selections From the Prison Notebooks*. (New York: International Publishers.)

GRO 347. Gloucestershire Record Office. Codrington Family Archive. Microfilm 347, C2. (Gloucester, England.)

GRO 351. Gloucestershire Record Office. Codrington Family Archive. Microfilm 351, D1610, C22. (Gloucester, England.)

Gutman, Herbert G. 1976. *The Black Family in Slavery and Freedom, 1750–1925*. (New York: Pantheon Books.)

Hall, Douglas 1959. *Free Jamaica, 1838–1865: An Economic History*. (New Haven: Yale University Press.)

Handler, Jerome S. 1974. *The Unappropriated People: Freedmen in the Slave Society of Barbados.* (Baltimore: The Johns Hopkins University Press.)

Hanley, Eric R. 1975. Rice, Politics and Development in Guyana. In *Beyond the Sociology of Development: Economy and Society in Latin America and Africa,* edited by Ivar Oxaal, Tony Barnett, and David Booth. (London: Routledge and Kegan Paul.)

Hanley, Eric R. 1979. Mechanized Rice Cultivation: The Experience of an East Indian Community in Guyana. In *Peasants, Plantations and Rural Communities in the Caribbean,* edited by Malcolm Cross and Arnaud Marks. (Department of Sociology, University of Surrey and Department of Caribbean Studies, Royal Institute of Linguistics and Anthropology, Leiden.)

Henfrey, Colin V.F. 1972. Foreign Influence in Guyana: The Struggle for Independence. In *Patterns of Foreign Influence in the Caribbean,* edited by Emanuel de Kadt, pp. 49–81. (London: Oxford University Press for Royal Institute of International Affairs.)

Henfrey, Colin V.F. 1981. Dependency, Modes of Production, and the Class Analysis of Latin America. *Latin American Perspectives* 8: 17–54.

Henriques, F. 1953. *Family and Colour in Jamaica.* (London: Eyre and Spottiswoode.)

Herrnstein, Richard J. and Murray, Charles 1994. *The Bell Curve: Intelligence and Class Structure in American Life.* (New York: Free Press.)

Herskovits, Melville J. 1937. *Life in a Haitian Valley.* (New York: Alfred A. Knopf.)

Herskovits, Melville J. 1941. Some Comments on the Study of Culture Contact. *American Anthropologist,* 43: 1–10.

Herskovits, Melville J. 1945. Problem, Method and Theory in Afroamerican Studies, *Afroamerica,* Vol. I: 5–24.

Herskovits, Melville J. 1952. *Man and His Works: The Science of Cultural Anthropology.* (New York: Alfred A. Knopf.)

Herskovits, Melville J. and Frances S. Herskovits 1934. *Rebel Destiny: Among the Bush Negroes of Dutch Guiana.* (New York: McGraw Hill.)

Herskovits, Melville J. and Frances S. Herskovits 1947. *Trinidad Village.* (New York: Alfred A. Knopf.)

Heuman, Gad 1981. *Between Black and White: Race, Politics and the Free Coloreds in Jamaica, 1792–1865.* (Westport, CT: The Greenwood Press.)

Higman, Barry W. 1976. *Slave Population and Economy in Jamaica, 1807–1834.* (Cambridge: Cambridge University Press.)

Higman, Barry 1978. *Domestic Service in Jamaica, England and the United States 1770–1970.* (Jamaica: University of the West Indies, Department of History.)

Hobsbawm, Eric 1983. Introduction: Inventing Traditions. In *The Invention of Tradition,* edited by Eric Hobsbawm and Terence Range, pp. 1–14. (Cambridge: Cambridge University Press.)

Hoetink, Hermanus 1967. *The Two Variants in Caribbean Race Relations: A Contribution to the Sociology of Segmented Societies.* (London, New York, and Toronto: Oxford University Press.)

Hoetink, Hermanus 1979. *Slavery and Race Relations in the Americas: Comparative Notes on Their Nature and Nexus.* (New York: Harper and Row.)

Holt, Thomas C. 1992. *The Problem of Freedom: Race, Labor, and Politics in Jamaica and Britain, 1832–1938.* (Baltimore: The Johns Hopkins University Press.)

IJMC. Institute of Jamaica Manuscript Collection. MS 1604. (Kingston, Jamaica.)

IJMC. Institute of Jamaica Manuscript Collection. Nuttall Papers, MST 209. (Kingston, Jamaica.)

Jagan, Cheddi 1966. *The West on Trial: My Fight for Guyana's Freedom.* (London: Michael Joseph.)

Jayawardena, Chandra 1960. Marital Stability in Two Guianese Sugar Estate Communities. *Social and Economic Studies* 9: 76–101.

Jayawardena, Chandra 1962. Family Organisation in Plantations in British Guiana. *International Journal of Cornparative Sociology*, Vol. III, No. 1.

Jayawardena, Chandra 1963. *Conflict and Solidarity in a Guianese Plantation.* (London: The Athlone Press.)

Jayawardena, Chandra 1966. Religious Belief and Social Change: Aspects of the Development of Hinduism in British Guiana. *Comparative Studies in Society and History* 8: 11–40.

JIRO. Jamaica Island Record Office. Wills, Lib. 131. (Spanish Town, Jamaica.)

Josselin de Jong, P.E. 1951. *Menengkabau and Negri Sembilan: Socio-Political Structure in Indonesia.* (Leiden: E. Ijdo.)

Kamerman, Sheila B. and Alfred J. Kahn (eds.) 1978. *Family Policy: Government and Families in Fourteen Countries.* (New York: Columbia University Press.)

Katzin, Margaret M. 1959. The Jamaican Country Higgler. *Social and Economic Studies* 8: 421–40.

Kerr, Madeleine 1952. *Personality and Conflict in Jamaica.* (Liverpool: Liverpool University Press.)

Kerr, Madeleine 1958. *The People of Ship Street.* (London: Routledge and Kegan Paul.)

Klass, Morton 1988 [1961]. *East Indians in Trinidad: A Study in Cultural Persistence.* (Prospect Heights, Illinois: Waveland Press Inc.) [New York: Columbia University Press.]

Kundstadter, Peter 1965. A Survey of the Consanguine or Matrifocal Family. *American Anthropologist* 65: 56–66.

Lamming, George 1953. *In the Castle of My Skin.* (London: Harborough.)

Land, Hilary and Roy Parker 1978. United Kingdom. In *Family Policy: Government and Families in Fourteen Countries*, edited by Kamerman and Kahn. (New York: Columbia University Press.)

Lazarus-Black, Mindie 1994. *Legitimate Acts and Illegitimate Encounters: Law and Society in Antigua and Barbuda.* (Washington and London: Smithsonian Institution Press.)

Leach, Edmund R. 1954. *Political Systems of Highland Burma.* (London: Bell.)

Leach, Edmund R. 1960. Introduction: What Should We Mean by Caste? In *Aspects of Caste in South India, Ceylon and North-Western Pakistan*, edited by E.R. Leach. (Cambridge:

Cambridge University Press.)

Leach, Edmund R. 1961. *Rethinking Anthropology*. (University of London: The Athlone Press.)

Lewin, Linda 1981. *Property as Patrimony: Changing Notions of Family, Kinship, and Wealth in Brazilian Inheritance Law from Empire to Republic*. (Unpublished manuscript.)

Lewis, Arthur 1961. Foreword, in Gisela Eisner, *Jamaica 1830–1930: A Study in Economic Growth*. (Manchester: Manchester University Press.)

Lewis, Oscar 1959. *Five Families: Mexican Case Studies in the Culture of Poverty*. (New York: Basic Books.)

*London Gazette*. No. 19656. Sept. 8, 1838: 2004–5.

Long, Edward 1774. *The History of Jamaica*. 3 Vols. (London: T. Lowndes.)

Lutchman, Harold A. 1974. *From Colonialism to Co-operative Republic: Aspects of Political Development in Guyana*. (Rio Piedras, Puerto Rico: Institute of Caribbean Studies, University of Puerto Rico.)

Maher, Vanessa 1987. Sewing the Seams of Society: Dressmakers and Seamstresses in Turin Between the Wars. In *Gender and Kinship: Essays Toward a Unified Analysis*, edited by Jane Fishburne Collier and Sylvia Junko Yanagisako. (Stanford: Stanford University Press.)

Mair, Lucy P. 1938. The Place of History in the Study of Culture Contact. In *Methods of Study of Culture Contact in Africa*, edited by B. Malinowski. Memorandum XV, International Institute of African Languages and Cultures.

Martinez-Alier, Verena 1974. *Marriage, Class and Colour in Nineteenth Century Cuba: A Study of Racial Attitudes and Sexual Values in a Slave Society*. (Cambridge: Cambridge University Press.)

Matthews, Dom Basil 1953. *Crisis of the West Indian Family*. (Trinidad: Extra-mural Department, University College of the West Indies.)

McKenzie, Hermione 1982. Introduction: Women and the Family in Caribbean Society. In *Women and the Family*. Women in the Caribbean Project, Vol. 2. (Barbados: University of the West Indies.)

Miller, Daniel n.d. *Modernity An Ethnographic Approach: Dualism and Mass Consumption in Trinidad*. (Manuscript.)

Miller, Daniel 1994. *Modernity An Ethnographic Approach: Dualism and Mass Consumption in Trinidad*. (Oxford: Berg Publishers.)

Miller, Walter B. 1958. Lower-Class Culture as a Generating Milieu of Gang Delinquency. *Journal of Social Issues* 14: 5–19.

Mintz, Sidney 1955. The Jamaican Internal Marketing Pattern: Some Notes and Hypotheses. *Social and Economic Studies* 4: 95–103.

Mintz, Sidney 1960. *Worker in the Cane: A Puerto Rican Life History*. (New Haven: Yale University Press.)

Mintz, Sidney W. 1961. A Final Note in *Working Papers in Caribbean Social Organization*, edited by Sidney W. Mintz and William Davenport. (Special number of *Social and Economic*

*Studies,* Vol. 10, No. 4.)

Mintz, Sydney W. 1974. The Caribbean Region. In *Slavery, Colonialism, and Racism,* edited by Sidney W. Mintz. (New York: W.W. Norton.)

Mintz, Sidney W. 1978. Was the Plantation Slave a Proletarian? *Review* 2: 81–98.

Mintz, Sidney W. and Douglas Hall 1960. The Origins of the Jamaican Internal Marketing System. In *Papers in Caribbean Anthropology,* edited by Sidney W. Mintz. (New Haven: Yale University Publications in Anthropology 57: 3–26.)

Mintz, Sidney W. and William Davenport (eds.) 1961. *Working Papers in Caribbean Social Organization.* (Special number of *Social and Economic Studies,* Vol. 10, No. 4.)

Moore, Brian L. 1987. *Race, Power and Social Segmentation in Colonial Society: Guyana after Slavery, 1838–1891.* (New York: Gordon and Breach.)

Moreton, J.B. 1790. *Manners and Customs of the West India Islands.* (London.)

Moynihan, Daniel P. 1965. *The Negro Family: the Case for National Action.* (Washington, D.C.: Office of Planning and Research, U.S. Department of Labor.)

Murdock, G.P. 1949. *Social Structure.* (New York: Macmillan Company.)

Murray, Charles 1984. *Losing Ground: American Social Policy, 1950–1980.* (New York: Basic Books.)

Myrdal, Gunnar 1944. *An American Dilemma: The Negro Problem and Modern Democracy.* (New York: Harper.)

Nadel, Siegfried F. 1951. *The Foundations of Social Anthropology.* (London: Cohen and West.)

Nath, Dwarka 1950. *A History of Indians in British Guiana.* (London: Thomas Nelson and Sons.)

*Negro Slavery; Or a View of Some of the More Prominent Features of That State of Society as it Exists in the United States of America And In the Colonies of the West Indies Especially in Jamaica.* 1823. (London: Hatchard and Son, Piccadilly.)

Newman, Peter 1964. *British Guiana: Problems of Cohesion in an Immigrant Society.* (London: Oxford University Press for the Institute of Race Relations.)

O'Loughlin, C. 1958. The Rice Sector in the Economy of British Guiana. *Social and Economic Studies* 7: 115–143.

Ostrowski, Bernice J. 1969. *Peasant Marketing in Antigua.* (Ph.D. Dissertation.)

Parsons, Anne 1969. *Belief, Magic, and Anomie: Essays in Psychosocial Anthropology.* (New York: Free Press.)

Parsons, T. and Bales, R. 1955. *Family, Socialization and Interaction Process.* (Glencoe, IL: Free Press.)

Parsons, Talcott 1952. *The Social System.* (London: The Tavistock Institute.)

Parsons, Talcott 1955. The American Family: Its Relations to Personality and to the Social Structure. In *Family, Socialization and Interaction Process,* edited by Talcott Parsons and Robert F. Bales. (Glencoe, IL.: Free Press.)

Patterson, Orlando 1967. *The Sociology of Slavery.* (Rutherford: Fairleigh Dickenson University Press.)

Patterson, Orlando 1982. Persistence, Continuity, and Change in the Jamaican Working-class Family. *Journal of Family History* 7: 135–61.

Post, Ken 1978. *Arise Ye Starvelings: The Jamaican Labour Rebellion of 1938 and its Aftermath.* (The Hague, Boston, London: Martinus Nijhoff.)

Premdas, Ralph R. 1992. *Ethnic Conflict and Development: The Case of Guyana.* Discussion Paper No. 30. (Geneva: United Nations Research Institute for Social Development.)

Radcliffe-Brown, A.R. 1950. Introduction. In *African Systems of Kinship and Marriage,* edited by A.R. Radcliffe-Brown and Daryll Forde. (London: Oxford University Press.)

Radcliffe-Brown, A.R. 1952. *Structure and Function in Primitive Society.* (London: Cohen and West.)

Radcliffe-Brown, A.R. and Forde, Daryll (eds.) 1950. *African Systems of Kinship and Marriage.* (London: Oxford University Press.)

Rainwater, Lee and William L. Yancey (eds.) 1967. *The Moynihan Report and the Politics of Controversy.* (Cambridge, MA. and London: The M.I.T. Press.)

Randolph, R.R. 1964. The Matrifocal Family as a Comparative Category. *American Anthropologist* 66: 628–31.

Reid, Stanley 1977. An Introductory Approach to the Concentration of Power in the Jamaican Corporate Economy and Notes on its Origin. In *Essays on Power and Change in Jamaica,* edited by Carl Stone and Aggrey Brown. (Kingston, Jamaica: Jamaica Publishing House.)

Reno, Philip 1964. *The Ordeal of British Guiana.* (New York: Monthly Review Press.)

Rex, John 1959. The Plural Society in Sociological Theory. *British Journal of Sociology,* Vol. X, No. 2.

Rex, John 1971. The Plural Society: The South African Case, *Race* 12: 401–14.

Richards, A.I. 1950. Some Types of Family Structure Amongst the Central Bantu. In *African Systems of Kinship and Marriage,* edited by A. R. Radcliffe-Brown and Daryll Forde. (Oxford: Oxford University Press.)

Roberts, G.W. 1957. *The Population of Jamaica.* (Cambridge: Cambridge University Press.)

Roberts, G.W. and L. Braithwaite 1959. Fertility Differentials in Trinidad, *International Population Conference.* (Vienna.)

Roberts, G.W. and L. Braithwaite 1960. Fertility Differentials by Family Type in Trinidad. *Annals of the New York Academy of Sciences,* Vol. 84, Article 17.

Roberts, G.W. and L. Braithwaite 1961a. A Gross Mating Table for a West Indian Population. *Population Studies,* Vol. XIV, No. 3.

Roberts, G.W. and L. Braithwaite 1961b. Mating Patterns and Prospects in Trinidad. *International Population Conference.* New York.

Roberts, G.W. and L. Braithwaite 1962. Mating Among East Indian and Non-Indian Women in Trinidad. *Social and Economic Studies,* Vol. 11, No. 3.

Roberts, George W. and Sonja Sinclair 1978. *Women in Jamaica: Patterns of Reproduction and Family.* (New York: KTO Press.)

Robotham, Donald K. 1970. *National Integration and Local Community Structure in Jamaica.* (Chicago: University of Chicago M.A. Thesis.)

Robotham, Don 1977. Agrarian Relations in Jamaica. In *Essays on Power and Change in Jamaica,* edited by Carl Stone and Aggrey Brown, pp. 45–57. (Kingston, Jamaica: Jamaica Publishing House.)

Rodman, Hyman 1963. The Lower-Class Value Stretch. *Social Forces* 42: 205–15.

Rodney, Walter 1981a. Plantation Society in Guyana. *Review* 4: 643–66.

Rodney, Walter 1981b. *A History of the Guyanese Working People, 1881–1905.* (Baltimore: Johns Hopkins University Press.)

Romalis, Rochelle S. 1969. *The Rural Community and the Total Society During Economic Change in St. Lucia: A Case Study.* (Montreal: McGill University Ph.D. Dissertation.)

Rosenfeld, H. 1958. Processes of Structural Change Within the Arab Village Extended Family *American Anthropologist* 60: 1127–39.

Roughley, Thomas 1823. *The Jamaica Planter's Guide.* (London: Longman, Hurst, Rees, Orme, and Brown.)

Rubbo, Anna and Taussig, Michael 1977. Up Off Their Knees: Servanthood in Southwest Colombia. *Michigan Discussions in Anthropology* 3: 41–65.

Schapera, I. 1962. Should Anthropologists be Historians? *Journal of the Royal Anthropological Institute* Vol. 92, Pt. 2.

Schapera, I. 1957. Marriage and Near Kin Among the Tswana. *Africa.* Vol. XXVII. No. 2.

Schlesinger, Arthur M. Jr. 1967. *A Thousand Days: John F. Kennedy in the White House.* (Greenwich, CT: Fawcett Publications, Inc.)

Schneider, David M. 1972. What is Kinship all about? In *Kinship in the Morgan Centennial Year,* edited by Priscilla Reining. (Washington DC: Washington Anthropological Society.)

Schneider, David M. 1980 [1968]. *American Kinship: A Cultural Account.* (Chicago: University of Chicago Press.) [Englewood Cliffs: Prentice Hall.]

Schneider, David M. and Raymond T. Smith 1978 [1973]. *Class Differences in American Kinship.* (Ann Arbor: University of Michigan Press.) [Englewood Cliffs: Prentice Hall.]

Shils, Edward 1968. Deference. In *Social Stratification,* edited by J.A. Jackson, pp. 104–32. (Cambridge: Cambridge University Press.)

Silverman, Marilyn 1979. Dependency, Mediation, and Class Formation in Rural Guyana. *American Ethnologist* 6: 466–90.

Silverman, Marilyn 1980. *Rich People and Rice: Factional Politics in Rural Guyana.* Monographs and Theoretical Studies in Sociology and Anthropology in Honour of Nels Anderson: Publication 16. (Leiden: E. J. Brill.)

Silverman, Sydel 1979. On the Uses of History in Anthropology: The Palio of Siena. *American Ethnologist* 6: 413–36.

Simey, T.S. 1946. *Welfare and Planning in the West Indies.* (Oxford: Clarendon Press.)

Singer, Philip 1967. Caste and Identity in Guyana. In *Caste in Overseas Indian Communities,* edited by Barton M. Schwartz. (San Francisco: Chandler Publishing Company.)

Singh, K.M. 1925. *Report on a Deputation to British Guiana.* (Calcutta: Government of India.)

Smelser, Neil J. 1959. *Social Change in the Industrial Revolution: an Application of Theory to the Lancashire Cotton Industry, 1770–1840.* (London: Routledge and Kegan Paul.)

Smith, Adam 1976 [1776]. *An Inquiry Into the Nature and Causes of the Wealth of Nations.* (Chicago: The University of Chicago Press.)

Smith, Adam 1978. *Lectures on Jurisprudence,* edited by R. L. Meek, D. D. Raphael, and P. G. Stein. (Oxford: Clarendon Press.)

Smith, Anthony D. 1981. *The Ethnic Revival.* (Cambridge: Cambridge University Press.)

Smith, M.G. 1955. *A Framework for Caribbean Studies.* (Mona, Jamaica: University of the West Indies, Extra-Mural Department.)

Smith, M. G. 1957. Dark Puritan: The Life and Work of Norman Paul. *Caribbean Quarterly,* Vol. 5, Nos. 1 and 2.

Smith, M. G. 1962. *West Indian Family Structure.* (Seattle: University of Washington Press.)

Smith, Michael G. 1965. *The Plural Society in the British West Indies.* (Berkeley and Los Angeles: University of California Press.)

Smith, M. G. 1966. Introduction. In Edith Clarke, *My Mother Who Fathered Me: A Study of the Family in Three Selected Communities in Jamaica,* i–xliv. (London: George Allen and Unwin.)

Smith, Michael G. 1984. *Culture, Race and Class in the Commonwealth Caribbean.* (Mona, Jamaica: Department of Extra-mural Studies, University of the West Indies.)

Smith, Raymond T. 1956. *The Negro Family in British Guiana: Family Structure and Social Status in the Villages.* (London: Routledge and Kegan Paul.)

Smith, Raymond T. 1957a. Economic Aspects of Rice Production in an East Indian Community in British Guiana, *Social and Economic Studies* 6: 502–22.

Smith, Raymond T. 1957b. The Family in the Caribbean. In Vera Rubin, ed., *Caribbean Studies: A Symposium.* (Kingston, Jamaica: Institute of Social and Economic Research.)

Smith, Raymond T. 1959a. Some Social Characteristics of Indian Immigrants to British Guiana, *Population Studies* 13: 34–39.

Smith, Raymond T. 1959b. Family structure and plantation systems in the New World. In *Plantation Systems of the New World.* Social Science Monograph No. VII. (Washington, DC: Pan American Union.)

Smith, Raymond T. 1963. Culture and Social Structure in the Caribbean. *Comparative Studies in Society and History* 6: 24–46.

Smith, Raymond T. 1967. Social Stratification, Cultural Pluralism and Integration in West Indian Societies. In *Caribbean Integration: Papers on Social, Political and Economic Integration,* edited by Sybil Lewis and Thomas G. Mathews. (Rio Piedras: Institute of Caribbean Studies, University of Puerto Rico.)

Smith, Raymond T. 1970. The Nuclear Family in Afro-American Kinship. *Journal of Comparative Family Studies* 1: 55–70.

Smith, Raymond T. 1971. Race and Political Conflict in Guyana. *Race,* 12: 415–27.

Smith, Raymond T. 1973. The Matrifocal Family. In *The Character of Kinship*, edited by Jack Goody, pp. 121–144. (Cambridge: Cambridge University Press.)

Smith, Raymond T. 1976a. Race, Class, and Political Conflict in a Postcolonial Society. In *Small States and Segmented Societies: National Political Integration in a Global Environment*, edited by Stephanie G. Neuman. (New York: Praeger Publishers.)

Smith, Raymond T. 1976b. Religion in the Formation of West Indian Society. In *The African Diaspora: Interpretive Essays*, edited by Martin L. Kilson and Robert I. Rotberg, pp. 312–341. (Cambridge: Harvard University Press.)

Smith, Raymond T. 1978a. The Family and the Modern World System: Some Observations from the Caribbean. *Journal of Family History* 3: 337–60.

Smith, Raymond T. 1978b. Class Differences in West Indian Kinship: A Genealogical Exploration. In *Family and Kinship in Middle America and the Caribbean*, edited by Arnaud F. Marks and René A. Romer. (Co-publication of the University of the Netherlands Antilles, Curaçao and the Department of Caribbean Studies of the Royal Institute of Linguistics and Anthropology, Leiden.)

Smith, Raymond T. 1980 [1962]. *British Guiana*. (Westport, CT: Greenwood Press.) [London: Oxford University Press for The Royal Institute of International Affairs.]

Smith, Raymond T. 1982a. Family, Social Change and Social Policy in the West Indies. *New West Indian Guide* 56: 111–142.

Smith, Raymond T. 1982b. Race and Class in the Post-Emancipation Caribbean. In *Racism and Colonialism*, edited by Robert Ross. (The Hague: Martinus Nijhoff.)

Smith, Raymond T. 1984. Introduction. In *Kinship Ideology and Practice in Latin America*, edited by Raymond T. Smith. (Chapel Hill: University of North Carolina Press.)

Smith, Raymond T. 1988. *Kinship and Class in the West Indies: a Genealogical Study of Jamaica and Guyana*. (Cambridge: Cambridge University Press.)

Smith, Raymond T. and Chandra Jayawardena 1958. Hindu Marriage Customs in British Guiana. *Social and Economic Studies* 7: 178–94.

Smith, Raymond T. and Chandra Jayawardena 1959. Marriage and the Family Amongst East Indians in British Guiana. *Social and Economic Studies* 8: 321–76.

Smith, Raymond T. and Jayawardena, Chandra 1967. Caste and Social Status Among the Indians of Guyana. In *Caste Among Overseas Indians*, edited by Barton Schwartz. (San Francisco: Chandler Publishing Company.)

Solien de González, N.L. 1961. Family Organization in Five Types of Migratory Wage Labor. *American Anthropologist* 63: 1264–80.

Solien de González, N.L. 1965. The Consanguineal Household and Matrifocality. *American Anthropologist* 67: 1541–49.

Solien, Nancie L. 1959a. *The Consanguineal Household Among the Black Carib of Central America*. (Ph.D. University of Michigan dissertation.)

Solien, Nancie L. 1959b. The Nonunilineal Descent Group in the Caribbean and Central America. *American Anthropologist* 61: 578–83.

Solien, Nancie L. 1959c. West Indian Characteristics of the Black Carib. *Southwestern Journal of Anthropology* 15: 300–307.

Solien, Nancie L. 1960. Household and Family in the Caribbean. *Social and Economic Studies* 9: 101–106.

Spence, Eleanor Jean 1964. *Marketing Activities and Household Activities of Country Hawkers in Barbados.* (Ph.D. Dissertation.)

Spiro, Melford E. 1968. Virgin Birth, Parthenogenesis, and Physiological Paternity: An Essay in Cultural Interpretation. *Man* 3: 242–61.

Srinivas, M.N. 1952. *Religion and Society Among the Coorgs of South India.* (Oxford: Clarendon Press.)

Stolke, Verena 1981. Women's Labours: The Naturalisation of Social Inequality and Women's Subordination. In *Of Marriage and the Market: Women's Subordination in International Perspective,* edited by Kate Young, Carol Wolkowitz, and Roslyn McCullagh. (London: CSE Books.)

Stolcke, Verena 1984. The Exploitation of Family Morality: Labor Systems and Family Structure on Sao Paulo Coffee Plantations 1850–1979. In *Kinship Ideology and Practice in Latin America,* edited by Raymond T. Smith. (Chapel Hill: University of North Carolina Press.)

Stone, Lawrence 1977. *The Family, Sex and Marriage in England 1500–1800.* (New York: Basic Books.)

Thomas, Clive Y. 1984. *Plantations, Peasants, and State: A Study of the Mode of Sugar Production in Guyana.* (Center for Afro-American Studies, University of California, Los Angeles and Institute of Social and Economic Research, University of the West Indies, Mona, Jamaica.)

Turner, Ralph H. 1964. *The Social Context of Ambition: A Study of High-School Seniors in Los Angeles.* (San Francisco: Chandler Publishing Co.)

Turner, Terrence S. 1976. Family Structure and Socialization. In *Explorations in General Theory in Social Science: Essays in Honor of Talcott Parsons,* Vol. 2, edited by Jan J. Loubser, et al. (New York: Free Press.)

Walkowitz, Judith R. 1980. *Prostitution and Victorian Society: Women, Class and the State.* (Cambridge: Cambridge University Press.)

Warner, W. Lloyd and Lunt, Paul S. 1941. *The Social Life of a Modern Community.* (New Haven: Yale University Press.)

Weber, Max 1946. *From Max Weber: Essays in Sociology.* Trans. H.H. Gerth and C. Wright Mills. (New York: Oxford University Press.)

Weber, Max 1968. *Economy and Society* (3 Vols). Edited by Guenther Roth and Claus Wittich. (New York: Bedminster Press.)

West India Royal Commission 1945. *West Indies Royal Commission Report (The Moyne Report),* Cmnd. 6607. (London: HMSO.)

Williams, Brackette 1989. A Class Act: Anthropology and the Race to Nation Across Ethnic Terrain. *Annual Review of Anthropology* 18: 401–44.

Williams, Brackette 1991. *Stains On My Name, War In My Veins: On the Politics of Cultural Struggle in Guyana.* (Durham: Duke University Press.)

Williams, Eric 1962. *History of the People of Trinidad and Tobago.* (Port of Spain, Trinidad: PNM Publishing Co., Ltd.)

Wolk, Daniel 1994. *The Making of Social Class and Status Among Assyrians Immigrants in Chicago.* (Unpublished Manuscript.)

Wright, Philip 1966. *Lady Nugent's Journal of Her Residence in Jamaica from 1801 to 1805.* (Kingston, Jamaica: Institute of Jamaica.)

Wright, Richardson 1937. *Revels in Jamaica, 1682–1838.* (New York: Benjamin Blom Inc.)

Yalman, Nur 1967. *Under the Bo Tree: Studies in Caste, Kinship, and Marriage in the Interior of Ceylon.* (Berkeley: University of California Press.)

# INDEX

**DATE DUE**

| | | | |
|---|---|---|---|
| 7/20/99 | | | |
| AG 07 '01 | | | |
| | | | |
| | | | |
| | | | |
| | | | |
| | | | |
| | | | |
| | | | |
| | | | |
| | | | |
| | | | |
| | | | |
| | | | |
| | | | |
| | | | |
| | | | |
| | | | |
| | | | |
| | | | |
| GAYLORD | | | PRINTED IN U.S.A |